CRITICAL SKILLS

CRITICAL SKILLS

The Guide to Top Performance for Human Resources Managers

William R. Tracey

American Management Association

*This book is available at a special
discount when ordered in bulk quantities.
For information, contact Special Sales Department,
AMACOM, a division of American Management Association,
135 West 50th Street, New York, NY 10020.*

Library of Congress Cataloging-in-Publication Data

Tracey, William R.
  Critical skills.

  Includes index.
  1. Personnel management.   I. Title.
HF5549.T712   1987   658.3   87-47762
ISBN 0-8144-5939-0

Printing number

10 9 8 7 6 5 4 3 2 1

To my grandchildren,
in the order of their appearance

Tamra Lee Letellier

Jacqueline Marie Tracey

Sean Keenan Letellier

Michele Marie Tracey

Laine Tracey Tarbania

William Raymond Tracey, III

Preface

As we approach the final decade of the twentieth century, the trends of the last 20 years continue and accelerate. We are in a period of rapid, substantive, and dramatic change—technological, social, political, and economic. It is an era of exciting growth in communication and computer sciences. It is a time of significant changes in the size, age, and ethnic origins of the population, in the composition of the workforce, and in the mix of jobs. It is an age of a puzzling anomaly: lingering unemployment and growing labor shortages and mismatches. It is an era of turbulence, of strikes and demonstrations, of chemical and nuclear accidents, of space spectaculars and space vehicle failures, of disinformation, evasion, dissembling, and misrepresentation, and, tragically, of terrorism and other forms of violence. It is also a period of economic change, of renewed growth, of fluctuating currency values, of towering national deficits, of massive negative balances of payments, of falling oil prices and lower interest rates, of increased domestic and international competition for markets, of enterprise restructuring and downsizing, and of rapid obsolescence of skills and career change.

The 1980s have seen the maturing of the human resources (HR) function, and its wide acceptance by top executives. They now see the importance of the HR manager's role in achieving and maintaining a competitive edge in enterprise efficiency and attaining the maximum possible return on investment.

Boards of control and CEOs are now beginning to recognize that company-sponsored or -operated HR programs can ameliorate the deplorable performance of the public educational system in providing workers with the communication, computational, and job skills—and their associated attitudes—needed for success in entry-level positions. They also understand that if the gap between the level of skill brought to the job by students and the competency needs of business and industry is to be closed, if the reduction in federal spending for job training and retraining is to be compensated or redressed, if the worker, technician, and engineer deficits are to be remedied, and if the needs of employees for training and development are to be met, HR programs and services must be exceptionally well designed. And they know that they must be executed under the leadership of topnotch, competent, and highly creative HR managers.

Recognition of the pivotal role of HR professionals in reaching enterprise goals and objectives has caused top executives and boards of control to demand consistently outstanding performance of their HR managers. They are holding their feet to the fire and requiring them to demonstrate the cost benefits, as well as the quality and effectiveness, of their programs and services.

Obviously, HR managers, like the managers of other business areas, must perform the usual managerial functions of planning, organizing, staffing, directing, and controlling. They must have in their repertoires the usual array of technical, conceptual, and human skills—and they must be able to use them with consummate proficiency. That requirement is certainly not new. The significance of those skills to outstanding performance has been recognized for many years. Yet recent surveys of HR managers reveal that their top-priority need is for greater human skills in general and for improved communication skills in particular. HR managers recognize that, if they are to survive, let alone prosper, they must learn to communicate better—up, down, and laterally.

All HR managers have communication needs in common. They need to:

- Match their personal goals with enterprise goals and communicate that convergence to top management.
- Measure and improve their own communication skills and performance and those of their subordinates.
- Perfect their problem-sensing, problem-solving, and decision-making skills.
- Overcome daily communication obstacles to progress and accomplishment.
- Extend their influence to everyone inside and outside the organization.
- Win support for their plans, programs, services, and objectives.
- Help their people to function independently and achieve more.

This book is about skills, primarily communication skills. It is designed to help HR managers improve the skills that are critical to effective communication—listening, speaking, and writing. It's about applying those skills to 12 other related skills that are crucial to HR management in all types of enterprise, large and small, public and private, profit and nonprofit: problem sensing, inquiring, problem solving, decision making, hiring, motivating, delegating, appraising, coaching, counseling, negotiating, and team building. Some of the skills, such as listening, speaking, writing, and problem solving, are used daily by all HR managers. Others, such as coaching and counseling, may not be used every day.

Nevertheless, all are critical skills that can have a significant impact on a manager's performance and the results achieved. They must all be mastered.

You will note that similar or closely related managerial activities are discussed in more than one chapter. That is deliberate, partly for emphasis but more because some tasks have more than one application. They are overlapping and reinforcing. Because you will probably want to deal with only one critical skill at a single sitting, I have tried to make each chapter self-contained, more or less independent of the others. This, too, creates a degree of repetition.

Admittedly, the literature of management, specifically in the area of communication, is extensive. However, I believe it has two shortcomings. First, materials are either too voluminous (whole books on a given communication skill such as listening) or too condensed (short articles on delegating or coaching). And, second, few, if any, address the communication skills from the perspective of HR managers and their needs.

I hope this book will overcome both deficiencies and fill an important gap in the literature of HR management. Each chapter of this book applies communication skills to the management of HR programs and activities. It is highly specific to HR and it focuses on the practical problems of HR managers. I also hope that this approach and framework will help HR managers, present and future, improve their communication skills and so enhance their performance as managers.

Contents

1 Listening: The Neglected Skill   **1**

2 Speaking:
     When You Are the Medium for the Message   **22**

3 Writing: The Demanding Skill   **43**

4 Problem Sensing:
     Managerial Preventive Medicine   **74**

5 Inquiring: Getting the Facts   **94**

6 Problem Solving:
     Managerial Diagnosis and Treatment   **117**

7 Decision Making:
     The Manager's Moment of Truth   **141**

8 Hiring: Matching People and Jobs   **166**

9 Motivating: Triggering Top Performance   **196**

10 Delegating: Multiplying Your Effectiveness   **220**

11 Appraising:
     Assessing Performance and Potential   **238**

12 Coaching: Fulfilling Performance Expectations   **264**

13 Counseling: Helping People Help Themselves   **283**

14 Negotiating: Win-Win Bargaining   **305**

15 Team Building: Engineering Synergy   **326**

     Index   **341**

1

LISTENING
The Neglected Skill

Although listening is central to all human endeavor and crucial to all management activity, it generally is not taught. So many people, including HR managers, have inadequate listening habits and skills.

To be successful as an HR manager, you must know what's going on, what people are thinking, what your boss really wants, what went wrong, how workers think it can be corrected or prevented in the future, and what potential problems are emerging. You must also know what other line managers and staff personnel think about your programs and services and what they want that you're not providing. You can't afford to be kept in the dark and you're not helped when your subordinates cover up or dissemble. You need facts to make decisions, to make plans, to remain productive. You certainly don't want surprises. And to do all those good things and prevent all the bad things, you must be a skilled listener.

Not listening creates problems in business, industry, and all other types of organizations as well as in the home between husbands and wives and parents and children. Listening says, "I care about you. What you say is important to me."

Of all the sources of information available to HR managers, of all the ways they can come to know and actually gauge the personalities of the people in the department, listening to individual employees is the most productive and rewarding. And listening to staffers is certain to result in good feelings, as in "My boss is great! She (or he) *listens* to me."

Listening is much harder to do well than most people believe; it takes a great amount of self-discipline. Helen Clinard, a well-known listening consultant, writes, "The assumption that you already know how to listen is probably the biggest barrier to improving listening skills."[1]

One of the most important lessons the HR manager should learn is this: Don't *talk* so much to the people in your department—*listen* to them.

1. Helen Clinard, "Listen for the Difference," *Training and Development Journal,* October 1985, p. 39.

They want to talk to you. If they wanted to listen to you, they'd say so. When you learn to listen to your subordinates (to say nothing of your superiors and peers), you'll learn what they really are telling you. You may even start listening to yourself to make sure that you're saying what you really mean. Then you'll start attending to the real needs of those you work with, and communicating your ideas and directions clearly, powerfully, and successfully to those who really need to hear and act on them.

Listening should occupy a far greater percentage of an HR manager's time on the job than any other form of communication. The relative amount of time spent on each probably should be something like this:

Listening, 65 percent
Speaking, 25 percent
Writing, 5 percent
Reading, 5 percent

Listening is the foundation for all other HR managerial activities and for all employee training and development programs. In an organizational setting, the costs of poor listening skills on the part of managers (particularly HR managers) can be staggering in terms of wasted time, materials, and funds, lower productivity, lost sales, reduced return on investment, missed opportunities, and poor interpersonal and labor-management relationships.

As HR managers you are in an excellent position to improve the listening skills of employees at all levels of an organization and thus avoid those negative results. But to achieve that objective, you must be aware of your personal listening strengths and weaknesses and become involved in a listening self-development program.

The Anatomy of Listening

Listening is much more than hearing. Hearing is a physiological function. Listening is a voluntary mental function. It is not simply the physical process of receiving sound waves.

> Listening is a complex, learned human process that comprises four stages, each equally important. *Sensing* is the first stage, where the sender's message enters, or does not enter, the listener's stream of consciousness (sensory mechanism). The second state is the *interpretation* of what was sensed, which leads to mutual understanding (or misunderstanding). The third stage involves *evaluation*. Evidence is weighed, fact is separated from opinion, the reasoning process is analyzed, agreements and disagreements are registered, and judg-

ments are made. Finally, the fourth stage of *responding* is necessary. Responding allows listening to come full circle and is crucial for judging the success of the listening act as a whole. *Sensing, interpreting,* and *evaluating* are internal acts; *responding* is an external act.[2]

Three Levels of Listening

Oddly enough, there are three levels of listening: nonhearing, hearing, and sensing/thinking/reacting. Only one of them is acceptable.

1. Nonhearing. The first level isn't listening at all. It occurs when we allow our minds to wander, to daydream or fantasize, to think about what we're going to do later, to worry about a personal problem, or even to consider what we're going to say next—while the other person is speaking. Although it may not be deliberate, it is not uncommon. This type of "listening" stymies communication. In purely social settings, nonhearing can be embarrassing. In business and professional situations, it can be ruinous.

Many times managers don't listen at all. Their preoccupation with other concerns, impatience, or lack of confidence in the speaker cause them to tune out, even though they may still be able to convey an attitude of attention and interest. The urge to comment sometimes prompts managers to cut people off before they can tell the complete story. But if communication is to be successful, the target of the communication must listen attentively and completely.

2. Hearing. At the hearing level, we hear the words and absorb and react to them in a very shallow or perfunctory manner. This might well be called nonattentive listening. We fail to absorb and comprehend the full meaning and intent of the message. Usually this level of listening is accompanied by verbal or nonverbal behavior (words, facial expression, and body language) that conveys lack of interest in the ideas or message being transmitted. Although potentially less damaging than nonhearing, incomplete hearing invariably results in misunderstandings.

3. Sensing, thinking, reacting. Unquestionably, the most important part of the listening process is understanding. If the listener fails to understand the content and intent of a message, or if he or she misinterprets what was said, the attempted communication has been unsuccessful.

True listening occurs only at the sensing/thinking level. At that level, we hear, evaluate, analyze, and comprehend the message; we fully receive and understand the communication as intended by the sender. Does that sound like a lot of work? Yes, understanding requires mental effort. But

2. Lyman K. Steil, "Communication Training: Listening," in *Human Resources Management and Development Handbook,* ed. William R. Tracey (New York: AMACOM, 1985), 1069–70.

full listening, as a sensing and thinking process, is the only way to get the meaning and intent of information that is transmitted orally. It is the only way we can successfully and accurately interpret what the speaker intends for us to receive.

The sensing/thinking/reacting level is usually accompanied by verbal or nonverbal behavior that shows others that you are interested in their ideas and that you want them to continue. It does not necessarily convey support, acceptance, or rejection of what is being said. It indicates neither agreement nor denial of the validity of the ideas—only interest in hearing them.

Management Uses

People need to listen for a variety of reasons: to do their jobs, to get information, to learn (change their behavior in some desirable way), to show affection, concern, interest, or some other form of emotional feedback, to persuade, and to interact socially. If an HR manager is to devote more than half the time on the job to listening to achieve those purposes, obviously listening skills will be predominant in many activities during the course of the typical work day. Here is a breakdown of some of those important day-to-day activities.

Exchanging job information. HR managers need to exchange information about programs, projects, problems, and issues with their superiors, peers, subordinates, and people outside the organization. Every person has knowledge, perceptions, and ideas that must be fully shared if maximum use is to be made of them. The way to get maximum use is full and free discussion. As an HR manager you must listen carefully to those with whom you work.

Receiving direction. HR managers, like all other managers in an organization, receive direction from their bosses. One of the best ways to miss direction from your supervisors—and alienate them—is to be inattentive. Inattentive managers cannot be successful simply because they are certain to miss or misinterpret the things that their boss considers important.

Seeking information for decision or action. Two of the most frequently used techniques for gathering information are inquiring and listening to oral briefings. Questions are posed to elicit information HR managers need to do their job. Oral briefings are a means of presenting information and proposals. For example, you may request a briefing from a supplier on a new interactive video training program. Or you could ask the chief of the organization development division to present an oral progress report on the results and costs of a team-building program. If you are to get a reasonable return on everyone's investment of time, you must listen attentively.

Accomplished HR managers will make full use of oral briefings by staff members and others to get the information they need to make plans and decisions. The content of briefings is so critical that HR managers must concentrate their attention fully and completely during presentations. Any instance of inattention could have very serious consequences. It probably goes without saying that HR managers must also listen attentively and with full concentration to briefings presented by other line managers, staffers, and outside personnel, such as vendors, consultants, and suppliers, if they are to be fully functioning members of their management teams.

Meetings and conferences. Staff meetings and conferences are other common means of sharing information and ideas and solving problems. In many HR organizations, staff conferences are held a minimum of once a week, sometimes more often. For example, you might call a special staff meeting to discuss ways of measuring your department's impact on corporate profit or return on investment. In addition, the chief executive officer of the organization in all probability conducts weekly staff conferences and frequently calls special conferences to deal with emergencies. Obviously, you must be an attentive listener at your own staff conferences as well as at those conducted by others. To do less is to invite disaster.

Coaching and counseling. As both a coach and counselor to your staff and as the receiver of coaching and counseling from your boss, you must be a good listener. You must listen attentively to staff members during coaching and counseling sessions if you are to provide the direction, assistance, and feedback they need. Similarly, when receiving coaching or being counseled, you must listen carefully if you are to get the full benefit of the direction, assistance, and performance feedback.

Training and development. Almost all learning activities, whether prerecorded or "live," have an aural component. Behavioral change, learning, cannot take place efficiently without understanding the audio component of the learning medium. For example, you might well call for a training session for yourself and the HR staff on the OSHA right-to-know laws. That training could not be conducted efficiently with visuals unsupported by audio.

Obviously, much of the communication in training and development programs and activities involves oral speech in one form or another—live lectures, small group discussion, role playing, audio and video recordings, motion pictures, and the like. Whether you are instructor or trainee, you must listen carefully. Otherwise you reduce your effectiveness as either.

Conducting performance reviews. One of the most delicate situations for any manager is the performance review, the discussion between manager and subordinate following a period of performance evaluation. It is also a significant event in the work life of the HR manager when the boss sits down with him or her to discuss performance. In both cases, the importance of careful listening during those emotionally loaded situations cannot be overstated. The person doing the appraisal and the person being appraised must be completely and totally attentive. Failure by either will result in less than optimal results from the discussion and also could be severely damaging to the relationship because of the potential for misunderstanding.

Job interviewing. The effective job interview, where the HR manager is attempting to find the right person to fill a vacancy in the HR department, is another critical event. Not only must managers be skillful questioners, with the ability to ask penetrating questions; they must also be very accomplished listeners, with the ability to hear what is really being said and what is not being said, to separate fact from fiction, to "hear" goals, to sense motivation, to uncover talent or the lack of it.

Exit interviewing. The exit interview is one of the best ways to get straight information about the quality of work life in an HR organization, insight into departmental problems and potential problems, and the reasons for such negative things as excessive turnover, unsatisfactory performance, and employee dissatisfaction. When anyone is terminated for any reason—layoff, firing, voluntary separation, or retirement—the HR manager should take the time to interview that person and try to identify the reasons for the termination and collect information that can help prevent costly turnover.

Negotiating. Another critical listening situation occurs during contract negotiations, or any other form of negotiating, including mediating and resolving interpersonal conflicts. HR managers cannot be successful in negotiating unless they are highly skilled listeners, with the ability to concentrate totally, to read between the lines, to "listen" with their eyes. Listening involves being attentive and sensitive to the nonverbal behavior of others, not just understanding their words.

Barriers to Effective Listening

Communication failure occurs when those who receive an oral message fail to understand the content and intent of a transmission or misinterpret what was said. Blocks and barriers to the effective transmission of communication are legion; some of the most common are discussed below.

Lack of interest, boredom, or laziness. People sometimes fail to listen because they are totally uninterested in the subject being discussed. Rightly or wrongly, they choose to tune out simply because they believe the subject has no real bearing on their job, their home life, or their concerns. Other people become bored with the presentation or discussion and just plain quit listening. Still others lose their concentration out of sheer laziness. Smart listeners look for something in the message that has value. They think in terms of "What's in it for me?" or "Is there something here that I can use?"

Noise or distractions. Some people can't listen because of external noise or distractions: street sounds (traffic, jackhammers, police or fire sirens, lawnmowers, piledrivers), conversations from adjoining rooms, bad acoustics, fans or air conditioners, side conversations, even the temperature and humidity of the room. They lose their train of thought and are unable to regain their concentration. The accomplished listener is able to exercise enough self-discipline to overcome distractions and concentrate on the speaker and the message. Failing that, you may have to move away from the distraction and closer to the speaker.

Language and vocabulary problems. People with limited English language skills or with meager technical or specialized vocabularies invariably find it impossible to keep their attention focused. They cannot understand large chunks of the message, so they become flustered, confused, mystified, frustrated, and finally they quit listening altogether.

There are at least three partial solutions to the problem. First, try to use context for clues to the meaning of unfamiliar words. Second, use the clues provided by tone of voice, posture, gestures, and body movements to discover the meaning. Third, if the situation permits it, ask the speaker for clarification.

Prejudgment. Sometimes we don't "hear" what people say simply because in earlier interaction with them we have been turned off. We may have decided that they have little of value to say, that they are not intelligent or perceptive, that they are biased, that they lack education and experience, or whatever, and so in subsequent contacts we pay them little attention. We have made the mistake of prejudgment. Typically people prejudge on the basis of one or more incidents, which may not be at all indicative of that person's potential for contributing to the solution of the problem at hand.

In other situations we listen to a speaker just long enough to place him or her in a category—someone who thinks and believes as we do, or someone whose beliefs are unacceptable. In the first case, we tend to react favorably and may even ignore information that is inconsistent with our position because of our overall identification with the speaker. In the second case, we tend to overlook comments that support our position and magnify or distort statements that conflict.

The solutions to the problem of prejudgment are easy to state but difficult to do: (1) listen more closely; (2) try to avoid putting people in either "sympathetic toward" or "biased against" categories; (3) if your first inclination is to be sympathetic, try to be critical of the content; or

(4) if you detect bias against, try to find the "good" things about the message.

Stereotypes. Unfortunately, people sometimes judge the credibility of others on the basis of their race, color, nationality, section of the country, religion, even hair color, weight, height, or some other observable attribute. Stereotyping is a form of generalizing, putting people into the same category on the basis of one characteristic. People who do this tend to see all members of the group as possessing or lacking the same traits. All fat people are jolly. All spinsters are bad-tempered. All Irishmen are hot-headed. All Italians are hot-blooded. All physicians are caring. All lawyers are mercenary.

Such biases can and often do get in the way of communication. That is indeed unfortunate, but it is a fact of life that must be recognized and dealt with. The truly regrettable thing about prejudice is that it frequently is unrecognized by the one who has it. And it affects day-to-day interaction and communication with others.

Here again the solution to the problem is easy to state but very difficult to do: Get rid of your prejudice. Perhaps a more realistic strategy is again to adopt the selfish attitude: "What's in this message for me? What can I get out of it that will help me?"

Distrust of the sender. A climate of distrust, conflict, animosity, and anxiety in an organization tends to reduce the amount and timeliness of information flow. It also causes people to block, screen, or distort communication upward, downward, and laterally. Under those conditions, people tend to keep their rears covered, play it close to the vest, share a minimum of information with others, and look at information passed by others with suspicion.

In any case, people's communication practices are strongly influenced by the kinds of rewards and penalties they experience as a consequence. For example, if subordinates report information that reflects unfavorably on their performance and if the HR manager responds with censure, more restrictive policies, more stringent controls, or outright punishment, communication upward is likely to be stifled—except for those items likely to receive a favorable reception. A little soul-searching will quickly reveal whether you are blocking information and legitimate feedback by punishing the bearers of bad news. If that is the case, the solution is simple: Mend your ways.

Speaker's delivery. Sometimes the root problem of communication breakdown is simply the speaker's delivery—voice, speech patterns, vocabulary, tone, inflection, accent, excessive use of vocalized pauses, stammering, or inarticulateness. Or it could be just the reverse—the glibness or fluency of speech, the richness or resonance of the voice could interfere with reception. But all those things are simply artifacts of speech. The competent manager can listen through them to get the message as intended. The only way to overcome this listening handicap is practice. Learn to concentrate on the content of the message, not on the medium.

Organizational distance. Differences in organizational levels often create barriers to communication. Horizontal communication—among executives, among supervisors, and among day laborers—is not so much of a problem as vertical communication—between supervisors and their subordinates, for example. The problem arises because people at disparate organizational levels have different goals and priorities, dissimilar perspectives and perceptions, and unique ways of thinking. In general, the greater the organizational distance between speaker and listener, the greater the possibility of communication failure.

From the standpoint of organizational distance, the HR manager encounters three somewhat different communication problems. The first involves the problem of getting accurate information orally from people who are only one or two levels removed—subordinate managers and supervisors and principal staff.

The second relates to the extremely difficult problem of getting information and feedback from the largest part of the department—the instructors, technicians, specialists, clerks, and hourly workers who are considerably lower in the organizational scheme of things. Their performance and ideas are important to the success of HR operations, yet it is exceedingly difficult to achieve genuine upward communication because of the widely differing perspectives from which problems and opportunities are viewed.

The third is often closely related to the first two: the potential problem of isolation. The uniquely powerful position of the HR manager also tends to generate a communication isolation that can create additional difficulties unless corrective action is taken. On one hand, HR managers may be denied access to valuable information; on the other, their capabilities for eliciting upward communication may be limited. They may be forced to make decisions on the basis of incomplete or unreliable information, and their communication to lower levels of the department may be distorted or blocked.

Semantic difficulties. Words often have varied meanings, and some words have high emotional content. The meaning intended by the speaker may often vary greatly from the meaning accepted by the listener. And the emotional "loading" interpreted by the listener may not have been intended at all by the speaker. People tend to interpret words in terms of their own experience and attitudes, and this affects the meanings they associate with the words other people use as well as the words they themselves use. So words, in and of themselves, are often confusing, and constitute yet another barrier to listening. Consider, for example, the emotional loading (at least for some) of the words *rate, appraise, monitor,* and *inspect* in the context of instructional supervision, or of *comparable worth* in the arena of job evaluation and pricing.

The main point to keep in mind is this: You must recognize that people on different levels of your department speak different languages, and so do people in other departments. Exercise great care when interpreting oral messages.

Physiological conditions. Inattention or failure to interpret oral communication correctly may be due to such permanent or temporary conditions as fatigue, emotional upheaval, pain, or illness. Extreme weariness makes concentration difficult. Similarly, emotional disturbance or agitation, whether job-related or acquired off the job, even if temporary, can severely impair your ability to focus on words. Illness or discomfort of any kind, from a simple headache to severe pain, can make concentration next to impossible.

Apathy, sophistication, or opposition. If you are apathetic, either toward the speaker or the subject of the communication, you will not hear what is being said. If, on the other hand, you feel that the speaker or the subject is too naive, elementary, or unsophisticated, your attentiveness is certain to suffer. If you are opposed to the speaker or the subject, your "all-knowing" outlook will cause you to dismiss the communication out of hand. Those three sins of commission can cause you a great amount of needless anguish. Avoid them.

Techniques of Effective Listening

There are many things you can do to increase your effectiveness as a listener. You can learn to listen actively and aggressively. You can develop the skills of evaluative and nonevaluative listening. You can learn to detect and resist propaganda and manipulation. You can learn to listen with your eyes. And you can become a better note taker.

Listening Actively

Work at listening. Get your listening skills up to the thinking level. Remember that human speech is articulated at a rate of 100 to 150 words per minute whereas people can hear at a rate of 600 or more. That is four to five times faster than the average speaker talks, and that difference allows you to think ahead, to analyze and evaluate what's being said while it is being said. While you are listening to the main points and the supporting illustrations and examples, you can be separating facts from opinions, mentally arguing with the speaker, predicting the next point, listening ahead, supplying examples to support points, paraphrasing ideas, making applications to your own situation, listening between the lines (to what is *not* being said), evaluating the speaker's position, and drawing your own conclusions. However, don't become so absorbed with analyzing what *has been* said that you miss what *is being* said.

Concentrate on the speaker and the message, not on yourself and your reaction. Give her your total, undivided attention. Look at the speaker directly, but don't stare at her eyes. Don't look at the floor or ceiling, or out the window. Don't rush or hurry the speaker. Let her digress, expand, elaborate, or repeat without getting impatient. Check your emotions at the door. Don't allow yourself to get overly excited, provoked, or stimulated.

Avoid listening solely for facts; locate the central idea. Evaluate the supporting evidence. Withhold judgment. Try to anticipate the speaker's thrust or direction. Evaluate the message. Respond appropriately. If it's a one-on-one situation, don't interrupt in the middle of a sentence, but do ask questions. Give the speaker feedback by saying, "I'm not too clear on what you mean," or "Would you mind repeating that?" or "Do you mean that . . .?"

> If you're actively listening, you'll constantly be asking yourself questions: "What does he have to back up that statement?" "Is this point relevant to what he's trying to prove?" "What does that word mean the way he's using it now?" Additionally, the active listener will also be asking questions out loud in an attempt to clarify the speaker's meaning. Not that the active listener is always interrupting, but whenever he or she finds the message becoming vague or confusing, questions are asked to let the sender know that he or she is off target. Active listeners help the speaker by asking what they need to know in order to understand the message.[3]

Here are some suggestions:

- Concentrate totally on the speaker.
- Shut out competing messages and other distractions.
- Listen in context.
- Act interested (with facial expressions, posture, and other nonverbal means).
- Ask questions and make comments.

Listening for Meaning

You should listen for meaning, not just words, or speech, or style of delivery. Don't be put off by a speaker's delivery or vocabulary. If you do, you might not hear what's really being said. Even if the topic is dull and the speaker is not exciting or accomplished, make the effort to focus on other aspects of the presentation to understand the real message. Be especially careful not to let individual words, especially red-flare words, create a block to your concentration and comprehension.

3. Susan Dellinger and Barbara Deane, *Communicating Effectively: A Complete Guide for Better Managing* (Radnor, Penn.: Chilton, 1980), 52.

Concentrate on the central theme, concept, or idea, not on isolated facts. Too many people try to remember the exact terms used by the speaker, assuming that they are then retaining the important facts. If you take notes, confine them to the central ideas.

Don't jump to conclusions before you hear the speaker out completely. If you judge too early, you can miss the essential meaning because you have already tuned the speaker out and are busy framing questions, rebuttals, and objections.

Evaluative Listening

Purpose is basic to effective listening. If you are to receive information and ideas successfully, you must have a clear, conscious objective. The HR manager who is a good listener knows at the outset of a one-on-one session, briefing, or conference what he or she ought to get out of the occasion. Whether it's an employment interview, a decision briefing, a status report on a project, or a problem-solving conference, the HR manager must focus on evaluating what is being said or presented.

In an employment interview, for example, the manager must evaluate the applicant's qualifications for the position in terms of education and training, experience, personality, personal drive and motivation, goals and objectives, all measured and evaluated against job requirements. That means that the manager must engage in evaluative listening. To do that, the interviewer asks questions designed to obtain information in depth about items listed on the application form. Even more important, the skillful listener will use the interview to assess certain intangibles, such as attitudes, interests, motivation, initiative, judgment, self-confidence, and emotional stability. You do this by listening attentively with your mind, eyes, and ears, and evaluating what you "hear."

Evaluative listening means:

1. Listening to understand, not to oppose, object, or argue.
2. Listening for inaccuracies, inconsistencies, and improper conclusions.
3. Evaluating the message and the supporting evidence.
4. Withholding judgment until the speaker has finished.

Nonevaluative Listening

This form of listening must be adopted by the HR manager who is serving as sounding board, mother or father confessor, mentor, or counselor. It is not the form used when conducting a performance appraisal. Nonevaluative listening is what you would use when counseling for career questions, job adjustment, social adjustment, and personal adjustment, whether the counseling is provided to individuals or groups.

In those roles, the HR manager should be helping people help themselves—to identify and solve their own problems, not to solve these people's problems for them. Specifically, the objectives of nonevaluative listening are to help employees gain self-understanding; attain objective acceptance of themselves, their thoughts and feelings, their aspirations and impulses; understand and deal with immediate problems; learn to deal with problems more effectively; eliminate or reduce deficiencies in personality, knowledge, or skills; make needed changes in their environment, or overcome other types of problems (substance abuse, marital, family, or financial problems).

Nonevaluative listening is just what it appears to be—the listener does not evaluate the person speaking, but simply displays an objective, interested, and concerned attitude. Attempt to convey by posture, eye contact, gestures, comments, and body language your regard for the employee, the problem, and the importance of the employee's ideas. You must be able to accept expressions of negative feelings and be unperturbed. Employees must be made to feel that you accept them as they are. Of course that does not mean you consider undesirable behavior acceptable, or that you don't want them to change for the better.

Nonevaluative listening

- Displays cordiality, warmth, and uncritical acceptance.
- Is forthright, sincere, and compassionate.
- Shows courtesy and attentiveness.
- Avoids evidences of pressure, boredom, irritation, or anxiety.
- Shuns displays of authority.
- Avoids antagonizing, embarrassing, or hurrying the speaker.
- Does nothing that could undermine the speaker's self-respect.

Listening with Your Eyes

The old saying "Actions speak louder than words" is true more often than not. Facial expressions, gestures, posture, body movements, dress, hairstyle, and voice cues (tone, volume, and pitch) frequently communicate much more accurately than the words being used. Some nonverbal behavior is inborn; it occurs naturally and is culture-free, a part of human evolutionary development. For example, hunched shoulders, angling the head to one side, or compressing the lips indicate disagreement or uncertainty. To show approval, people tend to face each other squarely; to show disapproval, they tend to turn their bodies away.

Other nonverbal behavior is learned and is culturally determined. For example, nodding the head in Bulgaria and Greece means *no* whereas in most other countries, it means *yes*. The rules for using the eyes are also culturally determined. The exception is the stare, which is almost universally regarded as showing hostility, disrespect, threat, or insult.

Verbal and nonverbal behaviors sometimes conflict. When they do, the nonverbal behavior provides better insight into the speaker's true feelings. For example, if someone says, "I'm really not upset," but his voice trembles, he probably *is* really upset.

Detecting Propaganda, Fabrication, and Deception

The good listener will be alert for cues that indicate that the speaker is propagandizing, dissembling, or deceiving. Here are some signs that can alert you to these deceitful (and often slick) messages.

Vagueness or imprecision. When the speaker uses unfamiliar, unclear, dubious, or inexact terms, or equivocates, watch out. For example:

"Many studies have proved . . ."
"I don't have the numbers, but . . ."
"I'll have to ask you to take this on faith but, it is a fact that . . ."
"From my experience over 25 years . . ."

Generalizations. One of the most common forms of deception is generalizing. Here the speaker attempts to extend his or her contention to a large number of people or cases. For example:

"Everyone knows that . . ."
"Most of our clients have found that . . ."
"They say . . ." (the infamous "they")

Exaggeration or embroidering. Here the speaker attempts to make the point by magnification, hyperbole, or overstatement. For example:

"The training program was a total disaster . . ."
"The results of the study were awesome . . ."
"This equipment is absolutely user-friendly and utterly foolproof."

Inconsistencies and self-contradictions. Identifying incompatible, incongruous, or contradictory statements requires concentration and full attention throughout a presentation. The listener must be on the alert to pick up numbers that do not track, remarks that do not conform to earlier observations, and conclusions that do not follow from earlier assertions.

Misrepresentation and exorbitant claims. A clever speaker can distort, color, or stretch the facts to make his or her presentation more convincing. For example, if a prospective employee who is being questioned about his experience in training system design and development says, "I was completely and solely responsible for designing, developing, and validating the six-month training program for electronics technicians at XYZ Corporation," he is probably misrepresenting his experience. It is highly unlikely that anyone could design, develop, and validate such a complex program without a lot of assistance.

Euphemisms. Sometimes speakers substitute bland or inoffensive expressions for ones that may offend or that suggest something unacceptable or unpleasant. For example, the speaker may use a term such as *lay off* instead of *fire, physical encounter* instead of *fight, labor dispute* instead of *strike, misunderstanding* instead of *argument.*

Epithets, invective, or ridicule. This tactic is typically designed to play to prejudices, biases, or emotions. Examples of such deliberate appeals would be referring to psychologists or psychiatrists as "head shrinkers," lobbyists as "influence peddlers," or politicians as "power brokers." Also:

Screaming liberals
Muddleheaded conservatives
Highbrows
Eggheads
Idiots
Clowns
Male Chauvinists
Wimps
Studs
Hippies
Yuppies
Women's libbers
Broads
Female jocks

Specious reasoning. This occurs when the speaker gives the *appearance* of being fair, just, or correct in assessing the facts or drawing conclusions, but in reality is being deceptive. Very often, such statements begin with

"To be honest . . ."
"To be perfectly candid . . ."
"Frankly . . ."
"Honestly . . ."
"It naturally follows that . . ."
"Now, I mean this sincerely . . ."
"You can count on this . . ."
"By the way . . ."

Clichés and metaphors. It is easy to get into the habit of using clichés and repeating metaphors. Most of us are guilty of using too many of them. But beware of speakers who pepper their talks with these "gems" in an attempt to build credibility:

Boilerplate
Bottom line
Game plan
Interface
Hang loose
A real bell-ringer
User-friendly
High performance
New dimension
Unprecedented
Power hungry
Blistering speed
Sophisticated software
The good news is . . . the bad news is . . .
Even as I speak
On a roll
Stay the course
Bear fruit
I'm not here to win a popularity contest . . .

Irrelevancies and gratuitous comments. Be on the lookout for speakers who introduce extraneous materials into their talks in an attempt to be more factual and believable. For example, when reviewing the credentials of candidates for a position in the organization, if the speaker says, "Nine out of ten candidates for the directorship are single," or "Only one of the five managers was reared on a farm," the remarks are irrelevant. Or a statement that begins with "It is interesting to note that . . ." or "Just as an aside . . ." is likely to be immaterial.

Gestures, facial expressions, and body movements. Another way to identify fabrication or deception is to watch gestures, facial expressions, and body language. Nonverbal behavior probably communicates feelings and attitudes far better than words. Hands and eyes provide fairly reliable clues to falsehoods. Covering the mouth, eyes, or ears with the fingers or hands, touching the nose, or rubbing the eyes, scratching the neck, or rubbing the ear frequently indicate that the speaker is being untruthful.

Gestures, too, have psychological coloring. Gestures and body movements should complement and reinforce the words that are being used. If they don't, something is amiss. Blushing, contraction of the facial muscles, giggling, nervous laughter, fidgeting or squirming, blinking, enlarged or reduced eye pupil size, silent staring, a "poker face," or forced smiles are clues to the real message. Remember that seeing is much more than looking. Looking is physical and objective. Seeing is mental—assimilating or taking in and comprehending what we are looking at—and subjective.

Guides to Better Listening

Here are some specific suggestions to improve your listening skills.

Encourage people to speak. Invite your subordinates to speak openly. Ask them to identify areas where they are concerned. Urge them to make suggestions and to ask questions. Don't interrupt them; hear them out completely. Give them plenty of feedback; summarize what they have said to verify that you have understood their messages.

Listen with purpose. If you're going to listen for meaning and ideas, you must have a clear and conscious objective. You must know at the outset what you should get from a communication. You should also be able to change your purpose if developments so dictate. Determine at the outset what your purpose is in listening to any communication.

Improve your concentration. To improve your concentration, sit up straight but not stiffly. Lean toward the speaker slightly. Maintain eye contact. Encourage the speaker by giving feedback. Nod your head, say, "Please go on. I'd like to hear more," or "I see," or "Uh-huh." Make periodic checks that you are understanding the message: "Are you saying that . . .?" or "Let me be sure that I am following you correctly."

Avoid stereotyping the speaker. Don't allow yourself to be distracted by the speaker's mannerisms, vocalized pauses, grammatical errors, or voice. Close your mind to interruptions, noises from the outside, or the side remarks or conversation of others. Remove all distractions. If necessary, shut the door and ask that you not be disturbed. Take notes. And remember that you can't listen while you're talking.

Be open-minded. Don't prejudge the content, and don't decide early on that you're not interested, disagree, or don't like the subject. Help the speaker feel free to talk, put him or her at ease. Show that you want to listen. Avoid defensiveness and don't put the speaker on the defensive. Listen to understand, not to object or oppose. Control your emotions, even when strong language or emotionally loaded words are being used. Don't overreact. Hold your temper. Avoid argument and criticism. Don't jump to conclusions. Don't tune out the speaker prematurely. Listen to the whole message, and don't interrupt. Give the speaker the courtesy of your undivided and unbiased attention.

Listen for ideas. Focus on the basic message, not on too much detail. Take full advantage of your thinking speed to think ahead, compare the point being made with your own experience, draw inferences and conclusions, identify areas of agreement and disagreement, consider applications to your own life or situation, develop questions for the question period, and review what you want to remember.

Check nonverbal behavior. First, monitor your own nonverbal behavior. Be sure that you are encouraging the speaker, not showing rejection, disbelief, or disdain. Be careful not to display negative facial expressions. Don't slouch, look at the ceiling or out the window, and don't make side remarks to others. Also, be sure to check on the speaker's nonverbal behavior to ensure that what he or she is saying is the complete message. Watch facial expressions, gestures and body movements, and posture; listen to voice tone, loudness, and pitch.

Ask questions. If the circumstances permit, ask questions to clarify meaning and to show interest in the message. Be sure that the questions you ask are not argumentative, off the point, or reveal that you have been inattentive. Make all your questions legitimate, clear and well phrased, and thought-provoking.

Take notes. Note taking is both an art and a science. Essentially it is the process of extracting, condensing, summarizing, and recording significant information from an oral presentation or discussion (or from written material). Your objective is to produce a record that is succinct (but not too brief), accurate to the nines, and undeniably complete. Notes should contain significant facts, important ideas, and all salient conclusions and recommendations.

Your purposes in taking the notes will determine the depth of detail. You must also consider those who will use your notes, particularly their education and knowledge of the subject. Is your purpose simply to record for future use? For research? To report? To reconstruct in fine detail? Although you should never try to record *everything*, you should always record enough detail that a week later you could reconstruct the presentation from your notes alone.

One further admonition: If you are going to quote someone, be scrupulously precise in recording the quote, and place quotation marks around it to preclude inadvertent plagiarism.

Summary

Of all the communication skills, listening is the most neglected. It is infrequently taught and rarely practiced. Yet it is the most critical skill for all managers, and particularly HR managers with their "human" orientation.

Every day on the job as an HR manager, you must work with and for people—planning and directing programs, services, and activities to make the most of the human assets available to the organization and, at the same time, provide those people with job satisfaction and opportunities to realize their full potential. If you are to be successful in doing those things, you must listen more than you talk, and you must learn to listen more effectively.

Here are some of the most important things to remember about listening.

Listening is a mental function. It involves three elements: sensing, thinking, and reacting. In HR, listening is used to get information, to receive direction, to learn, to coach and counsel, to train and develop, to evaluate performance, to interview, to provide emotional feedback, to persuade, to negotiate, and to interact socially.

There are many barriers to effective listening. Among the most important are prejudgment, stereotyping, distrust of senders, the speaker's delivery, organizational distance, semantic difficulties, temporary (or permanent) physical conditions, and apathy, sophistication, or opposition. These barriers must be overcome if you are to get the information and feedback you need to actuate, encourage, and inspire your subordinates and influence, persuade, or win over your boss.

Some of the most important listening techniques are listening actively, listening for meaning, evaluative listening, nonevaluative listening, and listening with your eyes. All require total concentration and attention and avoidance of such blocks to comprehension as prejudgment, stereotyping, semantic difficulties, and opposition.

The skilled listener can readily identify propaganda, fabrication, and deception. Clues include vagueness, generalizations, exaggeration, inconsistencies, exorbitant claims, euphemisms, epithets and ridicule, specious reasoning, clichés, gratuitous comments, and gestures, facial expressions, and body movement.

To improve your listening skills, listen with purpose, concentrate, be open-minded, listen for ideas, check nonverbal behavior, ask questions, and take notes.

FOR FURTHER READING

Adler, Mortimer J. *How to Speak, How to Listen.* New York: Macmillan, 1985.

Anastasi, Thomas E., Jr. *Listen! Techniques for Improving Communication Skills.* New York: Van Nostrand Reinhold, 1982.

Atwater, Eastwood. *I Hear You: Listening Skills to Make You a Better Manager.* Englewood Cliffs, N.J.: Prentice-Hall, 1982.

Axtel, Roger E. *Do's and Taboos Around the World.* Elmsford, N.Y.: Benjamin, 1985. (Available from Parker Pen Company, P.O. Box 1616, Janesville, WI 53547)

Bacheller, Franklin. *Listening and Recall*. Englewood Cliffs, N.J.: Prentice-Hall, 1986.

Banville, Thomas G. *How to Listen—How to Be Heard*. Chicago: Nelson-Hall, 1978.

Barker, Larry L. *Listening Behavior*. Englewood Cliffs, N.J.: Prentice-Hall, 1971.

Brownell, Judith L. *Building Active Listening Skills*. Englewood Cliffs, N.J.: Prentice-Hall, 1986.

Burley-Allen, Madelyn. *Listening: The Forgotten Skill*. New York: John Wiley & Sons, 1982.

Clinard, Helen. "Listen for the Difference." *Training and Development Journal*, October 1985, p. 39.

Dellinger, Susan, and Barbara Deane. *Communicating Effectively: A Complete Guide for Better Managing*. Radnor, Penn.: Chilton, 1980, chapters 4–7.

Feldman, Sandor S. *Mannerisms of Speech and Gestures in Everyday Life*. New York: International Universities Press, 1959.

Glatthorn, Allan A., and Herbert R. Adams. *Listening Your Way to Management Success*. Glenview, Ill.: Scott, Foresman, 1983.

Lucas, Stacey. "Listening Is a Learned Art." *Working Woman*, August 1983, pp. 45–46.

Maidment, Robert. *Tuning In: A Guide to Effective Listening*. Gretna, La.: Pelican, 1984.

Montgomery, Robert L. *Listening Made Easy: How to Improve Listening on the Job, at Home and in the Community*. New York: AMACOM, 1981.

———. "Are You a Good Listener?" *Nation's Business*, October 1981, pp. 65–66.

Morgan, Glen M. "Therapeutic Listening—A Communication Tool." *Training and Development Journal*, August 1983, pp. 44–46.

Nichols, Ralph G., and Leonard A. Stevens. *Are You Listening?* New York: McGraw-Hill, 1957.

Nierenberg, Gerard I. *The Art of Negotiating*. New York: Cornerstone Library, 1981.

———. "How to Recognize Needs." In his *Fundamentals of Negotiating*. New York: Editorial Correspondents, 1973.

——— and Henry Calero. *How to Read a Person Like a Book*. New York: Cornerstone Library, 1972.

Pease, Allan. "How to Tell If Someone Is Lying." *Reader's Digest*, December 1984, pp. 135–138.

Steil, Lyman K. "Communication Training: Listening." In *Human Resources Management and Development Handbook*, edited by William R. Tracey. New York: AMACOM, 1985.

———. *Listening: It Can Change Your Life*. New York: McGraw-Hill, 1985.

——— and George DeMare. *Listening—It Can Change Your Life: A Handbook for Scientists and Engineers*. New York: John Wiley & Sons, 1983.

————, Larry Barker, and Kittie Watson. *Effective Listening: Key to Your Success.* Reading, Mass.: Addison-Wesley, 1983.

Terris, Walter F. *Effective Listening.* San Jose, Calif.: Lansford Publishing (P.O. Box 8711, 1088 Lincoln Avenue, 95155), 1976.

Weaver, Carl. *Human Listening.* Indianapolis, Ind.: Bobbs-Merrill, 1972.

2

SPEAKING
When You Are the
Medium for the Message

Public speaking ranks number one as an intimidator. "Time and again the results are the same. When asked to name the things that daunt them, business people put 'giving a speech in public' at the top of their list of fears. It outranks senility, death, disease, fire, famine, flood and losing one's job."[1] Unfortunately, most people have little training in oral presentation skills. Those who have mastered the skills are in the minority, and they have usually acquired their proficiency on their own through trial and error.

As a human resources manager, you must be able to give your very best in training sessions, panel discussions, press conferences, speeches, employee orientations, staff briefings, sales and stockholders' meetings, and client or customer presentations, as well as in one-on-one dialog with your subordinates, superiors, and peers. Those situations are *always* important opportunities, and they are often crucial. Skill in oral presentations can influence the success or failure of an individual manager, a project, a campaign, or an organization, and public speeches affect the image of the HR manager and the organization he or she represents. Oral presentations are often make-or-break opportunities and challenges. They are also situations that inspire great anxiety, if not outright fear.

Being knowledgeable about your organization or well prepared with facts and figures often isn't enough to ensure success. As an HR manager you need to know how to make people listen and believe you. You need to develop your speaking skills to command attention, project credibility, establish rapport, and generate enthusiasm and support.

1. Ron Zemke, in a film review for *Training, The Magazine of Human Resource Development,* November 1985, © Lakewood Publications, Inc., Minneapolis, Minn. Reprinted with permission.

The Big Speech

Regardless of the form, purpose, or format, there are some guidelines that apply to almost every speaking situation: audience analysis, advance preparation, rehearsal, proper apparel, appropriate use of humor, voice, speech, style, and body language, and ability to handle questions.

Controlling Stage Fright

Do you become panicky or outright terrorized when you face a speaking engagement? Do your hands perspire, your knees tremble, and your mouth and tongue become dry when you are introduced to an audience? Does your voice quaver when you begin to speak? Have you ever drawn a complete blank for a second or two during a presentation? Do you sometimes grope for words, lose your train of thought, or become disorganized?

If any of these things happen to you, you are not alone. But don't despair, your affliction can certainly be moderated, if not completely cured. The experiences of many others have confirmed that fact. You can become an effective speaker. However, you cannot—and should not—completely overcome your nervousness. To be at your best, you need to feel some tension to get the adrenalin flowing and to sharpen your senses. Your objective is to learn to *control* your nervousness so that it is concealed and does not become dysfunctional.

Even if you are not gifted with a strong and rich voice, an imposing presence, an impressive vocabulary, or personal charisma, you can be interesting, engaging, and, most important of all, believable. All it takes is knowhow, preparation, and practice.

Setting Your Objectives

Although it should be obvious that a speaker must have clearly defined objectives, this is where many people come to grief. They fail to consider carefully what they want to accomplish—what idea, concept, message, emotion, or impetus to action they want to communicate to their audience. Keep firmly in mind from the very beginning what it is you want to achieve, what information, attitude, or feeling you want to leave with your listeners or what action you want them to take. Basically, there are four different objectives of oral presentations: to inform, to persuade, to inspire, or to entertain. HR managers are most often concerned with the first three.

Analyzing Your Audience

The more you know about your audience, the easier it will be to plan and prepare a successful presentation. Start your inquiry early.

Check on the type of group—approximate number, age range, sex, organization level (blue-collar or clerical workers, supervisors, executives), biases, and problems. Ask about their educational and experiential backgrounds. Find out how much they are likely to know about your subject. Learn why they will come to hear you and what, if anything, they will need to do with the information they receive. Pay special attention to potential audience antagonisms and resentments, particularly if listeners are forced to attend. Plan your strategy to overcome those obstacles.

You also need to find out what comes before you on the program— who is going to speak and what about—and how you fit in.

Writing Your Introduction

Always write your own introduction. Keep it short. Remember that it is an introduction, not your obituary. Tailor it to your purpose, the occasion, and your audience. Underscore items in your training and experience that are germane to your subject and most familiar to your audience.

Organizing and Sequencing Your Talk

Always write out your talk in full. This is not to suggest that you read a manuscript when you're at the podium. Later, you will convert the talk to an outline or a set of key words. Focus on the needs of your audience and you can't go wrong. Then, in addition to that basic rule, you need to consider an effective opening, a strong body, and a forceful closing.

The opening. You must grab the audience's attention within the first 30 seconds. To do that, you need a hook, something that will capture their interest. It can be a quote, a vital statistic, a personal anecdote, a startling statement, or a question. One of the most effective openings is to ask a rhetorical question that, when answered, will reveal benefits to the listeners. *Don't* open with a joke. If it falls flat, it will be very difficult for you to recover. Think carefully about your opening. Develop a strong one. Then *memorize* and *rehearse* it.

The body. Begin by briefly outlining what you plan to cover in your talk; tell them what you're going to tell them. Then tell them. Build your position, using statements, anecdotes, and examples that support your theme. Include personalized material when appropriate, but avoid extraneous content. Keep your remarks relevant to the subject and to the point. The keys are brevity and conciseness.

Give special attention to your main point, the idea or message that you want to leave with your listeners. Repeat it at least three times: at the beginning of your presentation, during your discourse, and at the end of your talk. Repetition is a very important factor in oral communication; it can add emphasis, promote understanding, elaborate key points, intensify feelings, or achieve dramatic impact. You can avoid sounding redundant by using synonyms or different phrases and by varying the format. For example, instead of "Don't fail to repeat your main point," say, "Be sure to restate your main theme" or "Paraphrase your basic thesis." Or change to the interrogative form: "Why is repetition so important?"

Avoid offensive content, any material that is racial, ethnic, sexist, off color, patronizing, insulting, or incompatible with national, regional, community, or audience values. If you use visuals, be sure that they are topnotch in design, color, readability, and focus. Likewise, your audio—that is, sound level, absence of distortion, appropriateness of music—should be of professional quality. Don't use humor unless it is appropriate *and* you can pull it off.

The closing. Don't preface your closing with "In conclusion . . . ." Get right to the summary and concluding statement. Tell them what you told them. However, be sure that your closing relates directly to your listeners and tells them something of value to them. Plan your close carefully, memorize it, and rehearse it.

Preparing Yourself

Now that you have prepared your talk, you are ready to prepare yourself. One of the things you can do is to exercise your voice. Speak often, read aloud, sing. Stretch your voice to strengthen it and give it more range, color, resonance, and power.

Rehearse, Practice, and Rehearse Again

Time your presentation and practice until you feel certain that you can present it confidently and competently. Read it over and over in front of a mirror. Underscore key words. Tape record it. Do a dry run with a colleague, a friend, your spouse, or your teenager. Get as much feedback as you can, make needed changes, and rehearse again.

Dressing for Your Talk

Speakers are judged in part by the image they project. Clothing is a prominent and important component of image. It has a positive impact on an audience, and it can also heighten your self-confidence. Women speakers must be especially careful about their apparel. Although there is no "uniform" that works as effectively as a business suit does for men, women should choose ensembles that are attractive, businesslike, and in good taste. Both men and women should select clothing that is comfortable and conservative, but not dull. They should avoid outlandish colors, flamboyant or eccentric styles, and wild fashions.

If the presentation is to be on TV, wear subtle, solid colors; avoid whites, bright reds, and solid blacks. Wear two solid colors but no more than one patterned item. Don't wear splashy prints or herringbones. Men should wear over-the-calf-length socks. Women should use a little more makeup than usual. Both men and women should use light pancake makeup on face and hands.

For any speaking occasion, dark and medium-tone clothing is best; use accessories for accents. Wear a base color with an accent color. Your suit is always the base color; your shirt and tie or blouse and scarf are the accenting color. Men can use strong, vividly colored ties and women bright scarves, belts, or costume jewelry.

Check the Setting

Get to the auditorium, meeting room, classroom, studio, or platform before the audience arrives, preferably 20 or 30 minutes early. Check the seating arrangements, the position of the podium, microphone, and audiovisual equipment and their controls. Familiarize yourself with the location of light switches and sound controls. If possible, arrange the seating to your preference. Conduct a check of the sound system, and adjust the sound level. Turn on the projector or recorder. Be sure that everything is operating, that there are spare lamps for projectors, and that all items are correctly positioned. If you are going to have a projectionist, work out your cues ahead of time. Do everything possible to avoid mishaps, surprises, and malfunctions.

If you can, mingle with your audience before you are introduced. Find out what interests them. Be on the alert for comments and questions that you may be able to incorporate into your remarks.

Final Preparations

If possible, spend the last two or three minutes alone and out of view of your audience. Get a few breaths of air or a drink of water; reduce your nervousness by swinging your arms and legs, rolling your head and shoulders, and stretching your facial muscles. Just before you are introduced, review your opening statement. Now the adrenalin should be flowing. You are ready.

Presenting Your Talk

All your advance preparations should make your talk effective. Your rehearsals should have helped you to make the most of your material, your voice, and your personality. In addition, here are some of the things that go into an effective and professional presentation.

The First Few Minutes

When you are introduced, stand tall, relaxed but alert. Look at the person who is introducing you and smile as modestly as you can. But *smile*. Then turn to your listeners, and establish eye contact with three people before you say a word. In the first 15 seconds, acknowledge the introduction, tell the audience about how long you're going to speak, establish your purpose, and identify the main reason for your listeners to be interested (what's in it for them). Two admonitions: *Never* tap the mike and ask, "Can you hear me?" *Never* apologize for not being the right speaker for the subject or for not having had enough advance notice to prepare properly.

Voice and Speech

Speak without a script or only with notes. Maintain eye contact. Talk with, not at, your listeners. Use simple, concrete words. Don't assume that words you commonly use are perfectly clear to others. Avoid words that are difficult to say. Use short sentences. Make effective use of pauses (make them two seconds in length). Pause briefly between sentences, and pause to change tempo. Vary your rhythm. Articulate carefully. Speak in a low voice, and use lots of jaw and lip movements to improve your diction and tone. Above all, work to eliminate your vocalized pauses, such as the ubiquitous and wearisome "you know" and the equally tiresome "I mean," "okay," and "um."

Remember that intonation conveys hidden messages. A flat or minor tone says, "I'm on the defensive"; a high-pitched or whining tone says, "I'm helpless or frightened"; a mumbling or muffled tone says, "I'm not sure of what I'm saying," or "I really don't want you to hear me"; a loud tone says, "I'm demanding that you listen to me"; and an angry or provocative tone says, "I'm being attacked so I'm counterattacking" or "I feel threatened so I'm making a preemptive strike."

Help the audience follow connections between ideas by using such phrases as "as a result," "on the other hand," (to show contradictions), "even more important," or "not so obvious," (to give emphasis). Summarize periodically.

Speak conversationally. Be enthusiastic, not gushy; forceful, but not overbearing. Avoid orating and dramatic whispering. Shun theatrical tricks. Don't shout or overenunciate. Speak clearly and crisply. Avoid chopping your speech into glib fragments. Vary the pitch and volume of your voice and the rate of delivery, but don't speak too fast or too slowly.

Style

The speaking style you choose depends on several things: your audience, your relationship with your listeners, your rapport with the audience, your message, and the interactions of these four factors. For example, you speak with different styles to very young children, teenagers, adults, employers or supervisors, employees or subordinates, construction workers, and other HR managers. Your style also varies when you have a one-shot speaking engagement and when you have a series of meetings with the same group of listeners. Your style must also change when you are simply giving information, when you are trying to persuade a group to accept a proposal, and when you are attempting to inspire confidence and extraordinary effort.

Although style is difficult to describe, it is easily recognized by your listeners. What are its key elements?

Tone of voice.   Your tone can be varied considerably. It can be forceful or restrained, humorous or serious, enthusiastic or subdued, impassioned or matter-of-fact.

Level of content.   You can be sophisticated or homespun, complex or simple, lofty or down to earth. Don't patronize or talk down to your audience, but be reasonable. Your audience may not need to understand every word you say, but they need to comprehend *most* of what you are trying to communicate.

Word choice.   Your vocabulary must be adjusted to your audience and your tone. Word choice must be appropriate to both. Consider, for example, the different connotations of *teacher* and *instructor, boss* and *superior, dollars* and *bread, use* and *exploit, investment* and *expenditure, productive* and *creative.* Be extra careful about the words you use. Be sure that they match your tone, convey your exact meaning, and can be readily understood by your listeners.

Body Language

Avoid head tossing, elaborate shrugs, pacing, and side-to-side movements. For emphasis, use body language and facial expressions, but don't exaggerate them. Make the size of your gestures in proportion to the size of your audience. Use full-arm gestures and forward and backward movements, but use them sparingly. Don't point with your finger. Instead, keep your hands open with your palms turned up when you gesture. Avoid closed-fist gestures. Smile occasionally, but only when it is appropriate. Be your natural, best self.

Using Humor

Use humor only to build rapport, make a point, or defuse a tense or awkward situation—not to get a big laugh. Keep all jokes and stories brief and, if possible, personalized. Make your stories realistic. Leave out extraneous details. Deliver them smoothly. Don't step on your lines. Insert only one pause—just before the punchline. Memorize your jokes word for word. Try them out beforehand and scrap the duds. Rehearse and rehearse until you can tell them with proper intonation and timing. Never, repeat *never,* tell a racial, ethnic, or off-color joke. Crude remarks or smutty anecdotes will immediately put you at the head of the list of the world's worst speakers.

Handling Questions

Don't start a question period with "Do you have any questions?" Be more direct and specific. Ask for expressions of feelings or reactions to the suggestions, proposals, or recommendations you have made in your talk. Listen to each question carefully, and be sure you understand the question before attempting to answer. Handle difficult questions by paraphrasing, briefly restating the question. This gives you more time to think about your answer, and it provides the questioner with an opportunity to correct your interpretation of the question. Don't argue, and never say anything off the record.

Controlling a Resistant Audience

Although resistance to speakers is not often blatant and open, it is not uncommon. At its best, it is characterized by icy stares, gaping yawns, snide remarks, or note passing. At its worst, it takes the form of heckling, side talk, debating, excessive questioning, disruptive behavior, or questions aimed at trapping the speaker.

Never ignore resistance. Troublemakers cannot be allowed to take control; they must be dealt with quickly and surely. If you don't, the result will be trampled decorum, wasted time, and failure to attain the objectives of the presentation. However, one thing must be avoided at all costs: threats to the audience or a show of annoyance. Never become defensive and never attempt to retaliate. You must keep cool and avoid getting into one-on-one battles, heated debates, or arguments with listeners. Don't use sarcasm, putdowns, or jokes at the expense of hecklers. They may cause neutral listeners to sympathize with the mischief-makers and not with you.

When you encounter resistance, the first thing you must try to do is to find out why it is occurring. There are several possibilities. Some people may have been forced to attend. Others may not see how the session is relevant to them or to their jobs. Others may have an overwhelming need to be the focus of attention. If you can discover the "why" behind the behavior, you will be in a better position to deal with it. Here are some specific suggestions:

- For those who have something to say on every topic or who try to dominate the question period, interrupt them when they pause for breath. Then say, "That's very interesting. How do the rest of you feel about that?" Then immediately break eye contact and move it to another part of the audience.
- For obnoxious hecklers, keep calm. When they criticize or disagree, acknowledge the legitimacy of their point of view, challenge them for specifics, and then see if the audience agrees with them. If it's a personal attack, keep cool and say something like this: "It's obvious that you and I should discuss this at another time." And then go on to the next question or comment.
- For the side-talkers, stop, smile, look directly at them, and pause until they stop talking.

Critiquing Your Presentation

There is one final step in the process—and one that should never be omitted or neglected—the critique. A constructive critique can improve your preparation and your performance the next time. Preferably, the critique involves others, independent and objective observers who can give you a fair, unbiased, and accurate rundown on your performance, its strengths and its weaknesses. If good observers are not available, you must do the critiquing yourself. What do you need to know?

1. Was your analysis of the audience on target? If it wasn't, where did you miss?
2. Was your objective realistic? Did you achieve it?
3. What features of your talk were especially well received by your listeners? Which ones were not so well received, and why?
4. What aspects of your delivery need shoring up?

Transcultural Presentations

Foreign audiences, or listeners whose second language is English, pose special problems for speakers. Be especially careful about:

- Puns and gags; TV and show biz one-liners.
- Buzzwords such as *feedback, interface, reentry,* and *burnout.*
- Idioms and figures of speech such as "don't make waves," "keep a low profile," "dog and pony show," "shotgun approach."
- Sports and military metaphors; your audience may not relate to:
    Ballpark figure
    That won't get you to first base
    Batting a thousand
    End run

    Slam dunk
    A new ball game
    On a roll
    Bush league
    On the ropes
    Run it up the flagpole
    Hat trick

- Acronyms and abbreviations, such as ASAP, FYI, IAW, POL, R&R, R&D, CEO, and ROI.

Remember that there are other pitfalls besides language; many are cultural. However, those difficulties can be overcome, especially if you remember that the actual words used are only one mode of communication (the other two are tonal and nonverbal), and some experts think they are by far the least important of the three.

Here are some suggestions for communicating with people from other cultural backgrounds:

- Know the cultural differences and the taboos of your audience to avoid misunderstandings and unconscious offenses.
- Know the educational level of your listeners and their English competency in listening, reading, and writing.
- Always speak slowly and clearly; enunciate.
- Allow more time to accommodate a slower pace.
- Avoid multisyllabic words and jargon; keep words simple.
- Use short and simple sentences.
- Write key words and special vocabulary on flip charts.
- Audibly punctuate; use pauses and full stops.
- Describe processes in short steps.
- Translate difficult, confusing, or ambiguous (but necessary) words into the language used by the listeners. (Get the help of a native speaker to do this.)
- Use plenty of examples and illustrations.
- Encourage questions and discussion during your presentation.
- Make certain that all problems and situations are appropriate and relevant to the lives of your listeners in their own country.
- Take more frequent breaks than usual.
- Allow role playing and breakout discussions in the native language.
- Summarize your talk in writing and, if possible, prepare your visuals in English and the native language of your listeners.

Visual Aids

Used properly, visual aids can facilitate communication and liven up a presentation. They must be relevant, necessary, current, and new to the audience. The most important thing to remember is that they should remain *aids* to the speaker and not become the primary means of communicating.

Visual aids include overhead transparencies (7½ by 9½), 35mm slides, 16 and 8mm motion picture film, video cassette and videodisc recordings, audio recordings, flip charts, chalkboards, and printed or duplicated handouts. They are used to stimulate interest, focus attention on critical elements of a presentation, provide illustration, effect emphasis, and summarize.

Visual aids should fit the maturity and interest of the audience. They must not be childish or naive, obscure or overly complex. They must also complement and reinforce the talk. Projected aids should be professionally made. Don't do your own lettering, artwork, or photography; homemade visual aids are seldom adequate. However, keep artwork simple. For slides, stick to either a horizontal or vertical format; don't mix them. Use print on slides that is one-quarter inch or larger and in a readable type style. Never use typewritten material. Never use more than six words per line or more than eight lines per visual. Mark slides for fail-safe loading and reference in the projector tray.

When using visual aids, be sure not to block the audience's view. Try to avoid turning off room lights; a darkened room promotes passivity and drowsiness. Keep projectors in focus. Never use a pointer on the screen when using an overhead projector; point on the overhead itself using a pencil. And don't talk to your visuals; face the audience at all times.

Other Speaking Situations

Although all the foregoing "rules," suggestions, and recommendations apply to just about every type of oral presentation, there are some special considerations that apply to one-on-one dialog, panels and symposiums, television appearances, transcultural discussions, and formal briefings.

One-on-One Dialog

As an HR manager, have you ever assigned specific tasks to subordinates and then found out that they worked on something very different from what you intended? Have you ever been in the middle of a disagreement and couldn't find a means of settling it? Have you ever discovered that your boss really didn't understand your proposal and now it's too late to do anything about it? Have you ever believed that you hired the right person, but now find out that he or she is not working out? If any of these things have happened to you—and they have to most of us—you have failed to communicate.

Objectives

Every day, HR managers must communicate one on one with subordinates, superiors, and peers. They must exchange facts, ideas, information, opinions, meanings, emotions, and perceptions. Such communication provides the information and understanding needed to attain the goals and objectives of the HR department and the total organization. That kind of communication is needed to build, maintain, and enhance employees' motivation, spirit of cooperation, and job satisfaction by providing guidance, assistance, encouragement, and feedback on performance.

Here are some of the specific uses of one-on-one communication:

1. To handle sensitive or confidential matters such as reprimands, personal counseling, and terminations.
2. To create openness, free interchange, involvement, candor, and warmth, and to personalize communication.
3. To save time, when deadlines are critical or information is needed immediately.
4. To assure maximum understanding by accepting questions and getting immediate feedback.
5. To supplement written communications.

Requirements

What does it take to get the results you want? To be successful as a one-on-one communicator, you must:

1. Get others to listen to you.
2. Control your voice, gestures, movements, and facial expressions to add authenticity, credibility, and power to your words.
3. Send clear messages and say what you really mean.
4. Get your messages across the first time.
5. Make your point and produce a positive impact with everything you say.
6. Use patterns of communication and words that turn people on.
7. Anticipate and avoid misunderstandings.
8. "Read" more accurately and respond more sensitively to people.
9. Understand how your words and behavior affect others.
10. Avoid defensiveness and defuse confrontations.
11. Get feedback to double check understanding.

Guidelines for Success

You should follow a few basic guidelines when communicating one on one. Although they apply to all types of communication, these standards are critically important in face-to-face situations.

Positive climate.   Effective communication depends on the existence of a positive climate, an atmosphere that will encourage the right attitudes, habits, expectations, and performance of subordinates. It is a climate of openness, trust, and mutual confidence and respect.

Appropriate objectives.   The HR manager must establish objectives that are realistic and acceptable to the people who must accomplish them. Unrealistic, unattainable, or unacceptable objectives build insurmountable obstacles to communication.

Proper address.   To be useful and effective, communication must be channeled to the right person. If communication goes to the wrong persons in the system, they may block, withhold, or distort it.

Clarity.   To be effective, oral communication must be understood, and to be understood, it must be clear. Don't use words that are not likely to be familiar to the receiver. Consider and respect the listener's position, orientation, interests, and capacity to understand.

Brevity.   Long and involved sentences make comprehension difficult. Brevity makes understanding easier. Avoiding communication overload is a must.

Precision.   Precise terms, words that have a standard meaning, should be used exclusively if semantic difficulties are to be avoided. Remember, too, that some words have heavy emotional loading and should not be used.

Integrity.   Speech should always be used as a means, never as an end. HR managers must say what they mean and mean what they say. Deceit, propagandizing, preaching, attempted brainwashing, or other hidden motives should not enter communication any time or anywhere.

Panels and Symposiums

Serving as the moderator or member of a panel poses considerably different problems from those encountered in a solo speaking effort. An effective panel presentation requires topnotch planning and execution by all participants. It also demands total cooperation and coordination.

The Moderator

The moderator plans the session, sets the stage for discussion of the subject or issue, manages the event to maximize the exchange of points of view, provides transitions between speakers, keeps the presentation on target and on time, and sums up at the end.

Specifically, when you serve as moderator, you should:

1. Plan carefully and thoroughly for the session.

    -   Develop a statement of objective, a set of ground rules, and time cues, and provide them to panelists well in advance.
    -   Prepare a brief introduction for each panelist, focusing on their expertise on the subject of discussion; double check on the pronunciation of their names.
    -   Prepare opening remarks that tell the audience what the discussion is about and why it is important; describe the format; set time limits and other ground rules.
    -   Prepare closing remarks, including a summary and concluding statement.

2. Conduct the session with aplomb, good humor, and efficiency.

    -   Introduce yourself simply—your name, the fact that you are the moderator, your job title, and your current affiliation.
    -   Introduce the panelists.
    -   Set the stage, atmosphere, and ground rules.
    -   Get agreement on purposes.
    -   Keep the group focused on purpose or problem.
    -   Help the group progress toward its goals.
    -   Intervene tactfully when a panelist exceeds the time limits.
    -   Provide transition comments to link presentations.
    -   Use visual (flip charts, chalkboards) and oral feedback.

3. Invite questions from the audience; assign them to the appropriate panelist.
4. Maintain order and decorum even when controversy flares up.
5. Conclude the session.

    -   Briefly summarize each panelist's view.
    -   Present a concluding statement.
    -   Thank the panelists and the audience.

The Panelists

The role of the panelists is to prepare and present brief, well-planned, and to-the-point remarks that represent their positions on the subject or issue. Specifically, as a panelist your responsibilities are:

1. Plan carefully and thoroughly for the session.

   ○ Review the objective statement, ground rules, and other information provided by the moderator.
   ○ Prepare your remarks, keeping the time limits in mind.
   ○ Try to anticipate questions the listeners will ask.

2. Help the moderator create an open, constructive atmosphere.

   ○ Address relevant questions to the moderator and other panelists.
   ○ Suggest new or better approaches and solutions.
   ○ Help get silent opposition or resistance into the open.
   ○ Ask for clarification of important ideas and suggestions.

3. Be attentive at all times during the panel session.

   ○ Be an active listener when not speaking; look at the speaker.
   ○ Take notes to show your attentiveness and to prepare for questions or for the transition statement.
   ○ Be careful with your facial expressions, posture, and movements; don't act bored, disapproving, or hostile.
   ○ Develop your own transition in case the moderator fails to provide one.
   ○ Present your remarks and concluding statement.
   ○ Be ready to answer questions.

Television Appearances

Speaking on television is different from speaking to a live audience, in several important ways. You must be aware of:

1. The camera itself. The red-eyed monster is to many people a frightening thing because they must face it and cannot hide from it.
2. The audience. Although it may encompass millions of people, it is much like talking to one person or a very small group. The audience is not obligated to listen to you; they can change channels or shut you off.
3. The clock. There are definite time limits to a commercial TV presentation, and they cannot be ignored.
4. The requirements of the medium. The speaker's movements and gestures must be slower and narrower in scope; the voice softer and more conversational; and the speaker must be clear, concise, and colorful. Brevity and succinctness are essential, but the overwhelming requirements are sincerity and naturalness.

To make the most of a TV appearance or interview, follow these suggestions. If you're overtired, postpone the appearance if at all possible. The camera exaggerates lines and wrinkles, circles under the eyes, and shadows. Get as much rest as possible beforehand. Don't eat a large meal; eat lightly, if at all. Be prepared for the glare of lights. Try to be personal, conversational, relaxed, and informal. Let your face and body show animation and some emotion.

The Interview

If the appearance is an interview, try to give the interviewer some questions in advance. Be sure that you know in advance the purpose of the interview and who will conduct it. Prepare fact sheets for distribution to media representatives. Include a contact name on all handouts. If possible, before starting the interview, establish some ground rules; for example, what will be covered, what will not be responded to, and how long the interview will be. During commercial breaks or between "takes" if the program is being prerecorded, suggest new directions for the conversation. Be sure that you make your points. Prepare in advance the information you want to cover.

Speak directly to the interviewer; occasionally look directly at the camera lens, particularly when you want to emphasize a point. Beware of panning, cutaways, and reaction shots, where the camera focuses on you while others are speaking; don't be caught fidgeting, scowling, or yawning.

Be ready for embarrassing questions. They are almost certain to be asked, so prepare for them in advance and turn them to your advantage. For example, say, "I don't know about that, but in our organization . . . " or, "Let's look at a larger issue . . . ."

In a crisis situation, take the time to prepare a statement that can be delivered in 60 seconds or less. Short statements stand the best chance of getting on the air without being cut.

Be on guard for the friendly interviewer who suddenly turns hostile, baits you, or tries to corner you. Concentrate on the question, not on the tone. Above all, keep your cool. Try tactfully to guide the interviewer back to the topic you came to discuss.

Never respond to a question with "no comment." But don't say anything that you don't want to be used as a story headline. Above all, don't show annoyance, anger, or confusion. Don't respond directly to questions that use statistics or quote reports you are unfamiliar with or disagree with. Explain that you are not familiar with the numbers (or conclusions or recommendations) and respond if possible to the thrust of the question.

Don't offer personal opinions when you are officially representing your organization. But do put realism into your press conferences by using a location-type background that is representative of your organization. For example, an oil rig for an oil company, a moving van for a transportation company, a cutter for a Coast Guard training officer. Answer all questions in 20 seconds or less. Don't be dull, immobile, or sonorous. And don't overstay your welcome.

Press Room Setup

If you are being interviewed at your company's offices, rather than at a professional TV studio, it's advisable to set up a room for the interview itself and for press briefings. The room should be large enough to accommodate both people and equipment, with a ceiling at least eight feet high. Make sure there are enough grounded electrical outlets to meet media requirements, and have adequate lighting. Telephones, typewriters, paper, and other incidentals should be readily available and accessible. Staff people should be on hand to assist.

Video Recordings

Most of the television suggestions apply equally to video recordings, whether video cassette or videodisc, produced for use in house or out, for information or for training. Of course, the recorded format offers one very important advantage: The presentation, discussion, or interview can be scripted, rehearsed, recorded, rerecorded, and edited so that the final product is smooth, clear, interesting, and believable, free from errors of fact and presentation, and timed to fit a predetermined number of minutes.

Briefings

The oral briefing is one of the tasks most crucial to effective and successful performance by HR managers at all levels in business, industry, government, and the military. There are two types, each with a distinctive purpose and a unique format.

Types

The **information briefing** is intended simply to inform. The primary goal is not to influence, provoke, indoctrinate, or inspire, although the briefing may do one or more of those things in addition. Information briefings are designed to familiarize, interpret, or report on something of importance or concern.

Here are some examples of information briefing titles:

"Progress Report on Project X"
"Quarterly Review and Analysis Report of the HR Department"
"Overview of the New Executive Compensation Plan"

The **decision briefing** is designed to obtain a verdict or judgment on an issue from an individual or group empowered to make that decision. The primary purpose of the decision briefing is to sell an idea, based on facts and logic.

Examples of decision briefing titles include:

"Proposed HR Department Budget Allocations for FY 1989"
"An Action Plan for Installing a Mentoring Program for Mid-level Managers"
"A Strategy for Dealing with the People Factor in the Proposed Merger"
"A System for Retraining Workers Whose Skills Have Become Obsolete"

Formats

The first three steps in both information and decision briefings are identical; the fourth and later steps are considerably different.

Step 1. State the purpose of the briefing at the outset: whether it is for orientation or information; to describe or report; to get a decision or approval.

Step 2. State the reasons for the briefing, how the action started.

Step 3. Outline the organization of the briefing.

Then, for the information briefing:

Step 4. Talk facts. Stick to essentials and get to the point. Clearly distinguish fact from opinion. Set forth the information concisely and precisely. Use visual aids where appropriate and helpful. Make them large enough and keep them simple.

Step 5. Summarize your main points directly, accurately, and succinctly.

Or, to complete the decision briefing:

Step 4. Identify potential costs and savings—your attention-getter. This is where you relate your proposal to company profitability. Compare costs and benefits in a one-sentence summary.

Step 5. Talk facts. Identify the facts that led to a definition of the real problem or issue. Include the 4 Ws: what, when, where, and who. Then express the real problem as a task.

Step 6. Identify and discuss the facts that bear on the solution to the problem or the resolution of the issue. Again include the 4 Ws. Use simple visuals to illustrate. Include the criteria for judging the adequacy of the solution.

Step 7. Identify and discuss alternative courses of action, the advantages and disadvantages, and the costs and benefits of each one.

Step 8. Present your conclusions. Make your statements direct and precise. Be blunt. Don't hedge. Again, emphasize costs and benefits.

Step 9. Present your recommendation. Put your recommended solutions in such a form that action may be taken by the decision maker. Make them specific. Be sure to include the kind and amount of support you will need from the boss as well as from others.

In sum, the oral briefing is one of the most important and useful tools in the repertoire of the competent HR manager. It *must* be mastered.

Summary

The oral presentation is one of the most important tools in the repertoire of the competent HR manager. Here, by way of review, are some of the most important things to remember about it.

You must develop and hone your oral presentation skills if you are to be able to command attention, establish rapport, project credibility, and generate enthusiasm and support for your organization and your HR programs and services. If you are to be effective, interesting, and believable as a speaker, you must have knowhow, and you must practice. Stage fright or extreme nervousness can be controlled by careful and thorough planning, preparation, and rehearsal.

Clearly defined objectives are basic to the development of an effective talk. There are only four types of objectives: to inform, to persuade, to inspire, or to entertain. Most presentations required of HR managers have as their objective to inform, persuade, or inspire.

The more you know about your audience, their interests, concerns, biases, and educational and experiential backgrounds, the easier it will be for you to prepare a winning presentation. The real key to an effective talk is to focus on the needs of the listeners. The opening 30 seconds are crucial. During that short span, you must seize the interest and attention of your audience. If you are unsuccessful, your chances of capturing their attention are remote.

Your speech should always be written out in full when you are preparing, but use only notes when you are presenting. The proper sequence to follow in developing content is to tell your listeners what you're going to tell them, then tell them, and finally tell them what you told them.

Your preparation for a presentation should include a wise choice of apparel since clothing is a prominent and important component of your image. Multiple rehearsals and feedback from others during your practice sessions are essential.

Don't overlook the importance of a preliminary check of the setting of your speaking engagement. That check should include seating arrangements, the sound system, and audiovisual equipment.

When you deliver your speech, use simple words, short sentences, and pauses. Speak in a low, conversational tone, use repetition for emphasis and dramatic impact, and adjust your style to match your audience and your message. If you use humor, do so with care, and then only to build rapport or make a point, not to get a big laugh. Racial, ethnic, sexist, or off-color jokes or anecdotes should never be used.

Television poses special problems for speakers because of the requirements of the medium itself, time constraints, and the nature and remoteness of the audience. Similarly, panels, interviews, and presentations to transcultural groups involve additional planning. Because they often involve considerable risk to your image and the reputation of the organization you represent, careful preparation is essential.

Of all the forms of oral presentation, information and decision briefings are the two tasks most crucial to successful performance of HR managers at all levels of the organization and in all types of enterprise. They must be mastered.

FOR FURTHER READING

Alexander, Roy. *Power Speech: The Quickest Route to Business and Personal Success.* New York: AMACOM, 1986.

Allen, S. *How to Make a Speech.* Del Mar, Calif.: McGraw-Hill Training Systems, 1985.

Axtell, Roger E. *Do's and Taboos Around the World.* Elmsford, N.Y.: Benjamin, 1985. (Available from Parker Pen Company, P.O. Box 1616, Janesville, WI 53547)

Berry, Susan E., and Robert J. Garmston. "Become a State-of-the-Art Presenter." *Training and Development Journal,* January 1987, pp. 19–23.

Bishop, Kathleen A. "The Silent Signals." *Training and Development Journal,* June 1985, pp. 20–21.

Bland, Michael. *The Executive's Guide to TV and Radio Appearances.* White Plains, N.Y.: Knowledge Industry Publications, 1980.

Cathcart, Jim, and Tony Alessandra. "When in Rome." *Training and Development Journal,* June 1985, pp. 22–23.

Detz, Joan. *How to Write and Give a Speech: A Practical Guide for Executives, P. R. People, Managers, Fund-Raisers, Politicians, Educators, and Anyone Else Who Has to Make Every Word Count.* New York: St. Martin Press, 1984.

Draper, Norman. "Training Managers to 'Meet the Press.' " *Training,* August 1986, pp. 30–38.

Dutton, John L. *How to Be An Outstanding Speaker.* New London, Wisc.: Life Skills Publishing, 1986.

Franco, John J. "Speaker, Know Thy Audience." *Training and Development Journal,* June 1985, pp. 20–21.

Hasling, J. *The Message, The Speaker, The Audience.* Del Mar, Calif.: McGraw-Hill Training Systems, 1982.

Holcombe, Marya W., and Judith K. Stein. *Presentations for Decision Makers.* Belmont, Calif.: Lifetime Learning Publications, 1983.

Humes, James C. *Talk Your Way to the Top.* New York: McGraw-Hill, 1980.

Jeffries, James R., and Jefferson D. Bates. *The Executive's Guide to Meetings, Conferences, and Audiovisual Presentations.* New York: McGraw-Hill, 1983.

Kennedy, Larry E. "Communication Training: Speaking." In *Human Resources Management and Development Handbook,* edited by William R. Tracey. New York: AMACOM, 1985.

Kenney, Michael, and the Editors of Eastman Kodak Company. *Presenting Yourself.* New York: John Wiley & Sons, 1982.

Leech, Thomas. *How to Prepare, Stage, and Deliver Winning Presentations.* New York: AMACOM, 1982.

Louw, Antoni A. "Stage Fright (How to Break Your Own Barriers and Become a More Effective Presenter)." *Training,* August 1986, pp. 55–57.

Lynch, Patricia L. "Surviving the Question and Answer Period." *Training and Development Journal,* June 1985, pp. 32–33.

Man at His Best: The Esquire Guide to Style. Reading, Mass.: Addison-Wesley, 1986.

Max, Robert R. "Wording It Correctly." *Training and Development Journal,* March 1985, pp. 50–51.

Muller, David G. "Effective Speaking: A Basic Takes the Limelight." *Training and Development Journal,* May 1984, pp. 102–106.

Nirenberg, J. *How to Sell Your Ideas.* Del Mar, Calif.: McGraw-Hill Training Systems, 1984.

Rodman, George R. *Speaking Out: Message Preparation for Professionals.* New York: Holt, Rinehart & Winston, 1978.

Sarnoff, Dorothy. *Making the Most of Your Best.* New York: Doubleday, 1981.

Severson, David. "When a Sales Pitch Won't Do." *Training and Development Journal,* June 1985, pp. 44–49.

Shea, Gordon. *Managing a Difficult or Hostile Audience.* Englewood Cliffs, N.J.: Prentice-Hall, 1984.

Tracey, William R. "The Oral Briefing: A Neglected Skill." *The Balance Sheet,* November-December 1984, pp. 29–31.

Valenti, Jack. *Speak Up with Confidence: How to Prepare, Learn, and Deliver Effective Speeches.* New York: Morrow, 1984.

Well, T. *Keeping Your Cool Under Fire: Communicating Non-Defensively.* Del Mar, Calif.: McGraw-Hill Training Systems, 1979.

3

WRITING
The Demanding Skill

Much of the communication in human resources must be in written form—letters, memos, reports, proposals, and the like. But in spite of its importance, many HR people are afraid of writing and others are not very good at it. "In a West Coast survey, the national consulting firm Communispond Inc. found that 93 percent of executives surveyed feel that business writing skills are essential for advancement. However, 91 percent feel that the ability to write is one of the most neglected skills in business."[1]

People often judge managers on their writing ability, on how well they express their ideas in reports and correspondence. Those who can present their thoughts efficiently and persuasively, and use correct grammar and spelling in doing so, are typically seen as competent managers. Those who cannot are considered to be less accomplished than they ought to be.

Another consideration is that bad writing costs money. One expert estimates that the cost of producing a single memo or letter has escalated to more than $7.[2] So a poorly written letter, memo, or report represents a sunk cost, unrecoverable to the organization. Even more important, ineffective or inadequate correspondence and reports may cause misunderstandings, mistakes, and lost opportunities, and they tarnish the image of the writer and the organization he or she represents. Cost-conscious HR managers must improve their writing.

1. "P.S. (For Your Personal Success): Execs Need Writing Guidelines," *Successful Meetings*, June 1986, p. 36. Reprinted with permission from *Successful Meetings* magazine, copyright © 1986, Bill Communications, Inc.
2. Robert R. Max, "Wording It Correctly," *Training and Development Journal*, March 1985, p. 50.

Uses of Written Communications

Basically, written communications in business and industry are used to inform, to persuade, to recommend, to inquire, or to record. The purpose will determine the tone, language, form, and format of the written communication used. But in every case, the objective is to get a positive response from the person to whom the communication is addressed, whether subordinate, peer, superior, customer, client, supplier, consultant, or the general public. A positive response is one that gets the results intended. In addition, competent HR managers will recognize that good writing will increase their influence and credibility.

Written communications are used to:

- Give and gather information and feedback.
- Disseminate policies, procedures, decisions, and commitments.
- Recommend actions and get decisions.
- Track and report progress and accomplishment.
- Communicate outside the organization, with customers, suppliers, colleagues, government agencies, community groups, prospective employees, and the media.

Written messages are used instead of oral communication when the objective is to:

- Exchange ideas over time or distance; for example, sending policy statements to offices nationwide.
- Store and retrieve information for immediate or later use; for example, records.
- Increase objectivity and precision; for example, proposals, agreements, and contracts.
- Enhance validity and reliability by the fact that ideas are committed to writing; for example, critical documents where careful scrutiny by many individuals is necessary.
- Increase impersonality and dispassionateness; for example, disseminating managerial decisions.
- Supplement oral communication; for example, meeting agenda and minutes; supporting documents for an oral briefing.

Limitations

Written communication has several limitations that are not characteristic of oral communication. First, as the subtitle of this chapter implies, written communication is more difficult and demanding; it requires the communicator to follow the rules of sentence structure, paragraphing, and grammar to an extent not needed in oral speech, not to mention the added difficulties of spelling. Second, nonverbal cues—tone of voice, facial expressions, gestures, and body language—are not present. Third, *immediate* feedback is totally lacking.

Elements of Written Communication

Effective written communication involves several important elements: form, tone, style, organization, paragraphing, sentence structure, word choice, grammar, spelling and punctuation, conciseness and clarity, format, appearance and layout, and use of graphics. Let's see what is involved in each.

Form

The most commonly used forms of written communication in HR activities are letters, memos, messages, status reports, trip reports, after-action reports, evaluation reports, critiques, minutes and summaries, staff studies and decision papers, proposals, policy statements, procedures manuals, course descriptions, training documents, job descriptions, applicant specifications, and press releases.

Tone

Tone may be formal or informal, enthusiastic or restrained, lofty or down to earth, forceful or unassuming. Tone is also determined in part by the audience, form of the communication, sophistication of the content, length of paragraphs and sentences, and vocabulary used. Here are some suggestions to achieve the right tone for *most* written communications:

- Pretend that you are talking to the reader in a face-to-face conversation.
- Don't talk down to, patronize, preach to, accuse, or insult the reader.
- Avoid overfamiliarity, coldness, insincerity, writer-centeredness, and emotionally loaded words.
- Never use sarcasm or ridicule, and don't try to be cute.
- Don't convey cynicism, annoyance, or anger.
- Write from the "you" frame of reference.
- Don't exaggerate; understate, but don't hedge.
- Always stress the positive.

Style

Style is determined mainly by the writer. It can be modified because of the person addressed, the relationship of the writer to addressees, the form and format of the message, and the interaction of these factors. Style can be rhythmic, breezy, smooth, animated, or whimsical; it can be brusque, pointed, serious, cadenced, or erudite. One style usually predominates for each writer. However, all writers must change their style to fit the age, educational level, and knowledge of addressees, and their status (subordinate, superior, or colleague).

Style has been defined as

> The art of clear, effective, and readable writing. The rhythm that makes a sentence sound right to the mental ear. The ruthless cutting out of phrases that only clutter and impede this special music. And always, always, the patient, painstaking search for the perfect combination of words and phrases that will create this mental music and express what is to be said in the most moving and effective way.[3]

Here are some specific suggestions for selecting the right style:

- Identify your readers; keep their needs firmly in mind.
- Don't worry about style with your first draft; concentrate on getting your ideas on paper.
- For most forms of communication, use a relaxed, conversational approach; speak directly to the reader.
- Be your natural self; don't try to assume a new personality when you write.
- Adjust your style to the subject at hand.
- Use active language; "I believe," not "It is believed."
- Write in the present tense as much as possible.
- Be consistent throughout your copy, whether long or short.

Organization

Organization refers simply to the way your written materials are put together. Basically, there are two forms of organization: *logical* order, in which the materials are presented in a reasoned arrangement of the content or subject matter, and *psychological* order, representing the best sequence for learning efficiently, persuading successfully, or eliciting truthful responses. Logical order has two forms: *inductive* order, which builds up to a conclusion, recommendation, or course of action; and *deductive* order, which starts with a recommended action, premise, or conclusion, and then provides supporting evidence or arguments.

3. Reprinted with permission from "Twelve Secrets of Style," by Marjorie Holmes, *The Writer*, August 1986, p. 10. Copyright © 1986 by The Writer Inc.

Here are a few specific recommendations for organization:

- Know your purpose and your audience.
- Know exactly what you want to say; organize your facts.
- Build an outline; try to let the subject organize itself.
- Capture the reader's attention in the first sentence.
- Organize the material sequentially by major components or divisions (logical order) or the best sequence to convince, influence, or win (psychological order).
- Use a strong close, a call for action of some kind.

Paragraphing and Sentence Structure

A good paragraph meets the following criteria: (1) it contains an explicit topic sentence; (2) it has a central theme, adequately developed with directly supporting ideas; (3) it is coherent in that it relates ideas through transitions; (4) it contains enough emphasis to make its point; and (5) it is the proper length. Good paragraphing separates thoughts, directs the reader's attention to changes in emphasis, and, through the use of headings, underlining, and white space, helps the reader to focus on each element.

Sentence structure refers to the balance of simple, complex, and compound sentences, and to the voice and tense used. Some suggestions:

- Use the active voice and present tense, if possible.
- Use short paragraphs, not more than 12 lines.
- Start a new paragraph for each new thought or subject.
- Use paragraph leads (the *few* words that indicate or cue the content of the paragraph) in bold-faced type, italics, or underlined, and separate paragraphs with white space.
- Use short (but not choppy) sentences (15 to 25 words).
- Use fewer than 150 syllables for each 100 words.
- Don't bury your main point in verbiage, intricate sentences, or disjointed paragraphs.

Word Choice

Word choice is simply the vocabulary you use. However, it involves much more than adjusting vocabulary to the educational and experiential levels of the readers. The words you use must also be appropriate to your tone and style. Here are some do's and don'ts.

- Use words that are appropriate for your readers.
- Use forceful words; avoid words like *generally, quite, rather, largely*.
- Use active voice and active words. Instead of "I am of the opinion that," write "I believe that."

- Use strong verbs. "Analyze," not "make an analysis of"; "decide," not "come to a decision"; "report," not "present a report"; "consider," not "take into consideration."
- Avoid jargon, acronyms, clichés, euphemisms, and unfamiliar words.
- If you use figures of speech, colloquialisms, technical or business terms, sports or military metaphors, or showbiz idioms or expressions, be sure your audience will understand them.
- Try to avoid vague or indefinite modifiers, such as *effective* or *efficient;* instead, use facts, numbers, or something definite; be exact.
- Don't generalize; avoid *all, right, wrong, true, false, always,* and *never.*
- Use strong, explicit nouns, such as *conflict* or *controversy* instead of *at variance* or *disagreement.*
- Use colorful words; for example, use gerunds (the "ing" forms of verbs used as nouns) and present participles (the "ing" forms of verbs functioning as verbs or as adjectives), such as caring, exacting, and growing practice.
- Use action words, descriptive adjectives, and contractions to make your copy lively. For example, use words like *rigid, gruff,* or *unyielding* instead of *stern;* use *don't* instead of *do not.*
- Make your writing positive; avoid *no* and *not.* "We're sure that you will be pleased with" rather than "We hope that you will not be disappointed with."
- Avoid redundant phrases, overworked words, and trite expressions (see specific suggestions later in this chapter).
- Read your copy aloud; use your ears to check how it sounds.

Grammar, Spelling, and Punctuation

Correct grammar is important in almost all forms of writing. On the other hand, stilted prose and rigid adherence to the formal rules are not only unnecessary but undesirable. So follow the rules, although not slavishly, and when in doubt consult a basic grammar book.

Taking liberties with spelling and punctuation is not wise. Incorrectly spelled words and poorly punctuated sentences indicate carelessness, or ignorance, or both. The rule here is simple: Always use the correct spelling and punctuation. If in doubt, look it up.

Conciseness and Clarity

Regardless of form or format, all written communication should be as brief as possible and crystal clear. Every word must contribute to the purpose of the message, and the meaning and intent of the communication must be readily understandable. Some specific do's and don'ts:

- Plan carefully before writing; know exactly what you want to say.
- Write clearly, concisely, and directly. Instead of "Please contact me as soon as possible" write "Please phone me before noon tomorrow."
- Avoid clutter, the excessive use of language flourishes.
- Make sure that every word contributes to the purpose of the message; avoid stating the obvious.
- Don't hedge. Instead of "In my judgment, I think this appears to have value," write "I believe this is a good suggestion."

Format, Layout, and Appearance

The general style, appearance, and arrangement of a written communication, its physical structure and configuration, must enhance and support your message. Use a variety of devices to make your message more readable, attractive, and interesting; break up imposing text, and highlight major points. Keep these suggestions in mind:

- Choose an attractive and appropriate format, type style, and font.
- Plan your layout before you go final.
- Make liberal use of titles, subtitles, headings, subheadings, and white space.
- Use arabic numbers, bullets (heavy dots), and underscoring for emphasis and to keep the reader on track.

Graphics

Well-designed graphics can contribute a great deal to the clarity and appearance of your message. However, illustrations must support and reinforce your material. For example, if your graphics are simple and your copy is elaborate, the message you send to your readers will be confusing. Follow these suggestions:

- Use graphics only to support your text and not just for effect.
- Plan your graphics carefully; if necessary, get professional help.
- Avoid overly complex charts, diagrams, and tables.

Guides to Better Writing

Although most of the preceding suggestions address some of the potential problems in writing readable prose, this section provides a strategy for improving your approach to writing tasks and getting better results.

General Guides

Writing is a sequential task; it involves a series of discrete steps. Each step in the sequence is critical to an interesting, readable, and persuasive piece of written communication.

1. Determine your objectives. The first step in writing is to establish your objective. You must know your purpose and keep it firmly in mind throughout the writing effort. Is it to persuade, to inform, to get a decision, to get information?

2. Consider your readers. To whom are you addressing your communication? A single reader or many readers? How will the reader use your communication? Make a decision? Digest the information? Distribute it to others? Upward in the organization? Down? Outside the organization? What's your basic message? What result do you want to get? State that result succinctly in writing, and use it as a guide throughout your writing effort. For example, "I recommend that we conduct a training needs analysis of all first-line supervisors in the Bigtown plant."

3. Gather the information. Collect all the documents, correspondence, or other materials that pertain to the subject. If necessary, do background research. Interview key people, observe, question (see Chapter 5). Take notes.

4. Select the form and format. Now you must consider the appropriate form and format of your communication. Should it be a letter? An electronic message? A memorandum? A proposal? A staff study or decision paper? Should it be continuous text or should it be broken up with headings and subheadings? Should it contain graphics? What kind? Graphs? Photographs? Maps? Tables? Should it be in color? Should it be produced on a word processor? Typewritten? Printed?

5. Build an outline. You have three options here: (1) a traditional outline, with content broken down by logical divisions; (2) a functional outline, with the substance of your communication divided by purpose or use (the basic message followed by the required actions—details of who, when, where, how, why); or (3) a combination of both approaches.

6. Anticipate special problems. Next, put yourself in your readers' shoes. How will they react to your basic message? Will they be skeptical? Surprised? Suspicious? Antagonistic? Disappointed? Satisfied? Delighted? Determine the most likely reaction, then think of ways to shore up your text to overcome adverse reactions and reinforce positive responses.

7. Write the first draft. Get started by warming up—write almost anything. Write the first draft quickly, nonstop if possible. Don't worry about tone, style, word choice, sentence structure, grammar, or punctuation. The objective is to get your ideas on paper, whether you use longhand, a typewriter, a word processor, or even a stenographer.

8. Edit for clarity, conciseness, logic, and flow. Now, read your draft. If possible, read it to someone else. Is the material clear? Does it make sense? Does it flow smoothly? If it doesn't, fix it. Review and rework every sentence, every paragraph, every page repeatedly until you get it right. Make changes right on the draft, correcting sentence structure, paragraphing, and word choice.

9. Write the second draft. At this point, depending on the importance of the message, you may go final. But in many cases you will want to produce a clean second draft. If possible, separate your second draft from the first by one day.

10. Edit for grammar, spelling, and punctuation. Again, read your draft slowly and carefully. Focus on grammar, spelling, and punctuation. Be on the lookout for redundancies, poor word choice, and inappropriate tone. Make editorial corrections on the draft. Be sure that everything is correct—paragraphing, centering, everything.

11. Produce the final text. Type or print the final text on good-quality paper. Read it aloud. Proofread meticulously, using a proofreader's card (permits viewing of only five or six words at a time) or read backward—bottom to top, right to left—to ensure that each word is carefully scrutinized. Double check spelling, punctuation, capitalization, and grammar.

Specific Guides

Each form of writing has special requirements or peculiarities relating to format or content.

Letters

Letters serve many different purposes: to get and give information, to seek help, to sell, to transmit other documents as enclosures, to collect money (dun letters), to acknowledge something, to refuse something, to thank someone, to commend another, or to recommend something.

Many of the do's and don'ts of writing apply to letter writing with a vengeance. You must plan carefully and thoroughly before writing a letter. You must know exactly what you want to say. You must keep your letter as short as possible, remembering that your reader probably will not give you very much time. If you use worn-out, hackneyed phrases, particularly at the start—"Please be advised that . . ."—the reader may quit reading. One writing trainer and consultant has identified some of the worst offenders used in business correspondence:[4]

4. Gary Blake "Utilize This," *Training and Development Journal*, February 1985, p. 16.

Trite	*Better*
At this point in time	At this time
Pursuant to your request or Per your request	At your request
Please do not hesitate to call	Please call
Enclosed please find	I've enclosed
Thanking you in advance for your cooperation	Thank you for your help
It should be noted that	[Don't "note" anything; just write your sentence]
Please contact me	Please call or Please write
Very unique	Unique
It has been recommended	I recommend
Utilize	Use

And here are some other hackneyed phrases:

Trite	*Better*
Afford an opportunity to	Allow or Enable
We are of the opinion that	We believe or We think
This will acknowledge receipt of	Thank you for sending (or replying)
On the basis of	By or From
I am pleased to note or It has come to my attention that	[Just write your sentence]
It is felt or It is the opinion of this office	We believe
In regard to	About
Will you be kind enough to	Please
Inasmuch as	Because
In view of the fact that	Because
This office interposes no objections	We approve or We recommend approval
We are not in a position to	We cannot or We are unable
In addition to the above	Also
Due in large measure to	Because
It is (or is not) contemplated or It is desired	We propose or We request
Despite the fact that	Although
During which time	While or Meanwhile
In recognition of this fact	Therefore

We are fully cognizant of	We know
Every effort will be made	[Say what effort will be made, when, where, and by whom]
Enclosed herewith	Enclosed
End results	Results

Here are some other specific suggestions:

- Pretend that you're talking to the reader; use a conversational style.
- Personalize your message; for example, "Here's how you can . . ."
- Capture the reader's attention right away, in the first sentence.
- Always refer to previous correspondence in exact terms; not "in reply to your recent letter" but "in your letter of June 30, 1988. . ."
- Keep foremost in mind what you want the reader to know or do.
- Lead with the main point.
- Avoid injecting your opinion; stick with the facts.
- Avoid qualifiers and vague modifiers.
- Shun exaggeration.
- Avoid "weasel wording"; for example, "Jones appears to need more suitable work" or "Perhaps Smith needs help." Don't qualify the statement—use "Jones should be transferred."
- If the message is good news, begin with the news; if it is bad news, use a cushion, some means of subduing or tempering the blow or easing the shock. Never deliver the bad news until after you have given the reasons for it.
- Don't bury your punch line in the middle of a paragraph, or your key paragraph in the middle of your letter.
- Highlight the point you are making, the action you are taking, or the request you are making in the first or last paragraph of your letter or first or last sentence of your paragraph.
- Don't hedge ("perhaps," "maybe," "seems"); be definite.
- Be sure that everything in the message is accurate.
- Close a letter by telling the reader directly what you expect or want done. Be specific and include a date, not "at your convenience."

Memos

Memos may be addressed to one person or to many. They can be used to transmit policies, procedures, or decisions. They can serve as the medium for reports, confirmation of discussions, recommendations, commendations, or reprimands.

Although many memos are too formal, when used correctly and in the right situations they can be very useful. For one thing, they can prevent misunderstandings because they are not spur of the moment communications. They can overcome filtering by subordinate managers and supervisors, and they can preclude barriers like inattention, distortion, or outright fabrication. Memos also help you get a reasonable response. Because there is usually no need for an immediate reply, receivers can relax their guard instead of erecting defenses to protect themselves. Also, because clear, concise words can get through barriers and provide ample opportunity for rereading and study, they are invaluable for introducing complex materials.

Usually memos should not be more than two pages long. Enclosures are sometimes used, but they should be restricted to material that is necessary to understand the paper.

There are three types of memos: (1) general information memos; for example, those addressed to large numbers of people to announce new policies; (2) specific information memos; for example, a message addressed to one person requesting action of some kind; and (3) memos for record.

The memo for record (M/R) or "cover your anterior" (CYA) memo is usually a record of an oral discussion, and is prepared immediately after the event. It can also be a record of an observation, a situation, an event, or an accident. The purpose of any M/R is to record the exact incident, decision, order, agreement, or commitment observed or reached. M/Rs should always answer the question "Who told whom to do what?" or "Who agreed with whom to do what?" or "Exactly what happened?" It is usually advisable to have the principals read and initial an M/R and correct the language so that it is thoroughly accurate.

To make sure an important memo is received, address it to the right person. Then ask that receipt be acknowledged in writing; the return message should state what is being done about the memo, by whom, and by when.

Messages

Here, *messages* refers to electronic communications, transmitted by computer, teletype, facsimile, or telex. The rules of letter writing apply to message writing, with two additional specifications. First, some messages must be formated to be accepted and read by scanners. Second, economy of language is essential to reduce transmitting time and costs. Therefore, all messages should be as brief as possible, with all unnecessary words eliminated.

Reports

Reports are usually time sensitive; those who receive and use them typically prescribe how frequently they will be written. All reports should be relevant, accurate, and timely, and they should meet a legitimate management or organizational need. They should have a clearly defined purpose, and be addressed to people who need them and are willing and able to understand and use them.

Reports should be prepared in an appropriate format, with facts, opinions, and evaluations clearly differentiated. Know your objectives, keep the language simple, double check for accuracy, and review them to be sure they say what they should say. Lengthy reports should always have an executive summary.

Trip Reports

In organizations where the jobs of managers and staff personnel involve travel, the trip report is an essential form of written communication. In most cases, trip reports should follow a consistent format because they will be used as a means of controlling travel expenses as well as for managerial information and decision making. A format for trip reports is shown in Figure 3-1.

Evaluation Reports and Critiques

Evaluation reports and critiques report on the adequacy of programs, including training and development programs, services, equipment, procedures, or any other aspect of the organization's operations. They are also used in appraising the performance of people, an application discussed in Chapter 11.

Minutes and Summaries

The only significant specifications for these documents are accuracy, brevity, and timely preparation and distribution. An inaccurate or error-laden summary or set of minutes is worse than useless; it is damaging. A lengthy set of minutes is a waste of everyone's time. In fact, it probably will not be read carefully. A late set of minutes or summary serves no useful purpose, with the possible exception of archival documentation of events.

Staff Studies and Decision Papers

Staff studies and decision papers are essentially identical; the only difference is length. A staff study may involve dozens of pages of copy; a decision paper is usually just a page or two. They are used to present the results of a problem-solving effort or the essential elements of a proposal to a decision maker. In addition to all the rules of effective writing, a good staff study or decision paper must be persuasive. A sample format is shown in Figure 3-2.

Figure 3-1. Sample format for a trip report.

TRIP REPORT

1. Name
   Title
   Office Location
	2. Dates of Trip

	3. Place(s) Visited
4. Mode(s) of Travel	5. Personnel Contacted

6. Purpose of the Trip

7. Significant Accomplishments

8. Significant Problem Areas

9. Other Comments

10. Recommendations

_____   _____

    Date Submitted   Signature

(Please use additional sheets if necessary)

Proposals

Proposals are written (or oral) messages designed to obtain acceptance or to get a favorable decision. Although they may be in-house suggestions about products, services, personnel policies, organizational arrangements, and the like, more and more frequently in HR they are written in response to federal, state, or local government requests for proposals (RFPs).

Writing winning proposals is both an art and a science. It is art because it invariably requires a marketing approach. When you respond to an RFP, or to an in-house requirement, you have a product to sell—a plan, a program, a service. To sell that product, you must make it sound fresh and original. However, proposal writing is also a science. You must respond to the RFP in such a way that your proposal makes good business sense. You must demonstrate that the proposal will meet requirements, that it will work. You must also identify the costs—including the hidden costs—and any risks. You must show how the plan, program, or service you are proposing will boost productivity, increase profits, reduce down time, or achieve any other worthwhile objective.

Government proposals. Proposals made to government agencies and offices should be prepared as simply and economically as possible. They should provide a straightforward, concise description of your commitment to satisfy the requirements and specifications contained in the RFP.

Fancy bindings, colorful displays, and promotional materials are neither needed nor particularly helpful. Accuracy, clarity, and completeness of response, however, are critical. You must never make claims or statements in your proposal that you are not prepared to commit yourself to contractually—because those items may be incorporated into the contract. A sample format for a response to an RFP is shown in Figure 3-3.

In-house proposals. Proposals made in house or to private organizations are somewhat easier to prepare because usually there are fewer restrictions on preliminary contacts with the client. The preparation steps are:

1. Conduct preliminary research. Read organization documents (mission, organization, objectives, and so on) unless you are familiar with the organization. Interview the potential buyer or decision maker and key staff. Discuss the problem that your proposal is to solve. Identify the target audience and the decision maker's concerns. Determine the support that will be made available to you (people, space, facilities, equipment, and the like). Identify any constraints (policies, contacts, restricted areas, costs, time, and schedules, for example).

2. Prepare a first draft. As soon as possible after your research and meetings with the potential buyer, develop a draft of your proposal.

(Text continues on page 59.)

Figure 3-2. Sample format for a staff study or decision paper.

STAFF STUDY or DECISION PAPER

                                                        Date _____

TO:

FROM:

SUBJECT:

1. *Purpose:* (State concisely and precisely the objective of the proposed action. Relate the action to company profitability or return on investment, efficiency, or other bottom-line result. The statement will invariably begin with "To . . .")
  2. *Facts defining the problem:*
     a. (Here describe the origin of the problem.)
     b. (State a fact—include the who, what, when, and where.)
     c. (State another fact.)
     d. (State another fact, and so on.)
  3. *Real problem:* (Identify the root problem by stating it as a task—"To determine policy regarding . . ."—or as a question: "What should our position be on. . . ?"
  4. *Discussion:* Discuss each of the facts that bear on the solution, identify alternative courses of action, and list the advantages and disadvantages of each alternative.
     a. (Fact leading to development of courses of action.)
     b. (Another fact.)
     c. (Another fact.)
     d. (Missing facts bearing on the solution.)
     e. (Alternative courses of action or positions.)
        (1). (First course of action.)
             (a). (Advantages of first course of action.)
             (b). (Disadvantages of first course of action.)
        (2). (Second course of action.)
             (a). (Advantages of second course of action.)
             (b). (Disadvantages of second course of action.)
  5. *Conclusion:* (State conclusions precisely and bluntly. Evaluate your proposal in terms of costs and benefits and state your findings clearly and pointedly.)

Figure 3-2, continued.

    6. *Recommendations:* (State recommendations boldly and without equivocation.)

        a. (First recommendation.)

        b. (Second recommendation.)

        c. (Third recommendation, and so on.)

Coordination: (Offices affected by the decision. Use only if needed.)

_____ Concur _____ Nonconcur _____ _____
(Name or Office)   (Initials)

_____ Concur _____ Nonconcur _____ _____
(Name or Office)   (Initials)

_____   _____
(Date)   (Signature of Preparer)

---

*Reason for nonconcurrence must be appended as an enclosure along with the action officer's rebuttal to the nonconcurrence.

---

    3. Do follow-up research to fill in any holes in your proposal.

    4. Prepare the final proposal and submit it.

A sample format for an in-house proposal is shown in Figure 3-4.

Policy Statements

Policies have been variously defined as company goals, enterprise plans, and decision rules; the most widely accepted definition is that a policy is a guide for action.

> A policy is a guide for *carrying out* action. It establishes a specific course of action that has been adopted as expedient in order to govern the operations of an organization. Thus it expresses the philosophy, principles, and purpose of the organization, as well as its values. A policy is also a declaration of intent about an organization's obligations and responsibilities. Since it indicates the manner in which the company wants to perform its activities, a policy serves as a guide for the achievement of objectives. In a word, a policy states *how* goals are to be reached.[5]

HR managers who want their policies to be understood and followed must state them clearly in writing, and provide suitable explanatory information. Anyone who has written a policy statement will testify that it is far from easy. Policies should not be vague, imprecise, dogmatic, or inflexible. Nor can they be inconsistent with overall company policies or with other HR policies. Usually, since HR managers are responsible for ensuring the consistency of directives throughout the organization, they

5. M. Valliant Higginson, *Management Policies I: Their Development as Corporate Guides* (New York: American Management Association, 1966), 21–22.

Figure 3-3. Sample format for a response to an RFP.

Letter of Transmittal

This part of a proposal is a letter signed by an individual authorized to bind you or your organization contractually. It should identify the length of time the proposal will remain in effect after the submission deadline noted in the RFP. The letter should also include the name, title, address, and telephone number of one or more people who can respond to requests for additional information, and one or more who are authorized to negotiate and sign a contract on your company's behalf.

Offeror Qualifications

Here you present your or your company's qualifications. In addition to education, experience, professional and technical skills, and other conventional qualifications, you should identify any special support equipment, facilities, or capabilities, and supply the names, addresses, and phone numbers of customers or clients who have purchased products or services similar to those proposed who may be contacted as references. You may be asked for financial statements covering your two most recent fiscal years. If you are part of a larger business entity, balance sheets and income statements should break out subsidiary data for your department.

Responses to Technical Requirements or Statement of Work

This section usually consists of responses to the technical requirements and specifications of the RFP. For example:

- The beginning and ending dates of the project.
- The minimum and maximum number of staff-days of service.
- The identity of those who will perform the services.
- The specific products and services you will provide.
- Where and when the products will be delivered and where the services will be performed.
- If training is involved, the number and types of participants.
- The management strategy and methodology you will use.
- The procedures, format, and standards you will apply.
- Assumptions and conceptual bases.
- The evaluation strategy you will use.
- The personnel, facilities, equipment, materials, and services you expect the client to provide.
- The reports (interim and final, oral and written) you will furnish.
- The work schedule you will follow.

Figure 3-3, continued.

Costs

This section identifies all costs associated with the proposal, separated as follows:

- Staff-hour costs (including overhead costs).
- Cost of equipment, materials, and supplies.
- Any additional costs (travel, meals, lodging, phone calls, postage, and the like).
- Total cost.

Additional Information

Here you may include additional relevant information such as clarification of responses, alternative approaches, or requests for additional action.

---

will write policy statements themselves. But, even if the task is delegated, HR managers cannot abdicate their responsibility; they must review (and often edit) those policies.

Policies typically found in HR organizations are:

Figure 3-4. Sample format for an in-house proposal.

Purpose. Define the purpose or objectives of the proposal.

Problem. Identify the underlying problem the proposal is intended to solve.

Solution. Describe the features of the solution: who does what to whom, when, where, and how.

Benefits. Identify the specific organizational and individual benefits that the proposal will provide, in both financial and (if applicable) human terms.

Costs. Identify all costs associated with the proposal—people, space, facilities, equipment, materials, supplies, time, and other costs, including hidden "people costs."

Follow-up. Describe needed follow-up actions, the "now what" actions to launch and evaluate the solution.

Scope of HR programs and
   services
HR plans and objectives
Public relations and media
Purchasing
Research
Travel
Tuition reimbursement
Financial accounting

HR goals and functions
Employee relations
Marketing HR programs and
   services
Contracts
Staff training and development
Physical plant
Evaluation
Use of consultants

An example of a policy statement is shown in Figure 3-5.
   Here are some suggestions for writing policies:

- Briefly define the subject matter and identify the purpose of the policy. Be sure to define technical terminology.
- State the policy as clearly and concisely as possible. Be sure that it is valid and accurate and conforms with government regulations when they are relevant.
- Make the policy flexible, broad enough to be useful to all managers, and specific enough to guide thinking and action.
- Establish the areas and limits of authority.
- Include reference to supporting policies.
- Provide for periodic review of policies.
- Subject the policy to review by subordinate managers and supervisors prior to implementation.

Procedures Manuals

Procedures describe what, when, where, how, and by whom an operation or task is to be performed. They include all steps necessary for completing the task. They are established to ensure maximum performance with minimum expenditure of resources. In the HR department, some typical subjects included in procedures manuals are:

Test administration
Equipment operation
Grievance handling
Safety checks
Recruitment and advertising
Records maintenance
Instructional materials
   development

Budget preparation and
   submission
Fund control
Screening and selection of
   personnel
Requisitioning supplies
Preparing travel requests and
   vouchers

An example of a procedure is shown in Figure 3-6. The formal and legalistic tone, an exception to the usual rules for good writing, is necessary in this case because the procedure will be a part of a collective

Figure 3-5. Example of a policy statement.

TRAVEL

Objective. The objective of this policy is to provide efficient travel services for employees at minimum cost.

General policy. Only travel necessary to accomplish the HR mission will be authorized. All travel arrangements, including air, rail, hotel, and car rental reservations, will be made through the travel office. In all cases, the most economical mode of transportation will be used.

Responsibilities. Travelers are responsible for reading, understanding, and complying with this policy, for initiating travel requests, for submitting travel vouchers and trip reports, and for filing written complaints about travel services. Travel requests will be submitted through the traveler's supervisor and the controller's office to the travel office at least ten working days before travel. Travel vouchers will be submitted to the controller's office within five days after you return. Trip reports will be submitted through the traveler's supervisor to the HR manager within three working days after return.

Supervisors are responsible for reviewing and approving all travel requests before submission to the controller and the travel office. Supervisors will combine trips whenever possible to reduce the number of people traveling and cut costs. Supervisors will also ensure that secretarial personnel who process travel requests and vouchers have completed the four-hour training program offered quarterly before working on those documents.

The controller's office is responsible for assuring that all travel requests and travel vouchers comply with company policy; it is the only office authorized to issue waivers. Employees requesting waivers must submit estimates of both the cost of a normal trip and that of the proposed trip.

The travel manager will make all travel arrangements and prepare itineraries. Itineraries will include full flight information, hotel reservations (with phone numbers and rates), designated car rental companies (with confirmation numbers and rates), and toll-free cancellation numbers. The travel officer will also serve as the contact for questions about travel requests and travel expense vouchers.

Review. This policy will be reviewed at least semiannually, based on quarterly review of travel files.

---

bargaining agreement and must be acceptable to legal counselors. Here are some suggestions for writing procedures.

- Briefly describe the purpose of the procedure.
- Clearly and simply describe the steps in the procedure in correct sequence. Include the what, when, where, how, and by whom.
- Subject the procedure to actual tryout by a sample of the people who will use it. Revise as necessary.
- Review procedures periodically.

Figure 3-6. Example of a procedure.

GRIEVANCE PROCEDURE

Section I. Purpose

The purpose of this document is to avoid, where possible, arbitration and litigation by providing an orderly means of settling disputes or allegations thereof between the parties of the collective bargaining agreement.

Section II. Definitions

A. The term "grievance" shall mean any dispute, claim, complaint, or allegation by an aggrieved employee or group of employees that there has been a violation, misinterpretation, or misapplication of the provisions of the collective bargaining agreement.

B. The term "grievant" shall mean the person(s) making such claim or allegation, including their designated representatives.

C. The term "management" shall mean any person(s) representing the corporation who, in order to solve a grievance, might be required to take action or who might have action taken against him or her.

D. The terms "bargaining representative" shall mean the individual(s) designated by the collective bargaining unit as its official representative(s).

Section III. Time Limits

A. All grievances shall be processed in accordance with the time limits specified in each grievance step.

B. Except for the initial filing of a grievance, such time limits may be extended by written agreement between the grievant and management provided that no such extension shall be made after the expiration of the time limits.

C. Failure to file or appeal a grievance within the specified time limits at any step of this procedure shall result in a waiver of the grievance.

D. Failure of management to respond to any grievance within the specified time limits shall be deemed a denial of such grievance and may be appealed to the next step.

Section IV. Informal Procedure

A. Nothing in this grievance procedure shall limit the right of an individual employee to present at any time grievances to management and to have such grievances adjusted without the intervention of the bargaining representative as long as the following conditions exist:

1. Adjustment is not inconsistent with the terms of the collective bargaining agreement.
2. The bargaining representative has been given opportunity to be present at such adjustment.

B. Any employee who feels that he or she has a grievance shall first discuss the

Figure 3-6, continued.

problem with his or her immediate supervisor not later than ten work days after the grievant knew, or should have known, or should reasonably be expected to have learned, of the action or condition on which the grievance is based.

    C. Any meeting held at this step of the grievance procedure shall be conducted at a time and place agreed to by the grievant and management.

    D. Any employee shall have the right to have his or her steward present at any meeting with management when he or she has reason to believe that a disciplinary action may result from the meeting.

Section V. Formal Procedure

    A. No grievance shall be filed under this section without first having gone through the informal procedure.

    B. Any grievance that cannot be settled informally shall be settled in the following manner and order:

    1. The grievant shall present the grievance in writing on forms provided for that purpose, and available at the employee relations office, either directly or through interoffice or United States mail to his or her immediate supervisor within 21 work days of the discussion. The grievance shall state the following:

        a. The nature of the grievance and the date of the action or situation giving rise to the grievance. The statement shall include all relevant facts and the provisions of the collective bargaining agreement alleged to have been violated.

        b. The relief sought by the grievant.

        c. The date of submission and the signature of the grievant.

    2. Within five work days of receipt of the grievance, the immediate supervisor shall provide a written response to the grievant's request for relief. The validity of the grievance shall be determined by gathering and analyzing all allegations, opinions, assumptions, and facts pertaining to the grievance (when, where, how, who, and why).

    3. If the grievant is not satisfied with the answer provided by management, the employee, or the bargaining representative, may appeal to the next higher level of management. Such appeal must be filed within ten work days of receipt of the immediate supervisor's response to the grievance. The appeal shall contain the following:

        a. The nature of and date of the occurrence giving rise to the grievance.

        b. Reference to the particular section of the collective bargaining agreement on which the grievance is based.

        c. The relief sought.

        d. The signature of the employee originating the grievance.

        e. A copy of the immediate supervisor's response to the grievance.

    4. Management's disposition of the appeal shall be submitted in writing to the grievant no later than ten work days following receipt of the appeal. The response shall include the reasons and rationale for any denial of the grievance.

    5. If the grievance has not been settled by the preceding steps, it may be referred to arbitration as provided in the document titled *Arbitration Procedures.*

Figure 3-6, continued.

Section VI. Records and Follow-up

A. Accurate records of the entire grievance process shall be prepared by the employee relations office and filed separately from individual personnel records. They shall include:
1. The written grievance and management's response.
2. The grievant's appeals.
3. Work-related facts, such as attendance, job records, training records, appraisals, interviews, and performance ratings of the grievant.

B. The case shall be followed up and evaluated by the employee relations office to determine:
1. The degree to which the parties involved were able to identify the real problem and agree on a solution.
2. The impact of the solution on management authority and understanding and communication between supervisors/managers and employees.

Course Descriptions

Course descriptions are very important documents in training and development, whether used only in-house or distributed outside. Essentially, they are marketing tools—they advertise the product. If they are to be successful, they must be well written. An effective course description is based on careful study of the target audience—the participants in the seminar, workshop, or course. There are some additional requirements. Course descriptions should include as a minimum:

- The need for and importance of the training.
- Course objectives in behavioral terms (what the participants will be able to do after the training).
- Description of the target audience, including prerequisite training and experience.
- Training content, including a sequential topical outline of the subjects and issues to be addressed.
- Instructional strategy and methodology used (lecture, discussion, small groups, role playing, individual assignments, and the like).
- Special features of the training such as individual assessment, video recording of performance, handouts, and follow-up.
- Training documentation provided (certificates of completion, continuing education units [CEUs], or academic credits).
- Length of training in hours per day and total number of days.
- Costs (tuition and fees).

Job Descriptions and Applicant Specifications

Two of the most important documents the HR manager must write (or at least contribute to and review) are job descriptions and applicant specifications. They also depart from the general rules for good writing because they are legal documents, often subjected to close scrutiny by lawyers during arbitration, mediation, and litigation.

Job descriptions. A job description defines the major duties, functions, and authority assigned to a position and the relationships between the position and other positions in the department, and, when appropriate, the relationship of that job to positions in the other departments. Job descriptions are used as a basis for job evaluation and salary administration, writing applicant specifications, designing training and development programs, conducting performance appraisals, and coaching and counseling. An example of a job description is shown in Figure 3-7.

Suggestions for writing job descriptions follow:

○ Review the statement of goals and objectives for the department.
○ Think about the work to be done in terms of functions, duties, and authority.
○ Make the job description an independent document so that reference to other documents or job descriptions is unnecessary.
○ Be specific in defining major duties, authority, and relationships; use precise terms to describe the work and authority.
○ Describe duties in terms of results rather than processes.
○ Define what is to be done, not how or how well it is to be done.
○ Have the draft checked by at least two knowledgeable people.

Applicant specifications. For each job description there should be a corresponding set of applicant specifications. These documents describe the education, training, skills, experience, competencies, personality, and any other qualifications needed for success in a particular job. Well-written applicant specifications are essential to proper and effective recruitment, screening, selection, assignment, training, development, and promotion of personnel. A sample set of applicant specifications is shown in Figure 3-8.

Here are some guides for writing applicant specifications:

○ Review the plans, policies, objectives, and programs of the department.
○ Analyze the job description—the duties, tasks, and functions performed by incumbents—to identify the professional and technical knowledge and skills required.
○ From these data, deduce the educational background, training, kind and amount of experience, and personal qualities needed for success on the job.
○ Write the specifications using direct, unequivocal, and nondiscriminatory language; be realistic.
○ Check the draft against the job description; have at least two other knowledgeable people check it.

Figure 3-7. Sample job description.

MANAGER, HUMAN RESOURCES DEPARTMENT

Functions

Operates under the general supervision of and reports to the executive vice president. Serves as principal adviser to the board of control, CEO, principal staff officers, and line managers on all matters relating to human resources planning, development, and utilization. Manages the HR department.

Duties and Responsibilities

1. Plans, organizes, staffs, directs, and controls the operations of the HR department. Exercises general supervision over all elements, activities, programs, and services of the department.
2. Is directly responsible for achieving annual objectives that support corporate goals as mutually agreed upon by the incumbent and the executive vice president.
3. Effects coordination among all elements of the department and between elements of the department and other line and staff elements of the company.
4. Coordinates with out-of-enterprise organizations, consultants, and contractors on human resources matters.
5. Performs other related duties as assigned.

Supervision Received

Enjoys an independent level of operation. Receives only general oral or written instructions from the executive vice president with respect to major corporate projects.

Supervision Given

Exercises direct supervision over the managers of the following elements:

> HR Requirements, Research, and Evaluation Division.
> Employee Relations and Services Division.
> Organization Development Division.
> Employee Training and Development Division.
> Training Support Services Division.

Press Releases

Press releases are a primary means of communicating information about the HR department, its people, and its activities to the general

(Text continues on page 70.)

Figure 3-8.   Sample applicant specifications.

MANAGER, HUMAN RESOURCES DEPARTMENT

Job Opportunities

Incumbent is eligible for intensive, short-term, out-of-enterprise graduate-level training and development in management and related disciplines. In-house development opportunities are available on a continuing basis through special assignments. Individual with potential for advancement, as demonstrated through job performance and the successful completion of special assignments and developmental experiences, will be eligible for promotion to the position of executive vice president.

Functions and Duties

1. Plans, organizes, staffs, directs, and controls the operations of the HR department. Exercises general supervision over all elements, activities, programs, and services of the department.
2. Is directly responsible for achieving annual objectives that support corporate goals as mutually agreed on by the incumbent and the executive vice president.
3. Effects coordination among all elements of the department and between elements of the department and other line and staff elements of the company.
4. Coordinates with out-of-enterprise organizations, consultants, and contractors on human resources matters.
5. Performs other related duties as assigned.

Authority and Responsibility

Is responsible to the executive vice president for performance of major managerial functions and duties. Provides general supervision to five subordinate division managers (HR Requirements, Research, and Evaluation, Employee Relations and Services, Organization Development, Employee Training and Development, and Training Support Services), general direction to a department administrative staff, and direct supervision to an administrative assistant. Advises and coordinates with all corporate officers, line managers, and out-of-enterprise organizations on matters relating to HR planning, development, and utilization.

Personal Specifications

1. *Education.* A master's degree in human resources development, organization development, business administration, industrial management, psychology, education, or related discipline, provided that graduate or undergraduate study included or was supplemented by a minimum of 18 semester hours or equivalent in HR-related subjects.

Figure 3-8, continued.

2. Experience. A minimum of ten years of successful and progressively more responsible experience in a specialized administrative, technical, or professional occupation directly connected with or having a close relation to HR planning, development, or utilization. Must have served at least three years in a supervisory or managerial capacity in a multiple-level HR activity in business, industry, government, the military, or education.

3. Skills and abilities. Candidates must be able to communicate effectively orally and in writing, possess skill in supervising people and managing resources, have the ability to prepare plans and articulate objectives, be able to analyze proposals, and be able to negotiate contracts.

4. Personal qualities. Candidates must be mature, self-confident, self-disciplined, emotionally stable, cooperative, articulate, perceptive, innovative, open-minded, ethical, and have a high tolerance for stress.

Salary Range: $60,000 to $80,000 per annum.

---

public via the news media or publications in your industry. To achieve maximum impact, the media release program should focus on critical jobs, programs, capabilities, products, and services; personnel changes, promotions, and awards; and feature stories on such subjects as organizational history, philosophy, policies, and human interest topics. A good press release never exaggerates, deceives, or distorts. It is never inaccurate, misleading, undignified, sexist, or in poor taste.

Although most large organizations have a public relations department, most small organizations do not. If you or your staff must prepare your own press releases, here are some ways to get maximum impact:

- Contact the editor of the target publication for guidelines.
- Fit the release to the specific needs of the media chosen.
- Begin with an attention-getting headline.
- Provide facts: who, what, when, where, and, on occasion, why.
- Be clear, accurate, and brief.
- Provide the name, address, and phone number of the HR department contact for clarification or additional details.
- If possible, send the press release to the publication one week before the release date.
- Include good-quality, interesting photos.

Summary

Skill in written communication is a must for every HR manager. Not only is your competence as a manager certain to be judged in part by your writing products, but your effectiveness as a leader is also certain to be affected. You use your writing skills to inform, persuade, recommend, inquire, and record, and to get positive responses from subordinates, peers, superiors, customers, clients, suppliers, consultants, and the general public.

Effective written communication involves thorough planning and execution. You must give careful attention to form, tone, style, organization, paragraphing, sentence structure, word choice, grammar and syntax, spelling and punctuation, conciseness and clarity, format, appearance and layout, and use of graphics.

Although not limited to these, the most common forms of written communication HR managers use are letters, memos, electronic messages, status, trip, and evaluation reports, critiques, minutes and summaries, staff studies, decision papers, proposals, policy statements, procedures manuals, course descriptions and training documents, job descriptions, applicant specifications, and press releases.

To improve your writing products, follow these steps: (1) determine your objectives; (2) consider your readers; (3) gather your data; (4) select an appropriate form and format; (5) develop an outline; (6) anticipate reader reaction; (7) write the first draft; (8) edit for clarity and conciseness, logic and flow; (9) write the second draft; (10) edit for grammar, spelling, and punctuation; (11) write the final copy; and (12) double check for errors and dispatch.

Although each form of writing has some special requirements or peculiarities relating to form or content, the general rules for writing apply to all written communications. Those rules are: (1) know your objectives; (2) when appropriate, use a conversational style; (3) when possible, personalize your message; (4) seize the reader's attention in the first sentence; (5) keep foremost in your mind what you want the reader to know or do; (6) avoid jargon, clichés, qualifiers, exaggeration, deception, and equivocation; (7) use active voice, strong verbs, and colorful words; use correct grammar, spelling, and punctuation; (8) don't talk down to, patronize, or preach to the reader; (9) avoid overfamiliarity, coldness, insincerity, and sarcasm; (10) use an attractive and appropriate format and type style; (11) edit and re-edit thoroughly; and (12) double check everything.

FOR FURTHER READING

Beaugrande, Robert de. *Writing Step by Step: Easy Strategies for Writing and Revising.* New York: Harcourt Brace Jovanovich, 1985.

Blake, Gary. "Utilize This." *Training and Development Journal,* February 1985, p. 16.

———. "A Writing Report Card." *Training and Development Journal,* April 1986, pp. 49–51.

Booher, Dianna. "Writing More But Enjoying It Less?" *Training and Development Journal,* November 1984, pp. 48–51.

Bowman, Joel P., and Bernardine P. Branchaw. *Business Report Writing.* Hinsdale, Ill.: Dryden Press, 1984.

DiGaetani, John L., Jane Boisseau DiGaetani, and Earl N. Harbert. *A Self-Help Guide to Clear Business Writing.* Homewood, Ill.: Dow Jones-Irwin, 1983.

Dumaine, Deborah. *Write to the Top: Writing for Corporate Success.* New York: Random House, 1983.

———. "Strategic Writing for Trainers." *Training and Development Journal,* January 1987, pp. 57–60.

Elbow, Peter. *Writing with Power.* New York: Oxford University Press, 1981.

Ewing, David W. *Writing for Results in Business, Government, the Sciences, and the Professions.* New York: John Wiley & Sons, 1979.

Fey, Carol. "Engineering Good Writing." *Training and Development Journal,* March 1987, pp. 49–54.

Gelderman, Carol. *Better Writing for Professionals: A Concise Guide.* Glenview, Ill.: Scott, Foresman, 1984.

Gilbert, Marilyn B. *Clear Writing: A Business Guide.* New York: John Wiley & Sons, 1983.

Gladis, Stephen D. *Survival Writing: Staying Alive on Paper.* Dubuque, Iowa: Kendall/Hunt, 1986.

Goodman, Michael. *Write to the Point: Effective Communication at the Workplace.* Englewood Cliffs, N.J.: Prentice-Hall, 1984.

Gordon, Karen Elizabeth. *The Well-Tempered Sentence: A Punctuation Handbook for the Innocent, the Eager, and the Doomed.* New York: Times Books, 1984.

———. *The Transitive Vampire: A Handbook of Grammar for the Innocent, the Eager, and the Doomed.* New York: Times Books, 1984.

Holcombe, Marya W., and Judith K. Stein. *Writing for Decision-Makers: Memos and Reports with a Competitive Edge.* Belmont, Calif.: Wadsworth, 1981.

Holmes, Marjorie. "Twelve Secrets of Style." *The Writer,* August 1986, pp. 10–13.

Holtz, Herman. *The Consultant's Guide to Proposal Writing: How to Satisfy Your Clients and Double Your Income.* New York: John Wiley & Sons, 1986.

Holtz, Herman, and Terry Schmidt. *The Winning Proposal: How to Write It.* New York: McGraw-Hill, 1981.

Joseph, Albert. "Writing Training Materials That Turn People On." *Training and Development Journal,* May 1981, pp. 111–114.

Kilpatrick, James L. *The Writer's Art.* Kansas City and New York: Andrews, McMeel & Parker, 1984.

Lamphear, Lynn. *Short Cuts to Effective On-the-Job Writing: How to Achieve an Immediate Improvement in Your Business Letters, Memos, and Reports.* Englewood Cliffs, N.J.: Prentice-Hall, 1982.

Lesikar, Raymond V. *How to Write a Report Your Boss Will Read and Remember*, rev. ed. Homewood, Ill.: Dow Jones-Irwin, 1984.

Longyear, M. *The McGraw-Hill Style Manual: A Concise Guide for Writers and Editors.* New York: McGraw-Hill, 1983.

Max, Robert R. "Wording It Correctly." *Training and Development Journal,* March 1985, pp. 50–51.

MacManus, Yvonne. "Unruly Writing." *Training and Development Journal,* August 1985, pp. 39–40.

McKay, Sandra. *Fundamentals of Writing for a Specific Purpose.* Englewood Cliffs, N.J.: Prentice-Hall, 1983.

Miller, Casey, and Kate Swift. *The Handbook of Nonsexist Writing.* New York: Harper & Row, 1980.

Paxson, William C. *Write It Now!* Reading, Mass.: Addison-Wesley Training Systems, 1985.

Roddick, Ellen. *Writing That Means Business: The Manager's Guide.* New York: Macmillan, 1984.

Spruell, Geraldine. "Teaching People Who Already Learned How to Write, to Write." *Training,* October 1986, pp. 32–35.

Strunk, William, Jr. and E. B. White, *The Elements of Style*, 3rd ed. New York: Macmillan, 1979.

Sweetman, Sherry. "Training Proposals That Sell Themselves." *Training and Development Journal,* May 1986, pp. 82–83.

———. *The Executive Memo: A Guide to Persuasive Business Communications.* New York: Wiley, 1986.

4

PROBLEM SENSING
Managerial Preventive Medicine

HR managers are problem solvers, right? Obviously, but is that their primary function? No. It's an ancillary function, necessary but not predominant. If it were their chief function, managers would be *reactive* rather than *active*, putting out destructive fires rather than fueling the company's engine. Unfortunately, many HR managers fit the reactive model.

As an HR manager you were hired to make good things happen in your organization and prevent bad things from happening. Both functions are active. Of course, you are also expected to fix things when they go wrong or when mistakes are made. That function is reactive. Admittedly, there must be tradeoffs between the active and reactive roles, but the normal balance must favor the active if crisis management is to be avoided.

The term *problem* is often misused or used to mean quite different things. Sometimes it is used in the sense of the deviation, variance, or abberation—the something that is out of line; sometimes as the source of the trouble or difficulty—the snag, pitfall, or tangle. A somewhat more precise definition is this: A problem is an unplanned and unwanted change or result.

Problem sensing is the technique of examining potentially troublesome areas to detect deviations either *before* they germinate or early enough in their growth cycle to prevent their flowering into truly serious and costly variations from plans.

Today senior executives are demanding that their HR managers and specialists provide more leadership in problem prevention, problem sensing, and problem avoidance. As manager you must learn to anticipate problems and head them off, rather than identifying them after the fact when they have become critical. The first step is to recognize that problem sensing and problem solving are separate skills.

Management development programs have traditionally emphasized problem-solving ability. The literature of the field, too, has been mostly concerned with solutions to problems. It's somewhat like the role of a medical pathologist, to discover the cause and the remedy after the patient has succumbed; it's useful for the next victim but of little help to the deceased. A far preferable strategy in business, particularly in HR, is to keep the injury or disease from occurring—preventive medicine. If managerial preventive medicine is to become a reality, HR managers must become expert problem sensers. Problem sensitivity is an essential managerial attribute, a critical determinant of timely and effective management control. And it can be developed.

Obstacles to Problem Sensing

Why do so few HR managers practice problem sensing and prevention strategies? There are several reasons:

1. "It's not my function." Too many managers believe that their primary role is to make decisions, solve problems, develop training programs, products, and services, serve as an in-house consultant, media expert, instructor, or perform some function other than problem prevention.

2. "I have enough problems without looking for more, and those problems must be solved first." Many HR managers are more concerned with solving the problems that are presented to them today by line managers or their subordinates than they are with identifying and preventing tomorrow's problems—or next month's.

3. "I'm too busy with paperwork." Other HR managers get too bogged down in paperwork to do problem sensing. They are victims of the cornucopian In Basket—letters, interoffice memoranda, message slips, sales reports, budget reports, inventories, equipment listings, review and analysis reports, staff studies, computer printouts, information papers, decision papers, requisitions, purchase orders, policy statements, contracts, minutes of meetings, and recommendations for promotions and awards. Plus the documents developed for outside use—the proposals, brochures, advertising copy, company newsletters, press releases, and of course the newspaper clippings, trade and professional journals, and books that someone has decided the manager must read. Although some paperwork is essential, much of it is unnecessary. It has become a self-induced malady.

4. "If there are problems out there, I'd know it." Some managers believe that their systems and procedures are so watertight and foolproof that potential problems cannot go undetected. They also believe that in

the unlikely event a problem should arise, it is certain to be of little or no consequence, something that can be easily corrected.

5. "It's safer in the office." A few managers don't know enough about the details of their operation to go problem hunting. They fear that if they go poking around the work areas, their ignorance will show. They don't know what to look for, and they are fearful that they will make fools of themselves by asking the wrong questions and failing to see what should be obvious deficiencies.

The Alpha and Omega of Management

Planning and control are the alpha and omega of management, the beginning and the end, the keys to effectiveness. Achieving goals and objectives hinges on developing and implementing well-conceived plans and well-designed controls. Both planning and control are receiving greater emphasis in all types of organizations, and more resources are being committed to those functions.

Planning. A plan is a guide to action. It is a map to get an organization from where it is to where it wants to be. Planning for HR involves assessing the status of the organization in general and the HR department in particular, predicting the environment of the future, determining goals and priorities, establishing objectives, anticipating problems, forecasting HR needs, establishing policies, developing procedures, preparing budgets, scheduling, establishing special programs, and designing HR strategies that will overcome barriers to the achievement of results.

Planning has become more sophisticated and better supported in modern business. Organizational activities and operations are heavily front-loaded with planning tools: forecasts, goals, objectives, priorities, budgets, schedules, policies, programs, and procedures. All of these tools are committed to writing. More and more we hear about the importance of strategic planning, including strategic planning for human resources. Similarly, the means of executing those plans—the organization and functions manuals, standard operating procedures, memoranda, disposition forms, contracts, and the like—are prepared in written form.

Controlling. Control is the way to ensure that HR events, activities, progress, and results match the plans. Effective control keeps plans and performance congruent. Adequate control is achieved by establishing measurable standards, comparing performance with the standards, identifying deviations and shortfalls, and applying corrective strategies to force performance to conform with plans.

Controls are many, varied, and documented. They mirror the primary function of the enterprise, be it financial, personnel, operational, marketing, production, or services. Budget, capital expenditures, cash flow, sales, production, inventory, unit cost, profit and loss, income, and audit reports are only samples of the many controls used by organizations.

To track progress and accomplishment, devices such as Program Evaluation and Review Technique (PERT), Critical Path Method (CPM), Performance and Cost Evaluation (PACE), Management Operation System Technique (MOST), and Line of Balance (LOB) are widely used. Still others include cost-effectiveness analysis, benefits-cost analysis, functional analysis, existential and operational analysis, opportunity analysis, risk analysis, catastrophe theory analysis, decision theory, sensitivity analysis, simulation, gaming, and modeling.

There are three broad categories of control: those that identify performance deficiencies *after* they have happened; those that identify deviations *while* they are occurring; and those that warn of shortfalls *before* they happen. Obviously, the last category is the most desirable.

Unfortunately, most management controls fall into the first grouping—the least desirable, least timely, and the most expensive (because unrecoverable resources have been invested in a project, product, or service). Remedial actions in this first group are also expensive; analyzing the reasons for the deficiency and reprogramming to remedy it take more resources. The second category has essentially the same costs, although the magnitude is smaller (theoretically) since the deficiency is identified before too much damage is done or too many resources have been irrevocably committed.

Potential Trouble Areas

Two of the best areas to search for potential problems are the performance of the HR function and the performance of HR managers and staff personnel.

The HR Function

To identify potential problems in the HR function, regularly ask yourself these questions:

- Do people assigned to the HR function demonstrate that they know and understand the business of the organization—what it is, what it does, how it does it, where it wants to be, and how it plans to get there?
- Does the HR function provide flexible and responsive training, career development, and organization development programs and services—those that will make direct and measurable contributions to improved employee performance and productivity?

- Does the HR activity provide solutions to problems—not just deliver programs and services?
- Does the HR department use the concepts and tools of business economics in planning, developing, conducting, and controlling HR programs and services; for example, benefits-cost analysis?
- Does the HR department provide tight and cost-effective training designs that exploit the power of new training technologies?
- Does the HR department evaluate programs and services through audits, self-studies, and on-site follow-up?
- Does the HR activity communicate the value of the HR function up, down, and laterally within the organization?
- Does top management view HR needs as a major consideration in business decisions and strategies?
- Has the HR function gained a major participatory role in top-level planning, policy formulation, and decision making?
- Do HR systems, programs, and services meet *both* company and employee needs? Where do shortfalls exist?
- Do the costs of HR operations compare favorably with those of other comparable-size organizations?
- Are the efforts of subordinate HR personnel directed toward department cost performance and other types of measurable objectives?
- Are HR systems, procedures, work methods, and equipment the best available for the intended purpose?
- Are deadlines for HR programs and services being met?
- Do HR managers and staff initiate improvements within the scope of their authority? Do they suggest changes and improvements in other areas?
- Do HR managers and staff work well under pressure?
- Are HR analyses and reports objective, accurate, and reliable?
- Are HR operations sufficiently well planned to produce reasonably uniform work load, work flow, and personnel needs?

HR Management

These questions point to critical areas of HR management; examine them periodically for potential or emerging problems.

- Has the HR staff been trained to communicate and cooperate with line management in the pursuit of organizational goals and objectives?
- Do HR personnel work effectively with line managers and operations people to develop strategies to improve workforce competence, job satisfaction, and productivity?

- Are company and HR department policies being carried out as intended?
- Are HR specialists, technicians, clerical, and other personnel being intelligently informed of the work to be done, its importance, and the performance standards?
- Is there cooperation between operating elements and HR, or is there evidence of friction, antagonism, or misunderstanding?
- Do key HR people delegate sufficiently to free themselves for their management tasks?
- Do key HR people evaluate their subordinates fairly, take action to correct deficiencies, train them, and reward outstanding performance?
- Do key HR people help their subordinates find the right answers to operating problems? Do they keep you informed of significant developments and problems?
- Do key HR managers fully understand applicable federal and state laws, collective bargaining agreements, and company rules and policies? Do they apply the rules and policies fairly and avoid allowing them to impair their effectiveness as supervisors?
- Does each key HR subordinate have a replacement trained?

Problem-Sensing Strategies

Ideal controls forecast problems before they occur and enable managers to take appropriate action. That smacks of pre-vision. Is it really necessary for an HR manager to have supernatural powers, to be an oracle, a prophet? No. There are means of prediction that are not supernatural. Most of them involve people. Here are some suggestions for preventing problems:

> Be proactive, not reactive. If you sense or identify a problem with HR systems, for which you are responsible, fix it quickly before it grows. If you can be proactive as a manager, do it. It will add much credibility to the HR function.
>
> Don't procrastinate. Managers and executives are characterized by initiative. If you can find a problem, you can find a solution. It's part of your responsibility to the organization.[1]

Sources of Potential Problems

Problems can crop up just about anywhere in an organization. However, there are certain situations or elements that tend to be contin-

1. Stephen P. Becker, "Correcting HR System Performance," in *Human Resources Management and Development Handbook,* ed. William R. Tracey (New York: AMACOM, 1985), 287.

uing sources of serious problems. To be ahead of the game, the HR manager should be particularly sensitive to those areas. Two of the best known authors and trainers in the problem-solving discipline have identified six sources.[2]

1. "Where something new, complex, or unfamiliar is tried." For example, the introduction of a new performance appraisal system, quality circles, or a performance management strategy.
2. "When deadlines are tight." For example, if a short-fused requirement is identified for media production to support a cross-cultural training program for newly-assigned foreign nationals.
3. "When a sequence is critical or has impact on others." For example, if a computer-assisted or interactive video troubleshooting program for a new item of electronic equipment is under development as a part or module of a larger training program.
4. "When an alternative is missing." For example, if it appears that the only action to avert a union walkout is to submit the issue to arbitration.
5. "When things involve more than one person, function, or department." For example, a plan to increase career support for women in all departments of the company.
6. "Where responsibility is hard to assign, or is outside the manager's area." For example, if an executive coaching program developed by the HR department is launched throughout the organization.

Questioning

The key to identifying problems is questioning. The ability to ask the right questions, in the right way, at the right time, to the right persons (including oneself), is a skill that will pay dividends to the HR manager over and over again.

Regardless of the problem-sensing strategy you use, questions are certain to be an important element. You need to know what to ask, when to ask, and how to ask. You must also remember that when you ask a question, the immediate reaction of the other person is, "Why does he (or she) want to know?" Questions often cause suspicion and anxiety. Here are some suggestions for questioning.

What to ask. Good questions are relevant, inoffensive, nonthreatening, and nondisciplinary. They may call for hard facts, estimates, opinions, or judgments. They are honest and straightforward; not traps for the unwary.

When to ask. Questions may be asked to get someone's attention:

2. Charles H. Kepner and Benjamin B. Tregoe, *The Rational Manager: A Systematic Approach to Problem Solving and Decision Making* (New York: McGraw-Hill, 1965), 215.

"Can you help me?" To get information: "Who, when, where, or what?" Or to stimulate someone to do some thinking: "What do you suggest? What do you think caused this situation?"

How to ask. Because questions can cause problems, you must take care in posing them. You will need to lay a foundation for difficult questions, cushion the potential shock by telling why you are asking. Other times you will need to make the answer easier to give by suggesting the answer in the question. In any event, you must try to avoid putting people on the spot.

Here are ten questions you can use to detect, identify, analyze, avert, neutralize, counteract, or solve latent HR problems.

1. What has gone wrong in the past? (Glitches during the last five years.)
2. What was the real problem in those cases? (People? Funding? Facilities? Equipment? Supplies? Policies? Procedures? Controls?)
3. What could get out of control or go sour in today's environment? (The sources of potential problems.)
4. What precisely would be the root problem in each instance? (What? Where? Why?)
5. How critical would each problem be if it materialized?
6. What are the odds that each potential problem will occur?
7. What are the possible causes of each potential problem?
8. How credible is each possible cause?
9. How can each credible cause be forestalled or its impact be diminished?
10. How should the potential problems with the greatest impact or risk be managed? (Who? When? Where? How?)

Types of Strategies

Basically, there are two categories of predictive strategies: casual or incidental, and conscious or planned. Both involve the judicious use of several approaches, including inquiring techniques, that are the subject of a later chapter. Some of those strategies are included here because they are indispensable means of sensing problems. However, more expanded coverage of these approaches will be provided in Chapter 5.

Casual

Opportunities to sense potential problems abound in all types of organizations. Unfortunately, many lead to dead ends. You must use judgment before you invest time and other resources in checking out potential problems that are identified by incidental means. Before resources are committed for following up on a lead, consider the potential value. That doesn't mean, however, that casual sources of information about potential problems should be rejected out of hand. What are some of the most common casual sources?

The grapevine. In most organizations a large amount of information is passed through an uncontrolled and informal communication system called the grapevine. In contrast with regular channels, the grapevine is not the result of deliberate attempts by people to get information they need; it is more a rumor mill than a communications network. The impulse to get the information needed to perform one's duties is very strong. The need to share concerns about the work environment with fellow workers is even stronger. When established communication systems fail to meet those needs, the tendency is to go outside the formal system. That is the origin of the grapevine.

The importance of the grapevine lies not in who is on it or how it works but what is being transmitted and why. Rumors usually start when information of concern to employees is not being provided through regular channels. People like to talk, so the formation of a grapevine seems to be inevitable. That being so, HR managers must tune in on the grapevine. It sometimes provides a warning about latent problems of great magnitude.

Incidental observation. Observation may be defined as a means of studying the behavior of people as they act, interact, and express themselves in ordinary work and social situations.

In the course of day-to-day contacts with people, either work-related or during social affairs, the HR manager has many opportunities to observe individual people, company operations, interpersonal relationships, and group interactions, and to ask probing questions. The astute manager stays alert to observe situations and people and to hear their casual comments. Sometimes what is left unsaid is just as revealing as a pointed statement or question. But here again, the HR manager must exercise caution and good judgment before taking any action.

Listening. HR managers must be alert to the casual comments from the boss, subordinates, superiors, peers, other employees, customers, suppliers, and visitors. The shop or office, the laboratory, the conference room, the cafeteria, the dispensary, the supply room, the warehouse, the assembly line, the training room, or any other place in the organization offers the opportunity to pick up clues that point to potential problems. Outside events such as service club meetings, concerts, conferences, exhibits, golf matches, and cocktail parties, provide chances to cull valuable fragments of information. Unfortunately, all too often managers do not listen at all; their preoccupation with other matters or their impatience causes them to tune out.

Suggestion systems.   A properly operating suggestion system provides another potentially fruitful source of information about latent problems. It offers employees at all levels a ready way to voice their complaints about policies, procedures, and practices, and equipment, materials, products, and working conditions, including hazards to health and safety. An effective suggestion system can provide a veritable flood of ideas to improve HR systems, programs, services, and activities. Periodic examination of suggestions will also reveal problems that otherwise might not show up until they become critical. The HR manager would do well to tap into this source regularly.

Tests and surveys.   Tests and survey instruments designed for other purposes can also be used for problem sensing. For example, psychological tests used to screen and select personnel can also be used to identify skills deficiencies that could pose serious problems if uncorrected. Achievement tests used to establish qualification for entry-level clerical, technical, or supervisory positions in the HR department can also be used to alert line managers and staff personnel about deficiencies of the personnel assigned to them. Surveys used to determine employees' expectations or to measure attitudes and morale, whether conducted by questionnaires or interviews, can also be used to identify potential problems.

Reports and records.   During the course of normal, day-to-day activities, the HR manager must review a great variety of reports and records: personnel, sales, production, review and analysis, training and development, equipment down time and damage, waste and spoilage, work backlogs, rejects and reworks, grievances, lost time, production bottlenecks, sick leave rates, accident rates, absenteeism and tardiness, turnover, unit costs, profit and loss statements, violations of company rules and regulations, and customer complaints. All these reports convey information from the point at which the action takes place to the accountable manager. However, from those same reports the HR manager can identify early on deficiencies, shortfalls, and failures that could severely affect company operations if they are not remedied.

Meetings and conferences.   Staff meetings and conferences, whether they are purely informational or involve problem solving and decision making, constitute another important source of information about potential problems. Status briefings, progress reports, proposals, and other forms of decision briefings frequently reveal situations and conditions that must be corrected; sometimes these conditions are the responsibility of the HR manager rather than the person making the presentation. The HR manager has an obligation to attend such meetings and conferences, and more than that, to be alert to identify those smoldering issues and take the action to investigate them further.

Planned

It is extremely important that HR managers not rely solely on incidental or accidental means of identifying potential problems. They must also take the time and expend the resources needed to collect and analyze information that may point to latent problems. These activities must be planned in advance, and they involve getting answers to what, who, where, when, and how.

Essentially, conscious or planned strategies are controls, systems for identifying either actual or potential variances in performance. Controls can be tailormade to provide early warning of results not conforming with overall company plans. This is the category of controls that needs more emphasis if the problem-sensing skills of the HR manager are to be sharpened.

The process of exercising adequate controls involves several sequential actions. The first step is to set quality, quantity, time, cost, or other *performance standards* for people or systems involved. The second step is to develop appropriate means of *measuring performance* against the standards, selecting or constructing yardsticks that will identify shortfalls or problems before they occur. Step three is to *apply the measures,* and step four is to *identify* the actual or projected variances.

The remaining five steps in the control process (analyzing the deviations, determining the causes, identifying and analyzing alternative courses of action and their probable impact, selecting and applying the most promising remedial action, and following up on results) are aspects of inquiring and problem solving, which are the subjects of the next chapters.

Forecasts.   Forecasts are projections of things to come; they represent an attempt to look into the future of an organization. Forecasts can be used to project the rate at which new technology will replace an older one, assist in managing R&D programs, determine the value and impact of developing managerial concepts and new hardware, evaluate new products and processes that present opportunities and threats to the organization, and determine future needs for personnel at all levels. Because the future is rarely crystal clear, forecasts are subject to error. However, the risk of prediction errors must be accepted because forecasts are absolutely essential to managerial planning.

Forecasts have two elements: inputs and outputs. Inputs commonly include such factors as organizational goals and objectives, results of market surveys, technological trends and developments, production plans, organizational arrangements, and staffing projections. Outputs consist of adjustments in policies, practices, and procedures, organizational changes, staffing modifications, and other actions designed to bring all company functions into line with anticipated requirements. Identifying and analyzing those factors is an important aspect of problem sensing.

Observation. Planned personal observation of activities of staffers in action is an important problem-sensing technique. To make observations count for something, the HR manager must plan carefully, knowing where to look, what to look for, and when. (Sometimes, as I discovered early in my career, the "right time" is the midwatch, between 12:00 midnight and 4:00 A.M.) In any case, haphazard observation will not be as fruitful as systematic observation. The HR manager must decide in advance what specific areas to visit and how often, what to check, and how to use the findings.

Inspections and visits. Inspections are one form of planned visits. Just about all departments and agencies of the federal government, most state governments, and many private organizations have an office or officer called the inspector general. The purpose is not only to look in depth at problems and issues identified by people within the organization, but also to conduct regular (usually annual) inspections to identify latent or potential problems and issues before they become acute.

Visits and inspections can provide answers to some key questions about a subordinate section or manager. For example: Are the people assigned to the section fully employed? Do they show spirit, motivation, and high morale? Are managers and supervisors fully informed about their sections (absenteeism, grievances, budget, expenditures, equipment problems, and the like)? Do subordinate managers have their sections under control? Are the work areas clean, orderly, and safe?

Here are some suggestions for conducting inspections and visits:

- Make a schedule. Set aside a definite amount of time for *daily* visits. Make them randomly, but be sure to include early Monday mornings, late Friday afternoons, and night shifts.
- Set targets. Review what you intend to inspect—and where.
- Stick with your plan. Don't let a subordinate manager or supervisor sidetrack you.
- Address your questions to the people doing the work, not their supervisor.
- Listen carefully to the answers you get. Find out from people what their problems are and how they think they can be solved.
- When possible, praise the accomplishments of both the manager and the employees. If there are performance discrepancies, don't criticize in public.

○ Make a brief record of your visits. List accomplishments, problems, and shortfalls.
○ Follow up. Send handwritten memos for noteworthy accomplishments. Take needed corrective action on discrepancies.
○ Reinspect after corrective action.

Problem sensing requires constant surveillance and scheduled inspections to recognize problems and good judgment to set priorities for solution in terms of urgency and seriousness. HR managers can put that principle to good use by conducting regular visits, and occasionally more formal inspections, to search out hidden problems.

Interviews.   Planned interviews with superiors, peers, subordinates, other employees, customers, and suppliers can provide additional insights. The interview may be useful to identify leads to new or unperceived problems (this is problem sensing) or to determine the seriousness of problems spotted by other means (this is inquiring). The interview permits you to collect information (or opinion) in depth. However, HR managers must guard against their own biases and prejudices, likes and dislikes, perceptions, and value judgments. Don't let those subjective factors get in the way of the facts.

Similarly, HR managers must be aware that interviewees may be guarded in their responses, will tend to remember incidents and situations subjectively and selectively, and may screen information. As a result the facts may be distorted or colored. The key to success in interviewing is to get people to talk, to level with you. You have to ask those kinds of questions that will elicit complete, pertinent, and useful information.

Formal and informal group discussion.   If properly planned and conducted, informal group discussions, such as rap sessions, are an excellent means of gaining insight into situations as employees and subordinates see them. They should, in fact, be a deliberate attempt to give people a chance to voice their problems and concerns, and offer suggestions for change or improvement, in a relaxed atmosphere. Informal sessions help to overcome the problems of size and organizational distance in large organizations and can provide HR managers with the feedback they need to identify problems before they become critical. They can also defuse potentially destructive or disruptive forces or issues in an organization.

Similarly, formal group discussions, such as quality circles, can provide the same kind of useful insight. Both formal and informal discussions should be used to the fullest extent as problem-sensing strategies.

Staff meetings.   We tend to get from something what we expect to get. This is true of meetings of any kind. What do you expect to get? If you expect to get the most out of a staff meeting in the context of problem sensing, you will hear about some events and situations that portend problems down the road. However, you must also be ready and willing to take some ambiguity.

Weekly or monthly staff meetings can be valuable sources of information. The HR manager must ensure that communication in staff meetings is omnidirectional (that is, with superiors, peers, and subordinates), that full and free discussion is encouraged, and that no penalties are imposed for disclosing bad news. Successful staff meetings require careful planning and skill in conducting them.

Spot reports.   Make conscious and direct use of your staff to sound the alert about conditions and events that could blossom into severe problems. HR personnel at all levels have a knack for problem sensing; that should be a part of their stock in trade. HR managers would do well to institute a system of spot reports—brief (one page), handwritten, formatted reports of observations by managers, supervisors, staff personnel, technicians, secretarial and clerical workers, and other employees. A format for a spot report is shown in Figure 4-1.

Attitude and opinion surveys.   Attitude and opinion surveys turn up valuable and often surprising information to help you make better decisions, avoid costly mistakes, plan more effectively, identify potential problems, and manage more competently.

Surveys can be designed to elicit information about attitudes on a whole range of managerial concerns, from problem identification to indepth analysis of potential problems identified by other means. They can uncover reasons for problems, probe feelings about situations or conditions, and get ideas for preventive actions. Here too, they must be meticulously planned and precisely executed.

Outside consultants.   HR and other types of outside consultants provide still another source of information about potential problems. They deal with a great variety of situations in many organizations of different types. Over a period of time they are exposed to issues and given access to information that can provide extremely useful insight. Often they can make that information available to you without compromising themselves or breaching confidentiality. Take full advantage of this source of information.

Meetings and exhibits.   Professional meetings and exhibits hosted by local and national trade and professional associations can provide insights into trends, developments, and other forces that pose potential problems for HR managers—often considerably in advance of their arrival. Such advance warning gives the manager time to take actions that

Figure 4-1. Format for a spot report.

SPOT REPORT

Date_____

From:

To:

Subject:

Situation or event observed:

(This section contains a brief description of what the reporter observed. It should contain the what, when, where, who, and why—facts only.)

Significance of the event or situation:

(Here the observer describes what the situation or event means, why it is important.)

Recommendations:

(Here the observer may make any suggestions about how to correct the situation.)

_____   _____
Department   Signature

                                        _____
                                        Title

---

will either diminish the impact or defuse the potential problem. Attendance at such meetings can repay the cost many times over. Examples of such meetings are the annual conferences sponsored by the American Management Association, American Society for Personnel Administration, American Society for Training and Development, and *Training* magazine.

Professional reading. Trade and professional books and journals can fulfill the same function as professional meetings but on a larger scale. Professional reading has an added advantage: Most books and articles propose alternative solutions to the problems identified, giving the HR manager a handle on a problem before it reaches his or her organization.

Professional reading is a must for the HR manager. Of the many periodicals currently available, some of the most useful are the *Training and Development Journal, Personnel, Training, Management Review, Business Week, Educational Technology, Educational Communications and Technology, Harvard Business Review, Northeast Training News, NSPI Journal, Phi Delta Kappan,* and *Technical Horizons in Education.*

Catalogs and brochures. The catalogs and brochures distributed by other organizations, particularly competitors, can provide information of value. New products and processes described in those materials can alert you to trends and developments. By inference, they can tell you what other organizations believe are important issues, challenges, wants, needs, and problems.

For example, if an organization is advertising an interactive video training program covering changes to a personnel law, it could be your first inkling that the law had been changed. Don't throw away those catalogs and brochures until you have at least skimmed them to see what the competition is doing. It could save you a lot of grief down the road.

Procedures

The challenge to HR managers is to assemble the resources needed to meet today's problems and tomorrow's uncertainties. They must identify the human and matériel resources and create the interactive environment needed to encourage better communication, innovation, leadership, renewal, and improvement in their organizations. In their search for potential problem areas, they must focus on *real* needs and results.

There are some procedures that will help organize and objectify your planned problem sensing. They will help you narrow your search and avoid wasting your time and effort on areas that are not likely to be fruitful.

1. Identify key result areas. To give your efforts focus, you need to start by identifying the key result areas for your organization. Those are the ones that spell the difference between success and failure. For some HR managers, the prime target may be executive succession, the selection and development of leaders. For others, the principal focus may be on marketing HR programs and services outside the organization. For still others, the primary thrust may be toward a linkage between HR strategy and business performance. The choices will be different for different situations and at different times, but the competent HR manager knows which areas represent the most pressing needs of his or her organization.

Let us assume, for example, that your HR department produces videotape training and development programs that are not only used within your company but are also marketed outside, to produce revenue to support in-house training and development efforts. In that situation, a key result area would be sales.

2. Develop a data collection plan. This step involves determining the specific categories of information required and the source of each one. You must now identify the data you need, their sources, the recording format, the procedures, and the time frame. Sticking with our example of marketing videotapes as the key result area, you must gather information about sales, such as total number of videotapes sold over a specific period of time, a breakdown of those sales by program title, type (VHS or Beta), geographic area, type of customer (educational institutions, banks, hospitals, charitable institutions, retail stores, and so on), and sources of sales (advertisements in professional and trade journals, retail stores, direct sales, over the counter at conferences and exhibits, and so on).

3. Collect and record the data. Systematically collect, tabulate, and record the data, using observation, interviews, surveys, spot reports, sales reports, and so on. Count, group, and prepare graphs and tables to depict the data. Use whatever techniques that allow you to examine the data efficiently and quickly spot problems and deviations.

Again, using our example of marketing videotaped programs, the task here is to gather all the information about sales, customers, and sources of sales, tabulate and collate the data, and then prepare a simple report that incorporates all the findings in readily understandable form.

4. Identify and define the problem. This is the most difficult step. It requires in-depth knowledge of the organization and the particular function under study—the product, production techniques, market, the competition, marketing and sales strategies and techniques, to mention only the most obvious. In addition, however, identification and definition also require the analyst to predict deviations, isolate the element that would be responsible for the shortfalls, and determine the direct cause of the potential deviation.

Continuing with our example, the HR manager would now study

the data to identify the pressure points. He or she would examine all information, criticisms, complaints, and suggestions made by superiors, peers, subordinates, salespersons, and customers about the quality of the videotapes (sequence, color, sound, and the like), short falls in advertising, promotion, delivery, inadequately trained salespersons, or any other deficiency. Every aspect of the situation would be examined to reveal possible organization, supervisory, training, production, advertising, marketing, or other weaknesses that could be the primary source of the problem. Next he or she would summarize the situation in the simplest possible terms and state the key facts that are still missing.

   5. Inquiring and problem solving. At this point the HR manager is ready to address the key facts or information that are still missing. To do that the inquiring techniques described in Chapter 5 should be used. Next, the problems are solved using the strategies and procedures described in Chapter 6.

Summary

Problem sensitivity is managerial preventive medicine. It provides a means of identifying potential problems before they have an impact on the organization or impede performance. You can develop problem-sensitivity skills, just as you can learn problem-solving ability. Three factors are essential: first, accepting the importance of and need for improvement; second, recognizing the means by which potential problems can be spotted; and third, practicing the skill.

   The ideal managerial control is problem prediction, based on the skill of problem sensing. The best places to prospect for potential problems are where some new program, service, policy, or process has been introduced, when shortage of time requires extraordinary coordination and effort, when a procedure involves several sequential and complex steps, when teams of people are involved, when a program or process requires the cooperation of several departments, or where the HR manager does not have control over the entire project or process.

   Although casual or incidental means of identifying potential problems should be fully exploited, major breakthroughs are more likely to come from planned and conscious efforts. Some of the most useful casual or incidental strategies are the grapevine, incidental observation, listening, suggestion systems, tests and surveys, reports and records, and meetings and conferences.

   Among the most useful planned or conscious means of prospecting for potential problems are company forecasts, observation, interviews, group discussions, staff meetings, spot reports, attitude and opinion surveys, outside consultants, meetings and exhibits, professional readings, and catalogs and brochures.

Problem sensing involves these steps: (1) identify key result areas; (2) develop a data collection plan; (3) collect, tabulate, and record the data; (4) identify and define the potential problem; and (5) use inquiring and problem-solving skills to delimit and solve the problem.

FOR FURTHER READING

Albert, Kenneth J. *Handbook of Business Problem Solving.* New York: McGraw-Hill, 1980.

————. *How to Solve Business Problems: The Consultant's Approach to Business Problems.* New York: McGraw-Hill, 1983.

Anderson, Barry F. *The Complete Thinker: A Handbook of Techniques for Creative and Critical Problem Solving.* Englewood Cliffs, N.J.: Prentice-Hall, 1980.

Andriole, Stephen J. *Handbook of Problem Solving.* Princeton, N.J.: Petrocelli Books, 1983.

Bibeault, D. *Corporate Turnaround: How Managers Turn Losers into Winners.* Del Mar, Calif.: McGraw-Hill Training Systems, 1982.

Bradley, John. "How to Interview for Information." *Training/HRD*, April 1983, pp. 59–62.

Delaney, William A. *The 30 Most Common Problems in Management and How to Solve Them.* New York: AMACOM, 1982.

Fogiel, Max. *Problem Solver in Business Management and Finance.* New York: Research and Education Association, 1985.

Hayes, J. R. *The Complete Problem Solver.* Philadelphia: Franklin Institute Press, 1981.

Hulett, Daniel G., and Jean Renjilian, "Strategic Planning." In *Human Resources Management and Development Handbook,* edited by William R. Tracey. New York: AMACOM, 1985.

Kepner, Charles H., and Benjamin B. Tregoe. *The Rational Manager: A Systematic Approach to Problem Solving and Decision Making.* New York: McGraw-Hill, 1965.

————. "Potential Problem Analysis." In *The New Rational Manager.* Princeton, N.J.: Kepner-Tregoe, 1981.

Leavitt, Harold J. *Corporate Pathfinders: Building Vision and Values into Organizations.* Homewood, Ill.: Dow Jones-Irwin, 1986.

Manzini, Andrew O., and John D. Gridley. *Integrating Human Resources and Strategic Business Planning.* New York: AMACOM, 1986.

Meltzer, Morton F. *Information, the Ultimate Management Resource: How to Find, Use, and Manage It.* New York: AMACOM, 1981.

Nathan, Ernest D. *Questions in Group Leadership,* 2nd ed. Reading, Mass.: Addison-Wesley Training Systems, 1979.

Nierenberg, Gerard I. *Fundamentals of Negotiating.* New York: Editorial Correspondents, 1973, chapter 8.

Odiorne, George S. *Management Decisions by Objectives.* Englewood Cliffs, N.J.: Prentice-Hall, 1969.

Olivas, Louis. "Auditing Your Training and Development Function." *Training and Development Journal,* March 1980, pp. 60–64.

Peters, Tom, and Nancy Austin. "MBWA (Managing by Wandering Around): The Technology of the Obvious." In *A Passion for Excellence: The Leadership Difference.* New York: Random House, 1985.

Roth, William F., Jr. *Problem Solving for Managers.* New York: Praeger, 1985.

Sanderson, Michael. *What's the Problem Here? Time-Saving Problem-Solving Techniques for Managers.* Englewood Cliffs, N.J.: Prentice-Hall, 1981.

Schoennauer, Alfred W. W. *Problem Finding and Problem Solving: A Guide to Aid Management in the Identification of and Solution to Operational Problems.* New York: Nelson-Hall, 1981.

Segal, Leon. *The Problem Solver's Universal Checklist.* Dayton, Ohio: Educator's Academy, 1983.

Slavens, Thomas P. *Informational Interviews and Questions.* Metuchen, N.J.: Scarecrow Press, 1978.

Tracey, William R. *Human Resource Development Standards: A Self-Evaluational Manual for HRD Managers and Specialists.* New York: AMACOM, 1981.

Van Fleet, James K. *The 22 Biggest Mistakes Managers Make and How to Correct Them.* West Nyack, N.Y.: Parker Publishing Company, 1973, chapters 5 and 15.

Vanston, John H., Jr. "Technology Forecasting." In *Human Resources Management and Development Handbook,* edited by William R. Tracey. New York: AMACOM, 1985.

White, Charles S. "Problem-Solving: The First Neglected Step." *Management Review,* January 1983, pp. 52–55.

5

INQUIRING
Getting the Facts

HR managers cannot afford to wait for their subordinates to tell them what they need to know. They will often need to ask their department people, as well as others in the organization, for information, ideas, impressions, opinions, and recommendations. This questioning process works upward too; HR managers must ask their superiors for the information and assistance they need to do their jobs. That is the essence of inquiring: the process by which facts, ideas, information, opinions, meanings, emotions, and understandings are obtained from others.

To get answers, you must ask questions. To get accurate and useful answers, you must ask penetrating questions about the right subjects, addressed to the right sources (including people) at the right time, with the right medium, format, and techniques.

Few HR managers can prosper, let alone survive in today's competitive business world, unless they are able to acquire, use, and manage information skillfully. A substantial part of that need is now being fulfilled by the convergence of the data processing and telecommunications technologies. Still, inquiring remains a basic method of collecting information and one of the key ways to put action-oriented management into effect. Inquiring is extremely necessary to competent planning, organizing, staffing, directing, and controlling—the essential functions of management.

Information is also a source of power in organizations. The manager who has the necessary information can perform well; the manager who lacks it cannot provide the leadership required. It is equally true that managers must have the information that others, particularly their subordinates, feel they need to do their jobs. Of course, the more information an HR manager gains that can affect the department, the more credibility the manager gains with line managers and top executives.

Information is used to inform yourself, to notify and influence other

Parts of this chapter are adapted with permission from William R. Tracey, "The New HRD Manager: How to Hit the Ground Running," *Training*, April 1984, pp. 44–51.

people, to solve problems, to make decisions, to innovate, and to evaluate. You need information to be knowledgeable about the status of your company and your department, and about current trends and future conditions. Information in today's age of discontinuity and ambiguity is a must. To get it, you need inquiring skills.

Applications

Three applications of the inquiring skill are particularly useful to HR managers: getting new or newly assigned HR managers up to speed; identifying opportunities to improve HR systems, programs, and services; and helping identify and solve the potential problems revealed by problem-sensing strategies.

Getting New HR Managers Up to Speed

For the new HR manager, or the manager new to the organization, the first order of business is to get up to speed. How shall we define that phrase? "Getting up to speed" involves specific, practical, and tested techniques for learning about the organization—collecting, assimilating, evaluating, and using information to create a firm basis for developing plans to improve things, and putting those plans into action.

Regardless of your skills and motivation, you cannot function competently and achieve outstanding results until you have studied your organization in detail. As an HR manager, you must know the answers to the following questions:

Why does the organization exist?
What does it do?
How does it do what it does?
Where does the organization want to be in the future?
How does it plan to get there?
How does it determine when it does get there?
Who are the principal players?
Where are the major power centers?

Inquiring strategies can help you get valid and pointed answers.

Improving HR Operations

Evidence of good HR decisions and top performance consists of verifiable progress and improvement in HR operations—in the quality

Note: Section titled "Getting New HR Managers Up to Speed" is adapted and expanded from William R. Tracey, "The New HRD Manager: How to Hit the Ground Running," *Training,* April 1984, pp. 44–51. Used by permission.

and effectiveness of HR systems, programs, and services. Improvement is ultimately more important to an organization than solving problems, particularly problems with minor impact. Exploiting major strengths, rather than shoring up minor deficiencies, is unquestionably a better way to use expensive resources.

Good decisions and topnotch performance depend on getting and using first-rate information. Getting good information depends heavily on the inquiring skills of the HR manager. Competent HR managers know when they don't have enough information to make good decisions or perform tasks well—and they know where and how to get the information they need.

To exploit opportunities to improve operations, HR managers must have answers to the following questions:

What HR systems and programs are in effect?
What HR services are provided?
How do the HR staff and users feel about them?
Can programs and services be improved?
How can they be made more efficient and effective?

Problem Solving

Whether brought to attention by HR personnel, line managers, employees, management control systems, or the problem-sensing strategies of the HR manager, solving actual problems (and preventing potential problems) depends to a great extent on the HR manager's skill at inquiring. The first step in preventing or solving problems is to get answers to questions like these:

Where did the problem originate?
What brought it to attention?
How serious is the problem? What is the potential impact?
Can it be ignored with impunity?
Who is involved? Who is responsible?
What are the alternatives?

Categories of Information

What is necessary to know? What is nice to know? What evidence is credible? What data sources are most appropriate for answers to critical questions? The HR manager must answer these questions before starting to collect data.

Obviously, all the information HR managers need cannot be collected in a day, a week, a month, or even a quarter. All the information collected in only a few weeks cannot be fully assimilated, let alone used, even by an HR manager with years on the job.

The process starts even before managers get hired. They acquire some information about the organization when they are being considered for employment or promotion. Obviously, however, the bulk of the data must be collected on the job—some in the first few days, much of it within the first few weeks. Thereafter, they must have a way to gather essential information regularly, quickly, systematically, and in the proper sequence. And it must be obtained from the proper sources using appropriate techniques.

The information you're after falls into three general categories: the current organization as a whole, the future organization, and the current HR organization.

The current organization as a whole. You need to learn about the company's origins, history, missions, functions, products and services; its formal structure, informal structure, goals and objectives, policies and rules. What collective bargaining agreements are in force or pending? How about its physical layout, its budget, its external relationships? Who are the key players?

The future organization. You need to identify projected changes in the firm's mission and functions, its products and services, formal structure, goals and objectives, and physical layout. Are there any plans for new equipment or systems? Are there any changes in the wind regarding external relationships or key personnel?

The current HR organization. Zero in on your functional area of responsibility—the mission, activities, position in the organizational structure, goals and objectives of the HR department, policies and rules, and programs and services. What about the HR budget, facilities, significant accomplishments, critical challenges, opportunities, problems and issues, current projects and key personnel?

Where do you look for all this information? Here's where—and also how.

Data Collection Sources and Methods

Many sources of information about your organization are readily available. Among the most common are organization documents, staff briefings, observation, interviews, meetings and conferences, inspections, questionnaires and surveys, and snowflakes/taskers (requests for information or opinion). The HR manager would do well to use most, if not all, of those means of getting the facts about the organization.

Here are some suggestions for getting the collection process underway:

- Identify and categorize the information you need.
- Establish a filing system for the data.
- Identify data sources and collection methods.
- Commit everything important to writing.
- Accumulate all the organization's key documents.
- Collect the data.

Document Review

One of the fastest and most productive ways to get information about your organization is to review organization documents: organization and functions manuals, policy and procedures manuals, budgets, supervisors' and employees' handbooks, collective bargaining agreements and contracts, industry and corporate forecasts, annual reports and audits, quarterly review and analysis reports, product catalogs, brochures, price lists, financial reports, and records of all types.

Those documents can provide important insights into the organization, its origins and history, mission and functions, financial status and budget, formal and informal organization structures, goals and objectives, policies and rules, programs and services, contracts and agreements, physical layout, facilities, equipment, external relationships, critical problems and issues, significant accomplishments, current projects, and personnel resources. Figures 5-1, 5-2, and 5-3 identify the types of documents that are most likely to yield information about the current organization as a whole, the future organization, and the HR function, on all organization elements.

Document review has several distinct advantages. First and foremost, materials are readily available for study, whenever and wherever you wish to use them. They can be taken home for leisurely study. They can be highlighted with colored marking pen to make it easy to find key items again. The only problem is their overabundance. In most organizations, there are so many documents that you must set priorities. Perhaps the best sequence is this: organization and functions manual, policy manual, collective bargaining agreement and contracts, budgets and financial reports, enterprise planning documents, and "summary" personnel records. That, of course, is a matter for individual decision.

Staff Briefings

Another time-saving means of getting information is to schedule a series of information briefings (as distinguished from decision briefings; see Chapter 2) by key staff, often coupled with visits to the briefer's area of operations. The sole purpose of the briefings is to obtain critical

Figure 5-1. Information you need about the current organization and where to find it.

Information	Sources
Origins and history	Organization manual Employees' handbook Supervisors' handbook Interviews Records and reports
Mission and functions	Organization and functions manual Policy manual Employees' handbook Supervisors' handbook
Products and services	Catalogs Brochures Price lists Advertising copy
Formal structure	Organization and functions manual Organization chart Interviews Staff meetings
Informal structure	Observation and visits Meetings and conferences Interviews
Goals and objectives	Planning documents Forecasts Interviews Policy manual MBO documents Staff meetings
Policies and rules	Policy and procedures manual Employees' handbooks Supervisors' handbooks Collective bargaining agreements Contracts
Collective bargaining agreement	Contracts Policy manual Interviews Staff meetings
Physical layout	Visits Maps Plot plans Photographs

Figure 5-1, continued.

Budget	Budget documents Interviews Quarterly reports Staff meetings
External relationships	Policy manual Catalogs and brochures Employees' manuals Annual reports Interviews
Key personnel	Biographical sketches Interviews Observation Job descriptions Staff meetings

information in a form that can be readily assimilated. Key executives, managers, supervisors, and staff personnel, such as the vice president for personnel, marketing manager, controller, director of research and development, purchasing manager, plant manager, subordinate HR staff, can be asked to provide 20- or 30-minute briefings on their areas of responsibility, focusing on their organization structures, goals and

Figure 5-2.   Information you need about the future organization and where to find it.

Information	Source
Projected changes in: Mission and functions	Enterprise planning documents
Products and services	Forecasts (political, economic, technological, social, demographic, industry)
Formal structure	Long-range plans for expansion, contraction, or diversification
Goals and objectives	Long-range financial plans
Physical layout New equipment and systems	Mid- and long-range plans for construction, rehabilitation, equipment and facilities, including automation, robotics, computer-aided design and manufacturing (CAD/CAM) systems
Key personnel External relationships	Interviews with key personnel (CEO, executives, line managers, staff officers)

Figure 5-3. Information you need about the HR organization and where to find it.

Information	Sources
Mission and functions	Organization manual Employees' manual Supervisors' manual Interviews Records and reports
Department structure	Organization and functions manual Organization chart Interviews
Goals and objectives	Policy manual Planning documents Interviews Staff meetings MBO documents
Programs and services	Catalogs and brochures Policy manual Employees' manuals Supervisors' manuals Collective bargaining agreements Contracts Records and reports Surveys and audits Interviews
Policies and rules	Policy and procedures manuals Employees' handbooks Supervisors' handbooks Collective bargaining agreements Contracts
Budget	Budget documents Financial reports and records Audit reports Quarterly reports Interviews Staff meetings
Personnel resources	Organization and functions manual Job descriptions Personnel surveys and audits Reports and records Interviews

Figure 5-3, continued.

Facilities	Inspections and visits Floor plans Interviews
Significant accomplishments	Annual reports Historical reports Quarterly reports House organs Interviews Briefings
Critical problems and issues	Annual reports Historical reports Quarterly reports Reports of audit Financial reports Personnel records Training and development reports Briefings and correspondence Interviews Observation Performance tests Attitude surveys
Current projects	Planning documents MBO documents Briefings Interviews Staff meetings Project boards
Key personnel	Biographical sketches Interviews Observation

objectives, budgets, staffing, major accomplishments and shortfalls during the past year, critical issues and problems, and current projects.

Observation

Observation is the most direct means of analyzing employees and the conditions that surround the job. It is the only way that certain aspects of the job environment—notably the interaction of people, equipment, and facilities—can be studied.

Although direct observation is time-consuming, and therefore expensive, HR managers must take the time to get out on the assembly line, into the training room, and in the employees' cafeteria to show interest in what their people are doing—and learn what they are thinking. Observation will often reveal things that subordinate managers or staff specialists either can't, don't, or won't report.

Observation is a deliberate and carefully worked out means of collecting information. It has these characteristics:

- *It is specific.* Planned observation is not just looking around or seeking general impressions. To be most useful, observation must be directed toward fact-finding objectives.
- *It is systematic.* Planned observation is not just dropping into the training or work area. The timing, length, and number of observations must be carefully scheduled.
- *It is quantitative.* As much as possible, measurable characteristics are the object of study, particularly when observation is used as a basis for evaluation.
- *It is recorded.* A record is made of the observation either during or immediately following the visit. The results are not entrusted to memory.

When planning for observation, the HR manager should ensure that critical aspects of the job environment come under scrutiny and that an adequate sample of all other facets of the job is included.

For effective observation, follow these steps:

1. Develop a plan that contains the who, when, and where.
2. Include activities that are truly typical (or atypical) of the job environment, but focus on critical areas.
3. Select your position in the work or training area carefully. Be sure that you can see and hear what is going on, but are not in the way.
4. Don't distract workers. Be as unobtrusive (but still visible) as possible; guard against displaying—in any form—disagreement, displeasure, or boredom.
5. Pay particular attention to employee reaction and performance.
6. Complete a record of observation as soon as possible after leaving the area.

Interviews

The interview is probably the most widely used method of eliciting and collecting information. There are two types: individual interviews with employees, and group interviews with employees who belong to the same team or organizational unit or have identical or similar jobs. For example, an individual interview might be conducted with the marketing manager; group interviews with first-line supervisors or with team members on a particular project.

Both kinds of interviews have their place in data collection. They enable HR managers to obtain information and observe behavior that might not otherwise come to their attention, either because it cannot be identified in any other way or because people are reluctant to put some things in writing. With skillful questioning, employees can be encouraged to express themselves freely about their jobs, the work environment, and their attitudes toward their co-workers (as a group), supervisors, and the organization.

The interview also gives employees an opportunity to explain their jobs, their accomplishments, and their concerns, to describe their satisfactions, and to identify resentments and frustrations that might otherwise go unnoticed. The major drawback to the interview is its potential for distortion of information—whether by screening, exaggeration, outright misrepresentation, or genuine misunderstanding on the part of interviewees or miscomprehension or misinterpretation of comments by managers.

Basically, there are two forms of the interview: nonstandardized, and standardized or structured. With the *nonstandardized* interview, the manager makes no attempt to obtain the same information from every interviewee. This type of interview is mainly used to explore broad problems or to search for explanations for unexpected situations.

The *standardized* or structured interview is used when the same information is to be collected from each respondent. The standardized interview also has two formats: the *schedule* interview and the *nonschedule* interview. In the schedule interview, every respondent is asked identical questions, usually read from a prepared schedule. The wording and sequence of the questions are determined in advance. With the nonschedule interview, standardization is achieved without the use of a prepared schedule. The interviewer depends on knowledge of the information required and then varies the wording and the sequence of the questions to attain maximum effectiveness with individual respondents.

Follow these procedures in interviews:

- Determine the objectives of the interview; know exactly what you are trying to find out.
- Select the topics or factors to be covered in the interview; be sure that they are relevant, specific, and can be described in terms that will be easily understood by all respondents.
- Develop an outline that groups similar or related items and establishes a logical sequence.
- Draft the questions using standard terminology; keep them short, clear, and direct.
- Select the interviewees by name, learn as much as possible about

them in advance, and set up an appointment for each one at a mutually convenient time.
- Select a place for the interview that is comfortable, private, and free from distracting noise and interruptions.

To get maximum return on the investment of time, there are several rules that must be followed when conducting interviews:

- Explain the purpose of the interview and the use to which the information will be put.
- Establish rapport, a friendly, cooperative working relationship with the interviewee; put the respondent at ease.
- Begin with questions that are easy to answer, those with no emotional loading.
- Let the interviewee talk; do not dominate.
- Be forthright and sincere with the interviewee; don't be pedantic, overbearing, or try to be clever.
- Avoid evidences of pressure, boredom, or irritation.
- Avoid antagonizing, embarrassing, or hurrying the interviewee.
- Keep control; don't permit the interviewee to go off on tangents.
- Be alert for leads; watch facial expressions, gestures, body language, and casual remarks.
- Don't be perturbed by expressions of negative feelings, such as hostility or highly subjective criticism.
- When the interview is over, summarize the main points to be sure that you have the facts as the interviewee presented them.
- Record all information immediately.

Meetings and Conferences

Meetings and staff conferences are much-maligned techniques for gathering and exchanging information. But when they are properly conducted, meetings and conferences are among the best means of communicating issues, problems, accomplishments, and results.

In addition to the obvious advantage of providing opportunities for face-to-face communication, meetings and conferences have several other benefits. They tend to reduce parochialism and foster greater loyalty to the organization as a whole. They go a long way toward ensuring that information passed is accurate.

If your meetings are to be most productive, you must meet certain requirements and follow certain procedures:

- Issue a meeting memorandum with adequate advance notice and a limited number of agenda items, distributed well in advance of the meeting.

- Have specific objectives.
- Streamline attendance by having only essential people present. If some people are needed only for a portion of the meeting, have them attend only for that period.
- Use a clean, well-lighted conference room with comfortable chairs and tables arranged in a U, circle, or semicircle.
- Supply a name placard for each person, and make water, coffee, or soft drinks available if the meeting is longer than 90 minutes.
- Start on time.
- Begin and end with noncontroversial items.
- Explain why the topic is important to the organization and to the members of the group.
- Never open a discussion with "I think"; it stifles ideas.
- Ask probing, open-ended questions, and don't ask questions that can be answered *yes* or *no*.
- Encourage full and free discussion.
- Be sure that no penalties are imposed on or by anyone for disclosing bad news.
- Maintain eye contact with the person speaking.
- Steer participants back to the point when they stray too far from the subject; repeat the issue to keep the discussion on track; stick to the agenda.
- Bring disagreements out into the open; stress the importance of getting different points of view on every issue to preclude "group-think."
- Require that two positions be presented about an idea or option before one negative comment is made (to focus on the positive and promote open-mindedness).
- Try to assign a devil's advocate (not the originator) and an advocate to every idea or position.
- Seek consensus on resolution of problems or issues.
- Summarize decisions at the end of the meeting.
- Develop a rough agenda for the next meeting.
- End on time.
- Follow through on every meeting by acting on recommendations and by distributing brief minutes.

An important variant of the staff conference is the discussion group, sometimes referred to as a rap session. Essentially, it is a meeting attended by the manager and a representative group of employees, *without* their supervisors; it provides them with an opportunity to voice their problems and concerns, discuss issues with a decision maker, and offer suggestions to improve the work environment. It not only provides a means of overcoming the bigness of organizations, but also gives the manager the feedback needed to determine real problems as the doers see them and without the inevitable screening that takes place when supervisory personnel report the problems and concerns of their workers. Rap sessions can defuse potentially destructive or disruptive forces by providing an outlet for negative feelings, give the manager firsthand feedback, and also demonstrate that management has a genuine interest in the problems and concerns of employees.

To be effective, rap sessions must be conducted as follows:

- Clearly communicate the purpose of the sessions to all concerned—participants and their supervisors.
- Keep the group small, not more than 12 people.
- Coordinate the time of the meeting with the participants' supervisors.
- Keep meetings informal and unstructured.
- Encourage an atmosphere that is open and elicits candor.
- Adopt and publicize a policy of nonattribution.
- Follow up problems and suggestions with the supervisors most directly involved.
- Report all actions taken to participants.

Inspections and Reinspections

Inspections are essentially semiformal visits to administrative, logistical, operational, maintenance, training, or other areas of HR operations. The purpose is to examine the effectiveness of policies and the adequacy of facilities, equipment, and supplies; to collect data on potential problems revealed by problem-sensing strategies; or to follow up on problem remedies. Usually a standard or locally developed checklist is used to identify strengths and weaknesses and the actions needed to bring the condition or facility up to standard and to eliminate actual or potential deficiencies and hazards.

Coverage may include general items, items relating to buildings and facilities, fixtures and controls, protective equipment, facilities and devices, exits and access, fire protection, machines and equipment, housekeeping, record-keeping, financial management, personnel, training and development, procurement, marketing, employee services, public relations, publications, and all policies and procedures.

Essentially, the task of the inspecting HR manager is to collect relevant data, using the checklist developed beforehand and carefully recording the results, then to compare results with the standard and determine whether they are within the tolerances allowed. This is how the manager identifies shortfalls and deficiencies, the areas that require attention and correction. To make the corrections, the manager must determine the cause—the who, what, where, how, and why of the deficiency.

Regardless of the function or activity being inspected, several key questions should be addressed:

- How well is the function or activity being performed?

    ○ Do systems, programs, and services meet the needs of *both* the organization and the individual employee? Where do shortfalls exist?
    ○ Do the costs of operation compare favorably with those of comparable-size organizations?
    ○ Are employees' efforts directed toward department cost performance and other types of objectives?
    ○ Are systems, procedures, work methods, and equipment the best available for the purpose?
    ○ Are deadlines being beaten or met?
    ○ Do employees work well under pressure?
    ○ Are reports and analyses accurate and reliable?
    ○ Are operations sufficiently well planned to effect reasonably uniform work load, work flow, and personnel standards?

- How well do subordinate supervisors manage?

    ○ Are organization and department policies being carried out as intended?
    ○ Are specialists and technicians being intelligently informed of the work to be done and the standards expected?
    ○ Do operating elements cooperate, or is there evidence of friction, antagonism, and misunderstanding?
    ○ Do key people delegate sufficiently to free themselves for their managerial or supervisory tasks?
    ○ Do key people evaluate their subordinates fairly and take action to correct deficiencies and reward outstanding performance?
    ○ Do key people help subordinates find the right answers to operating problems? Do they keep you informed of significant development and problems?
    ○ Are key people fully conversant with collective bargaining agreements? Do they apply the rules fairly and avoid allowing them to impair their effectiveness as supervisors?
    ○ Does each key person have a replacement trained?

To be most productive, inspections must be carefully planned and carried out. There are no shortcuts if you want results that are worth the time and resources expended. Follow these steps:

1. Select or develop a data-gathering instrument, preferably a checklist.
2. Develop a schedule of visits in coordination with the appropriate supervisors.
3. Make clear to all concerned the purposes of the inspection and how the findings will be used.
4. During the inspection, be as objective as possible. Don't overrate or underrate; don't nitpick.
5. Provide the supervisor with an oral summary of your findings immediately after your visit, then follow up with a detailed report.

Questionnaires and Surveys

Questionnaires and surveys are among the most popular means of collecting impressions of many people. They are used with a variety of subjects. Questionnaires can also isolate and describe elements of a situation for observation and reporting. Be aware, however, that they involve difficult techniques and require a heavy investment of time for development, tabulation, summarization, and interpretation. A well-constructed questionnaire defines the terminology respondents will use in reporting their impressions, preferences, attitudes, and observations.

There are two types of questionnaires: closed form and open form. The *closed form* questionnaire contains a list of items to be checked, a list of alternative responses to be selected, or blanks to be filled in by words or numbers. This type of form has two main advantages: It requires a minimum of time to complete, and it simplifies the task of tabulating and summarizing responses. However, it is more difficult to construct and anticipate all the responses people may want to make.

The *open form* questionnaire (sometimes called open-end or free response) allows the respondent to present a more complete description of a situation. Typically it encourages the respondent to go beyond the numerical or factual data to get into attitudes and feelings, the background of responses, or the reasons for preferences or opinions. It has two advantages: It is less restrictive than the closed form and permits more complete answers, and it is less demanding on the developer. However, it does require more time to administer, and tabulating and summarizing the data are more difficult and take more time.

In constructing a questionnaire or survey instrument, make sure these steps are followed:

1. Carefully define your objectives, considering the characteristics of the target group and how the results will be used.
2. Select the subjects or factors to be covered. Ensure that they are

specific, relevant, and can be defined in terms that will be clear to all respondents.

3. Group similar or related items and list them in a logical sequence.
4. Draft items using standard terms. Keep questions clear and direct. Avoid questions that can be answered *yes* or *no*.
5. Select an attractive format for the instrument; make it easy to use.
6. Draft directions to the respondents and a cover letter that includes the purpose of the survey, the approximate amount of time required to complete it, when and how the form should be returned, and how the results will be used.
7. Do a dry run with three to five people representative of the target group.
8. Administer the questionnaire.
9. Tabulate and analyze the results.
10. Revise the instrument as needed.

Snowflakes and Taskers

A snowflake or a tasker is a means of getting facts or opinions *in writing* on a specific subject from subordinate managers and staff specialists. (These papers are called snowflakes because they are often written on white 5″ by 7″ sheets and are widely distributed.) Taskers are deliberately designed to be short, usually one page or less. Identical taskers can be sent to several subordinate managers and staff personnel simultaneously to get a spectrum of responses to the same questions.

Taskers are often a much more productive means of getting thoughtful responses than face-to-face questions because employees have time to do some informal research or investigation, think through their answers, and commit themselves to writing. At the same time, taskers encourage rapid replies by establishing short but reasonable deadlines for responses.

Figure 5-4 illustrates the format for a snowflake or tasker, and Figure 5-5 displays the format for the reply to a tasker.

HR Self-Audits

Unquestionably, the most useful inquiry strategy is the HR self-audit or self-study. It is used to appraise the quality of the entire HR organization or any one of its elements, functions, services, or programs, and to institute changes to improve them.

The comprehensive self-audit is the most frequently used form of self-study. It appraises every major aspect of HR management, organi-

Figure 5-4. Example of a snowflake or tasker.

TO: All department managers.

FROM: Tom Murdock, VP Human Resources

SUBJECT: AIDS policy and program

1. PURPOSE: Three key employees have quit in the last week. They were preg-
              nant and resigned when they learned that a coworker who has
              AIDS was encouraged to return to work. Obviously, the women
              were not well-informed about AIDS. We need to do something to
              forestall additional resignations.

2. TASKING: Give me your ideas or recommendations for an AIDS policy and
              program. Should we develop and implement a mandatory training
              program for all employees? What else can we do? Please get your
              input to me before close of business on January 14th.

              _____   *Tom Murdock*
              January 11, 1988
                         Date   Signature

---

zation, programs, services, facilities, resources, and outcomes in relation
to the organization's goals. It examines and analyzes purposes and
objectives, policies, procedures, and budget, management, staffing, system, programs, services, and facilities (buildings, space, furnishing,
equipment, and materials).

Self-study involves both the total HR department staff and representatives of the constituencies served—from top management through
supervisory personnel and nonexempt employees to suppliers, customers, clients, and trainees. It employs a specific set of standards to measure
the results obtained from observation, interview, and review of documents.[1] It identifies strengths, weaknesses, and problems in organizational structure, services, and programs. The findings of self-study
projects are used to identify needed changes and to design detailed plans
for improvement.

1. See William R. Tracey, *Human Resource Development Standards: A Self-Evaluation Manual for HRD Managers and Specialists* (New York: AMACOM, 1981).

Figure 5-5.   Example of a reply to a snowflake or tasker (information sheet).

TO: Tom Murdock

FROM: Jane O'Neill

SUBJECT: AIDS Policy

REFERENCE: Your Snowflake of January 11th, subject as above.

PURPOSE: To give you my input on an AIDS policy and program.

DISCUSSION: We need a clear policy with respect to AIDS—and a well-planned and highly visible program, fully supported by the CEO. Information and education are essential to the success of the program. However, I do not favor mandatory training because employees would resent it.

               Here are my recommendations:

               • Develop and distribute a formal written policy on AIDS with a cover letter from the CEO urging employees to read it carefully.
               • Make educational materials on AIDS available to all employees; for example:

                   – The report of the Surgeon General of the US
                   – Newsletter articles

               • Establish and advertise an employee AIDS HOT LINE.

               • Schedule weekly informal and voluntary noon-time group sessions.

               • Schedule short TV presentations by cable into offices, work areas, and employee break areas.

January 12, 1988   *Jane O'Neill*
_____   _____
      Date   Signature

Using the Data

Once the information is collected, how should it be prepared for analysis and synthesis? What analytical methods are appropriate? These are important questions. Obviously, the HR manager must use analysis and synthesis to probe and interpret the information, always maintaining focus on the "must know." Some information is "nice to know," but it is not essential or crucial to HR management or operations; "must know" information *is* decisive. Time and effort are wasted analyzing "nice to know" info.

Analysis actually begins, or should begin, as you collect the data. You should be asking yourself, "What do the data show?" "What do they mean?" "What problems or issues are involved?"

Tabulating and Summarizing Data

The information you collected must now be tabulated, summarized, analyzed, and interpreted before it can be useful. How difficult that will be depends on the type of information you are working with. Where the data are quantitative, the problems are relatively straightforward, although you will need more than a nodding acquaintance with statistical measures to do what needs to be done (if you don't have the expertise, consult a statistician). Tabulating nonquantitative descriptive data poses more difficult problems. You will find it easier to get a handle on these "subjective" data if you recognize that the basic problem is to select appropriate summary categories.

The steps in tabulating and summarizing data are:

1. Review your notes.
2. Establish the categories of information to be used in summarizing. (Your filing system should help here.)
3. Determine the treatment to be applied to each category; that is, mathematical (rank order, mean, range, and the like) or other (listings, key words, and so on).
4. Make the appropriate entries in each summarizing category.

Analyzing and Interpreting Data

Once you have worked the data into manageable form, you are ready to tackle the most demanding and crucial step in the entire process: analyzing and interpreting it. This is the stage that depends most heavily on the competence of the manager. You must be able to examine the information you have gathered and answer two basic questions: What does the information reveal? What do these revelations mean? You must be able to identify significant strengths and weaknesses in the organization, in its plans for the future, and within the HR department. You must be able to draw conclusions upon which to base decisions or recommendations.

Logical steps in analyzing and interpreting data are:

1. Review the summaries for each category of information in turn.
2. Draft statements of your conclusions for all areas of strength.
3. Identify shortfalls or weaknesses and their underlying causes. Begin by isolating the part of the process or situation that is the probable source of the problem, then determine when and where the problem started and how long it has existed.
4. Draw conclusions and state them in simple and concise language.

The ultimate purpose of everything you have done is to improve HR programs, services, and activities to make them more efficient and to be sure that they provide real, recognizable benefits to the organization. The value of the whole process depends on what happens next. And that is the subject of the chapters on problem solving and decision making (Chapters 6 and 7).

Summary

The fundamental challenge to the HR manager is to deliver what the organization needs—to produce results. To meet the challenge, HR managers must be action-oriented; they must (1) focus on bottom-line outcomes; (2) demonstrate leadership skills and behavior; (3) build an open environment; (4) evaluate systems, programs, and services to identify accomplishments and shortfalls; (5) find and exploit opportunities to improve HR operations; (6) assist line managers to improve their use of human resources; and (7) communicate accomplishments up, down, and laterally within the organization.

The HR manager must study the organization to identify what it is and does, how it does what it does, where it wants to be in the future, how it plans to get there, who the players are, and where the power centers are.

To do that the HR manager must collect and file information in three categories: (1) the current organization as a whole; (2) the future organization, and (3) the HR organization. Primary sources of information include organization documents, staff briefings, personal observation, interviews, meetings and conferences, inspections and reinspections, questionnaires and surveys, snowflakes or taskers, and HR self-audits.

When information has been collected, it must be prepared for analysis and synthesis. That process includes (1) tabulating the data; (2) summarizing information; (3) analyzing data; and (4) interpreting findings.

The final step in the process is to use the information. That is, the ultimate purpose of inquiring is to collect information that can be used to improve HR programs, services, and activities, make them more efficient and cost-effective, and cause them to yield real benefits to the organization.

FOR FURTHER READING

Belson, William A. *The Design and Understanding of Survey Questions.* Lexington, Mass.: D. C. Heath, Lexington Books, 1981.

Black, James M. *How to Get Results from Interviewing: A Practical Guide for Operating Management.* Melbourne, Fla.: Kreiger, 1982.

Bradley, John. "How to Interview for Information." *Training/HRD,* April 1983, pp. 59–62.

"Correcting Common Discussion Leader Mistakes." *Training and Development Journal,* December 1982, p. 14.

Davidson, William L. *How to Develop and Conduct Successful Attitude Surveys.* Chicago: Dartnell, 1979.

Diebold, John. *Managing Information: The Challenge and the Opportunity.* New York: AMACOM, 1985.

Edwards, Allen L. *Techniques of Attitude Scale Construction.* New York: Irvington Publications, 1982.

Genua, Robert L. *The Employer's Guide to Interviewing: Strategy and Tactics for Picking a Winner.* Englewood Cliffs, N.J.: Prentice-Hall, 1979.

Goodale, James G. *The Fine Art of Interviewing.* Englewood Cliffs, N.J.: Prentice-Hall, 1982.

Gorden, Raymond C. *Interviewing Strategy and Tactics,* 3rd ed. Homewood, Ill.: Dorsey Press, 1980.

Gordon, Myron. *How to Plan and Conduct a Successful Meeting.* New York: Sterling, 1985.

Hon, David. *Meetings That Matter.* New York: John Wiley & Sons, 1980.

Housden, Theresa, and Jack Housden. *How to Design and Use Questionnaires.* Beaverton, Oreg.: Dilithium Press, 1983.

Joint Commission on Standards for Educational Evaluation. *Standards for Evaluations of Educational Programs, Projects, and Materials.* New York: McGraw-Hill, 1981.

Lees-Haley, Paul R. *The Questionnaire Design Handbook.* Huntsville, Ala.: Lees-Haley Associates, 1980.

Lippitt, Gordon L. "Criteria for Evaluating Human Resource Development." *Training and Development Journal,* October 1976, pp. 3–10.

Maher, John H., Jr. and D. Edward Kur. "Constructing Good Question-naires." *Training and Development Journal,* June 1983, pp. 100–110.

Meltzer, Morton F. *Information, the Ultimate Management Resource: How to Find, Use, and Manage It.* New York: AMACOM, 1981.

Nathan, Ernest D. *Questions in Group Leadership,* 2nd ed. Reading, Mass.: Addison-Wesley Training Systems, 1979.

Olivas, Louis. "Auditing Your Training and Development Function." *Training and Development Journal,* March 1980, pp. 60–64.

OSHA. *Training Requirements of OSHA Standards.* Washington: U.S. Department of Labor, Occupational Safety and Health Administration, February 1975.

Peterson, Dan. *The OSHA Compliance Manual,* rev. ed. New York: McGraw-Hill, 1979.

Phillips, Jack J. *Handbook of Training Evaluation and Measurement Methods.* Houston, Tex.: Gulf Publishing, 1983.

Richardson, Stephen A., Barbara Snell Dohrenwend, and David Klein. *Interviewing: Its Forms and Functions.* New York: Basic Books, 1965.

Slavens, Thomas P. *Informational Interviews and Questions.* Metuchen, N.J.: Scarecrow Press, 1978.

Sudman, Seymour, and Norman Bradburn. *Asking Questions: A Practical Guide to Questionnaire Design.* San Francisco: Jossey-Bass, 1982.

Tracey, William R. *Human Resource Development Standards: A Self-Evaluation Manual for HRD Managers and Specialists.* New York: AMACOM, 1981, chapters 6, 19, and 21.

———. *Managing Training and Development Systems.* New York: AMACOM, 1974.

Viladas, Joseph M. *The Book of Survey Techniques.* Greenwich, Conn.: Havemeyer Books, 1982.

6

PROBLEM SOLVING
Managerial Diagnosis and Treatment

Problem solving is a skill that all HR managers must use daily. Regardless of how skillful managers are at sensing and preventing problems, they will never be able to avoid them totally. They must be able to solve the problems that arise with confidence, competence, and consistent success.

Managers often solve problems inefficiently. The costs of inept problem solving, in terms of time, material, money, energy, and human grief, can be enormous. Any manager can recall a great number of botched problems and faulty decisions. Typically, they are the direct result of unsystematic and unsound thinking. HR managers need to know how to reason clearly about problems and their solutions. Although HR managers may apply automated systems to their problems, these mechanisms cannot make their decisions for them. They also need good judgment—an amalgam of past experience, sound values and standards, and learned and innate abilities. Unquestionably, the ability to reason is a basic requirement for anyone who hopes to manage well.

Problems are inevitable in organizational life, and they must be dealt with. Equipment breaks down, people make mistakes, plans go awry, controls fail to work. Dealing with conflict lies at the heart of managing any organization. An important part is being able to face issues squarely when there is disagreement over causes or solutions. Most issues cannot be put off, pigeon-holed, or ignored. Procrastination never solved anything. Worse, it typically results in decision by default.

HR managers must develop a systematic method of attacking problems, for these reasons: (1) to solve their problems with an acceptable level of success; (2) to determine whether their subordinates are solving their problems systematically; (3) to determine whether subordinates' recommendations are based on analysis rather than intuition; and (4) to be able to train subordinates to solve problems efficiently.

To be able to solve problems with short fuses or severe time pressure, a manager needs a systematic, logical, and efficient method. Anything less is certain to result in running up one-way streets, jump-starting stalled projects and programs, missing important data, repeating the same questions, and arriving at the wrong conclusions.

To be effective and efficient problem solvers, HR managers must:

- Know what the problem is (what's wrong and needs fixing) and how it came into being.
- Have an orderly means of determining whether the problem is critical.
- Have a systematic way of pinpointing the cause.
- Have a means of determining what information is needed to solve the problem.
- Be able to ask probing, rational questions that will elicit relevant information.
- Be able to identify alternative solutions.
- Be able to choose the best way to correct the problem.
- Be mindful of their problem-solving inadequacies.
- Be aware of what they are doing during problem solving so they can evaluate and improve their performance.

Definitions

In Chapter 4 we defined the term *problem* as an unplanned and unwanted change or result. In the context of problem *solving*, as differentiated from problem *sensing*, a problem is a situation that requires resolution and for which there appears to be no obvious answer.

Here's an expanded definition:

> Although they express the terms differently, most psychologists agree that a problem has certain characteristics:
>
> *Givens*—The problem begins in a certain state with certain conditions, objects, pieces of information, and so forth being present at the onset of work on the problem.
>
> *Goals*—The desired or terminal state of the problem is the goal state, and thinking is required to transform the problem from the given to the goal state.
>
> *Obstacles*—The thinker has at his or her disposal certain ways to change the given state or the goal state of the problem. The thinker, however, does not already know the correct answer; that is, the correct sequence of behaviors that will solve the problem is not immediately obvious.[1]

1. Excerpted from *Thinking, Problem Solving, Cognition* by Richard E. Mayer. Copyright © 1983 W. H. Freeman. Reprinted with permission.

Although some writers believe that problem solving is not entirely a rational process, in the context of HR management, its main characteristic is its reasoning, thinking quality. That is not to deny the role of feelings and values in problem solving; they are certainly involved in the process. However, when emotions and personal values come into play in problem solving, the process becomes less impartial and objective. Essentially, then, problem solving is a process that follows a deliberate and logical sequence. It is the means by which previously acquired knowledge, skills, and experience are used to take action in an unfamiliar situation.

Problem solving has been defined this way: "The term problem solving, as used in the psychological literature, usually refers to behavior and thought processes directed toward the performance of some intellectually demanding task."[2]

Another writer considers problem solving the equivalent of thinking and cognition.

> There are many definitions of *thinking, problem solving,* and *cognition* but [I] . . . use these terms interchangeably based on a single, general definition common to them all. . . . A general definition of thinking includes three basic ideas:
>   1. Thinking is *cognitive,* but is inferred from behavior. It occurs internally, in the mind or cognitive system, and must be inferred indirectly.
>   2. Thinking is a *process* that involves some manipulation of or set of operations on knowledge in the cognitive system, and must be inferred indirectly.
>   3. Thinking is *directed* and results in behavior that "solves" a problem or is directed toward a solution.[3]

Component Abilities

The problem-solving skill is a composite of several basic abilities: to classify patterns, to use past experiences to deal with the environment (to learn), to reason deductively, to reason inductively, to develop and use conceptual models, and to understand.

Deductive reasoning is the process of abstracting a general principle from a collection of experiences and then applying that principle to other identical or similar situations. It is the process of drawing conclusions from premises, from the implicit information at hand.

Inductive reasoning is the process of combining rules or principles to produce new conclusions, rules, or principles. It is the process of

2. Raymond S. Nickerson, David N. Perkins, and Edward E. Smith, *The Teaching of Thinking* (Hillsdale, N.J.: Lawrence Erlbaum Associates, 1985), 65.
3. Mayer, *Thinking, Problem Solving, Cognition,* 6–7.

generalizing, going beyond the information at hand to discover new rules and principles, arguing from particular instances to the general.

Blocks to Problem Solving

Beyond the obvious problem of lack of intelligence, there are several other barriers to effective and efficient problem solving, particularly the ability to develop novel or creative solutions. To be a skillful problem solver and to develop the skill in subordinates, the competent HR manager must be fully aware of these blocks.

Lack of knowledge and skill. Unquestionably, the biggest obstacle to problem-solving competence is lack of knowhow. Problem solving, remember, is a logical and sequential process. It is not a "seat of the pants," intuitive, or trial and error procedure. Nor is problem solving an innate skill. It must be learned, practiced, refined, and practiced again and again.

Rigidity. People develop habits, many of them dysfunctional. Among the most severe from the standpoint of problem solving is rigidity. Rigidity is a type of mental block, sometimes referred to as functional fixedness or, as clinical and experimental psychologists term it, *Einstellung* (attitude), problem solving mindset, or negative transfer. It may be characterized by fault-finding negativism.

Another form of rigidity is selective observation—the all too common fault of seeing only what we want to see, hearing only what we want to hear, and ignoring everything else. Rigidity is not an inborn trait; it is learned. Which means it can be unlearned. And it must be, if we are to be open to new solutions when faced with a new problem.

Suppressive education. In the past, and to an alarming degree in the present, public and private education tended to suppress or repress the natural desire to be creative in finding the solution of problems. We require children to solve mathematical problems by one "right" method (the method taught by the teacher or contained in the textbook), arrive at the "school solution" to other types of problems, and copy the artistic or musical creations of others. In so doing, we teach children to be conventional. In later life, such tendencies must be unlearned.

Lack of self-confidence. Some managers defeat themselves by undermining their own self-confidence. Where does this self-destructive attitude come from? Past failures, pessimism, apprehension about mistakes or being different, fear of ridicule by superiors, peers, and others, excessive modesty, and timidity. The tendency to be overly self-critical, to fear failure, to dodge derision, to shrink from display must be overcome.

The wise manager is also aware of the dangers of perfectionism. He or she knows that it is impossible to bat 1.000 all the time. A positive attitude and willingness to take risks are requisites for efficient and effective problem solving.

Negativism of others. Whether it comes from lack of confidence, narrowness, prejudice, envy, or some other type of negative attitude, discouragement by others can be a major block to problem-solving efforts. The most damaging discouragement comes from those we respect and those for whom or to whom we are responsible. For that reason, it is especially important for managers and supervisors to be supportive of the problem-solving efforts of their subordinates. Ideas are generated best in an organization where encouragement is the rule and where a pat on the back is the most common response to suggestions and innovation.

Poor concentration. Still another block is poor concentration. People can throttle their problem-solving talents by inattentiveness—from laziness, disinterest, distractions, wool-gathering, or lack of effort, motivation, or curiosity. Their creative powers and concentration can also be stifled by poor mental, physical, or emotional health and by worry, tension, anxiety, or emotional conflict.

HR managers and specialists must maintain their focus and concentrate fully on the problems they face. They must use their powers of concentration to think up ways to solve problems, create new programs, improve services, and develop new markets and new uses.

Types of Problems

HR managers must deal with a great variety of problems. Some of them affect individuals, others affect the entire organization, others affect organization-individual relationships, and still others relate to HR's role and functions.

Organizational problems. Some of the most crucial problems, from the standpoint of the viability and durability of the organization itself, come under the heading of organizational problems. Examples are low productivity, inadequate return on investment, executive succession, cost reduction, labor relations, public relations, compensation and incentives, job evaluation, and the quality of work life. Such problems get at the very heart of the organization and its reason for being.

Individual problems. A second category of problems, just as crucial to organizational wellness, is those that affect individual employees. Among the most common are problems relating to career development, orientation, training, job satisfaction, interpersonal relationships, job assignment, job performance, performance appraisals, absenteeism and tardiness, promotion and termination, and substance abuse.

Organization-individual relationships. The third category of problems, which also looms large in importance, includes problems in compensation and benefits, incentive systems, food services, recreation services, health services, promotion policies, training and development policies, composition of work teams, and career counseling policies.

HR role and functions. The problems in this category relate to the importance and viability of the HR function in modern business. Common ones are determining the proper role and function of HR in identifying organizational values, strategic planning, linking business forecasts to planning and action, budgeting, setting goals and objectives, profitability, return on investment, cost reduction, job evaluation, research, personnel services, cost benefits, the design and delivery of career development programs, and predicting the potential of people. Others relate to how HR can contribute to the solution of problems pertaining to mergers and acquisitions, budget deficits, tax credits, employee assistance, skills shortages, retraining, balance of payments, productivity, dislocated workers, and outside education.

Types of Problem Solving

There is more than one brand of problem solving. In fact there are two basic formats—individual and group—with the latter further subdivided into two subcategories: conventional and creative problem solving.

Individual Problem Solving

Despite the growing use of team problem solving, the innovative abilities and talents of the individual still predominate. And that dominance is likely to continue. The solitary, "lone wolf" thinker is not obsolete. Apparently, some people do their best thinking, their most creative work, all by themselves.

In fact, the individual approach to problem solving—an owner, the chief executive officer, a manager, or a supervisor makes all the decisions—is probably the most common. Why is that? One reason relates to size. In a sole proprietorship, or a small company without subordinate managers or staff, the person in charge is forced to make all the important decisions. Another reason relates to time. Sometimes, the problem is so critical it requires immediate corrective action. Also, group problem solving takes time—time that is not available in emergency situations. Under such circumstances, individual problem solving is certainly warranted.

The third reason has nothing to do with the size or complexity of the organization or the lack of time; it's a question of ego. Even today, many managers in all types of companies protect, preserve, and defend their power and authority by reserving the right to make all decisions unilaterally. Despite the fact that employees have proved time and time again that their unique talents, backgrounds, and responsibilities enable them to see problems from different perspectives, and therefore they can make substantive contributions to the solution of complex problems, frequently they are not allowed to do so.

Group Problem Solving

Despite the pervasiveness of the individual problem-solving approach, more and more managers and supervisors are enlisting the help of their subordinates or other groups of people to help them find solutions to problems. Many of the best ideas are now the products of research conducted by organized teams.

Reasons for Use

Most managers today recognize that not only do employees at all levels bring unique and valuable information and competencies to the problem at hand—they also want very much to help. Managers and supervisors now also realize that employees who have had a part in reaching solutions feel responsibility for making those solutions a success. They "buy into" solutions and try hard to make them work.

It has also been found that many people work better creatively when acting as a member of a team. Teamwork tends to inspire greater effort, promote friendly competition, stimulate the imagination, and facilitate the phenomenon of association—the chain reaction or contagion of ideas.

So, although group problem solving may take more time than individual approaches and may take people away from their regular jobs for prolonged periods of time, when the success of a solution depends on wholehearted acceptance by those who must implement it (as it very often does), the group approach is eminently preferable.

Many who have written on the subject of problem solving maintain that the only realistic and effective way to deal with problems in modern organizations is to attack them in group situations. Rensis Likert, the well-known social research specialist, for example, flatly maintains that participative management is the best kind of management, and for that reason group discussion is the only valid way to reach good decisions.[4] Norman Mayer states that almost all management problems are solved through the use of meetings and conferences.[5] He sees the problem-

4. Rensis Likert, *New Patterns of Management* (New York: McGraw-Hill, 1963).
5. Norman F. Mayer, *Problem-Solving Discussions and Conferences* (New York: McGraw-Hill, 1963).

solving meeting or conferences as the key to successful resolution of issues. Although I agree that many problems can be best solved in a group setting, I believe that there are many occasions when the HR manager must solve the problem more or less alone, although with the help of staffers in collecting and analyzing data.

Special Requirements

Group problem solving has some special requirements that, if not considered, will result in inadequate solutions.

Preparation and planning. The purpose of the problem-solving session must be clearly established. Objectives must be articulated. Be specific about what you hope to accomplish, and be realistic. Choose the participants carefully. Select those who have information bearing on the problem or have something to contribute to its solution. Select people for what they know, not for what department or special interest they represent. Limit the number of participants to between five and nine—and always have an odd number.

Set the date, time, and place of the meeting. Considerations here include the purpose, number of participants, length of the meeting, special equipment needed (projector, screen, easel, and so on), freedom from interruptions, easy access, and the like. Avoid Mondays, Fridays, and weekends. The best times are from 9:00 to 11:30 A.M.; 1:30 to 3:30 P.M.; and 6:30 to 8:00 P.M. for evening meetings. Make the time convenient; ask the participants for their preferences. Select a room that is large enough, pleasant and inviting, and comfortable. Arrange chairs and tables in a circle, semicircle, or hollow square.

Notify participants either personally, or by individual written notice, of the purpose and objectives, names and titles of participants, a brief description of their responsibilities, and the agenda. The agenda should detail the purpose and objectives, the sequence of events, and the time each item will have for both presentation and discussion.

Just before the meeting, do a final polish on your preparations. Check the meeting room, equipment, and seating. Set up notepads, pencils, name placards, and the like. Arrange for recording of minutes.

Conducting the meeting. In general, the usual procedures guide the conduct of problem-solving meetings. Every participant must understand the problem—the real problem. Every participant must have an opportunity to contribute. Begin by defining the problem. Assess the context of the problem. Move on to analyzing the problem. Determine the causes of the problem. Decide what would be a satisfactory solution; establish criteria or guidelines.

Use brainstorming techniques to generate possible solutions in volume. Select the most promising. Estimate the likelihood of success of each solution—its advantages and disadvantages. Along with rational thinking, and applying knowledge and experience, also consider feelings, values, beliefs, preferences, and other nonrational aspects. Select the best solution, using the criteria established earlier. Create an implementation plan.

Creative Problem Solving

An eminent psychologist defines creativity as "a cognitive activity that results in novel solutions to a problem." Creative solutions and products must be both significant and original. They "add insight, invention, and perspective to competence. Sound judgment, effective problem solving, and acute perception all figure in the making of creative products, but also in products the making of which requires great skill, but not invention."[6]

Nickerson describes two kinds of thinking: vertical and lateral. "Vertical thinking is . . . logical thinking. It is sequential, predictable, conventional. In contrast, lateral thinking is not necessarily sequential, it is unpredictable, and it is not constrained by convention."[7] And Edward deBono writes, "Lateral thinking generates the ideas and vertical thinking develops them. . . . Vertical thinking is digging the same hole deeper; lateral thinking is trying again elsewhere."[8]

Alex Osborn, the father of brainstorming, provides these four basic rules:

1. *Criticism is ruled out.* Adverse judgment of ideas must be withheld until later.
2. *Free-wheeling is welcomed.* The wilder the idea, the better; it is easier to tame down than to think up.
3. *Quantity is wanted.* The greater the number of ideas, the more the likelihood of winners.
4. *Combination and improvement are sought.* In addition to contributing ideas of their own, participants should suggest how ideas of others can be turned into *better* ideas; or how two or more ideas can be joined into still another idea.[9]

Other suggestions:

○ Don't let the team break down into smaller groups.
○ Keep a written record of all ideas suggested and give a copy to each participant.

6. Richard E. Mayer, *Thinking, Problem Solving, Cognition*, p. 327.
7. Nickerson and others, *The Teaching of Thinking*, 214.
8. Edward deBono, *New Think: The Use of Lateral Thinking in the Generation of New Ideas* (New York: Basic Books, 1986), 6, 26.
9. Alex F. Osborn, *Applied Imagination: Principles and Procedures of Creative Thinking*, rev. ed. (New York: Scribner's, 1958), 84.

○ Give frequent encouragement.
○ Use creative problem solving with specific problems only; if the problem is general, narrow it down.
○ Clearly state the problem and the objectives at the start of the session.
○ Organize groups of five to ten people, no more and no less.

Creative problem solving usually includes some or all of these phases:

1. *Orientation:* Pointing up the problem.
2. *Preparation:* Gathering pertinent data.
3. *Analysis:* Breaking down the relevant material.
4. *Ideation:* Piling up alternatives by way of ideas.
5. *Incubation:* Letting up, to invite illumination.
6. *Synthesis:* Putting the pieces together.
7. *Evaluation:* Judging the resultant ideas.[10]

Artificial Intelligence

A discussion of problem solving would be incomplete without at least brief and passing reference to a topic of growing interest—artificial intelligence (AI). During the past 15 years, artificial intelligence research has been supported by a number of organizations, including several academic institutions and the Department of Defense. Expert systems (computer programs based on syllogisms that can "reason" and manipulate data in a way similar to that of humans), robotics, machine vision, learning systems, and natural language understanding are being applied to management, defense, medicine, geology, mathematics, chemistry, and education and training.[11]

Achievements to date include such diverse advances as computer-aided diagnostics, computer-assisted and computer-managed instruction (CAI/CMI), automated planning and scheduling, dynamic situational assessment, and computer-aided design and manufacturing (CAD/CAM). All but the last two examples have HR applications. According to a recent survey of 42 trainers and related specialists, 14 percent of American Society for Training and Development (ASTD) members use expert systems in training.[12]

Very few technologies over the past two decades have so excited the imagination and generated such heated arguments as artificial intelligence. At the heart of the controversy is the fundamental issue of

10. Ibid., 115.
11. For further information on AI-enhanced management decision support systems, contact Roger C. Thibault, *AI Today,* 104 Frame Road, Elkview, West Virginia, 25071.
12. ASTD *National Report on Human Resources,* "Fieldgrass," September/October 1986, p. 5.

whether machines can duplicate the various forms of human activity that do not have computational aspects. Humans routinely perform tasks like reasoning and decision making, often without access to complete data or information of unproved validity, analyzing a problem and reaching a conclusion, learning to perform a specific task by repetition, introspection, and reflection, interpreting written and spoken materials to extract information relevant to an issue, and sorting quickly and efficiently through a massive amount of data using shortcuts based on understanding the type of information needed to solve a particular problem. Today, artificial intelligence researchers are trying to design and build automated systems that duplicate those activities.

In any event, artificial intelligence intrigues forward-looking HR managers. We do not yet have, nor are we likely to see, computers providing career counseling services, conducting performance appraisals, or interviewing candidates for positions. But we do have machines that can handle tasks that are too dangerous, such as gathering data in a damaged nuclear reactor, or too time-consuming. Automated systems do have the potential to increase HR managers' ability to respond to problems and situations more quickly, more surely, and more efficiently by making full use of the machine's ability to perform lower-level data tasks. That will free managers to concentrate on critical, higher-level problem solving and decision making.

Problem-Solving Strategies

Your objective as an HR manager is to provide logical, effective, mission-oriented solutions to problems. To do that, you must think logically and critically. You must be a devil's advocate to your own work. You must think in a mission-oriented manner, rather than from a personal perspective. You must determine in advance the total impact of the solutions and recommendations you develop—on personnel, facilities, equipment, and funds. Will work load increase, and if so for whom? Will additional or different equipment or procedures be needed? If so, how much and what kind? Can your organization afford them or will reprogramming of funds or additional funding be necessary? How do your recommendations fit in with the overall goals and objectives of the organization?

Planning

You must develop plans to solve the problems both you and your organization face. The most effective plans to solve problems have these characteristics:

- They establish priorities for each objective or solution.
- They address productivity, profitability, and growth matters separately.
- They are tough-minded—they often surprise, stun, or jolt people.
- They can be put into effect quickly.
- They often impose a new way of functioning on the organization.
- They delegate authority to people who have the boldness and nerve to take the needed action.
- They focus on measurable results.
- They establish a definite time frame for execution.

Ten Steps in Problem Solving

Problem solving is a deliberate, logical, sequential series of steps that, if followed resolutely, will result in suitable and workable solutions to problems. In addition to following the step-by-step procedure, there are two other requisites for efficient problem solving. First, there must be an organizational climate that allows full and free access to and use of information. Second, there must be recognition of the fact that all employees can contribute to the solution of problems.

Step 1: Identifying the Problem

Identifying the problem takes four substeps:

1. Problem sensing. Chapter 4 addressed in some detail the skill of problem sensing. Here we just need to note that identifying potential problems *early* will provide higher payback for the time, effort, and resources invested than any other management action. Even if a problem is not sensed before it occurs, the earlier it is identified the less damage will result. For that reason, the astute HR manager uses problem-sensing techniques as a regular part of his or her operation.

2. Inquiring. The techniques associated with the inquiring skill were described in Chapter 5; they will not be repeated here. The important thing to remember is that such techniques as visits and inspections, questionnaires and interviews, and meetings and conferences can be used to great advantage in gathering the information you need to identify, assess, and solve problems.

3. Identifying problems and establishing priorities. At this point in problem solving, the task is to identify all the things that are wrong. A conscientious survey of any aspect of operations or any department is certain to reveal several current or potential problems. For each problem identified, write a preliminary description. Include a list of its symptoms or evidence of the problem. Restate the problem in the light of the symptoms. Phrase it in terms of what you want to accomplish and what is the least you will accept. Once problems have been identified, the next step is to determine which ones are most critical, will cause the most grief unless they are remedied, and put the entire list in priority order for attack.

4. Identifying the real problem.   Before you can solve a problem, you have to define it. You must be able to determine precisely what the problem *is* and what it is *not*. You must define the problem's dimensions and boundaries—the who, what, when, where, why—and its impact.

- ◦ "Who" is just what it says—who (persons, organizations, groups, work units, and so on) is involved, and who is not.
- ◦ "What" deals with the policies, procedures, practices, issues, facilities, equipment, materials, processes, or other things that make up the problem—and, again, what is *not* involved.
- ◦ "When" relates to the time frame. Does it occur only on a certain shift? At a certain time of day? On a certain day of the week? Only after a holiday? When doesn't it occur?
- ◦ "Where" defines the location of the problem. Does it happen only at one plant? In one department or office? In one shop? Where doesn't it occur?
- ◦ "Why" refers to the circumstances surrounding the problem. Is there a sequence of actions that frequently or always precedes, accompanies, or follows the occurrence?
- ◦ "Impact" refers to how much of an effect the problem has on the organization, plant, department, or office and its people, facilities, equipment, materials, products, production, or profitability. How big, how many, how much, what percentage, and so on?

The Problem Analysis (Specification) Worksheet shown in Figure 6-1 can be used to specify the problem.

The old axiom "A clearly defined problem is half solved" is true. It is also true that a problem cannot be solved efficiently unless it is explicitly and accurately described. That should be patently obvious. No matter how important a problem may be, no matter how many people are affected, and regardless of how much money may be lost if it goes uncorrected, a problem cannot be solved unless its dimensions are stated specifically and succinctly. You must describe its limits, put a fence around it.

Summary.   To identify the real problem:

1. Study and analyze the facts and opinions collected.
2. Examine carefully all criticisms, suggestions, and complaints.

Figure 6-1. An example of a specification worksheet.

Problem Analysis (Specification) Worksheet

Deviation:

	IS	IS NOT	What is distinctive of the IS?	Any change in this?
WHAT: Deviation Object				
WHERE: On object Observed				
WHEN: On object Observed				
EXTENT: How much How many				
Possible causes for test:				

Source: Charles H. Kepner and Benjamin B. Tregoe, *The Rational Manager: A Systematic Approach to Problem Solving and Decision Making* (NY: McGraw-Hill, 1965), 75. Used with permission.

3. Judge the validity of each comment or item of information by checking it against other data collection means.
4. Summarize the situation or deficiency in simple terms so that anyone can grasp it.
5. State key facts that are missing and cannot be gathered so that allowances can be made for the gap in identifying courses of action.
6. Examine every aspect of the situation to expose organization, assignment, utilization, supervisory, or training weaknesses and means of improvement.
7. Summarize indicators of the problem in writing.

Step 2: Stating the Real Problem

The correct statement of the real problem is both the most important and the most difficult job in the problem-solving process. In the great majority of cases, once the problem is correctly defined, the solution is relatively easy to find.

One technique is to define the problem in different ways. Personalize the problem by asking, "In what ways might I . . .?" Or broaden the problem. Instead of "How can I improve Jane Smith's instructional skills?" ask, "How can Jane Smith's platform performance be improved?" Or instead of "How can I get Jones to be more productive?" ask, "How can I help Jones?" or "How could Jones help me?"

Another technique is to ask yourself, "What is the root problem? What am I trying to do?" When you have answered these questions, reformulate the real problem to give it the broadest statement. Then simplify the statement or break it into smaller parts. Finally, reword the problem statement.

When it comes to defining the real problem, the main pitfall to watch out for is this: Most of us are inclined to take the first possible solution that pops into our minds, and make the mistake of thinking that we have isolated the real problem. The result is that we sometimes overlook the real problem that requires corrective action and do not give ourselves a chance to consider all possibilities.

For example, an HR manager once posed the following problem to his staff: "Do you think that all training programs should be revised every year?" It should be obvious that annual review and revision is only one possible solution to the broad problem of how to make sure training programs are up to date and valid. Other possible solutions include evaluation of the products of the programs, feedback from first-line supervisors, analysis of test results, and analysis of work products of graduates of the programs, to name but a few. Any manager who takes the time to look at the total situation has a far better chance of defining the real problem and considering all possible solutions.

The real problem should always be stated as a task—"To determine the best course of action regarding executive succession"—or asked as a question—"How can we make organizational data more readily available to all HR supervisors?"

Step 3: Establishing the Criteria of Solution

Once the real problem has been defined, the next step is to set forth the specifications for the acceptable solution in terms of results desired, risks, degree of acceptability, and limitations of resources (people, funds, time, material, and so on) to be expended. The task is to describe the specific and concrete conditions that should exist when the problem is solved. One way to do it is to use questions about how the solution is to be implemented: "Who is involved? What is going to be done? Where is it to be applied? When will it happen? Why is this what I want?"

Another way to do it is to list specifications under two headings:

imperatives or "musts," and preferences or "wants." The "musts" set limits that cannot be exceeded by any of the alternatives. The "wants" do not set go/no-go limitations but they do express desirability. Here are some of the most common categories for both "musts" and "wants."

Effectiveness. Describe how well the solution must work to be considered effective. What is the least that you would accept in terms of the effectiveness of a solution? Now, what would you like to see as a mark of the effectiveness of a solution?

Efficiency. What is an efficient solution for this problem? How do you define efficient in this context? What must the solution do to be considered efficient? What would you like to see in an efficient solution?

Avoidance of unanticipated effects. What outcomes or results would you consider to be a totally unacceptable consequence of implementing a solution? What outcomes or results would you like to see avoided by any solution put into effect?

Costs. What are the outside limits of costs, including personnel, facilities, equipment, materials, time, funds, or other resources to be incurred by the solution? What costs would you like to see controlled by the adopted solution?

Summary. In this step, the criteria for judging the adequacy and practicality of the solution or remedy are formulated. These criteria are essentially yardsticks against which alternative courses of action will be measured. Criteria can be identified in terms of:

○ Results to be achieved, such as higher productivity or reduced costs.
○ The time and other resources required or allowable to achieve the results.
○ Any other goals, objectives, or limitations involved in reaching a feasible and workable solution.

Step 4: Analyzing the Problem

Problem analysis involves two substeps: collecting information and determining the cause of the problem.

Collecting information. The first step in problem analysis is to collect all the information you can about the situation. Don't jump to conclusions about the cause. Ask questions that bring forth relevant information. What could be wrong? What and who does it affect? Where does it occur? Under what circumstances? When does it happen? Fully explore what is known and unknown, the facts and the conditions that relate to them, and the gaps in data. Then determine what is relevant and irrelevant, what information to use and how to use it.

In all this, be careful to: make the distinction between truth and validity; not confuse consistency and validity; view your own opinions objectively; be objective about your hypotheses; and evaluate hypotheses rather than people.

Determining the cause.   It should be obvious that a problem cannot be solved until its origin is known. It should be equally evident that a solution based on an erroneous cause will be ineffective, costly, and sometimes out-and-out hazardous.

Although it may appear that a problem could be the result of any number of occurrences or events, the plain fact of the matter is that every problem has only one root cause. Before you attempt to isolate the cause, you must clarify the conditions that led to the problem and are sustaining it. Answers to the following questions must be found:

- How long has the problem existed?
- When and where did it start?
- Is it widespread or limited to one location or area?
- When was the deficiency noted? By whom?
- How do those closest to the problem explain how it happened?
- In what part of the process or situation is the probable cause of the deficiency most likely to be found?
- What is the direct cause of the problem?
- What is the hidden or underlying cause of the problem?

Although there is only one root cause of a problem, the problem solver must list *all* the possible causes by considering such questions as these: What preceded or followed the variance or deviation? What were the contributing factors? Economic? Historical? Environmental? Political? Social? People? Equipment? Materials? In-house? Outside?

The search for the cause of a problem should then quickly focus on the variation or deviation that could produce the exact effects observed during step 2, identifying the real problem. The deviation is found by analyzing the facts uncovered during that step. Analysis of the facts is the essence of problem solving. The key to analysis of this kind is to look for differences, the items that separate or make things dissimilar. The objective is to find the one change responsible for the problem. The clues to that variation lie in the facts that separate what the problem is from what it is not.

However, finding the cause of a problem is a separate task from identifying variations or changes. The deviations disclosed by analysis are only possible causes. Each possible cause must now be examined to determine which is the most likely, reasonable, probable, and believable.

Step 5: Identifying Alternative Solutions

The task here is to identify as many solutions to the problem as possible, using brainstorming techniques either as an individual or in a group. The keys to generating solutions are:

- Give yourself ample time in pleasant and comfortable surroundings, free from interruptions.
- Use the principle of association (where one idea or solution suggests another), visual imaging (seeing the problem and its solution in your "mind's eye"), analysis (breaking the problem into smaller pieces), and synthesis (merging and combining ideas and solutions to produce new ones).
- Ignore your internal critic; exclude criticism of ideas.
- Concentrate on the problem.

In sum, identifying alternative solutions involves two overall steps:

1. Brainstorm the problem; canvass all actions and procedures that could conceivably solve the problem, including "wild" or novel remedies.
2. Withhold judgment about the value of any solution until as many alternatives as possible have been identified.

Step 6: Selecting the Best Solution

This step requires that alternatives be tested, evaluated, adapted, and modified as needed before a decision on the best solution is reached.

Testing and evaluating ideas.   Now the task is to zero in on the best solutions. List the strengths and weaknesses and the advantages and disadvantages of each solution. Compare each solution with the list of "musts" and "wants," the criteria to be used in determining which solutions are acceptable. Select the solutions that best match the criteria—the ones that are most likely to solve the problem—and have the smallest number of potentially negative consequences. Then place the solutions in priority order starting with the best, the one with the greatest probability of successfully solving the problem. List all the reasons for rejecting any of the original list of solutions.

Review the top three solutions in the priority list. Do they make sense? Are there hidden issues that will invalidate any of them? Have you considered the impact of such limitations as budget, space, time, people, equipment, skills, and materials? How will your boss react to the solution?

Your subordinates? Your peers? If negatively, how will you counter their objections?

Adapting and modifying ideas.   This is the last-ditch effort to make solutions more efficient and effective—and more salable. What changes or modifications can be made to a solution to improve it? Such questions as these are germane: How can we modify this solution to make it more appealing? What can we substitute for this element of the solution? Would another procedure or process make the solution stronger? What department or person could do this better?

Making the decision.   If you are the decision maker, the decision was effectively made when you established the priority listing of solutions. Obviously, you will implement the number one solution if you have the resources and the authority to do so. If you don't have the authority, you must then get your boss, or a higher-level executive, to approve the solution and provide the resources to implement it. That is a selling job. If you have done your problem solving in the deliberate, objective, and sequential fashion described in this chapter, you should have no difficulty with the sale.

Step 7: Winning Support for the Solution

A solution must be supported if it is to be implemented. Two things are necessary: You must sell the decision, and you must get the solution approved in principle by the decision maker.

Presenting the solution.   Basically there are two means of presenting the solution to the decision maker. First is the written report which may be in the form of a staff study or a decision paper (see Chapter 3). A staff study presents all the steps in the problem-solving process in summary form. A decision paper presents the salient materials in a more abbreviated form. The written report is used when the solution to a problem requires staffing (review and comment by several other managers or staff personnel) before presentation to the decision maker. It is also used when a permanent record of the solution approach is required. A staff study or decision paper may also be used to support or supplement an oral decision briefing.

The second means of presenting the solution is the decision briefing, where all the steps in the problem-solving process, whether done by one individual or a group, are presented to the decision maker in abbreviated form. (See Chapter 2 for a more detailed description of the decision briefing.) The decision briefing is used when time is limited, when that is the format preferred by the decision maker, or when a staff study or decision paper requires it as a supplement.

To make the sale easier, you should outline the solution in broad terms for presentation to the boss. Include a list of the defects or shortfalls revealed by the problem-solving process, a snapshot of the proposed major changes to the situation or the system, the advantages, limitations, and risks of each aspect of the proposal, the costs of the change in terms of time, money, materials, equipment, personnel, and other resources, and the steps needed to put the solution into effect.

Getting the solution approved in principle. Your goal is not only to solve the problem but also to find a remedy that will be implemented. Before working out the details of the solution in the form of an action plan, it is wise to get acceptance of the proposed solution in principle before going to the work of preparing detailed implementation plans.

Summary. A complete summary of the proposal should be prepared for presentation to the decision maker. The summary should include the following:

- ○ The subject and scope of the study.
- ○ A definition of the problem and its causes.
- ○ The criteria to be met by the solution.
- ○ The proposed solution and its advantages, disadvantages, and risks.

Step 8: Translating the Solution into Action

At this point the task is to translate the decision you or your boss have made into an action plan. This is where you develop the remedy or solution in detail. This step requires that the detailed solution be so clearly and carefully worked out that it will be understood and used by those who must act on approved recommendations.

1. Creating the action plan. The action plan should be committed to writing. It should describe in fine detail what is to be done, who is to do it, when it is to be started, when it is to be finished, and to some degree how it is to be done (remembering that it is important to allow people to use their special knowledge, experience, and expertise to determine the "how").

The first draft of the plan should be submitted for review and comment to those who must implement it. That action is almost certain to eliminate the most blatant errors and preclude a complete fiasco when the solution is put into effect. Frequently, a meeting of all people involved in the implementation is held to discuss changes to the plan.

2. Refining the action plan. At this point the draft action plan is reworked to incorporate changes recommended by the reviewers either in writing or at a meeting. If time permits, it is wise to subject the product of this effort to a final review by the people who originally commented on the draft plan.

3. Implementing the solution. Get the needed resources. Assign people and delegate the authority they need. Install the changes, monitoring them carefully to ensure that they are put into effect by the right people at the right time, and in the correct way. Provide any guidance and assistance needed. Have some means of tracking progress in the implementation of the corrective action and reviewing results. Requiring periodic written reports is one way; others include periodic visits and observation and progress briefings by the principals.

Step 9: Following Up

The follow-up step involves evaluating the impact of the adopted solution and making any needed adjustments to the action plan.

Evaluating impact. The problem-solving effort is not complete with the installation of the remedies or solutions described in the action plan. A procedure and schedule designed to evaluate all changes after they have been implemented are also essential. The effects of the changes must be monitored for a reasonable period of time to ensure that they have been effective and that there is no need for either starting the problem-solving process all over again or making modifications to the solution implemented.

Making needed adjustments. If the problem-solving process has been carried out conscientiously and deliberately as described in this chapter, there should be no need for drastic changes to the solutions approved by the decision maker. However, minor modifications are usually required to eliminate small glitches and to make the solution work even better. Such changes should be subjected to review by those responsible for the activity before they are installed. And again they must be monitored for effectiveness.

Step 10: Reporting Results

There is one more step—one that is essential and often overlooked. Be sure to report the results to all concerned. That includes the people within the organization that are either interested in the outcome or are affected by the solution. It also includes people outside the organization who are affected by the change.

Summary

HR managers must deal with a great variety of problems; some are routine, but many are of critical importance to the wellness of the organization and its people. Some problems affect the entire organization, others affect organization-individual relationships, others affect individual employees, and still others affect the HR department itself.

All HR managers must develop and polish a systematic method of attacking problems to improve their batting averages and those of their subordinates in finding workable and cost-effective solutions to problems. Effective problem solving is a rational process; it follows a deliberate and logical sequence of steps and uses to the maximum the previously acquired knowledge, skills, and experience of the manager.

The first action the manager must take to improve problem-solving skill is to avoid or overcome barriers to efficient problem solving. In addition to lack of knowledge and skill, the most common blocks are rigidity, suppressive education and training, lack of self-confidence, negativism of others, and poor concentration.

There are two general types of problem-solving: individual and group. Both are extremely useful and must be mastered by all HR managers. Individual problem solving is a must for emergency situations or where time is short, and group problem solving is an important means of getting the help and commitment of employees in finding and implementing creative solutions to critical problems.

Major steps in problem solving are:

1. Identify the problem.
2. State the *real* problem.
3. Establish the criteria of solution.
4. Analyze the problem.
5. Identify alternative solutions.
6. Select the best solution.
7. Get support for the solution.
8. Translate the solution into action.
9. Follow up.
10. Report results.

FOR FURTHER READING

Albert, Kenneth J. *How to Solve Business Problems: The Consultant's Approach to Business Problems.* New York: McGraw-Hill, 1983.

Allen, Jane Elizabeth. "How to Solve the Right Problem." *Training,* February 1987, pp. 39–45.

Anderson, Barry F. *The Complete Thinker: A Handbook of Techniques for*

Creative and Critical Problem Solving. Englewood Cliffs, N.J.: Prentice-Hall, 1980.

Andriole, Stephen J. *Handbook of Problem Solving.* Princeton, N.J.: Petro-celli Books, 1983.

Baugh, James R. *Solution Training: Overcoming Blocks in Problem Solving.* Gretna, La.: Pelican, 1980.

Brightman, Harvey J. *Problem Solving: A Logical and Creative Approach.* Atlanta: Georgia State University, Business Publishing Division, 1980.

Cohn, A. G., and J. R. Thomas. *Artificial Intelligence and Its Applications.* New York: John Wiley & Sons, 1986.

Edgar, William J. *The Problem Solver's Guide to Logic.* Lantham, Md.: University Press of America, 1983.

Finlay, Joel S. "Diagnose Your HRD Problems Away." *Training and Development Journal,* August 1984, pp. 50–52.

Fogiel, Max. *Problem Solver in Business, Management and Finance.* New York: Research & Education Association, 1985.

Ford, N. *How Machines Think: A General Introduction to Artificial Intelligence.* New York: John Wiley & Sons, 1987.

Frohman, Mark A. "How to Improve Your Problem-Solving Capability." *Management Review,* November 1980, pp. 59–61.

Grossman, Stephen R. "Releasing Problem Solving Energies." *Training and Development Journal,* May 1984, pp. 94–98.

———. "Brainstorming Updated." *Training and Development Journal,* February 1984, pp. 84–87.

Hayes, J. R. *The Complete Problem Solver.* Philadelphia: Franklin Institute Press, 1981.

Hines, William Watson III. "Vertical Slice: A Problem-Solving Technique." *Training and Development Journal,* February 1981, pp. 96–98.

Kepner, Charles H., and Benjamin B. Tregoe. *The New Rational Manager.* Princeton, N.J.: Kepner-Tregoe, 1981.

Lyles, Richard L. *Practical Management Problem Solving and Decision Making.* New York: Van Nostrand Reinhold, 1982.

Mayer, Richard E. *Thinking, Problem Solving, Cognition.* San Francisco: W. H. Freeman, 1983.

Meltzer, Morton F. *Information, the Ultimate Management Resource: How to Find, Use, and Manage It.* New York: AMACOM, 1981.

Nickerson, Raymond S., David N. Perkins, and Edward E. Smith. *The Teaching of Thinking.* Hillsdale, N.J.: L. Erlbaum Associates, 1985.

Nierenberg, Gerard I. *The Art of Creative Thinking.* New York: Cornerstone Library, 1982.

Nilsson, Nils J. *Problem-Solving Methods in Artificial Intelligence.* New York: McGraw-Hill, 1971.

Osborn, Alex F. *Applied Imagination: Principles and Procedures of Creative Thinking,* rev. ed. New York: Charles Scribner's Sons, 1958.

Prince, George M. *The Practice of Creativity: A Manual for Dynamic Group Problem Solving.* New York: Harper & Row, 1970.

Raphael, Bertram. *The Thinking Computer: Mind Inside Matter.* San Francisco: W. H. Freeman, 1976.

Roth, William F., Jr. *Problem Solving for Managers.* New York: Praeger, 1985.

Sanderson, Michael. *What's the Problem Here? Time-Saving Problem-Solving Techniques for Managers.* Englewood Cliffs, N.J.: Prentice-Hall, 1981.

Scharlatt, Harold. "Beyond Brainstorming." *Training and Development Journal,* August 1984, pp. 8–9.

Segal, Leon. *The Problem Solver's Universal Checklist.* Dayton, Ohio: Educator's Academy, 1983.

Taylor, Jack W. *How to Create New Ideas.* Englewood Cliffs, N.J.: Prentice-Hall, 1961.

Ulschak, Francis, Leslie Nathanson, and Peter Gillan. *Small-Group Problem Solving: An Aid to Organizational Effectiveness.* Reading, Mass.: Addison-Wesley Training Systems, 1981.

Whimbey, A., and J. Lockhead. *Problem Solving and Comprehension: A Short Course in Analytic Reasoning.* Philadelphia: Franklin Institute Press, 1979.

White, Charles S. "Problem-Solving: The First Neglected Step." *Management Review,* January 1983, pp. 52–55.

7

DECISION MAKING
The Manager's
Moment of Truth

Decision making is unquestionably the central job of all managers; they must constantly choose what is to be done, who is to do it, when, where, and very often how. Rational decision making involves a tangible objective; for example, to reduce training costs by a certain amount, get a development program on schedule, cut training time, or reduce hazards to people or equipment.

The decision, therefore, is the linchpin of the HR manager's leadership and control. It comprises the manager's concept of forthcoming activities, the mission and functions of subordinate elements, and major problems involving coordination, cooperation, support, and control of participating people and organizations.

Three Kinds of Decisions

Let us say, by way of definition, that a decision is a choice from among two or more ways of getting something done or achieving a wanted result. It is the actual selection of a course of action from among alternatives.

Not all management decisions are problem-connected; many are oriented toward goals or objectives. For example, an HR manager's decision to develop an intensive executive development program for women may be made primarily to support the goal of providing equal opportunity for women to advance in the company. Or the decision to install an MBO program in the HR department may relate to a desire to increase the participation of subordinate managers and supervisors in setting objectives.

On the other hand, many critical decisions *are* problem-driven. They are made—or at least should be—after careful study of the facts surrounding a problem. Most of these decisions represent a compromise between idealism and reality, falling somewhere between utopian and utilitarian, and are aimed at getting the most benefits at the least cost. A third category of decisions includes routine, noncritical choices, such as selecting agenda items for a staff meeting.

In summary, in order of importance, decisions are made to meet one of the following requirements:

1. To achieve the goals and objectives of the organization.
2. To solve immediate or potential problems of varying magnitude.
3. To carry out day-to-day functions and activities.

Importance of a System

The dynamics of HR programs and services limit the amount of time a manager has to formulate a decision. Decision making is a complex process of logical, analytical, and intuitive activity accomplished under conditions of uncertainty. Although the HR manager may have a staff to assist, insufficient information, compressed due dates, a rapidly evolving situation, and other constraints demand foresight, an ability to forecast potential problems.

HR managers need a *conscious* and *deliberate* system for making decisions, not only to improve their performance as managers but also to teach their subordinates how to make better decisions. There are many different systems of decision making. Some are esoteric. Others are very complex and mathematical. Still others are quite simple. Of course, there are nonsystems—where decisions are based on hunch, intuition, or past experience alone. And there are nondecisions—where the manager allows a situation to percolate until no decision is possible and the issue is resolved by default.

The nontechnical, conceptual decision system advocated here is somewhere between simple and complex. It will not do your thinking for you, but it will make your decisions more rational because they are arrived at systematically. It's also flexible: If you don't like some parts of the system, you don't have to junk the whole process, just use the parts you do like. You'll still make better decisions with the remnants than you would without them.

To make timely, sound decisions the HR manager must use both logical and qualitative methods. However, without quantitative support and substantiation, it is often impossible to make a correct, let alone optimal, decision. Mere common sense, experience, or intuition, is not enough; the trial-and-error method is altogether unacceptable.

The consequences of indecision or poor decisions can be disastrous for the organization and the manager: financial loss, employee dissatisfaction, work slowdowns and strikes, excessive turnover, reduced production, failed programs, tarnished company image, wasted time and resources, and, in the case of the manager, being passed over for promotion or perhaps reassignment, transfer, or firing. For those reasons HR managers must learn not only to make correct decisions but also to make them when needed and implement them as economically as possible.

Options for Action

When confronted with a serious problem, the manager has more than one option—and sometimes must use more than one.

1. *Interim action.* This is frequently the first action. It buys the time a manager needs to find the cause of a problem.
2. *Adaptive action.* This action is taken after the cause has been found, but it does little or nothing to eliminate the cause—either because the manager does not have sufficient authority, influence, or control or because the solution is too expensive to implement. The action lets the manager live with the quite "tolerable effects of a problem or with an ineradicable cause."
3. *Corrective action.* This action eliminates the deviation by eliminating the cause.
4. *Preventive action.* This action removes the possible cause of a problem before it occurs or reduces the probability that it will appear at all.
5. *Contingency action.* This action provides "stand-by arrangements to offset or minimize the effects of a serious potential problem."[1]

Decision Blockers

Indecisiveness can be just as costly as a poor decision. For whatever reason, failure to make timely decisions strongly affects both the manager and the organization. There are several possible reasons for managerial indecisiveness.

Insufficient authority. Authority is inherent in positions. The hierarchical structure of most organizations results in the allocation of separate and specific authority that enables managers to make decisions

1. Charles H. Kepner and Benjamin B. Tregoe, *The Rational Manager* (New York: McGraw-Hill, 1965), 132–133.

relating to their part of the organization. Sometimes the limits of authority are defined in the job description. Too often, however, they are not, and managers must determine where their authority begins and ends by trial and error—frequently at considerable personal and organizational cost. A common cause of what appears to be indecisiveness is simply a failure to act because the manager does not have the authority to do so.

Fear of making mistakes. Another major cause of indecision is simply apprehension about the consequences of error. In most organizations there are price tags attached to bad decisions. The price on critical decisions may be very high—demotion or termination. Yet even the consequences of poor decisions of less importance can be intimidating—ridicule, reprimand, or censure. Where the aftereffects of mistakes in judgment are severe, the likelihood of indecision or procrastination is greatly increased.

Lack of information. Inadequate, incomplete, or questionable information, or the total absence of factual evidence, sometimes makes a timely and considered decision impossible. Rather than succumb to impulse or implement a seat-of-the-pants decision, many managers prefer to wait until they have what they consider to be adequate information before commiting themselves to a course of action.

Perfectionism. Some managers establish the goal of impeccable performance. In their pursuit of perfection, they delay decision until they have exhausted every resource, pursued every avenue of investigation, left no stone unturned to gather the information they believe they need to arrive at a sound decision. Sometimes the strategy backfires simply because when the manager gets to the point where he or she is ready to act, the time for decision has long since passed.

Impaired judgment. Sometimes decisions are deferred or simply not made because the manager's judgment is impaired. The cause may be temporary—a headache, mild emotional distress, or tension—or chronic—severe mental, physical, or emotional illness. And, to an alarming degree, judgment is being impaired by substance abuse—alcohol and drugs.

Wishful thinking. Occasionally, managers make the mistake of deferring decision in the vain hope that the problem will cure itself, or just go away. Or they delude themselves into believing that there really isn't a problem, that someone has blown a small, unimportant deviation into a catastrophe. Unwarranted optimism invariably results in serious shortfalls in achieving goals and objectives.

Why Decisions Fail

Decisions miss the mark or turn out badly simply because the decision maker overlooked, misjudged, or underrated crucially important factors.

When a decision turns out poorly and doesn't work, one invariably finds that some factors necessary for success have been ignored or misassessed. Almost always, the critical information was available. It was missed because the decision maker failed to ask the right questions. A poor decision produces surprises: Things happen that weren't expected, and other things that were expected and relied on don't happen at all. A good decision goes right to the heart of the matter, accomplishes what needs to be accomplished, wastes neither time nor resources, and is productive. A poor decision is unproductive because it leaves much undone, incurs patch-up and retrofit costs, and creates new problems to be dealt with tomorrow.[2]

Types of Decisions

Decisions range all the way from nondecisions through intuitive to logical and analytical. They are made by individuals and groups. They may be either routine or critical.

Nondecisions

Nondecisions—absence of or avoidance of decisions—are, unfortunately, not uncommon. Some managers decide to do nothing about a situation or problem in the hope that it will evaporate. Others defer decision, hoping that the problem will resolve itself, that conditions will change, or that someone else will do something about it. Some managers ignore a problem simply because they cannot face it. The unfortunate thing about a nondecision is that it is decision making by default. Whether the manager realizes it or not, some resolution of almost every problem or issue is inevitable—someone will take an action, or something will happen—and often the consequences to the organization, and to the manager who failed to act, are severe.

Intuitive Decisions

Intuitive decisions are not based on logic, hard facts, or experience but on instinctive knowledge or gut feelings. Managers who use this approach do not (usually) think they are clairvoyant, but they do believe they have an innate sense of what needs to be done in a situation. They are sometimes, but not always, right. Certainly, there are occasions in the life of every manager where he or she has to go on inspiration or intuition simply because there are no precedents, no facts, no hard

2. Charles H. Kepner and Benjamin B. Tregoe, "Decision-Making Training," in *Human Resources Management and Development Handbook*, ed. William R. Tracey (New York: AMA-COM, 1985), 1137.

numbers, and no experience. In other situations, decisions are made on the basis of incomplete knowledge, resulting in a combination of logic and intuition. But in all other cases, logical analysis should predominate, if not prevail.

Roy Rowan, however, contends that logic is only one part of the decision process. When carried to excess, he maintains, it results in "analysis paralysis"—a condition caused by too much inquiry. "Constantly accumulating new information and numbers, without giving the mind a chance to percolate and come to a conclusion intuitively, can delay any important decision until the time for action expires." That is "substituting study for courage." Rowan says that it is often the daring, instinctual leap that can make the difference in decision making; he calls it the Eureka factor. "Hunch is an odious word to the professional manager," he writes. "It's a horseplayer's or stock market plunger's term, rife with imprecision and unpredictability. Yet . . . the old-fashioned hunch continues to be an important, though unappreciated, managerial tool."[3]

Logical/Analytical Decisions

The logical approach is a rational and restrained method of arriving at decisions. It involves precise planning and rigorous analysis. Logical and analytical decisions come in two forms: The first is based mainly on thought processes and other nonmathematical approaches, and the second involves symbolic logic, mathematical theories, and, more and more today, computers.

Nonmathematical Processes

The bases for nonmathematical, analytical decisions are experience and research and experimentation.

Experience. Although reliance on past experience plays a larger role in decision making than it probably should, it still has validity as long as HR managers realize that the things they have accomplished and the mistakes they have made in the past do not furnish an infallible guide to future decisions.

Experience is still the best teacher, and the very fact that the HR manager has reached the present position indicates that his or her judgment is above average. If a certain program succeeded elsewhere or sometime in the past, there may be good reason to believe that, if the same set of conditions is present, the program will succeed again. It is equally true that if a manager recognizes that a bad decision was made in the past, and has accurately analyzed the reasons for the mistake, the likelihood of repeated error is diminished.

3. Roy Rowan, *The Intuitive Manager* (New York: Little, Brown, 1986), 91, 93.

The greatest danger in relying on past experience is that situations are rarely identical; even slightly different objectives, premises, and events demand at least slightly different actions.

Research and experimentation. One of the best ways to decide among alternative courses of action is to try them out. That is the method used in scientific inquiry, and it does have some applications in HR. Frequently, it is used to determine the most cost-effective strategies, methods, and techniques for conducting instruction—actual tryout of approaches to learning—under controlled conditions. Of course there are many other HR uses. However, experimentation is the most expensive of all approaches and should be reserved for those areas where even very accurate records of experience cannot assure the manager of a good decision, and where the potential for a return on the investment of time and other resources is substantial.

Mathematical and Scientific Techniques

In other disciplines, mathematical models are being used to examine and evaluate different scenarios, based on specific factors and conditions, and to forecast the outcome. These models provide the computer-generated results needed to substantiate decisions and plans. Model functions are distributed between humans and machines so that the automated equipment does what it does best and relieves the human of routine, noncreative work.

However, we must not forget that models provide only quantitative data to substantiate or verify a decision. They do not *constitute* the decision. They are but one input among many at the manager's disposal. They are most useful in finding answers to such questions as: What are the anticipated results of this decision? What resources have to be allocated to achieve the goals? What strategy or methodology should be selected?

Although mathematical models, computers, and automated systems are here to stay and will have a growing role in HR management, the human factor is crucial in all stages of automated systems.

Marginal analysis. The evaluation of alternative courses of action may involve the use of marginal analysis, the process of comparing factors that can be expressed in numbers. Its major advantage is that it emphasizes the variables in a situation and deemphasizes averages. For example, marginal analysis can be used to underscore additional costs or revenues from additional quantities. Therefore, when the objective is to maximize profits from the sale of internally developed training materials, the objective will be reached when additional revenue from increased sales and additional costs from stepped-up marketing and production efforts are equal. At any other point, either more revenue could be obtained at less added cost or any additional revenue gained would be less than the additional costs incurred. In either case, profits would not be maximized.

Operations research (OR). OR is the application of the scientific method to the study of alternative courses of action. Its objective is to provide a quantitative basis for arriving at optimal solutions to problems in terms of the objectives sought. It involves careful definition of the problem and the objective, systematic collection and assessment of facts, orderly development and testing of hypotheses, precise establishment of relationships among facts, meticulous formulation of predictions based on hypotheses, and painstaking design of measures to evaluate the effectiveness of courses of action.

The construction of models is the central tool of OR. However, other scientific and mathematical techniques, such as *probability theory, game theory, queueing theory, linear programming,* and *servo theory* have also been used.

In brief: *Probability theory* is based on the assumption that certain outcomes are likely to happen in accordance with a predictable mathematical pattern—the laws of probability. *Game theory* is based on the postulate that when people compete, they seek to maximize their gains and minimize their losses, and that they tend to act rationally under such circumstances. *Queueing* or *waiting-line theory* uses mathematical formulas to balance the cost of queues (waiting lines) against the cost of preventing queues by providing increased service. The theory is based on the premise that although queues are costly, the expense of eliminating them may be even higher. *Linear programming* is a technique used to determine the best mix of limited resources to achieve an objective. It is based on the assumption that a straight-line relationship exists between variables and that their limits can be determined. *Servo* or *feedback theory* is based on the thesis that when information is fed back to correct for deviations, the optimal operation of the system can be achieved.

The complexity of these tools precludes full description here. Information about them can be found in the selected readings at the end of this chapter.

Individual Decisions

The great majority of decisions—large and small, routine and crucial—are made by individuals and not groups. The reasons for this are many, but probably the most prevalent is that typically only one individual in the organization or organizational element has the authority to make certain decisions. Whether this is by design or by accident is immaterial.

Individual decisions have important consequences. Their aftereffects go far beyond the area in which they are made; they affect decisions and functions in other parts of the organization. There are also important behavioral consequences. Failure to coordinate and relate decisions may result in inconsistent actions throughout the organization.

Group Decisions

Some organizations and HR managers have rejected participatory decision-making strategies because they tend to degrade or at least threaten the manager's power, authority, and prestige. That attitude flies in the face of one of the most important employee motivators—opportunities to share in making the decisions that affect them.

Participatory management has a long history. For about 50 years, multiple management has been practiced at McCormick and Co. (the spice company). Until recently, however, the cooperative management strategy made little headway in other companies. Now, however, many larger firms are experimenting; among the most prominent are General Electric, General Motors, Boeing, and Xerox.

For example, in 1981 Xerox implemented a multiple management strategy in its copier engineering, design, development, and manufacturing organizations—the Reprographic Business Group. The approach Xerox used involved identifying specific behaviors characteristic of an effective management style. Out of a total of 44 behaviors in five categories, many dealt with some aspect of sharing power and authority. Xerox's decision-making category identified these behaviors:

> *Decision-making—an effective manager:*
> Allows decisions to be made at the lowest appropriate level in his/her organization.
> Considers employees' opinions in making decisions which affect their work.
> Encourages employees to participate in the decision-making process in areas in which they believe they can contribute.
> Explains his/her rationale for decisions with which employees disagree.
> Manages decision making in a way that maximizes employee commitment.[4]

It appears likely that group decision making will increase as more and more workers demand opportunities to participate in making the decisions that affect them.

4. Norman Deets and Dr. Richard Morano, "Xerox's Strategy for Changing Management Styles," *Management Review*, March 1986, p. 33.

Routine Decisions

During the course of everyday business, the HR manager must make many routine decisions. Although they may relate to the efficiency with which the operation is conducted, they are not crucial to achieving the department's objectives. Such decisions as how much time to spend on correspondence, how much copy paper to order, which typewriter to purchase, who to consult on a project, when to visit a new supervisor, and where to find information about new products and services, while important, are not momentous. They are routine.

Crucial Decisions

Without question, many of the decisions HR managers make are crucial. The importance of any decision depends on three things: its impact on the goals and objectives of the organization, its effect on people, and the extent of the responsibility of the manager making it. Here are some factors you should consider when trying to determine how critical a decision is.

1. The magnitude or duration of the commitment. If a decision commits the organization to a substantial investment of time, talent, or funds, or to a key program, such as executive development or technical training, or if the program extends over a relatively long period of time, invariably it is crucial and must be subjected to very careful scrutiny by the HR manager or a higher-level executive.

2. Specificity and quantifiability of variables. Where the objectives, inputs, and other variables are general, rather than specific, or difficult or impossible to quantify, as is very often the case when dealing with the human element—characteristic of HR decisions—the decision tends to be more important than in situations where quantification is relatively easy.

3. Changeability or adaptability of plans and actions. Some decisions involve courses of action that are not easily changed. Others are quite easily changed or modified. Decisions that are difficult to alter are usually crucial and deserve more than a quick and superficial look.

4. People impacts or consequences. If the people impact of a decision is substantial, its importance is inevitably high. Decisions that may be practical and advantageous from a purely business perspective (such as profit or return on investment) may well be unworkable from the standpoint of the people affected by it. For example, a decision to convert all technical training programs to a self-instructional, "home assignment" mode might be both feasible and cost effective, yet the potential for negative reaction and resistance by technical workers might make it unwise.

Levels of Decision-Making Authority

Most large organizations are faced with a difficult choice: tight management controls and centralized decision making on one hand and discretionary decision-making authority at lower levels on the other hand. The first choice means at least some loss of individual initiative; the second brings increased requirements for communication and coordination.

Douglas Basil, industrial consultant and professor of management, has this to say: "In a highly centralized organization, it is necessary not only to refer decisions to higher authority for action but also to provide the information that will permit higher echelons to make the decisions . . . The individual who controls the information really controls the decision."[5]

Top-Level Decision Making

Why are decisions so often made at the top levels of the organization? Because:

- Managers at the top have proven ability and more experience.
- Top managers have a better grasp of corporate goals, objectives, and priorities.
- Lower-level managers may not know when a decision is really one of policy (rather than an operating decision) that should be referred to a higher level.

Lower-Level Decision Making

What are the justifications for pushing decision-making authority downward in the organization?

- Top managers have too much to do; they suffer from task overload.
- Routine decisions are frequent, and they consume too much of the valuable time of top managers.
- Too much communication and coordination are required when top managers make all decisions; communication channels often become gridlocked.
- Decision making at the top leads to rigidity and inability to adapt to new conditions.
- Lower-level managers know more about a particular situation than higher-level managers and should be able to respond more appropriately.
- Lower-level managers need practice in making decisions.

5. Douglas C. Basil, *Managerial Skills for Executive Action* (New York: AMACOM, 1970), 89.

- Lower-level managers are more likely to know what decisions their subordinates will willingly support.
- Operating managers and supervisors control the information needed for good decisions.
- Employees want to have a say in decisions that affect them.
- Participation of employees is one key to job satisfaction and high morale.
- To do otherwise is to fail to use subordinates to the limit of their abilities.

Guides for Determining the Proper Level

Although there are no hard and fast rules for determining at what level decisions should be made, there are some useful guides.

- Decisions should be made at the lowest effective level possible.
- The cost of making the decision (the salary of the decision maker plus the loss of income he or she could be generating by spending time on other matters) should be reasonable and acceptable.
- A timely decision is needed to avoid excessive costs.
- Savings or income from a decision must exceed the costs of its implementation.

"To make the optimum use of managerial resources, decision making should be allocated on the basis of the cost of the decision. Decentralization of authority for decision making thus becomes a matter of cost alternatives, not a philosophy of management."[6]

Sources and Types of Authority

In all types of organizations, there are three sources and at least four types of power and authority.

Status

One important source of authority is directly associated with the individual's status in the organization. Status is usually determined by position and title. CEOs have more status than vice presidents, and hence greater power and authority. Supervisors have more status than technicians and therefore have more decision-making authority.

Supervisors and managers at all levels have a critically important power that is status-rooted—coercive power, the power to reward or

6. Basil, *Managerial Skills*, 90.

punish. Although firings, reassignments, and promotions are often restricted by collective bargaining agreements, statutes, and other legal constraints, managers retain the threat to deprive people of their livelihoods or to limit their earning power or prestige.

Expertise

Authority can also be acquired exclusively by having special expertise, information, or skills in areas that others need. The extent of that authority is determined by the importance of that expertise to the organization and the number of people in the organization who are masters of the discipline. For example, if there is only one systems analyst in an organization and much of the work of the organization is computerized, the systems analyst is likely to acquire a great deal of decision-making authority in developing or purchasing both hardware and software—and even in other areas.

This example, by the way, points to a potential problem for HR managers. If they are truly to be the people who manage and make decisions, they must develop computer literacy, even fluency. They must be able to review computer-related options and speak the language of computer specialists. If they cannot, many important managerial decisions will be made by computer specialists, whose legitimate role is that of technician, not manager.

Delegated

All authority below the highest level in any organization (such as the board of directors, or the CEO or president where there is no board) is delegated, and the amount and kind of authority delegated can vary considerably.

Complete. Complete authority is effectively an independent level of operation. The incumbent of a position is assigned a broad, all-encompassing area of functional responsibility, and he or she determines which jobs are to be performed, when, where, by whom, and to some degree how. The incumbent may be subject to ordinary legal and regulatory controls, but is independently responsible for the activity within the functional area. At this level, the responsibilities of the incumbent usually include supervising others and invariably involve delegating some authority.

Permissive. With this type of authority, the incumbent of a position is assigned a broad area of work activity. He or she is given the authority to decide which specific activities within that broad area must be performed, in what priority they must be performed, and by whom. The incumbent also decides how the functions, activities, and tasks should be performed and selects the tools, materials, equipment, and procedures to perform them. The incumbent's supervisor is available for consultation on any aspect of the delegated function.

Limited. Here the supervisor provides specific instructions about *which* duty or task to perform, but allows the incumbent to determine *how* the work is to be done. The incumbent selects the tools, equipment, materials, and procedures. The supervisor is available for consultation about how to do the work.

Encumbered. At this level, the authority of the job incumbent is extremely circumscribed. The incumbent is not permitted to proceed to any new work activity until further instructions have been given. The supervisor provides all necessary tools and materials, or specifies which ones will be used for a given job or task. The incumbent is not permitted to make judgments about additional requirements and is not allowed to proceed independently. Before anything is done, consultation with the superior is required.

The Decision-Making Process

Several errors are commonly made by decision makers. The process of decision making involves a series of activities and a sequence of steps. We'll take a look at both.

Common Errors

Among the many errors made by decision makers, these are the most common, and the most damaging:

1. Making unnecessary decisions. All decisions involve risks, so it is sometimes wiser to make no decision, to leave well enough alone.
2. Solving recurring problems. They should be resolved by implementing new policies or procedures, not by repetitive decisions.
3. Proposing unrealistic solutions. Always carefully consider the cost and other consequences of decisions.
4. Making a decision precipitously or too soon. Always consider proper timing.
5. Delaying decision to the point where no decision is needed because it has been overtaken by events. Always make timely decisions; do not permit decision by default.

Major Considerations and Actions

The decision-making process should set into motion six major actions:

1. Determining the purpose of the decision (what you must decide and why).
2. Ascertaining when you must make the decision (the matter of timing).
3. Determining how the decision should be made (independently and unaided, or with collaboration and assistance).
4. Identifying what you need to know to make a good decision (what facts you need).
5. Considering available alternatives (how best to achieve the results you want).
6. Assessing the risks and consequences of available options (which action is likely to be safest, soundest, most productive, and most cost effective).

Steps in Decision Making

As noted earlier, the decision-making process involves a deliberate, logical, and sequential series of steps, all of which are critically important in reaching a good and workable decision.

Step 1: Determine Purposes and Objectives

This is identical to the first step in problem solving, discussed in Chapter 6. Unfortunately, it is often overlooked or given short shrift. For example, the objective "to develop better measures of performance" is too vague to be of much use. It must be made more specific. Whose performance? What kind of performance? What is meant by better measures? Who is to use the measures? When? How often? The statement should describe the objective precisely in terms of the who, what, when, where, how, how much or how often, and sometimes why.

"Objectives . . . must be stated in terms of gains, risks, expected values, utility, or other criteria which will indicate change, or indicate the degree to which action has been effective."[7]

When phrased specifically and completely, the purpose defines the standards by which alternative actions can be assessed and, ultimately, the success and effectiveness of the decision can be measured.

Five factors energize and drive decision making: the criticality of the decision, the desired outcomes, the information needed, the resources (including time available), and the skills of the manager.

The astute manager usually starts with the results he or she wants to achieve. To get that information, put your questions to the right people. What specifically is to be done? What are we trying to accomplish? What

7. George S. Odiorne, *Management Decisions by Objectives* (Englewood Cliffs, N.J.: Prentice-Hall, 1969), 33.

shortcomings are we trying to remedy? What processes or situations are we trying to improve? How much are we willing to invest? What returns do we want for our investment? What pitfalls are to be avoided? What outcomes are to be prevented?

The perceptive decision maker listens, observes, and reads. When the facts have been collected, you should check or test them for relevancy and accuracy. In doing that, you get rid of irrational notions and attitudes—preconceptions, prejudice, wrong assumptions, and emotions.

When gathering information about resources to be committed, you should examine quantitative units—people (number, types, skills, and staff-hours), funds (overhead costs, capital expenditures, rates of return on investment, and profit), market forecasts and projected sales, production (units of output), materials (space, facilities, equipment, and supplies), and time.

Then you should examine nonquantitative or intangible factors—employee relations, company image, tactics of competitors, product and services quality, new technologies, and new markets. Using this list, the manager asks: What resources are available? What are the limits within which I must operate? What resources should be used sparingly? Economized? Kept in reserve? Expended freely? Maximized?

Step 2: Place Objectives in Priority Order

When all the objectives have been identified, they must be placed in order of priority. Some objectives are "nice to accomplish," but they usually don't have very much effect on the situation one way or another. Others are very useful but not critical. Still others are absolute musts—extremely important. Obviously, you should attempt to achieve all the objectives, but the focus of the decision-making process is on achieving the "must" category. All alternatives considered must address that classification, and for it minimum limits for results and maximum limits for resources must be established.

One way to place objectives in priority order is to assign a weight to each one according to its importance, starting with the least consequential and giving that a weight of 1. The priority of the next item is determined by comparing its importance with the item of lowest priority, and giving it a weight of 3. And so on. Another method is to use a numerical scale of 1 to 10, assigning a number to each objective in relation to its importance.

Either procedure is, in effect, deciding priorities on the weight of the total evidence. However, you must remember that both procedures involve human judgment. Few decisions can be so accurately quantified that judgment is unnecessary. If every variable could be accurately measured, all the manager would need to make decisions is a computer.

Step 3: Identify Alternatives

Assuming that you have clearly defined objectives listed in priority order, the next step in decision making is to develop alternatives. And there almost always are alternatives, even when it appears that there is only one possible action. HR managers must always force themselves to consider ways other than the obvious one, the one that first presents itself. For every situation, issue, or problem, alternative courses of action exist, and effective management involves a thorough search for the option that represents the best route toward the desired objective.

In this step, you examine each objective in turn. You ask yourself, What does this result imply? What actions might meet this requirement? This is where managers bring their experience in similar situations to bear. They develop the best possible list of alternative actions. If they lack experience they must forge, improvise, or synthesize choices "from scratch." However, this is not a seat of the pants operation; it is a systematic and methodical search for the most promising courses of action.

Step 4: Weigh and Compare Alternatives

Now you must check each option against the objectives, gauging to see how practical, functional, or effective it will be. Systematically measure the alternatives against each one of the "must" objectives separately, on a "go/no-go" basis. If any alternative fails to yield what a "must" objective requires, it must be rejected.

This might well be called the search for the crunch factors. It simply means that when choosing from among alternatives, primary attention and emphasis must be given to those factors that are strategic to the decision involved, the ones that determine whether the objectives will be achieved. For example, if an HR manager were considering a tuition reimbursement plan for employees, the crunch factor might be the availability of funds, or employees' attitude toward the plan, or perhaps the availability of outside educational opportunities.

The search for the crunch factor never ends, because what is strategic to a decision at one point becomes less important later. For example, the HR manager might decide to acquire a computer-driven, interactive video training system when the determining factor was the availability of funds. But later the strategic factor might become delivery, or training the users, or repair of malfunctions.

Alternatives that pass the crunch-factor test may then be measured against the "nice to have" objectives. A weight or score can be assigned to each option on the basis of how it performs against the "nice to have" objectives. Or they can be placed in rank order.

A useful technique for weighing alternatives is called worst-case planning. This is how it works. Before deciding, list your options. Determine the worst possible outcome that could occur. Decide how likely the worst case would be. For example: You are considering asking for financial support for a new employee participatory management program. Determine the worst possible outcome: You might lose the confidence of your boss if the project goes sour. Then determine the maximum possible loss if your boss begins to question your judgment and the maximum loss if you don't ask for the support. Then figure out how likely it is that you'll suffer the maximum loss, and then make your decision.

A form like the one shown in Figure 7–1 can be used to judge the adequacy of options. To use the form, first enter the short titles of each option under "Optional Choices." Then you can determine the Action Priority Rating of each option by either of the following means.

Enter in each box under "Criteria" a number from 1 to 5 (with 1 being the best) to denote its rank in comparison with the other options with respect to each "Desired Outcome." Sum the ranks horizontally and enter the total score in the column headed "Action Priority Rating." The lowest score will represent the "best" option, and the highest score the "worst" option.

Figure 7-1.   Criteria for judging options.

OPTIONAL CHOICES	CRITERIA					
	Contribution to Objectives	Cost	Feasibility	Time	Unwanted Side Effects	Action Priority Rating
1. ____ A						
2. ____ B						
3. ____ C						
4. ____ D						
5. ____ E						
Desired Outcome	High	Low	High	Short	Low	

Adapted from George S. Odiorne, *Management Decisions by Objectives* (Englewood Cliffs, N.J.: Prentice-Hall, 1969), 68. Used by permission.

Or, assign a weighted score to each criterion. For example, contribution to objectives might be given a weight of 10, cost a weight of 8, feasibility a weight of 7, time a weight of 5, and unwanted side effects a weight of 5. Then judge each option on that scale and enter the appropriate number for each option under each criterion. Sum the results horizontally. The option with the highest weighted score is theoretically the best course of action.

Step 5: Make a Tentative Decision

Although the alternative that receives the best score on performance against the objectives is theoretically the best available course of action, this should be only a tentative decision. Inevitably options represent tradeoffs, and any one high-ranking option may not be the best choice when *all* consequences are taken into account. Choices invariably involve change, and most managers are fully aware that change of any kind inevitably causes problems. It is even conceivable that a change dictated by a decision will cause even more serious consequences than the initial problem. Therefore, you must carefully evaluate the consequences of you choice.

It is important to remember that when making a decision, your objective is to make the *right* decision—one that is well considered and logical—and also the decision that people will *accept.*

Step 6: Assess the Consequences of the Tentative Decision

At this point, you ask, "If I were to implement this decision, what would happen? What could go sour?" You should question the potential effect of each of the most promising options on other things and the effect that other events could have on it—the potential but unexposed or unexpected consequences.

Where should you look?

○ People impacts—in terms of performance, productivity, attitudes and motivation, skills and abilities, growth and development, and health and safety.
○ Organizational consequences—in terms of relationships among teams, units, shifts, functions, and persons; formal and informal communication; responsibility, cooperation, coordination, and delegation.
○ External factors—in terms of economic trends, technological advances, foreign and domestic competition for markets, company image and reputation, and laws and government regulations.

○ Space, facilities, equipment, and supplies—in terms of location, flexibility, accessibility, adaptability, compatibility, safety, and costs.
○ Materials—in terms of sources and availability, quality, distribution, packaging, handling, and storage.
○ Funds—in terms of capital or fixed costs and expenses, return on investment, and profit.
○ Products and services—in terms of quality, quantity, and timing of output and customer/client satisfaction.
○ Personal considerations—in terms of career goals and objectives, plans and programs, skills, abilities, and interests, strengths and weaknesses.

Step 7: Make the Final Check and Decision

Before implementing a decision, you should make a final check: In effect, "review the bidding" before committing yourself to a course of action. The key is to worry before you decide—and not after.

If the decision is based on your own analysis of the problem, follow these steps:

1. Discuss the tentative decision with your staff. Identify the other alternatives you considered and your reasons for rejecting them. Get their reactions, comments, and reasoning.
2. Ask your staff for new alternatives and discuss their advantages and disadvantages.

If your decision is to be based on the analysis of other individuals or groups, follow these steps:

1. Identify the opportunities or challenges the recommendation or proposal applies to.
2. Determine how completely the proposal or recommendation has been circulated among your staff for comments and concurrence.
3. Find out the reasons for nonconcurrences and why the proposer rejected the objections of other staffers.
4. Review the alternatives that were considered and rejected in arriving at the recommendation—and why they were thrown out. Look for the logic behind the reasons given for the rejection. Ask the proposer to explain the factors taken into account and the reasoning behind their use.

Regardless of whether the decision is based on your own solo problem solving or on the efforts of other individuals or groups, these steps mark the end of the final check:

1. Determine the extent to which the recommendation or proposal complements (and does not conflict with) other decisions, proposals, or recommendations.
2. Determine what value will be added to the total organization, department, system, policy, procedure, equipment, or whatever (profit, performance, time-saving, efficiency, effectiveness).
3. Determine how the proposed "item" is to be provided. Must it be manufactured, developed, fabricated, or can it be obtained or purchased?
4. Find out how the performance of the proposed item or change can be proved effective—or at least adequate. Identify the criteria to be applied.
5. Determine the cost of the proposal or recommendation—in dollars, time, materials, talent, facilities, equipment, skills—including negative costs, such as decreased job satisfaction, motivation, and the like.

If everything checks out, you now give the necessary orders to go ahead, making sure to take every possible action to prevent bad consequences or, if that is not possible, deciding on a contingency action.

Step 8: Develop the Action Plan

It is in this step that you take precautions to implement the decision properly. Two actions are needed.

1. Establish controls. Set up reporting procedures, reporting dates, and other controls so that the progress of plans can be tracked. Controls tell you whether the action plan is being carried out, whether it is working, and whether the decision itself was correct. Controls may already be built into the organization, but frequently you must design and implement special controls to provide the information and feedback you need.

2. Follow up. You must make plans to follow up on your instructions to see that they have been received and understood. This is something that cannot be left to chance. The best decision will be totally wasted if the people who must implement it don't fully understand what is to be done and how.

Step 9: Implement the Decision

Now you put the action plan into effect—activate the reporting procedure and begin monitoring progress. Sometimes, this simply involves an order to execute the plan. More often, however, a sequence of orders is needed to activate the decision by stages. In any case, your attention is required to ensure that the decision is put into effect in a timely manner and that there is no "foot-dragging" among those who may have been lukewarm about the decision.

Step 10: Follow Up and Evaluate

In this step, you systematically follow up on the implementation of the decision. The basic purpose of this step is to analyze, assess, and appraise the effect of the decision on the people, the organization, and other important elements and factors identified earlier. Another objective is to develop a list of lessons learned. This type of feedback is used to improve future decisions.

Managing a Bad Decision

No manager can hope to bat 1.000. Some of your decisions are certain to be less than perfect, and occasionally one will be very poor, perhaps even a minor disaster. What to do then? Thre are several things that the competent manager can and should do.

Admit error. The most important thing to do is admit error—not just to yourself (although that is very important and a necessary first step) but also to those who are affected by the bad decision. The coverup never solves any problem, it only serves to complicate and exacerbate a situation. So the first thing you should do is admit that a mistake has been made.

Reverse the decision. If the decision is reversible or retractable, do that immediately, to limit the damage. Procrastination is not the solution to a decision gone bad. Time will only make the situation more difficult to deal with, and may result in irrevocable damage or irretrievable loss of resources. Bad decisions must be overturned as soon as they are identified.

Apply other damage-control measures. Once the decision has been reversed or retracted, apply interim measures to limit or reduce the damage. Once that has been done, identify reasons for the failure of the decision and repeat the process of problem solving and decision making. Of course, this time around you have the advantage of hindsight, as well as the fruits of the earlier effort in the form of a priority listing of alternatives. The replacement decision should be a winner.

Summary

A decision is a conscious choice of one course of action from among two or more alternatives designed to achieve a wanted result. It involves the use of logical approaches and quantitative factors, qualitative methods and experience, and common sense—and, on occasion, intuition or hunch.

Decision making is a distinct skill. It is not another term for problem solving, although it is sometimes the final step in arriving at a solution to a problem. In addition to its problem-solving application, decision making is also used to support organization goals and objectives, management strategies and tactics, and to make routine, day-to-day choices.

The consequences of poor decisions can be serious from the standpoints of the organization as a whole, departments, individual employees, and the managers themselves. For that reason, HR managers must not only make good decisions, they must also make them in a timely and cost-conscious way.

Managerial indecisiveness is all too common in organizational life. The major causes of failure to act are insufficient authority, fear of mistakes, lack of information, perfectionism, impaired judgment, and wishful thinking. Decisions fail because critical information, although available, was ignored, missed entirely, misassessed, or misused.

Basically, there are three types of decisions: nondecisions, intuitive decisions, and analytical/logical decisions. From a different perspective, there are individual and group decisions. All except nondecisions, and to a limited degree intuitive decisions, have application to HR programs and activities.

The degree of importance is determined by assessing the following factors: (1) the magnitude or duration of the commitment; (2) the specificity and quantifiability of the variables; (3) the changeability or adaptability of plans and actions; and (4) the impact on people.

Although there are valid arguments for both centralized and decentralized decision-making authority, accepted rubrics for determining the appropriate level of decision-making authority are: (1) decisions should be made at the lowest level possible; (2) the costs of the decision must be acceptable, and (3) savings or income from a decision must exceed its costs.

The steps in a logical and systematic decision-making process are:

1. Determine the purpose and objectives of the decision.
2. Place the objectives in order of priority.
3. Identify alternative courses of action.
4. Weigh and compare the alternatives.
5. Make a tentative decision.
6. Assess the tentative decision.
7. Double check, then make a final decision.
8. Develop an action plan.
9. Implement the decision.
10. Follow up and evaluate results.

FOR FURTHER READING

Anderson, David, and others. *An Introduction to Management Science: Quantitative Approaches to Decision Making,* 4th ed. St. Paul, Minn.: West Publishing Company, 1985.

Basil, Douglas C. *Managerial Skills for Executive Action.* New York: AMACOM, 1970.

Behn, Robert D., and James W. Vaupel. "Quick Analysis: Analytical Thinking for Busy Decision Makers." *Management Review,* September 1983, pp. 8–13.

———. *Quick Analysis for Busy Decision Makers.* New York: Basic Books, 1982.

Chou, Ya-Lun. *Probability and Statistics for Decision-Making.* New York: Irvington Publications, 1982.

Cotton, John L. "Why Getting Additional Data Often Slows Down Decision Making—and What to Do About It." *Management Review,* May 1984, pp. 56–61.

Croucher, John S. *Operations Research: A First Course.* Elmsford, N.Y.: Pergamon Press, 1980.

Daggett, Willard, and Martin J. Marrazo. *Solving Problems, Making Decisions.* Cincinnati: South Western Publishing Company, 1983.

Deets, Norman, and Dr. Richard Morano. "Xerox's Strategy for Changing Management Styles." *Management Review,* March 1986, pp. 31–35.

"Getting a Handle on Decision-Making." *Training,* August 1985, p. 73.

Grove, Andrew S. "Decisions, Decisions . . . How High-Output Managers Reach Agreement in a Know-How Business." *Management Review,* December 1983, pp. 8–13.

Harvey, C.M. *Operations Research: An Introduction to Linear Optimization and Decision Analysis.* New York: Elsevier Science Publishing Company, 1979.

Hickson, David J. *Top Decisions: Strategic Decision-Making in Organizations.* San Francisco: Jossey-Bass, 1986.

Hill, Percy H., and others. *Making Decisions: A Multidisciplinary Introduction.* Reading, Mass.: Addison-Wesley Training Systems, 1979.

Huber, George P. *Managerial Decision Making.* Glenview, Ill.: Scott, Foresman, 1980.

Keegan, Warren J. *Making Judgments, Choices, and Decisions in Business: Effective Management Through Self-Knowledge.* New York: John Wiley & Sons, 1984.

Kepner, Charles H., and Benjamin B. Tregoe, "Decision-Making Training." In *Human Resources Management and Development Handbook,* edited by William R. Tracey. New York: AMACOM, 1985.

———. *The New Rational Manager.* Princeton, N.J.: Princeton Research Press, 1981.

Leigh, Andrew. *Decisions, Decisions: A Practical Guide to Problem Solving and Decision Making.* Brookfield, Vt.: Gower Publishing Company, 1984.

Lyles, Richard I. *Practical Management Problem Solving and Decision Making.* New York: Van Nostrand Reinhold, 1982.

McCall, Morgan W., Jr., and Robert E. Kaplan. *Whatever It Takes: Decision Makers at Work.* Greensboro, N.C.: Center for Creative Leadership, 1985.

Meltzer, Morton F. *Information, the Ultimate Management Resource: How to Find, Use, and Manage It.* New York: AMACOM, 1981.

Miller, Marc. "Practical Insight into DSS: Putting More Power Into Managerial Decisions." *Management Review,* September 1984, pp. 12–16.

Moody, P. E. *Decision-Making: Proven Methods for Better Decisions.* New York: McGraw-Hill, 1983

Moskowitz, H., and G. Wright. *Operations Research Techniques for Management.* Englewood Cliffs, N.J.: Prentice-Hall, Inc., 1979.

Murnighan, J. Keith. "Group Decision-Making: What Strategies Should You Use?" *Management Review,* February 1981, pp. 55–62.

Odiorne, George S. *Management Decisions by Objectives.* Englewood Cliffs, N.J.: Prentice-Hall, 1969.

Philip, Tom. *Improve Your Decision Making Skills.* New York: McGraw-Hill, 1985.

Rothenberg, Ronald J. *Linear Programming: A Problem Solving Approach.* New York: Elsevier Science Publications, 1980.

Rowan, Roy. *The Intuitive Manager.* Boston: Little, Brown, 1986.

Rudolph, Barbara. "Hailing the Eureka Factor.' *Time,* April 21, 1986, p. 65.

Swanson, Leonard W. *Linear Programming: Basic Theory and Applications.* New York: McGraw-Hill, 1979.

Taha, Haml A. *Operations Research,* 3rd ed. New York: Macmillan, 1982.

Taylor, Ronald N. *Behavioral Decision-Making* Glenview, Ill. Scott, Foresman, 1984.

Woolsey, Robert E., and Huntington S. Swan. *Operations Research for Immediate Application: A Quick and Dirty Manual.* New York: Harper & Row, 1975.

Zeleny, M. *Multiple Criteria Decision Making.* Del Mar, Calif.: McGraw-Hill Training Systems, 1981.

8

HIRING Matching People and Jobs

The process of finding new employees for your organization can be complicated, time consuming, and costly. Getting the right people for the right jobs while conforming to the law is a significant challenge. Competence in strategic planning or setting objectives, competitive salaries, innovative training programs, exemplary development plans, top-notch facilities, and state-of-the-art equipment have little value or effect on productivity unless you can hire the people who can transform those resources into results.

The hiring process is so important that it justifies as much time and effort as the HR manager can give to it. Even when the final hiring decision is made by another departmental manager, the HR professional will be a major participant in the screening and selection processes. HR managers should work with other managers and supervisors throughout the organization to ensure that effective procedures are established and followed. This will enable the organization to hire the right people and to make the best use of available personnel resources.

Selecting a person for a position involves a considerable financial investment. If the employee remains with the organization for a full career, the investment in salary alone may amount to $1 million or more. Even if the person leaves within a year or two, the investment is likely to amount to $50,000 or more (depending, of course, on the individual's salary). But the investment is also a human one. When people are employed, they are investing in their well-being and that of their families—and so is the organization.

To hire the right people, HR managers must master the skills and techniques needed to select high achievers—people with a proven track record for key positions and people with high potential for outstanding performance for lower-level positions. Lack of those skills and techniques will inevitably result in recycling hiring errors back into the overall worker pool—not to mention the costs associated with high turnover and the poor company image terminated employees can engender.

Employee recruitment and selection techniques must be sound, valid, reliable, and nondiscriminatory. They must also be fair and equitable, free of favoritism and irrelevancies, administratively manageable, and cost effective. Research has demonstrated a reasonable and consistently high correlation between hiring techniques used and on-the-job performance.

Hiring Misconceptions

Miscalculations, misinterpretations, and mistakes abound in organizations, the result of several prevalent misconceptions about employee selection. Too many managers believe that hiring strategies and techniques are of little importance because the best candidate will invariably get the job, no matter which process is used. They also believe that the best candidate will accept the first job offer and that he or she will cost the most money in salary. Others are naive enough to believe that the references supplied by candidates are usually reliable sources of information.

When advertising vacancies, some managers mistakenly believe that a blind ad will attract as well as an ad that uses the company name. When conducting employment interviews, there are many who believe that the best way to get a truthful and direct answer is to ask a direct question. Or that a stress interview is the best way to weed out weak candidates. In fact, however, all these beliefs are wrong—dead wrong.

Characteristics of the Hiring Process

A good selection system is:

- *Standardized.* Every applicant for a specific position goes through the same system; that is, the same number and types of interviews, tests, and the like.
- *Efficient.* It avoids unplanned duplication or overlap of information about applicants.
- *Comprehensive.* It evaluates all factors required for success on the job.
- *Marked by clear decision points.* It consists of a series of go/no-go hurdles.
- *Cost effective.* The results obtained are worth the investment.

The hiring process includes several elements, all critically important to success in matching jobs and people.

- Formulating job descriptions and applicant specifications.
- Designing application forms and interviewer evaluation forms.
- Constructing or selecting tests and other forms of evaluation instruments.
- Preparing advertisements for position vacancies.
- Administering and interpreting tests.
- Conducting employment interviews.
- Using group selection procedures such as assessment centers.
- Making reference checks.
- Arranging for medical examinations.
- Evaluating candidates and making the hiring decision.
- Assigning, orienting, and training the new employee.
- Following up.

Selection and the Law

The entire selection process must be in compliance with Title VII of the Civil Rights Act of 1964 as amended, the EEO Commission's *Uniform Guidelines on Employee Selection Procedures* (1978), and state and local regulations on employee selection. That means that your screening and selection instruments and procedures must be unassailable from the standpoints of legality and nondiscrimination. Use the wrong procedures, or ask the wrong questions, and you can be sued! For example, probing into the wrong areas by asking questions relating to religion, age, sex, marital or family status, physical handicaps, criminal record, or financial status are grounds for charges of discrimination.

Today a growing number of legal problems surrounds the hiring and firing of employees. Labor, civil rights, and other employee safety and welfare laws, and the tendency of the courts to side with employees, are restricting the right of employers to discharge employees without running the risk of legal liability.

HR managers must give special attention to several items with the potential to evoke charges of implied contracts and the venerable "employment at will" principle. These include oral statements during or following employment interviews, employment correspondence, application forms, and salary and benefits statements. HR managers would do well to determine the potential for litigation of company documents and hiring practices, including having them reviewed by legal counsel.

Recruitment Procedures

Recruiting procedures and advertisements must be analyzed to identify and avoid or eliminate discriminatory practices and content. Recruitment sources must be notified that your organization actively seeks women, minorities, and the handicapped to fill vacancies. All vacancies must be openly advertised both internally and externally. Women and minorities should be included on all search and recruiting teams.

Advertisements must include statements that the organization is an equal opportunity employer and that members of minority groups are encouraged to apply. They do not refer to the gender of applicants unless sex is a bona fide occupational qualification (BFOQ). They do not specify age except to indicate the mandatory retirement age under existing laws or unless there is a legitimate BFOQ or statutory exception. They must not use discriminatory terms or expressions or specify attributes or qualities that tend to favor one gender or any other category.

Screening and Selection Procedures

Preemployment inquiries are made with care and thorough planning. Whether directed to prospective employees or their current or past employers, inquiries must avoid discriminatory questions. Questions relating to age, race, color, national origin, language fluency, disabilities, educational level, financial situation, arrest or criminal records, military service, affiliations, or religion are avoided in application forms and correspondence or are phrased in such a way that discrimination cannot be inferred.

Screening and selection procedures, instruments, forms, and standards are based on position descriptions and advertised selection criteria. All position descriptions and applicant specifications are reviewed to guard against inadvertent discrimination against women, minorities, and the handicapped. Standards of physical, mental, emotional, character, educational, experiential, marital or parental, financial, or other personal characteristics used to measure an applicant's suitability for a position must not disproportionately affect the employment prospects of any race, sex, or ethnic group.

Tests and Other Evaluative Instruments

Tests, scored interviews, personal history forms, ratings, and other evaluative instruments used in screening and selection must not discriminate against minorities, women, or the handicapped. They must be professionally developed and validated unless there is empirical evidence that they (1) do not screen out minorities disproportionately; (2) measure specific skills that are related to job performance; (3) have pass-fail rates for minorities and women that are comparable or equivalent for all groups of applicants; and (4) are objective tests of skills. They must be available in forms designed for persons with impaired sensory, motor, or speaking skills; they must be selected and administered in a manner that ensures that the applicant's impaired sensory, motor, or speaking skills are not reflected (unless those are the factors the test purports to measure); and they must be administered in facilities accessible to the handicapped.

Further information on testing appears later in this chapter.

Records

Applicant records are maintained to analyze, monitor, and report recruiting activities and procedures. In addition to completed application forms and résumés, completed candidate evaluation forms, and the results of tests and other screening devices, these records contain the referral source of each applicant, the position applied for and the date of the application, whether or not a job offer was made, which job was offered and why, whether the applicant accepted or rejected the job offered and why, and the name and title of the individual making the employment decision.

For tests and other scored evaluations used in screening and selection, the following records must be maintained: (1) statistical data, indexes, and graphics demonstrating the relationship between the instruments and job performance; (2) mean, median, and modal scores on the instrument for all relevant company subgroups, by sex, minority, and nonminority groups; (3) cutoff or minimum qualifying scores for each test or measure; and (4) the names of test or instrument administrators, scorers, and evaluators, together with the dates of each action, for each measure applied.

Records of all interviews must be filed. They should contain the following information: (1) the name of the candidate; (2) the title of the position; (3) the date of the interview; (4) the identity of the recruitment source; (5) the tests or other instruments administered and scores; (5) the ratings and comments of the interviewer; (6) the date of hire or the reasons for nonselection; and (7) the name and title of the interviewer.

Recruitment

Recruitment is the process of matching job descriptions and applicant specifications with people. That means that the manager who undertakes recruitment, screening, and selection must have a clear understanding of the position to be filled, including future changes in that position, and the skills, capacities, and personality requirements of candidates.

Recruitment is much more than evaluating and hiring new employees or promoting and assigning current employees to new positions. It involves job analysis, attracting suitable applicants, assessing current skills and potential, making employment decisions, assigning duties and authority, orienting and training, and following up.

Forms of Recruitment

Position vacancies can be filled by either internal or external recruitment and selection. Both have a place in the organizational scheme of things.

Internal

Internal recruitment is the process of attracting and screening current employees for promotion or assignment to vacant positions in the organization. It is very important to both the organization and its employees to make use of internal recruitment whenever possible to achieve the following objectives:

- To make full use of the talents and potential of current employees.
- To provide incentives for current employees and opportunities for advancement and career development.
- To reward and retain good people.

Internal recruitment involves use of any or all of the following: self-nominations by employees, employee referrals (friends and relatives), nominations by managers and supervisors, and in-house advertisements or job posting.

External

External recruitment is the process of seeking applicants for openings from outside the organization. It is used to serve the following purposes:

- To obtain the services of people with skills, knowledge, and experience needed by the organization but currently unavailable in-house.
- To ensure an adequate and continuing supply of new employees to meet expansion or diversification requirements.

External sources of applicants include walk-ins, direct mail (using association lists or the directories of professional organizations), telephone recruitment or sourcing (calling qualified individuals), college recruitment, advertisements, public and private employment agencies, and executive search specialists (headhunters).

Recruiting Objectives

Regardless of the source of candidates for vacant positions, hiring objectives must be based on a carefully developed personnel planning system that, in turn, is based on organization forecasts, goals, and objectives. That system must establish recruitment levels by anticipating staffing requirements. To develop accurate personnel recruitment objectives, certain records and statistics must be maintained:

1. Forecasts of workforce trends likely to affect plans; for example, job changes, salary adjustments, and demographic shifts such as in age, sex, or skills.
2. Technology forecasts that may affect jobs and skill requirements.
3. A list of future vacancies reflecting corporate goals and plans and employee turnover; for example, resignations, dismissals, promotions, transfers, retirements, deaths, and leaves of absence.
4. A list of people, classified by types of positions, with potential for advancement.

Advertisements

To be effective, advertisement of position vacancies must reach the target audience, produce an adequate number of qualified replies, minimize the number of unqualified respondents, and enhance the image of the organization. They can be placed in company publications, on bulletin boards, and in trade and professional journals and newspapers.

Advertisements may be any one of four types:

1. Classified (appear in the classified section of the newspaper or magazine);
2. Display (appear in the display section, usually include artwork, and may run wider than the standard column);
3. Blind (may be either classified or display, do not identify the company, and use a newspaper or magazine box number or P.O. box number for replies);
4. Open (may be either classified or display but do reveal the company name)

Regardless of the medium used, ads should be a synopsis of the job description, written and printed in a format and layout designed to attract suitable candidates. To do that, ads must be informative, comprehensive but brief, logical and understandable, relevant to the people to whom they are addressed, and nondiscriminatory. It's better not to use blind ads; identify your company.

An effective ad:

- Captures the reader's attention by clearly identifying the target respondents and providing an incentive to read further.
- Arouses interest in the organization and the position by describing what the organization does, its size, structure, and products or services, and its achievements and prospects.
- Describes the position by title and hierarchical placement (the position to which the job incumbent reports), major duties and authority, career ladder, salary range and benefits, and training and development opportunities.
- Describes position requirements in terms of qualifications—education, training, experience, skills, and personal traits.
- Stimulates the reader to take immediate action to apply—to write or phone for an application form and early interview.

Documents for Screening and Selection

The processes of screening applicants and selecting employees from among candidates require selecting or developing and using several important documents and forms.

Job Descriptions

The HR manager needs to have a written job description for every position. A job description is a means of defining the duties, functions, and authority assigned to a position. As a minimum, each job description should specify the functions and major duties of the job, scope of authority, the relationships between the position and other positions in the particular department, and, when appropriate, the relationship of the job to positions in other departments. Every HR manager needs position descriptions to inform job applicants, incumbents, and others what they are expected to do and what they will be held accountable for doing.

An effective job description:

- States why a job exists—its basic purpose or function.
- Is based on detailed job analysis conducted, when possible, by observation and interview of job incumbents.
- Defines the scope and nature of the work to be done by indicating relationships, such as "reports to the HR manager" or "as directed by the instructor supervisor."
- Uses precise terms to describe the work, its complexity, the skills required, and the amount of authority to be delegated to the incumbent.

○ Describes duties in terms of results rather than processes.
○ Defines *what* is to be done, not *how* or *how well* it is to be done.
○ Identifies clearly the functions and duties performed by the incumbent.

Applicant Specifications

For each job description there must be a corresponding set of applicant specifications. In general terms, applicant specifications describe the education and training, experience, skills, personality, and other qualifications needed for success in a particular job. Put another way, applicant specifications describe what an applicant for a particular position should *know* (the technical, professional, and managerial knowledge needed), what the candidate should be able to *do* (the technical, professional, and managerial skills required), and what the applicant should *be* (the personal qualities, educational background, and kind and amount of experience sought).

An effective set of applicant specifications contains the following:

○ The title of the position and its location within its department.
○ A description of principal job functions and major duties.
○ The kind and amount of authority the incumbent will be delegated.
○ Personal specifications:

Type and level of education.
Kind and amount of experience.
Skills and abilities essential to success on the job.
Temperament and personality demanded by the job, in straightforward, nonpsychological terms.

○ Identity of positions to which incumbents can aspire.
○ Salary range and benefits, including training and development opportunities.

It is also useful to identify three categories of information under each heading:

1. Essential (must have for satisfactory job performance).
2. Desirable (nice to have in addition to essential factors).
3. Exclusory (a basis for automatic rejection).

Application Forms

Well-designed application forms are essential to the process of screening, interviewing, and selecting employees. They also become an important part of an employee's permanent personnel record, and they are useful documents when developing a future vacancies file and performing workforce market analysis and planning.

A good application form:

- Is clear and concise; simple, but not superficial.
- Uses appropriate format, layout, and type styles.
- Is tailored or adapted to specific categories of positions.
- Is easy for applicants to complete and for interviewers to review.
- Has adequate space for responding to questions.
- Uses suitable paper stock, durable and color-coded by position classification.
- Is designed to be an aid to the interviewer; provides space for interviewer's notes.
- Groups identifying information, personal items, and education and experience items together.
- Asks only for information needed for selection and not for other purposes.
- Contains a disclaimer with respect to its status as a noncontractual document.
- Avoids projective-type, personality assessment items.
- Has been tested before regular use.

Résumés

Résumés submitted by applicants for positions are valuable sources of information for two different but closely related hiring activities: initial screening and preparation for the employment interview. Review of résumés can prevent the enormous waste of time that occurs when people who are obviously unsuited or unqualified for a position are interviewed. Where an interview is indicated by the review, careful scrutiny of the document will provide leads for questions during the interview to elicit information of great value. However, the HR manager must remember that the résumé is designed to put the best possible face on the candidate and his or her credentials. They often exaggerate education, experience, skills, and other employment considerations.

Tests and Ratings

Tests are simply samples of performance taken under standardized conditions. They are used to measure knowledge, skills, abilities, aptitudes, interests, and personality. Other types of evaluative instruments are rating scales and standard interview forms. Rating scales are used to transform observations of personal characteristics, behavior, or performance into objective evaluations. The interview will be discussed separately in a later section of this chapter.

To the maximum extent possible, tests and other evaluative devices used in screening and selecting personnel should meet certain standards:

- Validity. An instrument is valid to the extent that it measures what it is supposed to measure.
- Reliability. An instrument is reliable when it yields consistent results.
- Objectivity. An instrument is objective when the judgment or bias of the rater or scorer is eliminated.
- Nondiscrimination. An instrument is nondiscriminatory when it does not disadvantage persons of a certain age group, sex, race, creed, or color, or the physically, mentally, or emotionally disabled.
- Administrability. An instrument is administrable when it can be given with relative ease and with excellent potential for communicating to the subject and the administrator what is to be done.
- Standardization. An instrument is standard when a systematic sample of performance has been obtained under prescribed conditions and scored according to definite rules.
- Comprehensiveness. An instrument is comprehensive when it takes liberal samples from whatever it is measuring.
- Economy. An instrument is economical when a minimum of time, equipment, materials, and personnel is required to administer and score it.

Psychological Tests

In the 1960s and 1970s, many companies stopped using psychological tests as screening and selection instruments because they were afraid of discrimination suits. Today, more and more, larger organizations are returning to the use of quantitative procedures simply because they have the potential to improve their batting averages in hiring effective people.

Although it is true that tests are not cures for all staffing ills, or substitutes for good judgment, when selected wisely or developed expertly, when administered and analyzed properly, they can measure knowledge and skill, identify aptitudes, predict job performance, and analyze temperament and personality. Continuing attacks on them notwithstanding, tests and inventories, when used in conjunction with other screening and selection techniques, can and do contribute to effective screening and selection for jobs.

When tests are used to evaluate knowledge or skill, the major concern is that the competencies measured by the test are similar to those required by the job, and that the test can be proved to have predictive validity. The latter is a major factor in meeting the requirements of equal opportunity laws and standards. That is, tests must be nondiscriminatory.

When test results are used to predict job performance, there must be statistical proof of the relationship between test scores and success on the job. When used to assess temperament or personality, test results must be supplemented by professional psychological appraisal by a clinical psychologist or psychiatrist, involving in-depth interviews, study of background information, self-reports, and records.

To avoid litigation or charges of discrimination, the HR manager must ensure that tests used for screening, selection, and promotion are specifically related to job performance requirements, fair and reasonable in their contents and requirements, administered in good faith and without discrimination to determine aptitudes and abilities, and properly interpreted by qualified personnel. In addition, tests must be demonstrably valid (measure and predict what they purport to measure and predict—the ability to learn and perform a specific job); they must be reliable (measure the same thing consistently); they must not discriminate against any group, minority or otherwise.

Tests are commonly used to measure general mental ability (intelligence or scholastic aptitude); specific mental abilities (such as deductive, inductive, and spatial reasoning); specific information, job knowledge, and trade knowledge; mechanical aptitude and psychomotor skills; supervisory and managerial abilities; interests; and personality and temperament.

Because no single test is a perfect selector, test batteries are commonly used to evaluate applicants for positions. However, you must also remember that tests can measure only what an applicant *can* do, not what he or she *will* do; that tests have a large margin of error, sometimes as much as plus or minus 10 points from the actual score; and that tests alone are not very accurate predictors of job success.

The selection, administration, scoring, and interpretation of tests is a time-consuming and expensive process. Training, skill, and experience are necessary for proper test interpretation, but the results are often worth the investment.

The keys to maximizing the value of tests in the screening and selection process are:

- Develop accurate job descriptions and applicant specifications to define the target population clearly and precisely.
- Use tests only as a supplement to other means of collecting information about job applicants.
- Know *why* you are using a test and make this clear to all applicants.
- Use caution in interpreting all test results, particularly the results of personality measures.
- Feed back the results of tests to each applicant.

Ratings

Ratings (that is, evaluating people's traits and performances through observation and judgment) may be adjectival or numerical. They may be based on judgments made with or without a scale that describes behavior at several levels. They are easy to administer and score, and they are very reliable, as long as five or more raters evaluate the behavior, performance, or trait and the ratings are averaged. Rating scales have the following limitations: (1) individual ratings typically have low reliability; (2) rating scales are difficult to construct; (3) raters require training in their use; and (4) rating procedures are time consuming and therefore expensive.

There are two classes of rating methods: relative and absolute. Relative methods are frequently used in selection because they compare the performance or traits of two or more persons. No attempt is made to assign meaningful values. Although relative rating methods include rank order, paired comparisons, and equal intervals, rank order is the most common approach.

Absolute methods of rating require the rater to assign an absolute value to the trait or performance being measured without any reference to the traits or performance of any other candidate. Four types of absolute rating scales are used in selection: numerical, descriptive, graphic, and checklists.

For management positions, the following dimensions of behavior are typically included in rating forms or other means of screening and selecting personnel: analytical/problem-solving ability, judgment, decisiveness, planning ability, delegation, independence, stress tolerance, leadership, initiative, motivation and personal drive, creativity, writing ability, speaking ability, and sociability.

Medical Screening

Pre-employment medical examinations should be used primarily to make the best use of all employees by placing them in suitable positions, jobs where they can make the maximum contribution to the organization and at the same time obtain job satisfaction. There is also a "protective" element to medical examinations. They are used to reduce absenteeism and turnover, avoid workmen's compensation and other claims against the organization, make needed adjustments to the work area or the work schedule of the new employee, safeguard the health and safety of the employee, other employees, clients, and customers, and identify substance abusers before they are hired. Typically, particular attention is paid to such vulnerable groups as the very young and very old, the physically disabled, the emotionally and psychologically handicapped, epileptics, diabetics, people with cardiac conditions, and the hearing deficient and visually impaired.

Recently, a great deal of controversy has arisen over proposals or actions to screen prospective or current employees for AIDS (acquired immune deficiency syndrome) or ARC (AIDS-related complex). Pressures are being brought to bear on management by workers who fear that working with people with AIDS or ARC constitutes a risk of infection, despite widely publicized statements from the Centers for Disease Control and other medical experts that there is no evidence that the virus can be tansmitted by casual contact. In addition, the potential magnitude of the AIDS epidemic and the anticipated cost of treatment raise serious questions about the ability of company health insurance plans to cover the increased disability costs.

More and more information about the medical, legal, insurance, and management aspects of the AIDS question becomes available daily. The HR manager would do well to obtain the advice of knowledgeable legal and medical counsel before taking any action with respect to the illness.

Self-Reports

Biographical information has proved to be a good source of data on which to base a prediction of success in instructional, supervisory, and management positions. Essentially, self-reports are personal histories or inventories of biographical information that have been systematically designed and statistically validated in much the same way as psychological tests. Although the ways in which properly constructed and validated biographical inventories can be used are probably numerous, it is important for the HR manager to remember that the inventory must be tailormade for each position.

Interviewer Evaluation Forms

Forms used by interviewers during the selection process must be constructed to facilitate fair and objective evaluation of candidates and, at the same time, be easy to use. A rating scale-type form best serves those purposes. The form should employ an odd-numbered scale, say 1 to 5, for each item to be evaluated, and it should provide adequate space for the interviewer's comments.

Items typically evaluated include physical appearance and manner; experience, in terms of kind, amount, and relevance; education, general and specialized; intelligence, as revealed by responses to questions, ideas, career goals, and sense of purpose; special aptitudes, such as technical or mechanical; skills, such as course development, instructional, writing, or speaking; interests and activities, in terms of breadth, depth, type, and job relevance; motivation, disposition, and personality, such as dependability, persistence, sociability, and self-confidence; and overall assessment. The form should of course also include identifying information—name of applicant, position for which he or she is applying, interview date, and signature of the interviewer.

The Interview

Although its specific purpose, form, or content may differ, the interview is basically a means of collecting information directly from others in face-to-face contacts. In hiring, the personal interview is the heart of the process. The screening devices discussed earlier should weed out the obvious nonemployables or nonpromotables. The interview can focus on a shortened list of candidates that should yield the most promising applicant.

Interviews are *always* necessary to (1) pass information about the organization and the job to the candidate; (2) assess characteristics that can only be evaluated in face-to-face contacts; (3) obtain information that candidates are not likely to put in writing; (4) draw out information, follow up on leads and take advantage of small clues, including nonverbal ones, that would be impossible to get any other way; (5) form an impression of the candidate, make judgments, and gauge the truth of statements and answers to questions; (6) meet the candidate's expectation for personal contact with prospective employers; and (7) validate the results obtained by other means of screening.

However, the interview has limitations. Among the most important are:

1. Costs. The interview takes a considerable amount of time for planning, development, and actual conduct.
2. Danger of distortion. The candidate may have a faulty memory, may distort reports unconsciously, or may deliberately mislead the interviewer.
3. Lack of relevance. Information obtained by interview often contains much unrelated and therefore useless information.
4. Interviewer faults. Deficiencies in the interviewer's qualifications, background, personal values, perceptions, training, or experience can lead to an inadequate interview.

The reliability of the data collected in the interview and the quality of the judgments reached depend on the skill of the interviewer. Interviewer biases and prejudices, likes and dislikes, and value judgments often get in the way of the facts. The tendency to talk too much and listen too little is another common fault. In addition, the typical guard-up posture of the interviewee, as well as his or her lapses in memory and tendency to screen information and even to deceive or distort, often make the interview ineffective.

The validity of an interview is governed by how relevant the questions are to the purpose of the interview but even more by how relevant the candidate's responses are. To make sure the responses are on target, do a preliminary tryout of structured interview materials with representatives of typical candidates. The results of that trial should prove whether the questions are clear, whether their implications are understood, whether they are concerned with items that are reasonably stable and important, and whether the information collected is consistent with data collected by other means.

Types of Interviews

Two types of interviews are commonly done to obtain additional facts about candidates for positions: standardized or directive and nonstandardized or nondirective.

Standardized or directive. This form of interview is the one most commonly used in hiring, simply because it is important to collect the same information from each candidate. That being true, the answers of all interviewees to all questions must be comparable and classifiable; that is, they must deal with exactly the same subject matter. Differences between responses must reflect actual differences between candidates and not differences that can be attributed to the questions they were asked or the meanings they attach to the questions.

Standardization is achieved by either reading the questions from a prepared schedule or by thoroughly briefing the interviewer on what information is required and then allowing him or her to vary the wording and the sequence of the questions to achieve maximum informality and effectiveness with individual candidates.

A standard interview schedule:

- Includes a clear introductory statement of the purpose and ground rules.
- Deals with items that the candidate is likely to feel are important.
- Avoids trivial and irrelevant questions and unnecessary detail.
- Employs clear and unambiguous questions.
- Avoids leading questions but encourages the candidate to be specific without forcing definiteness where it is inappropriate.
- Uses questions that elicit responses of sufficient depth to be useful.
- Avoids questions that are embarrassing, tricky, or illegal.

Nonstandardized or nondirective. With this type of interview, little or no attempt is made to direct the candidate's conversation. The interviewer simply listens carefully and occasionally comments in ways that encourage the applicant to talk freely about any subject of interest.

Those who prefer this type of interview claim that (1) it puts the applicant at ease; (2) because the candidate chooses the subjects, it reveals his or her true interests; (3) information tends to be more reliable because the candidate is unable to judge what evaluation is made of his or her comments.

Interview Formats

In terms of format, there are three types of selection interview: (1) individual interviews conducted by two or more managers sequentially and independently; (2) group interviews conducted by two to five managers simultaneously; and (3) stress interviews, which may be conducted either individually or by a group of managers. Group interviews and stress interviews have legitimate applications and their share of advocates. However, individual interviews, followed by pooled judgments, provide the soundest basis for hiring decisions. The stress interview, in which the interviewers speak, behave, and question the candidate provocatively, is of doubtful value, particularly if the position to be filled is in the HR department itself.

Being a Good Interviewer

The following procedures should be used in preparing for and conducting a selection interview. In addition, a review of the listening techniques outlined in Chapter 1 may be helpful.

Preparation

Determine the purpose and objectives of the interview. Know specifically what you are trying to find out. Study the interview schedule so that you won't have to read every question to achieve standardization. Do some preinterview profiling; find out as much as you can about the applicant by studying the completed application form, and, if available, the résumé. If the applicant is currently an employee in your organization, do some discreet checking with the current supervisor and fellow workers, and review records of performance and work history.

Develop a plan for conducting the interview. Select topics and frame questions to unravel items that are unclear, fill in holes in information, and the like. If they are available, study test results and reports of earlier interviews for other jobs (not the one for which the person is currently applying). Set up an appointment at a mutually convenient time, and allow enough time for discussion. Choose a place that is private, pleasant, comfortable, reasonably quiet, and free from distractions and interruptions.

Conducting the Interview

All your advance preparations should go a long way toward achieving the objective of collecting the information you need for a hiring decision. But there are still some critically important things to do to ensure success.

Opening

It is important to get the interview off to a good start. To accomplish that, courtesy, concern for the applicant, informality, and rapport are essential. The traits of the skillful interviewer are a positive attitude, empathy with the candidate, objectivity, and self-confidence.

Establishing rapport. Observe the usual amenities. Stand up, get out from behind your desk, greet candidates warmly, meet them halfway between your desk and the door, introduce yourself, shake hands, and invite the person to be seated. If possible, conduct the interview in comfortable chairs facing each other, without a desk in between.

Explain the purpose of the interview, how you plan to proceed with it, and how the results of the interview will be used. Invite questions about the procedure. Make it clear that applicants can say whatever they want without waiting for questions. Put candidates at ease. Try to establish a friendly, cooperative relationship before getting to the task at hand.

Questioning. Begin with questions that are easy to answer and that are not in any way emotionally loaded. Avoid questions that can be answered *yes* or *no*. Use open-ended questions that permit the candidate some leeway in composing the answer. Don't ask double-headed questions. Ask only one question at a time. Make every question and answer count.

Try to learn more about applicants' work history and background than are included in the application form or the résumé. Ask for opinions and judgments. Use hypothetical situations and ask how they would handle them. Encourage applicants to offer ideas on how the job would be done, what the priorities would be, and what problems are anticipated.

Use follow-up questions to clarify responses. Don't use leading questions, such as "I assume that . . ." or "Presumably . . ." or "I expect that . . ." The form of the questions suggests the answers.

Avoid illegal, discriminatory questions. For example, do not use questions about sex, family, marital status, religion, age, race, national origin, or veteran's status. Do not ask, "Do you have children?" "How do you plan to avoid absence from the job when your children are ill?" "Are you married?" "Is your wife (husband) employed?" "Have you ever been arrested?" "What is your nationality?" "Do you (or have you ever) belong(ed) to any social clubs, fraternities, or sororities?" "Do you attend religious services on Saturdays or Sundays? "Are you a World War II (Korean or Vietnam) veteran?" "Do you own your own home?" Don't ask for *any* information from minority or female applicants not routinely asked of white or male applicants.

Construct and deliver your questions to elicit responses that can help you determine "will he or she do it?" and not just "can he or she do it?" Develop questions that will draw out information, and that will encourage truthful responses. Be assertive but not aggressive. Encourage candidates to reveal more information by pausing before responding to comments.

Let the candidates talk. Encourage them to feel free to express themselves. Phrase your responses briefly. "Tell me more." "That's interesting." "What were the circumstances?" "What happened then?" "I see." Other suggestions are listed in Figure 8-1.

Above all, don't dominate. Avoid evidences of pressure, boredom, or irritation. Deal with applicants in a sincere, forthright manner. Don't be pedantic, and don't try to be clever. Give candidates an opportunity to clarify or qualify their answers. Avoid antagonizing, embarrassing, or hurrying them. Don't push ahead too rapidly, but don't dawdle.

Keep control. Don't allow applicants to go off on extended tangents. At the same time, be alert for leads. Encourage applicants to state their views completely. Allow them to show their talents and qualifications in relevant situations. Raise questions to elicit responses about areas not covered in their responses. Watch facial expressions, gestures, and casual remarks. Don't put applicants in situations where they must respond emotionally. Don't put them on the defensive. Don't rush them into giving off-the-cuff answers.

Prepare applicants for difficult or sensitive questions, such as those

Figure 8-1.   Interviewer responses to applicant comments.

TO ENCOURAGE THE APPLICANT TO CONTINUE:

I see.	I get what you're saying.
So you tend to . . .	You had a very hard . . .
In other words, you . . .	You find it satisfying to . . .
I understand.	You have to feel . . .

TO GET CLARIFICATION OF A STATEMENT:

Are you saying that . . .	If I understand you correctly . . .
I gather that you mean . . .	I'm not sure that I follow you, but . . .
You're saying that . . .	Let's see if I really understand that . . .
Is that it?	In other words, you would . . .
You mean that . . .	You are saying that . . .

---

pertaining to unexplained breaks in their work records. Preface the questions with such words as, "This may be a difficult question for you to answer, but it is important for a complete and accurate picture of your qualifications." Or, "Please bear with me while I explore this area a little further."

Don't fret about pauses in the conversation. Allow candidates time to overcome such difficulties as lapses in memory or concentration, finding the right word, or composing a response. Use silence to your advantage. Wait patiently for responses, but don't permit lengthy pauses.

Figure 8-2 lists key interview questions in several categories that are designed to get candidates to reveal important information.

Interpreting responses. Your assessment of a candidate should be based on several key areas: intelligence, skills, experience, abilities, accomplishments, attitudes, goals, motivation, personal drive, and personality. To do that you must listen actively as well as ask the questions that will reveal critical incidents, situations, and activities in the applicants' work life. Give applicants your undivided attention. Show interest by your responses, nods of the head, and facial expressions. Listen fully and completely. Don't interrupt, change the subject, challenge, or disagree.

Don't confuse voice, manner, appearance, or dress with intelligence, or some other job-related attribute. You are looking for clues to employability and emotional stability, cooperativeness, dependability, integrity, sociability, interest, attitudes, motivation, or leadership capacity. Observe what really exists. Don't allow selective perception, seeing what you expect or want to see and hearing what you want to hear, to get in the way of objective judgment. The way to do that is to (1) be aware of the phenomenon; (2) be tough-minded in probing to find answers to inconsistencies and anomalies; and (3) use factor-by-factor evaluation, not a global assessment of the candidate.

The task of making a fair hiring decision is one of avoiding prejudgments, biases, and stereotyping; listening to understand, rather than oppose; being alert for inaccuracies, inconsistencies, distortions, and falsification or dissembling; evaluating responses and supporting evidence; and withholding judgment until the interview is over. However, don't fail to check exaggerated claims of competence or to distinguish between skill and enthusiasm.

Providing information. Remember that an employment interview is not a one-way process. Candidates have every right to expect that information about the organization and the job for which they are applying will be furnished freely, completely, and accurately. The interviewer has the further obligation of being certain that the dimensions, requirements, challenges, and opportunities afforded by the position are fully described and that applicants are given the chance to ask questions.

Figure 8-2. Key interview questions.

Openers

How did you learn about this job vacancy?
What attracted you to our company?
What do you know about our organization?
Why are you applying for this position?
Why do you want to change jobs?
Why do you feel qualified for this position?

Education

How does your educational background qualify you for this job?
What was your major field of study and why did you choose it?
What subjects did you like best and why?
What subjects did you like least and why?
How would you describe your academic record?
Did your grades reflect your true ability? If not, why not?
What activities did you participate in while in school that have a bearing on the position for which you are applying?
What leadership positions did you hold while in school?

Experience

What experiences have you had that you feel qualify you for this job?
Can you describe a typical day in your present job?
What duties and tasks do you enjoy doing most? Least?
How many people do you supervise?
What aspect of the supervisory job do you like best? Least?
What aspect of supervision are you best at doing? Have the most difficulty performing?
What are your greatest (technical, professional, or managerial) strengths?
What are your most important (technical, professional, or managerial) limitations?
What was the biggest (job or professional) risk you ever took and how did it turn out?
What is the single accomplishment that you are proudest of?
What was your biggest professional failure or near miss? What were the consequences? Why did it happen?

Skills and Abilities

What are your top three job-related skills?
How competent do you feel about (e.g., conducting instruction, making a public speech, being interviewed by the media, presenting a briefing to top management, chairing a meeting of managers or supervisors, writing a proposal, designing a course)?

Figure 8-2, continued.

What do you consider to be the most important elements of a _____system?
What do you think it takes to be successful as a (trainer, course developer, technician, manager)?
How would you go about developing a _____system or _____program?
What process do you go through to make important or critical decisions?
If you were given the task of (marketing, designing, planning a _____), how would you go about it?
If you discovered that one of your subordinates was incompetent, what would you do?
What kind of recommendation do you think you present boss would give you?
Do you have any physical problems that might interfere with your ability to perform the job for which you are applying?
Are you willing to take a physical exam at our expense?

Motivation and Aspirations

Why did you get into the _____field?
What is the most potent motivator for you?
What in this field turns you off?
Where do you want to be professionally in three years? Five years?

Pay and Benefits

What is your current salary? What benefits do you receive?
What salary do you expect for this position? Benefits?
What is the minimum salary you will accept?
How much do you hope to be earning in two years? Five years?

Detecting deception. The skillful interviewer must use eyes and ears to uncover fabrication, deception, or exaggeration. Indications of those tactics include vagueness, generalizing, inconsistencies, equivocation, and irrelevancies. Visual signs of fabrication and deception include gestures, facial expressions, and body movements. Be particularly alert for blushing, contraction of the facial muscles, nervous laughter, squirming, blinking, or forced smiles. Watch out for gestures that do not complement or reinforce the candidates' words.

Interviewing the handicapped. Interviewing handicapped persons provides some special challenges. Obviously, the situation is extremely sensitive and tension-producing, probably for both parties. With a little thought, advance planning, and consideration by the interviewer, the situation can be handled. Here are some suggestions:[1]

1. Adapted from Ruth S. Bragman, "Interviewing the Handicapped Job Applicant," *Training and Development Journal*, October 1984, p. 10. Used by permission.

- Study the job description very carefully, paying particular attention to requirements as they pertain to the physical demands of the job itself and the work environment.
- Develop a file of information about specific and common handicapping conditions, the potential hazards to the individual, other workers, and equipment associated with them, and adjustments or accommodations that will ameliorate or eliminate the risk. Have the list checked by medical and legal consultants.
- Identify areas of potential difficulty for the position for people with specific disabilities.
- Attempt to match the job requirements with the individual's abilities.
- Develop job-related questions in advance of the interview.
- During the interview, attempt to match the applicant and the job, making accommodations as necessary.
- If the applicant is not hired, document the specific reasons for rejection.
- If the applicant is hired, document the job modifications needed to accommodate the person's handicap.

Interviewing members of minority groups. When interviewing members of any group, the most important thing is to communicate a sincere desire to treat people equally and to put them at ease. That is especially important with members of minority groups. Failure to succeed in achieving that objective will interfere with proper and objective evaluation of the candidate.

If a person is clearly not qualified for the position at hand, give him or her the straightforward reasons why and suggest other avenues to pursue. In any event, be informal, understanding, warm, and show concern for the applicant. Be sure to write up the interview report immediately and keep it on file. It is important to maintain records to protect the organization against "burden of proof" in the event of a charge of discrimination, an investigation, or a lawsuit.

Closing the Interview

Although interviews should not be rushed, they should be terminated when all the information required by both parties has been shared. The interview should be closed by the interviewer. First, give candidates another opportunity to ask questions. Then, briefly summarize the actions to be taken by the organization. Tell candidates approximately when and how they will be informed of the decision. Don't promise what you can't deliver. The interview should end with the usual courtesies—a sincere thank you for applying for the position, accompanied by a warm smile and a handshake.

Making Reference Checks

Inadequate reference checking is one of the major causes of poor hiring decisions. In recent years there have been many cases of misrepresentation, even outright falsehoods, in application forms, résumés, and interviews—claims of academic degrees and military and civilian experience and training that were discovered to be out-and-out lies after the individual was hired.

Reference checks are made to confirm or validate information obtained by other elements of the selection system, and to gather other information not provided by the system. They are used to check an applicant's character and habits and to follow up leads obtained during interviews or from other elements of the selection system. Reference checks are vital to successful hiring.

Reference checks should be made near the end of the selection process. When done properly, they serve a critical function whether they involve the applicant's past employers or educational institutions. The more recent the references, the better they serve as sources of information that are predictors of behavior in the new position. Obviously, they should be people who have observed the applicant in situations similar to the job at hand, preferably the immediate supervisor. It is usually advisable to first get a signed form from the applicant permitting inquiries to be made to reference sources.

There are three methods of making reference checks:

1. By mail. To confirm basic facts, such as dates of employment, positions held, reasons for termination, and, by means of checklists, evaluation of personal traits and performance. Or, in the case of schools and colleges, confirmation of attendance, graduation, and degrees or certificates granted.
2. By phone. In addition to basic factual data, detailed information about the candidate's work, job performance, strengths and weaknesses, examples of behavior, and relationships with superiors, subordinates, and associates.
3. By face-to-face contacts with people listed on application forms as well as individuals identified through the candidate's associates and superiors. Basic factual data and information in depth about the candidate's performance, personal qualities, strengths and limitations, behavior, accomplishments, and relationships.

Other Selection Techniques

Two other valuable selection techniques are visits and observation and assessment centers.

Visits and Observation

When selecting a senior supervisor or manager, or when considering a trained teacher for a position in the training element of the HR department, the HR manager should visit candidates on their home ground to discuss their candidacy and to observe them in action. Of course, such visits should be coordinated with the candidates well in advance. When an instructor position is to be filled, the observation visit is most important. Although it is true that an hour's observation of an instructor in action cannot provide complete information on competence, it does provide insights unavailable by any other means.

If the successful applicant will be involved in the development of instructional materials or the design of instructional systems, an examination of work products is very useful. Course developers, technical writers, artists, and illustrators fall into this category. Samples of their work products must be reviewed before hiring.

Assessment Centers

Assessment centers are typically used to select people for executive, managerial, or supervisory positions. Basically, the approach is a structured method of identifying the potential of individuals for success in specific kinds of jobs. It differs from other types of screening and selection techniques in that it processes several individuals at the same time.

Although assessment schemes differ markedly in objectives, dimensions assessed, length, staffing, and costs, the general approach is always the same. The process works like this. Applicants for position vacancies, including current employees either nominated by their supervisors or self-nominated, undergo assessment in a group. Over a period of two or three days, and under the direction of a team of trained and qualified evaluators, participants deal with a variety of realistic management problems and situations. They engage in simulations and business games, in-basket exercises, role playing, and decision-making exercises; they undergo psychological tests and projective techniques; and they engage in group discussions and self-evaluation. Observers/evaluators assess and record participants' behavior and performance, critique group exercises, interview participants, and combine their appraisals into a formal report.

Like any other screening and selection technique, assessment center results must be of proven validity in terms of prediction of job performance, and they must be nondiscriminatory. Probably the biggest problem with the technique, however, is cost. Nonetheless, assessment centers have great promise for making the executive screening and selection process more objective and more reliable.

Making the Hiring Decision

Don't decide too quickly that a person is not right for the job. The decision to hire or to reject a candidate must be made on the basis of an assessment of all the objective evidence collected during the entire screening and selection process—application forms, résumés, test results, review of records, ratings, employment and reference checks, and employment interviews.

Basically, there are two approaches to the hiring decision:

1. Clinical approach. The decision maker reviews all data and, on the basis of knowledge of the job and the applicants, makes the hiring decision.
2. Statistical approach. This involves identifying the best predictors of job success and weighting them through statistical methods.[2]

To the maximum extent possible, subjective evaluation, biases, hunches, and intuition should be kept out of the decision. The best way to do that is to have a group discussion of each candidate's credentials and performance by a small group of people who had ample opportunity to review the evidence and interview the candidates. Nevertheless, the final decision should be made by the manager to whom the new employee will report.

Here are a few final cautions. Be sure that (1) the individual selected is qualified (but not overqualified) for the position (an overqualified person is likely to become bored and nonproductive); (2) the applicant has the right skills for the job; and (3) job requirements are relatively stable and not subject to radical change in the immediate future.

And two remaining actions: (1) make the job offer to the successful candidate, and (2) notify *all* applicants of the hiring decision by phone call or letter.

Maintaining Records

It is important that records pertaining to all personnel actions be retained for at least one year from the date of the action. That includes (1) job applications, résumés, and any other form of employment inquiry or response when submitted to your company in response to an advertisement or other notice of an existing or anticipated job vacancy; (2) records pertaining to failure or refusal to hire an individual; (3) records of

2. For a brief discussion of both approaches, see Herbert J. Cruden and Arthur W. Sherman, Jr., *Managing Human Resources* 7th ed. (Cincinnati: South-Western Publishing Company, 1984), 163–165.

promotion, transfer, selection for training, layoff, recall, or discharge; (4) job orders for recruitment by an employment agency; (5) test papers showing the results of company-administered aptitude or other tests considered in connection with any personnel action; (6) results of physical examinations given in connection with any personnel action; and (7) ads or notices to the general public or to employees relating to job vacancies, promotions, or training programs.

Following Up

Good follow-up can make the assimilation of newly hired personnel as smooth as possible by orienting them to the organization and the job, following their progress during the early months of their affiliation, and reviewing the effectiveness of the selection process.

An effective orientation program can go a long way toward developing loyal, effective, and productive workers, developing favorable attitudes toward the company, its policies, and its personnel, engendering a feeling of acceptance and belonging, and generating enthusiasm, high morale, and job satisfaction among new employees. In terms of content, the orientation and induction program should include an overview of the organization and its mission, organization of the company and the department, functions of major organizational elements, compensation and benefits, and company policies, rules, and regulations.

In addition, a workplace induction program, conducted by the new employee's immediate superior, will ensure quick and easy assimilation into the workforce. Such a program should include a welcome to the work area, review of rules and regulations, tour of the work area, introductions to co-workers and key personnel, and ample opportunity to ask questions.

Summary

Hiring a new employee is important to the viability of an organization and to the success of the HR manager. Hiring mistakes are costly and must be avoided. The way to avoid them is to have a systematic personnel search, screening, and selection program.

A well-designed selection system is based on organization goals and objectives, staffing forecasts, personnel and skills inventories, projections of position vacancies, and detailed job descriptions and applicant specifications for all jobs to be filled. Application forms are tailored to major categories of jobs. They are complete, and conform with EEO statutes and regulations.

Nominations and applications are used to eliminate obviously unqualified applicants. If tests are used, they are administered and interpreted by fully qualified personnel. Interviews are conducted to collect information about each candidate's qualifications and to provide information about the job and the organization.

Assessment centers may be used to screen and select top managers. Physical examinations are used primarily for assignment unless the results are clearly disqualifying for the job at hand. Reference checks are made for all candidates in the final stages of the selection process. All information is synthesized, reviewed, evaluated, and interpreted in terms of the whole person with due consideration for a proper balance of strengths and weaknesses. All recruitment, screening, and selection documents, forms, and data are filed.

The relative ranking of candidates is established on the basis of ability and fitness for the position. The final hiring decision is made by the manager to whom the new employee will report, based on the recommendations of a selection committee, all of whose members were involved in the screening and selection process.

The successful candidate is selected solely on the basis of merit and fitness as required by sound management and applicable legal and regulatory requirements. All candidates are informed immediately after the decision is made; unsuccessful candidates are thanked for their interest and time.

FOR FURTHER READING

Acuff, Hall A. "Recruitment." In *Human Resources Management and Development Handbook,* edited by William R. Tracey. New York: AMACOM, 1985.

AIDS: The Workplace Issues. AMA Management Briefing. New York: AMA, 1985.

Aldrich, John W. "Staffing Concepts and Principles." In *Human Resources Management and Development Handbook,* edited by William R. Tracey. New York: AMACOM, 1985.

Anastasi, Anne. *Psychological Testing,* 5th ed. New York: Macmillan, 1982.

Arthur, Diane. *Recruiting, Interviewing, Selecting and Orienting New Employees.* New York: AMACOM, 1986.

Brinkerhoff, David W. "The HR Professional Staff." In *Human Resources Management and Development Handbook,* edited by William R. Tracey. New York: AMACOM, 1985.

Byham, William C. "Screening and Selection." In *Human Resources Management and Development Handbook,* edited by William R. Tracey. New York: AMACOM, 1985.

Conducting the Lawful Employment Interview. New York: Executive Enterprises, 1983.

Dessler, Gary. *Personnel Management: Modern Concepts and Techniques,* 3rd ed. Reston, Va.: Reston Publishing Company, 1984, especially chapters 2, 4, 5, and 6.

Dobrish, Cecelia, and others. *Hiring the Right Person for the Right Job.* Danbury, Conn.: Franklin Watts, 1984.

Drake, John D. *Interviewing for Managers: A Complete Guide to Employment Interviewing,* rev. ed. New York: AMACOM, 1982.

Goodale, James G. *The Fine Art of Interviewing.* Englewood Cliffs, N.J.: Prentice-Hall, 1982.

Goodwin, C. T. *Effective Interviewing for Employment Selection.* Brookfield, Vt.: Brookfield Publishing Company, 1983.

Half, Robert. *Robert Half on Hiring.* New York: Crown Publishers, 1985.

Hodes, Bernard S. *The Principles and Practices of Recruitment Advertising: A Guide for Personnel Professionals.* New York: Frederick Fell Publications, 1982.

Jaffee, Cabot L., Frederic D. Frank, and James R. Preston. "Assessment Centers." In *Human Resources Management and Development Handbook,* edited by William R. Tracey. New York: AMACOM, 1985.

Lipman, Burton E. *The Executive Job Search Program.* East Brunswick, N.J.: Bell Publishing, 1982.

Mackey, Daniel Murnane. *Employment at Will and Employer Liability.* New York: AMACOM, 1986.

McCulloch, K. *Selecting Employees Safely Under the Law.* Englewood Cliffs, N.J.: Prentice-Hall, 1981.

Manzini, Andrew O. "Human Resources Planning and Forecasting." In *Human Resources Management and Development Handbook,* edited by William R. Tracey. New York: AMACOM, 1985.

Manzini, Andrew O. and John D. Gridley. *Integrating Human Resources and Strategic Business Planning.* New York: AMACOM, 1986.

Mathis, Robert L., and John H. Jackson. *Personnel: Human Resource Management, Fourth Edition.* St. Paul, Minn.: West Publishing Company, 1985, especially chapters 4, 8, and 9.

Mueller, Joan. "Transfer and Promotion." In *Human Resources Management and Development Handbook,* edited by William R. Tracey. New York: AMACOM, 1985.

Newell, David. *Understanding Recruitment Law.* Elmsford, N.Y.: Pergamon Press, 1984.

Ramsay, Roland T. *Management's Guide to Effective Employment Interviewing.* Chicago: Dartnell Corporation, 1980.

Rice, Craig S. *Your Team of Tigers: Getting Good People and Keeping Them.* New York: AMACOM, 1982.

Robbins, Stephen. *Personnel: The Management of Human Resources.* Englewood Cliffs, N.J.: Prentice-Hall, 1982.

Sanders, Norman. *President's Guide to Attracting and Developing Top Caliber Employees.* Englewood Cliffs, N.J.: Executive Reports Corporation, 1981.

Taylor, A. Robert. *How to Select and Use an Executive Search Firm.* New York: McGraw-Hill, 1984.

White, Christine, and Abbie W. Thorner. *Managing the Recruiting Process.* New York: Harcourt Brace Jovanovich, 1982.

Federal Laws

Veterans' Readjustment Act of 1952
Equal Pay Act of 1963
Title VII of the Civil Rights Act of 1964
Age Discrimination in Employment Act of 1967
Occupational Safety and Health Act of 1970
Equal Employment Opportunity Act of 1972
Rehabilitation Act of 1973
Vietnam Era Veterans Readjustment Act of 1974
Pregnancy Discrimination Act of 1978

9

MOTIVATING
Encouraging
Top Performance

Traditionally, human relations in business have been formal, detached, and impersonal. That is changing. Younger workers increasingly expect more personal satisfaction from their jobs. The work environment and relationships with other workers can be a major source of job satisfaction—or dissatisfaction. All people, young and old, however, will be motivated to produce more and better in a setting where they believe that they are understood and valued. Managers must say to their people in effect, "You matter. You're important. Your contributions are valuable."

HR managers must remember that people are not machines. They need something far different from maintenance, proper servicing, and an appropriate energy supply to function properly and do the job they were employed to do. Nor is it simply a matter of telling people what to do, rewarding them if they do it, and firing them if they don't. Managers must train, encourage, and inspire the people who work with them and, in coordination with them, create the conditions and the environment in which they can, as the Army enlistment slogan says, "be all they can be," give their best and realize their full potential. HR managers can apply these principles directly when dealing with their own subordinates and can guide other managers throughout the organization in doing the same.

Motivation and management are irrevocably connected. The results managers get will be determined in large part by the motives of those they attempt to manage. Motivation is not *given* to subordinates; how workers behave is, to a considerable degree, determined by the internal motivations they bring into the workplace. On the other hand, failure to realize that behavior is also determined by surrounding circumstances would be a serious mistake. Personal motivations, therefore, are major, although not the sole, determinants of behavior. For everyone in an organization, environmental factors combine with personal ones to create individual patterns of motivation. All that an HR manager can do is establish and maintain the conditions that will foster strong motivation. For each individual, the particular combination of factors is unique.

What Is Motivation, Anyway?

Motivation is not simply a matter of getting people to work hard; it is far more a matter of getting them to subordinate personal ambitions and individual goals to organizational requirements and objectives, to cooperate with the manager and with each other, and to display initiative and teamwork.

Motivation has been defined as "the general condition of relatively high rates of responding produced by reinforcement. In the past, motivation has been considered an internal process or state. It is now understood that motivation is the result of reinforcement and is identified by a relatively high response rate."[1]

Looking at it from a somewhat different perspective—the organizational one—motivation is a goal-directed drive; its components are needs, wants, and desires. Essentially, then, for our purposes, motivation may be defined as the willingness of people to meet their personal needs, wants, and aspirations by directing their efforts and talents toward attaining organizational goals and objectives.

What can motivation do? What effect can it have on the results achieved by an organization and its people? Motivation can help control absenteeism, reduce turnover, get new workers off on the right foot, develop team spirit, and encourage group competition and individual initiative. It can build employee participation, encourage creativity, overcome resistance to change, provide individual fulfillment and job satisfaction, and improve productivity while maintaining quality standards.

How do you get your people to do what you want them to do—what the organization needs to have them do? Why do some people work harder and longer than others? Why do some workers seek additional responsibility while others duck it? The answer lies in motivation.

Each employee in the organization is a person, an individual who has a certain position and status in the department. Underlying the behavior required by organizational roles are the personal motives that cause people to perform in a unique way. Most people in management and professional positions find ample opportunity to create their personal work patterns out of a range of alternatives. Given that latitude, people interpret and execute their roles in accordance with their partic-

1. Lawrence W. Miller, *Behavior Management: The New Science of Managing People at Work* (New York: John Wiley, 1978), 338.

ular needs and abilities. Despite that freedom, management and professional jobs make numerous demands that have a powerful impact on personal motivations. One of the most obvious is the fact that these people must perform well in positions that often significantly affect the lives of others.

HR managers must be concerned not only with what an employee *can do* but also with what an employee *will do*. The *can do* is largely determined during the hiring process; the *will do* is only predicted at that point. The *will do* is determined by two factors: (1) the motivational factors that lie deep within the individual, the personal pattern of motivations that make up and characterize the employee; and (2) the professional values, goals, and other attributes of the workplace subculture that surround the individual and become a part of him or her—the work environment.

In more specific terms, what employees will do is determined by these factors:

- Within the individual:

    ◦ Needs, wants, and drives that energize and excite behavior.
    ◦ Goals and objectives that channel, direct, and control behavior.
    ◦ Forces, pressures, and constraints that reinforce needs and goals to maintain the desired behavior.

- Within the work environment:

    ◦ The job itself, its challenges and opportunities.
    ◦ Working conditions, physical, mental, and organizational (policies, rules, and regulations).
    ◦ The work group and interpersonal relationships.
    ◦ The kind, amount, and quality of supervision received.
    ◦ The reinforcement, incentives, and rewards provided.

But of all these, the quality of job performance of any person, manager, technician, or office worker is the result of applying energy and effort to their skills and abilities.

Albert Ellis, renowned counseling psychologist, puts it this way: "Motivation is the desire to do something. It includes the willingness to work at it, but also the work itself. Motivation has to include will power as well as will. Will power has action as a part of it. Will alone can just be in your head and you'll never accomplish anything until you act on your will."[2]

2. L. B. Gschwandtner (quoting Ellis), "The Rational Way to Sell," *Personal Selling Power*, July/August 1986, p. 17.

HR managers cannot succeed unless they understand their people—superiors, subordinates, and peers alike. The success of any organization, large or small, depends on the people who work in it. No matter how brilliant managers may be, no matter how creative and innovative their plans and programs, unless they understand and can motivate those they depend on to carry out programs and projects, they are doomed to failure.

Because what motivates one person will be ineffective with another, learning what each person will respond to requires observation, listening, and empathy. When you empathize with people, you are able to stand in their shoes and view the world as they see it. You can almost guess what they will say even before they say it.

Motivation comes from within the person when conditions are right. Part of creating those conditions is knowing when *not* to tell people what to do, being supportive but not paternal or patronizing, being loyal but not a patsy, being flexible in approach, remembering that each employee is an individual and that no two individuals, even identical twins, are truly identical, that everyone is unique in personality, knowledge, goals, skills, attitudes, experiences, capabilities, and learning style.

Individual Differences

Why are individuals different? Because they have different aptitudes, abilities, skills, knowledge, and habits. Even more than that, they are different because their attitudes, values, ideals, interests, appreciations, feelings and emotions, and personalities are different. They have these differences because of the singular combination of genes they inherited from their forebears and their unique experiences in the home, church, school, neighborhood, and workplace.

We have used many terms to describe individual differences. What do these terms really mean?

- An *aptitude* is an innate or natural mental or physical behavioral capacity. Examples are inductive and deductive reasoning and manual dexterity.
- An *ability* is an innate or learned physical or mental capacity or faculty. Examples are walking, talking, seeing, and hearing.
- A *skill* is a learned mental or motor behavior that requires some degree of facility in the performance of all or part of a complex act. Examples are writing, calculating, problem solving, counseling, and interviewing.
- *Knowledge* consists of facts, concepts, principles, meanings, understandings, and ideas. Examples are nomenclature, terminology, symbols, concepts, and understandings.

- A *habit* is an acquired tendency to act in a certain way when certain conditions are present in the environment. Examples are cleanliness, observing safety precautions, and showing concern for others.
- An *attitude* is a person's predisposition or sentiment, favorable or unfavorable, toward other persons, objects, institutions, practices, or ideas. Examples are respect, receptiveness to change, prejudice, and tolerance.
- A *value* is an object, activity, principle, or concept that an individual considers important in his or her life. Examples are independence, integrity, and industry.
- An *ideal* is a standard, often a standard of perfection, relating to persons, traits, objects, or ideas, that are accepted by an individual (or group). Examples are managership, leadership, and craftsmanship.
- An *interest* is an acquired concern for or about an object, person, process, or idea. A feeling of excitement usually accompanies attention to or perception of the interest area. Examples are sports, handicrafts, and politics.
- An *appreciation* is a recognition and comprehension of worth in some person, trait, object, idea, or process. Examples are appreciation of work, of modern art, of national traditions, of democratic institutions.
- A *feeling* or *emotion* is a sentiment or sensibility that creates an impulse to action, usually accompanied by some physical reaction—fear, anger, joy, grief, disgust, surprise, and so on.
- *Personality* refers to enduring personal traits or characteristics that make each individual truly unique—assertiveness, self-reliance, dependence, responsibility, dogmatism, defensiveness, openness, warmth, coldness, haughtiness, and the like.

Theories of Motivation

Theories about the underpinnings of motivation abound.[3] Most of them relate motivation to human needs. Probably the most popular theory is the work of a major figure in the humanist school of psychology, A. H. Maslow.[4] That theory explains human behavior in terms of a hierarchical structure of needs. In order of priority, they are:

1. Physical. The need for food, water, air, rest, and so on to maintain and sustain life.

---

3. For an excellent summary of several motivation theories, see R. M. Steers and L. W. Porter, *Motivation and Behavior*, 3d ed. (New York: McGraw-Hill, 1983).
4. A. H. Maslow, *Motivation and Personality*, 2nd ed. (New York: Harper & Row, 1970).

2. Safety. The need for physical and psychological safety and security.
3. Belonging. The need for acceptance, attention from others, for affection, and a sense of belonging.
4. Esteem. The need for self-respect, achievement, independence, freedom, recognition, approval, and prestige.
5. Self-actualization. The need for self-fulfillment, the realization of one's potential.

Frederick Herzberg developed the motivation-hygiene theory to explain the relationship between Maslow's needs hierarchy and the work environment. He proposed that there are two types of needs relating to the job: (1) hygiene factors, which operate to cause or remove obstacles in the work situation but *do not* motivate or improve performance (physiological and safety needs, for example) and (2) motivation factors, higher-level needs, which can motivate people to higher levels of performance (self-esteem and self-realization/actualization needs).[5]

Two writers on organizational behavior maintain that "such widely disseminated theories as Maslow's needs hierarchy and Herzberg's motivation/hygiene theory are unproven in the critical area of predicting employee performance."[6] They identify five theories of improving employee performance that they say *are* research-supported:

1. *Achievement motivation theory.* This theory states that challenging tasks and their successful completion elicit feelings of pleasure. Therefore, the solution to the motivation problem is to hire people with a high need for achievement, give them challenging tasks, permit innovative and novel solutions, and provide clear and unambiguous feedback on degree of success.
2. *Goal-setting theory.* This theory suggests that the way to maintain the motivation of all employees is to set difficult but specific and attainable goals and provide feedback on goal accomplishment.
3. *Expectancy theory.* This theory states that if workers see high productivity as leading to personal goal attainment, they will tend to be high producers. In other words, people tend to maximize pleasure and minimize pain. Therefore, set performance goals and standards that are attainable, communicate them clearly to workers, provide training or coaching if required, and make the performance outcome (rewards) clear and individualized.
4. *Equity theory.* This theory holds that when people compare their work/effort, educational level, or experience with those of other

5. Frederick Herzberg. *Work and the Nature of Man.* Cleveland, Ohio: World Publishing Company, 1966.
6. Martin J. Kilduff, and Douglas D. Baker, "Getting Down to the Brass Tacks of Employee Motivation," *Management Review*, September 1984, p. 56.

employees, their performance will be affected if they perceive inequity in pay, benefits, or prestige. Both overreward and underreward equal inequity. Managers should provide outcomes (rewards) that employees perceive as relevant, and should design compensation systems that employees perceive as equitable.

5. *Organization behavior modification.* This theory suggests that people behave in ways that help them avoid unpleasant outcomes (punishment) and attain pleasant ends (reward). Therefore, managers should identify critical and observable job performance behaviors, measure the frequency of their occurrence to establish a baseline, determine the conditions that trigger the behavior, develop a reinforcing strategy for desired behaviors, and evaluate the effect of the strategy by comparing the frequency of occurrence before and after.

Forms of Motivation

Motivation may be extrinsic or intrinsic, external or internal, tangible or intangible.

Extrinsic and Intrinsic

Extrinsic motivators are not controlled by the individual; they are controlled by the organization, the work group, the boss, a work partner, a spouse, or a friend. Extrinsic motivators include pay, fringe benefits, promotions, and incentives—and also praise, smiles, nods, and pats on the back.

A reward is a means of recognizing achievement, a contribution to the organization, or performance above and beyond what is expected. It says that an important "someone" noticed and cares.[7] Note that pay is not a reward; it is compensation for work done.

Incentives usually involve monetary awards, including additional compensation, for employees who perform well. However, they also include nonmonetary awards such as certificates, plaques, and trophies, vacation travel, tickets to sporting events, memberships in recreational organizations, or special recognition of some sort (letters of commendation, handwritten thank-you notes, feature articles in company publications, and the like).

When extrinsic motivational devices are used, they should be linked as directly and as closely as possible to performance and productivity.

7. For a list of 45 ways to recognize and reward people, see Rosabeth Moss Kanter, "Holiday Gifts: Celebrating Employee Achievements," *Management Review*, December 1986, pp. 20–21.

They should be personally delivered by the manager and be personalized, tailored to the recipient. They should be timely, presented close to the act. They should communicate clearly to both the recipient and others why the recognition is given and the criteria used to give it.

It is critically important that employees see a direct relationship between their effort and the reward. Rewards must be equitable and, at the same time, must provide for individual differences; there must be different types of awards to appeal to different people.

Intrinsic motivators are ones over which the individual has a great deal of control. They are a natural outcome of the job and the tasks associated with the work environment. Examples are: the feelings of satisfaction and accomplishment following a highly successful presentation or the completion of a complex research project, or the pleasure felt when a worker stands back to admire a piece of furniture he has just restored. Intrinsic motivation may be either internal or external, tangible or intangible. Intrinsic reinforcement is extremely important because of its potential for increasing individual employee performance and productivity and for improving the general level of employee morale and job satisfaction.

It must be noted that extrinsic and intrinsic motivation are closely related. That is, extrinsic reinforcers typically increase the effects of intrinsic reinforcers. For example, the HR instructor who is given a $500 savings bond for being chosen "Instructor of the Year" has been extrinsically motivated, but undoubtedly also feels better about the job performance itself. Although he or she may have received intrinsic reinforcement simply by being a capable instructor, the external reinforcer added considerable value to the intrinsic reinforcer.

Internal and External

Another way of looking at motivation is to consider whether it comes from within the individual or outside.

Internal motivation refers to thoughts or feelings, such as pride or satisfaction, that are evoked in an individual by some behavior.

For example, seeing a need to propose an important program to top management, planning the decision briefing, and presenting it involve external behavior and motivation. A feeling of satisfaction with delivering a good briefing is an example of internal motivation. Internal motivation may reinforce behavior that is either internal or external. The internal feelings of satisfaction at achieving some result considered worthwhile may occur in response to an external action, such as selling an important program to the chief executive officer of the company.

External motivators are reinforcers that occur outside the individual and include any reinforcer other than thoughts and feelings. Internal motivation is often confused with intrinsic motivation. Intrinsic motivation is intrinsic to the behavior being demonstrated or the task being performed. However, many intrinsic reinforcers are *external.*

For example, conducting a problem-solving seminar involves many behaviors, such as stating the objectives, introducing the problem, getting participation, asking questions, paraphrasing comments, and the like. As a result of these behaviors, the seminar leader can see results—the interaction of people in a problem-solving situation. Intrinsic motivation (or reinforcement) occurs as a natural result of conducting the session. Nonetheless, many of these intrinsic reinforcers, such as seeing and hearing usually shy people enthusiastically contributing to the discussion, are external. Although a natural result of the task of conducting the session, they occur outside of the seminar leader.

Intrinsic motivation may also produce internal reinforcement. After conducting the session, observing the interactions of people, and evaluating the quality of the solutions developed by the group, the seminar leader may say to himself or herself, "That was the best problem-solving session I have ever conducted." The results obtained by the seminar are external reinforcers and the "best session ever" thought is an internal reinforcer. Both of these outcomes are intrinsic to the task of conducting a problem-solving seminar.

Although HR managers can do little to manage the internal motivation of subordinates, they can take some solace in the fact that the process of arranging the work situation and the consequences of the work can produce external motivation, both intrinsic and extrinsic. As a result of this external motivation, employees also experience internal satisfactions. External motivation teaches people that certain behaviors are desirable. That increases the probability that similar behavior in the future will result in internal motivation.

Tangible and Intangible

Another distinction between types of reinforcers is tangible and intangible motivation. This is an area that has received a great deal of attention in recent years by consultants and organization development practitioners, particularly those who employ behavior management strategies.

Tangible motivational devices involve the presentation of rewards for behavior or performance in concrete or touchable forms, such as bonuses, savings bonds, trophies, plaques, certificates, or items selected from a gift catalog. Tangible reinforcers may be effective and appropriate in some situations and highly ineffective and inappropriate in others. Used in the right situations, they can result in significant behavioral change.

Intangible motivation includes nonmaterial reinforcers, such as social approval in the form of praise, smiles, and nods. It is particularly effective if it involves the approval of people who "count." Intangible reinforcers include such other things as assignment to prestigious work groups, committees, and task forces, and special individual assignments, as well as such forms of recognition as public acknowledgment of achievements, honorary titles (Supervisor of the Month), or pats on the back. Social reinforcement is an essential part of any successful behavior management program because it increases and enhances both job performance and job satisfaction.

Feedback as a Motivator

Although feedback has long been recognized as an important means of influencing employee behavior, in recent years it has received increased emphasis as a management strategy. Feedback is information given to people about their behavior and performance. Most organizations have several sources of feedback information, including data processing systems.

Feedback not only works, it virtually *always* works, because it is a strong motivator. It is also a powerful productivity tool and an instructional device. It corrects errors, clarifies misconceptions, and creates both internal and external consequences.

To be a potent motivator, feedback must meet these criteria: (1) It must be given to the person who is responsible for achieving the desired result; (2) it must relate to specific performance; (3) it must reinforce only good performance; and (4) it must be given as soon as possible after the performance. Providing feedback to the wrong person or work group, or providing it long after the fact, will do nothing to change behavior or performance.

Incentives

Incentives are tangible motivational devices. Because they are frequently used in modern business as "incentive systems," they deserve special attention. Incentives are tangible rewards for changes in behavior or performance. They go behind statutory benefits mandated by federal and state laws and the customary company-paid employee benefits or entitlements such as medical and hospitalization insurance, dental and vision care plans, life insurance, and sickness benefits. There are group incentives, individual incentives, and another category of individual incentives called executive perquisites or "perks."

Individual and Group Incentives

Several types of incentives are commonly used as motivational devices: commissions, bonuses, stock-sharing plans, and cash-deferred plans.

Commissions. These are cash payments based on someone's performance or the performance of workers that person supervises. Typically, they are used in marketing and sales organizations—or, in the case of HR organizations, the marketing and sales element of the department. Usually, they are based on a percentage of the income derived from the sale of company-developed training materials or programs.

Bonuses. These are lump-sum cash payments made to individuals or divided among work groups based on performance standards specified in advance.

Profit-sharing plans. Here a designated portion of the company's profits is committed to participants of the plan and usually paid out as a supplement to a retirement annuity. Shares may be fixed by formula or determined each year, based on that year's profits.

Cash-deferred [401(k)] plans. Under this plan, employees are given the options of either deferring part of their income to be invested in a group plan or receiving that same amount in cash on a current basis. If the individual qualifies under very rigid IRS requirements, the deferred amount, plus any accrued interest and dividends, can be completely sheltered from current taxation (as of 1987).

Incentive stock option plans. Under these plans, companies grant stock options to employees and receive tax relief in the form of tax deductions or credits in accordance with specific IRS rules (as of 1987).

Performance-based supplemental compensation. Here cash or stock in the company is awarded to employees who attain prestated short- or long-term targets. Usually, such plans are a part of a management by objectives (MBO) program.

Executive "Perks"

Perquisites are a distinct area of generic incentives that involve special privileges and considerations in addition to salary and benefits. Usually "perks" are associated with organizational rank and status, although sometimes they are granted on an individual basis. Some of the common perquisites are company-provided cars, chauffeur-driven limousines, free reserved parking, country club or luncheon club memberships, executive dining room privileges, first-class travel accommodations, paid travel for spouses, and interest-free loans.

Determinants of Motivation

What are the factors that determine, or at least strongly influence, the motivation and thus the behavior of people in organizations? Basically, there are two types: (1) factors that arise out of the unique needs of the individual, and (2) factors directly associated with the values and goals of the individual's occupation or profession.

Personal Patterns of Motivation

Among the many factors that influence employees, one of the most potent is the desire for success. At the higher levels of management, the sense of actively participating in important work may be a powerful motivator. Related to that may be the need to exploit an energetic personality through organizing and directing people and other resources and making decisions that have far-reaching consequences. For most people, however, the motivation to perform effectively is essentially of two kinds:

1. The performance of organizational duties provides a means of achieving some goal not directly related to performance. Thus, by performing a job well, a person may receive recognition, promotion, or some other reward that is personally satisfying. That kind of motivation is probably more important at lower levels of organization and in production or support jobs, where the duties themselves are somewhat less challenging than at the professional levels. However, even at the higher levels, the desire for advancement is a strong motivating factor.

2. The performance of a given task can provide intrinsic satisfaction; the individual can obtain real and important satisfactions from performing well. Here there is satisfaction not because the activity leads to other rewards, but because the activity is rewarding in itself. Intrinsic satisfaction may take several forms:

- Opportunity for self-expression. The activity gives the individual a chance to develop and demonstrate skills and abilities.
- Opportunity to gain new experiences. The activity gives the individual the chance to pursue interests through a variety of tasks and challenges.
- The feeling of self-determination. The activity fosters a sense of freedom by providing opportunities to make choices and decisions.

- ○ Completion. The activity promotes the satisfaction that comes from the successful completion of tasks.
- ○ Self-esteem. The activity provides opportunities for increase in self-esteem either through pride in accomplishment or through identification with the achievements of the organization.

There is considerable evidence that, for people at higher levels in the organization and for professionals, intrinsic satisfaction is by far the most important kind of motivation. For them, the real motivators are the opportunities to exercise initiative and ingenuity, meet challenges, handle problems in their own way, and do their jobs well. The challenge of their duties, rather than other forms of tangible reward, is the prime motivation. The more lasting motivation comes from such things as being assigned to stimulating work, having considerable authority and responsibility, and being given projects of great importance. The key to sustained motivation seems to lie in assignments that push individuals to the limits of their ability (but not beyond) and that match growth, ability, and skill with newer and bigger challenges.

The drive for achievement is likely to be a highly subjective, personalized experience for the individual manager. It is potentially the most powerful motivator of all because it can never be fully satisfied. Therefore, that type of motivation can play an important role in a person's performance over a long period of time despite repeated success. In fact, repeated success keeps such motivation alive, and lack of success is likely to squelch it. Thus, every success reveals a greater challenge. The individual accepts the challenge in the hope of getting the satisfaction of scoring again.

Professional Values and Goals

Motivation is not determined exclusively by deeply ingrained personal needs. It is also influenced by ideas, shared by others, of what is desirable behavior in a given situation. Any activity is the result of a combination of the requirements of a situation and the personal drives and value commitments of the individual.

For the performance of HR professionals, value commitments have special and particular significance. They are the result of all the education, training, and experiences to which they have been exposed throughout their careers. To a large extent, individual HR managers and specialists have value systems that were determined by their education and the immediate supervisors under whom they have worked. In addition, the informal working practices of their immediate superiors and colleagues do much to shape their habitual behavior.

Much of what HR workers do, say, and think is determined by professional norms and standards, and most of them—certainly those who, by training and accomplishment, deserve the name "profession-als"—share many values, ideals, customs, and beliefs. Obviously, sharing values means being influenced by them in making decisions and taking actions. When people identify themselves with the HR profession, their careers will be shaped largely by their ability to perform in relation to the value system prevailing in that profession.

In general, the HR profession today places high value on accomplishment of organizational goals and departmental objectives, acceptance of responsibility in all its forms, loyalty to the organization, improvement in results, and service to people. That does not mean that all HR practitioners are motivated by a single set of values; in fact, there is sometimes considerable conflict between the values of the HR profession and the values of the individual HR manager or specialist. However, people do operate on the basis of some sort of value orientation that usually results in a reasonably consistent approach to work, a career, and life in general, and that leads them to approach problems along roughly predictable paths.

Characteristics of a Sound System

Developing a sound motivational system is not easy. Preaching about the Protestant work ethic or repeating clichés like "We expect an honest day's work for a day's pay" won't do it. A truly sound motivational system is people oriented, competitive, comprehensive, flexible, and productive.

People-Oriented. An effective motivational system focuses on people—people at all levels of organization, from the assembly line to the executive suite. It is not concerned with production, productivity, profits, and return on investment, although those may well be some of the results expected from the system. It begins with caring for people, their needs and goals, their concerns, aspirations, and hopes.

Competitive. A complete motivational system includes elements with a definite price tag. That price tag is not confined to the time and effort that supervisors and managers put into the task of establishing conditions to promote the motivation of their people. Extrinsic motivational devices, such as extra compensation, benefits, awards, and other types of incentives represent costs. In an era of strong competition for markets, the motivational system must be competitive in its industry, maybe competitive across the board. But the most important consideration is this: In any business, the cost of any system should never exceed its productivity. In other words, comparable input costs must yield comparable results.

Comprehensive. An effective motivational system must be comprehensive; that is, it must provide for more than the satisfaction of needs that salaries and benefits are designed to meet. It must also encompass the needs for acceptance, belonging, participation, self-determination, self-development, and self-realization—the higher needs of people in organizations.

Flexible. An effective motivational system must be flexible from two standpoints. First, it must be flexible in time. That is, it must be modifiable in the light of new knowledge about motivation and changes in the organizational and larger environment. Second, it must be flexible with respect to the people it is designed to serve. That is, since the power of specific motivational devices differs with individuals, the system must be adaptable to meet those individual employee differences.

Productive. Finally, the system must be productive, not only in the sense of inducing people to work more efficiently and effectively and therefore more productively, but also in terms of its success in increasing the job satisfaction and loyalty to the organization of employees. In short, the system must produce the results intended.

Building and Maintaining Motivation

As we have seen, the HR manager must be concerned about employee motivation within his or her own department and throughout the organization. The only alternative is to place sole responsibility for performance squarely on the shoulders of employees themselves. That, in effect, creates a make-or-break situation: Workers stand or fall on their efforts alone. Although the manager can operate in that way, the wisdom of disregarding motivational conditions is questionable. There are much more effective ways to direct an organization.

So, what can HR managers do to build and maintain a high level of motivation among their own departments and to help other managers do the same with theirs? Here are some positive answers.

Develop an Appropriate Organizational Environment

Several actions will go a long way toward developing the kind of organizational environment in which motivation prospers. You must develop a climate in which subordinates can feel secure—a feeling that they can trust you and that you trust them. You must treat every employee as an individual—as a worthwhile, important *somebody*, not a human zero. Remember that a person's respectability and self-respect are based on his or her job, and that *every* job is important to its holder. Encourage your people to see the job as *my* job, *my* contribution to the organization—as well as *our* work and *our* job as a member of a team. Encourage cooperation rather than competition.

Let your people know where they stand. Make frequent face-to-face contacts on *their* turf, not just in your office. Show personal interest in them and in their aspirations, concerns, and accomplishments. Discuss their goals and ambitions frequently. Give credit freely for a job well done. Recognize positive accomplishments. Give frequent pats on the back. Give praise publicly when earned; criticize privately and sparingly. Criticize orally; praise orally *and* in writing. Praise for progress as well as for accomplishment. Ensure that your feedback is timely, appropriate, honest, and focuses on improved performance.

When you praise in writing, follow these simple rules:

- Do it now. Don't wait even a day after noting the accomplishment.
- Keep it brief. Three or four sentences, without fancy language, is about right.
- Be specific. Avoid general terms and use numbers where possible to describe what merited the recognition.
- Write personally and informally. Use "I" instead of "management" or "the company," "you" instead of "the employee."
- Distribute the memo. Send copies to the person's superior and to the personnel office for insertion in the individual's file.

Believe in the potential of your subordinates. Build up their ego. Use positive thinking and reinforcement. Take the "I know you can do it" approach. Show that you have confidence in them by avoiding becoming immersed in their activities and by permitting them to exercise judgment. Be receptive to their ideas and suggestions.

Involve them in decision making. Focus on their concerns, not on yours. Delegate authority in increasing amounts as people demonstrate their ability to handle more and more challenging assignments. Give proven performers more autonomy. However, keep your expectations realistic. Don't ask too much too soon.

Avoid "killer phrases" when reacting to the ideas or suggestions of subordinates. Some of the most common idea murderers are:

Are you nuts (crazy) (a dreamer)?	Let's study that some more.
Be realistic (sensible).	Let's talk about that later.
It's a great idea, but . . .	Maybe next year.
It's been tried before.	It doesn't have enough potential (glitz) (pizzazz).
It's too far out.	So what else is new?
It's too risky.	The boss will laugh.
The company is not ready for that.	We've got enough problems.
What for?	You're on the wrong track.
Where did you get that?	You've got to be kidding!

Give awards and recognition. Link them to performance. Make them "winnable" or accessible to the majority of employees to prevent the few "star" performers from winning repeatedly. Don't pick just one winner; have second, third, and honorable-mention awards. Where possible, tailor individual awards and recognition to individual needs. Award bonuses on the basis of performance ratings—measured against specific objectives. Where possible, give bonuses to work teams and not to individuals.

Link reward to performance. Tailor recognition and rewards to individual needs. Show that good work is appreciated and rewarded by praise, attention, understanding, and esteem.

Develop Yourself as a Leader

Get *yourself* motivated. You must believe in what you're doing, enthusiastically and wholeheartedly. You must be ready to share your experience and give information to your people freely—and not insist on justification or "need to know." You must be open and approachable.

Differentiate your role from the roles of your subordinates. Address yourself to broader objectives, policies, and plans; involve yourself in operational details to a lesser degree. Avoid becoming overly close and specific in your direction. To the maximum degree possible, focus your attention on such activities as setting objectives, issuing mission-type directives, and providing general, rather than specific, supervision. Use your skills to develop collaborative teams within your department.

You must train your subordinate supervisors to develop cooperative relationships with their subordinates, superiors, and peers. You must train them to be trainers, coordinators, counselors, consultants, and team leaders. You must help them to become more aware of their own behavior and its effect on others. You must get them to examine their own assumptions about and attitudes toward others and increase their knowledge of people and work and their skills in analyzing "people" problems and human situations.

Always publicize changes before they are implemented. Provide, whenever possible, immediate oral responses to questions. But provide *written* responses to significant employee questions, comments, and complaints. Send them to their homes to assure anonymity.

You must remember that although showing displeasure, even anger, about a situation or event can be motivating, it usually motivates people to do the wrong thing. You must also remember that yelling, screaming, swearing, or whining are not only unacceptable but downright destructive. Recognize that showing disappointment with an *action* (or failure to act) and not with the *person,* usually motivates people to try to do better.

You must be able to admit freely that you don't have all the answers, that you don't know *everything* about your organization or even the HR business. You must be ready and willing to learn *from* your subordinates. Finally, you must be ready to make the really tough decisions yourself, and not push them up or down; be ready to bite the proverbial bullet.

Lower the Potential for Failure

You must recognize the importance of self-fulfillment, self-development, and realizing one's potential. Help your staffers set personal goals and objectives—goals that are realistic and reasonable, require stretching to achieve, and make people feel successful when accomplished. You must establish and maintain the conditions that will enable people to achieve their own personal goals by meeting the goals and objectives of the organization.

You must know the personal characteristics and professional skills of each of your subordinates and use that knowledge to help them exploit their strengths and shore up their deficiencies. You must assist and support them whenever they falter. But, more than that, you must provide them with the training, coaching, development, and experiences that will preclude failure.

You must develop clear job descriptions and define standards of performance. Tell people exactly and specifically what is expected of them. Give them immediate feedback and provide recognition and reward for doing well. Keep controls reasonable; don't hobble creativity and initiative. Do everything possible to "turn people on and then turn them loose."

You must ensure that your people know that they have the right to express their ideas, suggestions, opinions, and anxieties to you without fear of rejection or retribution. Be sensitive to the needs and motivations of your people so that you can judge the possible reactions to and outcomes of the various courses of action that are open to you. Be willing to act in a way that takes the motives of others into account.

Finally, you must put people in situations where there is a high likelihood of success and avoid placing them in situations where failure is likely. If, despite your precautions, failure does occur, communicate a quiet sense of composure and enough emotional support to restore the person's self-confidence and motivation.

Reduce Physical and Emotional Stress

Be sure to do all you can to protect your people from physical and emotional stress. Ensure that physical working conditions are safe, comfortable, and attractive. Protect people from concerns about hazardous situations and substances and dangerous equipment. Conduct frequent, systematic, and thorough inspections of equipment and facilities to identify and eliminate potential hazards. Train people in safe habits and practices.

It is equally important to do everything you can to protect people from the debilitating effects of mental and emotional stress, strain, and tension—from threats, deprivation, unfairness, discrimination of any kind, and loss of job. Encourage people to keep regular hours, to quit unhealthful practices, to get adequate rest, and to take vacations. Be concerned, too, about their compensation—that they receive a fair return for their investment of talent, time, and effort.

Motivational Strategies

In addition to the specific things that managers can do to motivate their staffers, there are several broader strategies that will do much to generate motivation among individuals and groups.

Goal setting. Goals identify both the direction and the degree of improvement sought. In other words, goals describe where an organization or an individual wants to be three, five, or ten years in the future. Because goals are a means of steering an individual, the cooperative development and articulation of a statement of goals, involving both the superior and the subordinate, or a superior and a work unit, can be a strong motivational strategy.

Triggering action. Most of the actions that people take on a day-to-day basis are routine. They accept these actions as a part of the job, make only reasonable demands about them, and perform them without question. However real progress in improving operations does not come from routine actions, but from actions that go beyond the routine. Managers have the obligation to effect improvements; therefore, they must motivate subordinates to higher and higher levels of achievement. That involves making extraordinary demands. Under those conditions, managers must acknowledge freely and openly that they are asking for more than ordinary effort, and they must afford people an opportunity to discuss the problems involved and develop strategies to achieve the desired results.

MBO programs. Management by objectives (MBO) is a constructive strategy for improving performance. Basically, it involves a cooperative approach to identifying objectives for a definite period, such as a month or a year. It encompasses five steps: (1) identify key result areas (areas that are important to the individual employee and to the department); (2) establish standards of satisfactory performance; (3) identify objective measures of performance; (4) appraise performance; and (5) mutually determine ways to improve performance. MBO is a particularly effective motivational device because it offers a means of providing regular and meaningful feedback at each step.

Delegation. This is the process of assigning tasks to subordinates, giving them enough authority to complete the tasks successfully, and exacting responsibility for acceptable performance. Because delegation demonstrates trust and confidence in subordinates, it is effective as a motivational strategy. It also provides a bonus to the manager because it enables him or her to devote attention to the broader problems of planning, directing, and controlling the department.

Job enrichment or enlargement. One of the more useful strategies for increasing motivation is job enrichment or enlargement. This may be defined as redesigning jobs to give an employee increased responsibility, more autonomy, or greater challenge. The basic objectives of the strategy are to motivate people to work to their highest level of capacity and ability, improve employee relations, attract and retain quality employees, reduce absenteeism, improve quality and productivity, and increase return on investment.

Development of supervisors. Training supervisors to develop collaborative relationships with their subordinates, superiors, and peers— training them to be trainers, coordinators, consultants, team leaders— will go a long way toward the goal of improving the motivation of the entire workforce. Improving the behavior and performance of those in supervisory positions multiplies the manager's effectiveness.

Participative management. Participative management has enormous potential for raising productivity, improving motivation and morale, job satisfaction and commitment. There is no substitute for encouraging people to share in making the decisions that affect them and their jobs.

Key concepts of this strategy are: (1) participation means mental and emotional involvement; (2) it motivates initiative, creativity, and contribution; and (3) it encourages and promotes acceptance of responsibility and commitment to the success of the organization.

At all costs the manager must avoid "counterfeit" or halfhearted participation. It will quickly and inevitably be sensed by subordinates, with ruinous results.

Other prerequisites for an effective participatory management system include: (1) costs should not exceed the benefits, financial or otherwise, that the system produces; (2) participants must have the knowledge and abilities to participate effectively; 3) participants must be able to communicate effectively; (4) participation should not threaten the authority or reduce the responsibility of managers; and (5) participation is limited to areas that are within the decision-making authority of members.

Steps in Motivation

To develop effective motivational systems, the manager should follow the following steps.

Step 1. Determine which motivational strategies are appropriate for implementation in his or her department. Consider the possibilities we described:

Goal setting
Triggering action
MBO program
Delegation
Job enrichment/enlargement
Training and developing supervisors
Participative management

Step 2. Develop procedures and a timetable to install the selected strategies.

Step 3. Install the strategies.

Step 4. Identify the personal needs, aspirations, and motives of each immediate subordinate and the priority of each need.

Step 5. Establish conditions that will result in strong motivation for each subordinate to perform up to the level of his or her capabilities and eliminate demotivating factors to the maximum extent possible. Consider the strategies discussed earlier:

Develop yourself as a leader.
Provide opportunities for new experiences, self-expression, and self-determination.
Develop a supportive climate.
Lower the chances for failure.
Reduce physical and emotional stress.

Step 6. Provide appropriate recognition of and formal awards for special acts or services, superior accomplishments, or other efforts that contribute to efficiency, economy, or productivity.

Step 7. Evaluate the effectiveness of the strategies in improving the motivation and performance of individuals and work teams.

Step 8. Make adjustments to the program to improve results.

Summary

Motivation is the willingness of people to meet their personal needs, goals, and aspirations by directing their energies and talents toward the achievement of organizational goals and objectives. The challenge facing the HR manager is to use the best strategies to get people to subordinate their needs to those of the organization and to produce more and better.

Basically, motivating people is much more than telling them what to do, insisting that they do it, rewarding them if they produce, and punishing them if they don't. It involves creating the conditions and the environment in which people feel that they are understood, valued, and trusted and that they, in turn, can understand and trust their superiors.

Motivation, the desire to excel, is determined by three factors: the unique personal pattern of needs and wants that make up and characterize the individual subordinate, the professional values and goals that surround the individual, and the amount of effort and energy the individual expends to employ his or her skills and abilities. The latter two factors are strongly influenced by the work environment and the kind and quality of supervision received.

Although they vary in their strength and effectiveness, motivators of all types, intrinsic and extrinsic, internal and external, tangible and intangible, feedback and incentives, should be employed. A sound motivational system must be people-oriented, competitive, comprehensive, flexible, and productive.

To build and maintain motivation, the HR manager must develop a supportive organizational climate, develop himself or herself as a leader, lower the potential for failure of subordinates, reduce physical and emotional stress in the job environment, and adopt broader motivational strategies such as goal setting, MBO programs, delegation, job enrichment, training and development of supervisors, and participative management.

FOR FURTHER READING

Apter, M. J. *The Experience of Motivation*. New York: Academic Press, 1982.

Cherrington, David J. *The Work Ethic—Working Values and Values That Work*. New York: AMACOM, 1980.

Clark, Charles H. *Idea Management: How to Motivate Creativity and Innovation*. New York: AMACOM, 1980.

Collins, Samuel R. "Incentives and Awards." In *Human Resources Management and Development Handbook*, edited by William R. Tracey. New York: AMACOM, 1985.

Cruden, Herbert J., and Arthur W. Sherman, Jr. *Managing Human Resources*, 7th ed. Cincinnati: South-Western Publishing Company, 1984. See especially Chapter 11.

Freedman, Arthur M. "Stress-Management Training." In *Human Resources Management and Development Handbook*, edited by William R. Tracey. New York: AMACOM, 1985.

Grant, Philip C. *Employee Motivation: Principles and Practices*. New York: Vantage Press, 1984.

Kilduff, Martin J., and Douglas D. Baker. "Getting Down to the Brass Tacks of Employee Motivation." *Management Review,* September 1984, pp. 56–61.

Merrill, David W., and Roger H. Reid. "Performance Feedback Based on Behavior Measurement." In *Human Resources Management and Development Handbook,* edited by William R. Tracey. New York: AMACOM, 1985.

Miller, Lawrence M. *Behavior Management: The New Science of Managing People at Work.* New York: John Wiley & Sons, 1978.

Myer, Mary Coeli. "Motivation." In *Human Resources Management and Development Handbook,* edited by William R. Tracey. New York: AMACOM, 1985.

Leidecker, Joel K., and James J. Hall. "Motivation: Good Theory—Poor Application." *Training and Development Journal,* June 1981, pp. 152–155.

Locke, Edwin A., and Gary P. Latham. *Goal Setting: A Motivational Technique That Works,* Englewood Cliffs, N.J.: Prentice-Hall, 1984.

Needell, Cheryl K., and George W. Alwon. "Recognition and Reward: Keys to Motivating Supervisors." *Management Review,* November-December 1982, pp. 53–56.

Miller, William B. "Motivation Techniques: Does One Work Best?" *Management Review,* February 1981, pp. 47–52.

Odiorne, George S. "An Uneasy Look at Motivation Theory." *Training and Development Journal,* June 1980, pp. 106–112.

Ozley, Lee M., and Judith S. Ball. "Quality of Work Life." In *Human Resources Management and Development Handbook,* edited by William R. Tracey. New York: AMACOM, 1985.

Petri, H. L. *Motivation: Theory and Research.* Belmont, Calif. Wordsworth, 1981.

Pinder, Scott C. *Work Motivation.* Glenview, Ill.: Scott, Foresman, 1984.

Rosenbaum, Bernard L. *How to Motivate Today's Workers: Motivational Models for Managers and Supervisors.* New York: McGraw-Hill, 1982.

Rychiak, Joseph F. *Personality and Life-Style of Young Male Managers.* New York: Academic Press, 1982.

Schermerhorn, John R., Jr. "Team Development for High Performance Management." *Training and Development Journal,* November 1986, pp. 38–41.

Smith, Howard R. "Who's in Control Here?" *Management Review,* February 1980, pp. 43–47.

Steers, Richard M., and Lyman W. Porter. *Motivation and Work Behavior,* 3rd ed. New York: McGraw-Hill, 1983.

Ullrich, Robert A. *Motivation Methods That Work.* Englewood Cliffs, N.J.: Prentice-Hall, 1981.

"Understanding Motivation and Behavior." *Training.* July 1985, pp. 12–13.

Westcott, Russell T. "Behavior Management Training." In *Human Resources Management and Development Handbook,* edited by William R. Tracey. New York: AMACOM, 1985.

Yankelovich, Daniel. *New Rules—Searching for Fulfillment in a World Turned Upside Down.* New York: AMACOM, 1981.

10

DELEGATING Multiplying Your Effectiveness

Of all the problems facing HR managers today, few are more important—or more misunderstood—than delegation. Strangely enough, the managers most affected by this problem are the ones who are the most principled and industrious. They find it difficult to yield control or trust others with tasks they themselves are responsible for. They are in fact being held back by performing trifling tasks or tasks that could be performed better by their subordinates. They become overworked, overtaxed, and overwrought—and at the same time, miss opportunities to foster initiative, revitalization, motivation, and expertise among their subordinates.

The solution takes knowledge, understanding, experience, and skill. It is far from simple. HR managers must learn how to plan for delegation, how to identify tasks that should be delegated, how to select the right person for each delegated task, and how to train people before delegating. Once unburdened from some of their tasks, HR managers will be free to deal with significant problems and issues, improve the department, train subordinates, and take on additional responsibilities. They need to know how to begin, when is the right time, what can go wrong, how it is done properly, how to choose the right person, and how to pick up the pieces when things go wrong.

We can define delegation as that part of the organizing process by which the manager deliberately makes it possible for subordinates to share in the work to be done. It is the process by which authority is shared throughout an organization. Delegation, then, is the technique of assigning functions, duties, and tasks to subordinates, along with sufficient authority to complete the assignment.

Delegation has three elements: (1) assigning functions, duties, and tasks; (2) allocating sufficient authority to command the resources needed to accomplish the assignment; and (3) creating an obligation on the part of the employee to complete the assignment satisfactorily.

The employee must assume a shared responsibility for the performance of the delegated duty or task. However, the manager cannot abdicate his or her responsibility—only *authority* is delegated.

Accountability is the flip side of delegation; the employee must accept accountability to the manager for acceptable performance. Accountability grows out of responsibility and goes hand in glove with it.

Although objective evidence may be hard to find, I am convinced that a considerable percentage of failures among HR managers can be traced to inability or unwillingness to delegate. Delegation is truly one of the critical skills of the HR manager.

Delegation is an act of trust. It is vital to the growth and development of an organization. It is a necessary accompaniment to decentralization. It makes executives, managers, and supervisors more effective because it relieves them of repetitive or noncritical tasks and permits them to spend their time on matters of great importance to the organization. It therefore affects the profitability and efficiency of an organization. It is also central to the development of people.

Oddly enough, the delegation process has the effect of leaving the manager with as much authority and responsibility as he or she had before. No matter how much authority a manager delegates, no matter how much the employee is obligated to perform satisfactorily, the manager still retains ultimate authority and responsibility for whatever happens. The manager must continue to direct, guide, assist, and hold accountable the subordinate to whom he or she has delegated the authority. In short, the HR manager's responsibility for the actions of subordinates is absolute and cannot be delegated.

For example, if the HR manager delegates authority to the director of training to approve training schedules for the company, the manager must assume the responsibility if there are glitches in the schedule that result in lost time and unnecessary employee travel costs. Obviously, the training director should share the criticism and any adverse action that is taken as a consequence of the foul-up, but the HR manager cannot be held blameless.

Benefits of Delegation

To the organization. Delegation increases the flexibility and adaptability of the organization and makes possible better and more rapid response to change. It speeds up decisions. It encourages maximum use of the experience and talents available within an organization. It makes it possible for executives and managers to use their time more effectively. It produces better decisions because they are made closer to the action.

Delegation jettisons the notion of the "indispensable" executive or manager. It compensates for specific skill deficiencies among key managers. It reduces tensions. It develops a built-in supply of potential supervisors, managers, and executives for succession. It helps employees identify with organization goals and objectives. It improves employee morale and job satisfaction, thereby reducing turnover and its associated costs.

To executives and managers. Delegation multiplies and extends the personal influence and effectiveness of executives and managers. It enables them to maximize the use of their own talents, resources, skills, and leadership capacities. It makes their own functions and duties more manageable. It reduces executive stress.

Delegation allows the manager's superior to see him or her as a person who develops people. It allows managers to be away from their job, even for prolonged periods of time, without worrying about what is happening in the department while they're gone. It builds initiative and confidence and increases the productivity of subordinates. It reduces such negative attitudes as defensiveness, suspicion, impatience, resentfulness, and frustration among subordinates. It creates an atmosphere conducive to teamwork. It provides an effective means of training subordinates and a sound basis for evaluating their readiness for promotion.

To subordinates. Delegation gives people opportunities to participate in the organization. It allows them to share in making the decisions that affect the organization and its employees. It improves their motivation, morale, and job satisfaction. It builds initiative and self-confidence. It develops responsibility.

Delegation also supplies truly effective training and development. It provides people with more control over their jobs and their destiny. It reduces the frustrations that arise from indecision or untimely actions by higher levels of management. It provides an effective means of recognizing and rewarding progress and accomplishment. It demonstrates trust in subordinates.

Barriers

There are many potential blocks to effective delegation. Some of them are attributable to the organization, others to executives and managers, and still others to subordinates.

From the Organization

There are two organizational factors that can and often do have the effect of blocking the delegation of functions, duties, and tasks. The first is organizational climate. Some organizations have an autocratic climate, an atmosphere that tends to discourage the dispersal of authority. Whether such a climate is just a hangover from the early days when the organization was small and authority was in the hands of the owner, or a distinct philosophy of today's management, is immaterial. The result is identical—strong, centralized control.

The type of work performed in an organization also affects the amount and kind of delegation permitted. If much of the work is research oriented or at the growing edge of technology, the tendency is to delegate more authority to subordinates—the managers, scientists, or engineers—simply because as professionals they are in the best position to make important decisions.

On the other hand, if the work requires only a low level of skill or is highly repetitive, or if employees are not highly trained, a lesser amount of delegation is likely. Another organizational factor relates to the pre-dictability of events that control the distribution of work or workflow. Where the predictability is low, the amount of delegation is also likely to be limited.

From Executives and Managers

The roster of blocks to delegation that come from executives and managers is the longest of the three lists. Some represent the "right" reasons for not delegating, but most are the "wrong" reasons.

The "Right" Reasons

Some authority must be reserved simply because the decision is critical to the viability, efficiency, or profitability of the organization. Such reserved authorities will be discussed later in this chapter. Some-times delegation is deferred because at that moment, no subordinate is capable of assuming the task (we would hope that someone is currently being trained for it). In any case, there is a need to proceed slowly with the delegation. A third legitimate reason for not delegating is a lack of needed controls. Again, this should be only a temporary block to dele-gation. A capable manager will quickly take action to establish the needed control mechanisms and then delegate the function or task.

The "Wrong" Reasons

The most common reasons for failure to delegate are (1) lack of knowledge and skill in delegating (the manager simply does not know how to do it); (2) failure to recognize the benefits of delegation; (3) fear of loss of authority; (4) ego, passion for power, or the desire to retain tight control over their organizational element; (5) perfectionism ("no one can do it as well as I can"); (6) lack of trust or confidence in subordinates; and (7) insecurity—fear that the subordinate may develop enough managerial potential to take the manager's job.

Other reasons for failing to delegate, although less frequently observed, are (1) fear of loss of a capable subordinate due to recognition of his or her talents by either outside organizations or other departments; (2) fear of loss of control from a reduction in day-to-day contacts with lower-level employees; (3) reluctance to give up duties and tasks that are particularly enjoyable to the manager; and (4) uncertainty about the reaction of collective bargaining units to delegation.

From Subordinates

Subordinates are not always receptive to the idea of delegation. Among the most common reasons for negative reactions to delegation are (1) delegation makes the job more time-consuming, difficult, risky, or stressful; (2) lack of self-confidence—subordinates feel that they don't have the skills, information, or resources needed to perform well; (3) fear of failure and its consequences—second guessing, criticism, and censure by their bosses, demotion, or loss of job; and (4) lack of appropriate recognition, incentives, or rewards for performance.

Indicators of Failure to Delegate

There are many indicators of poor delegation. Some of the most common are:

- Shortsightedness. The manager is so busy with current problems that he or she is unable to devote any time to long-range planning and innovation.
- Inaccessibility. Subordinates must often wait for hours, even days, to get on the manager's calendar.
- Time wasting. The manager can often be found performing trivial tasks (such as opening mail or answering the phone) that should be performed by others.
- Inefficiency. The manager spends many evening and weekend hours either in the office or at home catching up with work.
- Anxiety. The manager is reluctant to schedule needed travel or vacations for fear that things will get off the track.
- Egocentricity. The manager uses secretaries and assistants as mere messengers.

Why Delegation Fails

If everyone understands the importance, benefits, and need for delegation in modern organizations, why does delegation sometimes fail? There are many potential pitfalls in the delegation process. Again, some are attributable to the organization, others to the delegators, and still others to the delegatees.

Organizational Reasons. Two organizational conditions can foredoom delegation to failure. The first is counterfeit delegation—an organization merely gives lip service to the concept, and managers just go through the motions of delegating authority. In this situation, functions appear to be delegated, but the constraints are so rigid that the employee cannot make a decision without going to his superior for "guidance." In effect, the superior retains the "delegated" authority and shares none of it with others.

The second potential pitfall is the establishment of arbitrary or unrealistic standards for performance. Performance standards that are imposed by the organization, without the participation of employees, standards that are unreachable, inevitably will result in negative feelings and frustration of both managers and subordinates.

Weakness in the Process. Most of the potential pitfalls in delegation come from managerial ineffectiveness or outright failures. Some of the most common: poor selection of delegatees; overestimating the skills and abilities of subordinates; oversupervision—annoying the subordinate by constant checking; undersupervision—taking a completely hands-off approach and not checking on performance at all; giving the subordinate insufficient authority, lack of latitude in selecting methods to produce the desired results, or inadequate direction, guidance, and assistance; setting goals and standards that are too high or too low; applying inadequate or inappropriate measures of performance; and failure to train subordinate managers and supervisors in the delegation process.

Some of the pitfalls in delegation come from delegatees themselves: (1) failure to accept the obligation to perform because of laziness, lack of interest, or lack of responsibility; and (2) unconsciously or deliberately taking action or seizing authority beyond the scope of the authority delegated—or bending, ignoring, or manipulating the authority granted. Both application and dedication of subordinates are needed if delegation is to succeed.

Three Methods of Delegation

There are three basic methods of dividing and delegating the work to be done in any type of organization: incremental, sequential, and functional.

1. Incremental. With this method, the limits of authority to perform a duty or task are defined in terms of specific positions, people, locations, numbers, or periods of time. For example, an instructor in a training organization could be delegated authority to develop a pretest for a specific technical training program. Or an instructor-supervisor might be delegated authority to schedule training for the Boston branch of the operation.

2. Sequential. Here the limits of authority to perform a duty or task are defined in accordance with the sequence of actions, from beginning to end, that are required for the complete and proper performance of that duty or task. For example, the manager of a consulting firm could be given authority for the complete hiring sequence for the Chicago branch—recruitment, screening, selection, assignment, and orientation of all new personnel.

3. Functional. The limits of authority for performing a duty or task are determined by the content, subject matter, or discipline involved in the performance of the task. In effect, functional delegation recognizes the need for highly developed knowledge and skills or specialization. Functional delegation should *always* be carefully restricted. Typically, it grants authority over activities or procedures to a specific individual or position in a well-defined area of enterprise operations. It usually involves authority over the "how," sometimes over the "when," and only rarely the "who," "where," or "what."

Principles of Delegation

The HR manager would do well to consider very carefully what to delegate. Three categories of principles apply. The first set of principles concerns identifying legitimate bases for delegating functions, duties, and tasks. The second set has to do with how the scope of the authority delegated to subordinates should be determined. The third set is concerned with the specific functions that should and should not be delegated.

Bases for Delegation

There are four legitimate bases for making decisions about delegating functions, duties, and tasks: logic, work flow, work load, and skills and abilities.

Logic. The guideline here is to assign functions, duties, and tasks to people because their normal functions and responsibilities are logically related to the tasks to be delegated. For example, it is logical to assign the additional function of determining the weighting of various factors used to select personnel to the manager or supervisor who makes the final hiring decision.

Work flow. This criterion indicates that functions, duties, and tasks should be assigned on the basis of complete work flow—and not necessarily on how much the function is related to other duties the person performs. For example, although the functions of *developing* and *validating* training materials, such as interactive video programs, are quite dissimilar, they represent a complete package of work; therefore, approving authority for both should probably be assigned to the same manager.

Work load. When a manager's or supervisor's work load becomes excessive or verges on the unmanageable, delegation of some functions, duties, and tasks is an essential action to preclude slowdowns, bad decisions, or inaction. For example, an unanticipated vacancy in a key position either immediately above or below the HR manager is certain to result in additional duties and responsibilities for the HR manager. If the position remains unfilled for any length of time, some of the HR manager's regular duties and some of the duties assumed because of the vacancy must be delegated to others.

Skills and abilities. This criterion says that functions, duties, and tasks that exceed the skills and abilities of the manager, or that can be performed substantially better by subordinates, should be delegated to those subordinates. No HR manager can be an expert in all the skills and abilities represented within the HR function. Whether the staff is large or small, it is almost certain that some subordinate HR personnel will have expertise in areas where the manager has little or none. Those are the functions, duties, and tasks that should be delegated.

Scope of Authority Delegated

The scope of authority delegated to subordinates depends on four important factors: organization policies, the authority held by the delegator, the duties, tasks, and activities of the delegatee, and the competencies of the delegatee.

Policies. Consideration must be given to organization policies and rules about the types of delegated authority that are permissible. In some organizations, delegating some functions—such as strategic planning, organization planning, capital expenditures, purchases above a stated amount—are not permitted below a certain level in the hierarchical structure.

Authority of the delegator.   In all organizations, a determining factor in delegation is the actual authority held by the delegator—that is, the authority conferred by his or her boss. Simply stated, you can't delegate authority that you don't have—unless you're willing to risk censure, even termination.

Duties of the delegatee.   Consideration must be given to the duties, activities, and tasks embodied in the job of the subordinate; authority delegated must be consistent with the job description and the results expected of the person holding that job. Never *require* subordinates to do something that is totally unrelated to their jobs. You can request, but don't demand. If you do, you will almost certainly guarantee failure.

Competencies of the delegatee.   Finally, the delegator must be attentive to the competencies of those to whom functions, duties, and authority are assigned. This is the human side of delegation. Never require subordinates to perform functions that exceed their capabilities. To do otherwise is to be imprudent, if not downright foolish. The outcome is predictable—failure to complete the assignment satisfactorily. Delegate up to the limits of the employee's ability, but not beyond.

Three Levels of Delegation

Although the amount and kind of delegated authority for the performance of HR functions, duties, and tasks can vary from zero to infinity, three levels of delegation are sufficiently discrete and different to be distinguished from each other.

1. Accountability for specific tasks. This is the lowest level. Here the degree of freedom and initiative that the employee has in performing a specific task varies greatly with the amount of supervision involved and the importance and complexity of the task.

In terms of ascending difficulty, subordinates may perform tasks that involve (1) standard procedures; (2) definite skills but under fairly precise instructions on methods; (3) well-defined skills but with only general or "mission-type" instructions, given with a focus on what to produce but not how (methods are left to the delegatee); and (4) skills that either the manager doesn't have at all or that the subordinate is better at, so that the subordinate has almost complete autonomy for the task.

2. Authority over others. At this level of delegation, the employee is granted authority to supervise, direct, and control other employees. The amount of freedom the employee will delegate are the same as the first three in paragraph 1 above.

3. Complete authority. Here the employee is given complete authority and autonomy for a major function or subdivision—marketing, sales,
training, organization development, research and development, or
branch managership.

Another Perspective on Levels

Another way of looking at the amount of authority delegated involves the degree of independence that the manager allows. There are
four levels:

1. Await direction: await authority and instructions before acting.
2. Ask before acting: authority to act only after getting permission.
3. Act and report: authority to act but with the stipulation that the
   delegatee must report to the delegator what was done.
4. Act: authority to act autonomously and independently.

Extremes in Level of Delegation

As we have just seen, delegation is a relationship between the delegator and the delegatee. The degree of delegation may vary considerably,
depending on the philosophy and attitude of the delegator and the
degree of supervision he or she exercises. It may also vary with the
attitude, skill, initiative, and dedication of the delegatee. The extremes
are illustrated by the following two examples.

Tight Delegation

Sally Jones is principal of a small training and consulting firm in
Kansas City. She has recently hired Joe Smith, a recent graduate of
Central University's master of arts program with a major in HR, as an
associate. Initially, Sally expects that Joe will listen to what she says and
carry out instructions on the elementary operations she entrusts to him,
such as preparing seminar rooms, operating audiovisual equipment, and
registering participants. Gradually, Sally will show Joe how to perform
more complex functions, such as assisting with management surveys and
developing draft proposals. Ultimately, she will allow Joe to carry out all
the tasks involved in his special skills, such as acting in an advisory
capacity to a client.

Initially, Sally will watch and check *how* Joe goes about each assigned
task. Later, she will be satisfied with simply checking the *results*. When
Joe becomes sufficiently competent to hold the title of "professional
consultant" and be entrusted with complex consulting assignments, he
will have completed his training and become accepted by Sally as a full-
fledged associate.

Autonomous Delegation

Jim Teller is the trusted manager of the Seattle office of a large HR corporation headquartered in New York City. He is neither visited regularly nor called to New York except in unusual circumstances. Jim has been given complete responsibility for all the affairs of the branch, and corporate officers are totally satisfied with his annual results. The New York office merely keeps Jim informed of developments in other branches of the company and honors his requests for assistance from financial, marketing, or R&D departments.

Corporate officers have complete confidence that Jim has trained his subordinates so well that, should he become ill or incapacitated, branch operations would continue without interruptions or major problems. New York headquarters relies on Jim to take action to develop and market workshops and training programs, and supports his requests for financial backing, compatible with other corporate budgetary commitments. In short, Jim enjoys the complete confidence of his superiors and has as much freedom of action as he would have if he owned the business.

Guidelines for Delegation

The HR manager has an obligation to foster conditions that make for proper delegation, to select functions, duties, and tasks that are appropriate for delegation, to choose the people for the assignments, and to make the delegations effectively.

Good Conditions for Delegation

The very first thing HR managers must do to ensure the success of the delegation process is to accept the need for delegation. Then they must discuss delegation with their superiors to get approval in principle of their plans for delegation. Then they must create and maintain an atmosphere in which subordinate managers and supervisors can feel confident and secure. They must do everything possible to remove the elements of fear, lack of trust, and frustration. They must also keep in mind that employee and union-management relationships must be harmonious.

Next, they must train their subordinates in the delegation process and continuously provide coaching to improve their performance in delegating their own authority. Then they must develop goals and plans for delegation and appropriate and effective controls. They must select the functions and duties to be delegated and the individual managers and supervisors to whom the delegations are to be made. They must establish clear and unequivocal lines of authority and responsibility—and then ensure that they are understood through constant clarification, refinement, and reinforcement. There must be no doubt as to what authority each manager and supervisor has. Use published and distributed organization charts, job descriptions, policy manuals, periodic discussions with the people involved, and personal observation and checks of performance.

Last, they must adopt a constructive and permissive managerial attitude. They must reward effective delegation, make it a factor in performance appraisal, and use it as a standard for promotion. In addition, they must demonstrate patience and forbearance with their subordinates as they develop their skills in delegation. Above all, they must allow some latitude for mistakes in judgment. Subordinates' errors should be used as educational devices rather than as occasions for destructive criticism or punishment.

Here are some specific recommendations:

- Give each subordinate manager and supervisor opportunities to participate in developing the HR department's goals, objectives, and policies.
- Cooperatively develop with all managers and supervisors clearly expressed, written objectives and the results they are accountable for accomplishing.
- Delegate authority to plan, schedule, and program major activities and projects.
- Set budget limits broadly enough to permit final decision by managers and supervisors on most activities included in approved programs.
- Establish performance standards that are at least in part based on cost or profit.
- Require periodic reports on progress, performance, and results.
- Provide opportunities for subordinate managers and supervisors to win incentive awards that are directly tied to performance.
- Provide opportunities for all subordinate managers and supervisors to participate in an enterprise-sponsored management development program.

What to Delegate

Delegations may be specific or general, written or oral, but they must be accompanied by the assignment of functions, duties, or tasks. That brings us to the question, "What authority should an HR manager delegate?" The answer, as we have noted, depends in part on the skills and abilities of subordinate personnel. Here are some additional guidelines.

If a subordinate is to be held accountable for performance of a function or task, delegate enough authority to get the job done correctly and expeditiously. Delegate all routine, recurring jobs and tasks. But don't stop there; delegate *all* types of tasks—difficult, challenging, unique or one of a kind. Whenever possible, delegate a total job or task, not just a part of one.

Select tasks and functions that require research, study, and recommendations. Choose *some* activities that stretch the scope of the subordinate's present job. Select activities that tap talent and either further the organization's goals or expand the employee's outlook. However, keep the list of delegated tasks short. Delegate matters that concern only one person to that very person. Delegate all tasks where consistency and coordination are relatively unimportant. Delegate functions and tasks where technology permits individual discretion.

Keep in mind that all delegations are subject to recall. This usually happens because things change—goals, policies, programs, organization structure, departmental objectives, or personnel—or because the employee, for one reason or another, fails to perform satisfactorily.

What Not to Delegate

What authority should an HR manager retain? Obviously, a definitive list is impossible, but we can make some generalizations. First, the manager should usually retain authority to take actions that involve two or more subordinate HR elements, other departments, or other organizations. Where consistency and coordination of critical decisions are needed, the HR manager should remain in charge. The manager should also reserve final decision-making authority over the broad aspects of departmental planning, organizing, staffing, and controlling, and policies relating to those functions. Specifically, if the decision involves approving items like these, the HR manager should *not* delegate:

Department budget	Sales prices of programs and
Department policies	services
Large-dollar purchases	Price quotations
Capital expenditures	Proposals and contracts
Sale of capital equipment	Credit
Travel expenses	Staff salary increases
Major new programs and	New staff positions
services	

The Delegation Process

The actual process of delegation requires careful planning and skillful execution. Let's look at the elements one by one.

Plan the delegation. Decide *what* you are going to delegate using the guidelines described earlier. Identify the functions, duties, and tasks that you *can* delegate, that you *must* delegate, and that you *cannot* (for strategic reasons) delegate. Select functions and tasks that are appropriate for a particular position and within the capabilities of the incumbent of that position. Start with routine, recurring duties. Don't limit functions and tasks to those the employee has done in the past. Move on to developmental tasks. Broaden people's skills by assigning tasks that are new but for which you believe they have the potential to complete satisfactorily. Tap the talents available. Assign functions and tasks that are difficult (but do-able), challenging, and unique.

Assign functions, duties, and tasks. Select the delegatee. Consider the nature of the task and the skills, knowledge, experience, motivation, and developmental needs of the employee. Match the individual to the task.

Delegate in advance; don't drop problems on someone without warning. Assign work gradually; don't dump on the employee all at once. Delegate at the end of a day to avoid disrupting the employee's plans and schedules. Meet with the person selected for the delegation. Get his or her ideas about work load and priorities before giving additional assignments. Discuss the task before it is delegated. Tell delegatees what's in it for them. Show the relationship and importance of the task to their personal goals and objectives.

Clarify what you want done. Explain the "why" of the assignment. Spell out the results you expect in terms of specific action and in relation to the organization as a whole. Identify the principal steps to the objective. But don't do it autonomously. Find out what subordinates know about the task. Get their ideas: how should the task be approached, what standards can be met, and how much authority can they handle? Of course, you make the final decision, but the participation of employees is essential to success.

Delegate the authority to act. Delegate enough authority to get the job done—authority to use resources, to make commitments and decisions, and to take action. Remember that if you give people too little authority, they will find it difficult, if not impossible, to complete the job. But also set limits on the authority delegated so that subordinates will not make decisions or take actions that they should not.

When you delegate a function or task, say what you mean and mean what you say. For example, don't tell subordinates they have full authority to purchase materials and supplies (of course, within budget) and then require them to submit all purchase orders to you for approval. If the delegation or the function is critical, put the scope of authority in writing.

Delegate authority to subordinates as long as it is needed—and as long as they use it effectively and wisely. Don't be whimsical in your delegation—granting it one month and retracting it the next without any sound reason.

Withdraw authority only when a task has been completed, a responsibility has been fulfilled, or a subordinate has conclusively demonstrated lack of readiness or ability to perform the task.

Obtain commitment. Be sure people understand that they have an obligation to perform the task up to standard and within the time frame. Make them feel responsible for achieving the desired results. Ask questions to make sure there is no doubt about what is to be done and when. Again, be sure that subordinates understand the extent and limits of authority. Mutually establish means and times for reporting progress.

Monitor performance. Encourage employees to perform on their own. Once a job is delegated, leave them alone to do it. Allow sufficient freedom to achieve objectives. Never suggest that a job be done "your way." Balance your supervision of delegated tasks somewhere between benign neglect and looking over someone's shoulders.

Keep communication open. Review and measure both progress and results. Request status reports. Indicate that your door is open for help should they really need it, but don't encourage them to double check each and every step with you. Simply explain what help is available if needed. If subordinates come to you with questions, don't provide an answer. Instead ask, "What do you think should be done?" Get them to answer their own questions.

Providing feedback. If the task is complex or long-term, provide feedback on performance regularly but not on a set schedule. If the person is doing well—making good progress, meeting the standards, and remaining on schedule—say so. If, on the other hand, the subordinate makes mistakes or is failing the task, review the initial assignment. Was your delegation faulty: inadequate information, insufficient authority, inadequate resources, unrealistic standards, or too short a time frame? If so, make the needed changes and proceed from there.

If the subordinate is at fault (poor judgment, inadequate hustle, lack of attention), you can—depending on the severity of the deficiency—provide assistance and continue the assignment, or delegate it to someone else. If at all possible, however, try to make good use of errors; remember that delegation is a form of training. In any case, always tell subordinates exactly what they did well and identify areas where improvement is needed.

Evaluating results. Periodically, every HR manager should review the results of delegation to determine where improvements can be made. Sometimes the review will point to a need for greater attention to the delegation process itself—*how* authority is delegated. Other times the review will indicate that some functions and duties should be taken from one person and reassigned to another—to *whom* authority is delegated. In any event, evaluation of both the process and results is essential.

Steps in Delegation

In summary, the HR manager who delegates a task or function and the authority to carry it out, will follow these steps:

1. Accept the need for delegation.
2. Develop a detailed plan for delegation.
3. Get your supervisor's approval of your plans for delegation.
4. Establish the proper climate for delegation; remove the elements of fear and lack of trust, and replace them with mutual confidence and trust.
5. Train your subordinate managers and supervisors in the delegation process; set the example.
6. Select the functions, duties, and tasks to be delegated and assign them to individual managers and supervisors.
7. Establish clear lines of authority and responsibility and ensure that they are understood by all.
8. Adopt a constructive managerial attitude; demonstrate patience and forbearance when subordinates make mistakes.
9. Monitor performance and provide frequent feedback.
10. Reward effective delegation.
11. Periodically review and evaluate delegation efforts.
12. Improve the delegation process.

Summary

In delegating, the HR manager assigns functions, duties, or tasks to subordinates and creates an obligation on their part to perform in accordance with established standards. Although the manager must delegate authority, and in turn the subordinate must accept the obligation to perform, the manager retains ultimate authority and responsibility for whatever happens as a result of the delegation.

Delegation produces benefits to the organization, the HR manager, and the subordinate. Among other things, delegation increases the flexibility of the organization, fosters maximum use of available talent, improves decisions, reduces stress, develops subordinates, builds confidence and initiative, develops responsibility, increases productivity, and enhances employee job satisfaction, motivation, and morale.

When delegation fails, the failure can be from organizational conditions, flaws in the delegation process, managerial ineffectiveness, or lack of interest or responsibility on the part of subordinates.

Decisions about what should be delegated should be made on the basis of logic, work flow, work load, or available skills and abilities. The amount of authority delegated should be determined by organization policies, the authority of the manager, and the competencies and attitudes of the employees.

FOR FURTHER READING

Anthony, William P. *Participative Management.* Reading, Mass.: Addison-Wesley, 1978.

Balfour, Campbell, ed. *Participation in Industry.* Harwood Heights, Ill.: Roman, 1973.

Brannen, Peter. *Authority and Participation in Industry.* New York: St. Martin's Press, 1984.

Bristol, Poly. *Leadership and Delegation.* New York: State Mutual Book & Periodical Service, 521 Fifth Avenue, 10017.

Child, John. *Organization: A Guide to Problems and Practice.* New York: Harper & Row, 1984.

Dessler, Gary. *Organization and Management.* Englewood Cliffs, N.J.: Prentice-Hall, 1982.

Engle, Herbert M. *How to Delegate: A Guide to Getting Things Done.* Houston, Tex.: Gulf Publishing, 1983.

Galbraith, Jay. *Designing Complex Organizations.* Reading, Mass.: Addison-Wesley, 1973.

Jenks, James M., and John M. Kelly. *Don't Do. Delegate! The Secret Power of Successful Managers.* Danbury, Conn.: Franklin Watts, 1985.

Kolasa, Blair J. *Responsibility in Business: Issues and Problems.* Englewood Cliffs, N.J.: Prentice-Hall, 1972.

Krein, Theodore J. "How to Improve Delegation Habits." *Management Review,* May 1982, pp. 58–61.

LeBoeuf, M. *Working Smart: How to Accomplish More in Half the Time.* Del Mar, Calif.: McGraw-Hill Training Systems, 1979.

McConkey, Dale D. *No-Nonsense Delegation.* New York: AMACOM, 1979.

Massarik, Fred. *Participative Management.* Elmsford, N.Y.: Pergamon Press, 1983.

Steinmetz, Lawrence L. *The Art and Skill of Delegation.* Reading, Mass.: Addison-Wesley Training Systems, 1976.

Taylor, Harold. *Delegate: The Key to Successful Management.* New York: Beauford Books, 1984.

Varney, Glenn H. *Organization Development for Managers.* Reading, Mass.: Addison-Wesley, 1977.

Vinton, Donna. "Delegation for Employee Development." *Training and Development Journal,* January 1987, pp. 65–67.

Williams, Ervin. *Participative Management: Concepts, Theory and Implementation.* Atlanta: Georgia State University, Business Publishing Division, 1976.

11

APPRAISING
Assessing Performance and Potential

Few HR managers today would question the need to improve employees' performance. Most are faced with the demands for greater efficiency, productivity, and return on investment. Specialists in the use of "human resources," HR managers have a major role to play in meeting those challenges.

The HR manager's job is to get results through the contributions of people. One important facet of this involves appraisal of their work and the results achieved. Effective performance appraisal includes explicit performance standards—what you expect of subordinates, what aspects of the work will be evaluated, when you expect the work to be completed, and how much you expect to be accomplished.

Some managers view performance appraisal as more of a millstone than an effective management tool. Yet with computerization and automation so pervasive today, employees need to know that their bosses truly care about their technical, professional, managerial, and personal development. They need personal contacts to make them feel valued, appreciated, respected, and enable them to become more productive and effective. A skillful performance appraisal can accomplish that.

In practice, however, performance appraisals do not always live up to expectations. Organizations are constantly reassessing their programs, asking: What purpose does performance appraisal serve? What makes it work? What makes it go wrong? What is the most we can expect from it? Does it increase efficiency and productivity?

Definition and Purpose

Performance appraisal is a systematic, periodic, collaborative review and analysis of employees' performance with the objective of improving that performance so that employees can realize their full potential. It involves measuring how well subordinates do the job as compared with a set of performance standards, communicating that information to employees, getting their own evaluation of performance, agreeing on strengths and deficiencies, and developing a plan of action to enhance strengths and shore up weaknesses.

Performance appraisal is much more than filling out forms once or twice each year and sending them to the personnel office. It involves difficult and important decisions by a manager about what is expected of subordinates and how they measure up to those expectations.

Performance appraisal is not an isolated event. It is needed for economic, legal, and social reasons. It is an active process characterized by six distinct sequential components: (1) identification of critical job requirements, (2) communication of those requirements and standards to employees, (3) collection and evaluation of performance data, (4) documentation of progress and accomplishment during the performance period, (5) performance appraisal interview, and (6) follow-up.

The primary purpose of performance appraisal is to assess and improve job performance. In addition, it can also serve several important secondary purposes.

- To establish job objectives.
- To delegate authority and responsibility.
- To communicate expectations with regard to standards of performance.
- To change the attitudes and behavior of subordinates.
- To tell subordinates where they stand.
- To facilitate use of subordinates' skills and talents.
- To build on strengths and remedy weaknesses.
- To identify employees' goals and aspirations.
- To provide a sound basis for making job assignments, transfers, and promotions.
- To provide motivation and incentives.
- To obtain information from subordinates.
- To provide information to subordinates.
- To document personnel actions to prevent legal difficulties.
- To provide data for forecasting personnel needs.
- To provide feedback on performance.
- To reward outstanding performance.
- To determine readiness for advancement.
- To serve as a basis for career counseling.
- To provide a basis for coaching interventions.
- To identify training and development needs.

Should performance appraisals be used as a basis for salary decisions? No. They are two totally different actions, intended to serve entirely different purposes. Performance appraisals are carried out to improve performance; they focus on specific job requirements and standards, the details of job performance, and are (theoretically) objective and cooperative. Salary decisions consider employees' overall performance, compare their contributions to employees of equivalent rank and position, tend to be more subjective, and include factors other than performance—seniority, credentials, industry salary range, and fund availability.

Three Kinds of Benefits

Performance appraisal is important to the organization, the manager, and the subordinate. All three stand to benefit from an effective appraisal system and suffer substantial losses under an ineffective system.

1. Organizational benefits. To survive in today's competitive environment, organizations must do more than encourage topnotch performance. They must also measure, evaluate, and reward performance. HR managers must view appraisal as an investment in the future of their organizations.

An effective appraisal system can provide (1) improved efficiency, productivity, and return on investment; (2) relevant and objective information on which to base placement, training and development, promotion, and other personnel actions; (3) information about current workers upon which to base long-term human resources plans; and (4) improved employee performance, job satisfaction, and morale.

2. Benefits to managers. An effective performance appraisal system provides managers with several important benefits: (1) better understanding of their subordinates, their motivation, capabilities, deficiencies, and aspirations; (2) information on which to base their coaching, training, and development interventions; (3) feedback on their own performance as managers; and (4) improved efficiency and effectiveness of HR programs and services.

3. Benefits to subordinates. Employees stand to gain a great deal from an effective appraisal program. It lets them know where they stand in the organization; provides realistic objectives and standards against which they can measure their own progress and performance; helps identify career opportunities and blocks; and gives feedback on their performance. The plain fact of the matter is that people not only expect appraisal, they demand it.

"Never lose sight of the fact that your employees want to be measured accurately; they want feedback and they want to be rewarded accordingly. Performance assessment is a much maligned subject, but it must be given greater attention in response to employees' demand for a vital and accurate process."[1]

Types of Appraisal

Performance appraisal may take many forms and use different formats. Each represents a different philosophy of management or, at the very least, a different approach to the process.

Informal

Informal performance appraisals might better be called casual or seat-of-the-pants evaluation. Personnel decisions, such as promotion, tenure, reassignment, or termination, may be based on nothing more than periodic observation by supervisors that involve no constructive feedback or attempt to improve performance and potential. No standards of performance are identified and no objective measures of performance are employed. The result is likely to be evaluation of personal traits, bias, inconsistency in judging subordinates, and lack of fairness. Although not uncommon in small organizations, informal evaluation has nothing to commend it. It should be avoided.

Formal

Formal performance evaluation is structured assessment designed to eliminate subjectivity, bias, inconsistency, and unfairness. It makes use of standards and measures of performance, frequent observation and measurement of performance against the standards, feedback to employees, and written records of the process and its results. However, there are four quite different forms of formal performance appraisal: directive, collaborative, reciprocal, and peer.

Directive. This is one-way or one-sided evaluation. The superior observes, evaluates, and provides feedback on performance to subordinates, who are allowed little or no input into the process. The manager establishes the standards, chooses the measures, does the evaluating, reports findings to subordinates at an appraisal review, makes suggestions for improvement, and records the results. Although better than informal appraisal, directive appraisal is not recommended.

Collaborative. This kind of appraisal is cooperative evaluation involving both manager and subordinate. Together they establish the

1. John H. Zimmerman, "Human Resource Management at MCI," *Management Review,* April 1986, p. 51.

standards, choose the performance measures, jointly evaluate progress and accomplishment, identify needed improvements, and establish an action plan. The subject of the evaluation, however, is the subordinate alone. This is the most common form of performance appraisal.

Reciprocal review. More and more organizations are instituting reciprocal review programs, in which the performance of *both* the manager and the subordinate is evaluated. The subordinate evaluates the manager and the manager evaluates the subordinate based on performance criteria and measures agreed to in advance by both parties. Together they determine progress and accomplishment, identify shortfalls, and establish action plans. Records of the appraisals are maintained.

Peer. Peer performance appraisal is performed by an employee's peers—colleagues, team members, or other employees of equivalent rank who have adequate opportunities to observe performance. Employees rate each other. Although this can be used as a substitute for other forms of appraisal, it typically is used as a supplement to either collaborative or reciprocal performance appraisal. It employs predetermined performance standards, some form of rating scale, and feedback of results to the individual.

Qualifications of Raters

It is true, of course, that every supervisor and manager inevitably is involved in rating subordinates. However, to do the job well, there are several important qualifications.

Knowledge of job requirements. The rater must always have a thorough knowledge of job requirements and standards. Without a detailed knowledge of the functions, duties, tasks, and authority delegated to the subordinate, a rater is in no position to evaluate performance, progress, or accomplishment.

Opportunity to observe and evaluate. No one should appraise anyone unless there has been ample opportunity to observe the performance or the results of the performance and collect relevant data. That does not mean that the appraiser must have continuous, daily, or even weekly personal contact with the subordinate. It does mean, however, that the rater must have some way of arriving at an objective judgment of performance, based on regular review of work products and at least occasional personal contact, personal observation, or both.

Objectivity. Perhaps the most difficult qualification is objectivity, freedom from bias. This means having the ability to judge performance, not personality. It is not an innate trait; it must be acquired over time. It requires continuous surveillance by both parties to see that subjectivity does not creep in. A later section of this chapter will address some of the most common rating errors—errors that are a reflection of subjectivity in one form or another.

Attitudes. Although it should be obvious that the manager's attitudes toward appraisal and subordinates are crucial, it might be useful to identify them here. Managers must not only accept performance appraisal as necessary but also see it as a means of improving both their own performance and that of subordinates. Managers must also have concern for people, respect subordinates, believe in their ability to improve, want to help, and encourage their improvement efforts.

Skills. Although many separate skills are involved in the performance appraisal process, three are of paramount importance: listening, observing, and interviewing. All three require training and supervised practice, focusing on the development of standards, listening, observing, rating, providing feedback, and recording information. Refer to Chapters 1, 5, and 8 for detailed discussion of these skills.

Criteria for the Appraisal Program

To be successful, performance appraisal programs must meet certain criteria relating to management support, clarity of objectives, format, and procedures.

Organizational support. First and foremost, the performance appraisal program must have the unconditional support of all organizational constituencies—top executives, managers and supervisors, the union, and workers at all levels. Appraisal must be based on a sound system in which all participants have confidence. If any one of those groups resists the program, even passively, the program cannot succeed. That support cannot be won unless the importance of appraisal is clear to all concerned, users participate in the design of the system, and managers are adequately trained and rewarded for carrying out the program conscientiously.

Regular schedule. Performance appraisal cannot be a sometime thing. It must be conducted on a regular schedule. A good schedule involves more than one annual review—do it quarterly, or at the very least semiannually.

Objective and results oriented. The third criterion underscores the need for objectivity and a "results" orientation. The review must be confidential, fair, impartial, ethical, honest, and must avoid both positive and negative bias. That is, the system must focus on job requirements and performance and not on personality. Ratings must be based on agreed-upon standards. They must be founded on specific, measurable performance objectives. Forms used must be standardized for specific jobs and consistently applied to similar positions. Ratings must be based on truly representative, sufficient, and relevant observations by the rater, not only of performance, but also of *results*. Recommendations for changes or improvements must be clearly stated and recorded.

Cooperative and collaborative. The system must emphasize cooperation between rater and subordinate. It must provide for the participation of the subordinate in establishing standards and measures of performance, evaluation of progress and accomplishment, and the determination of next steps toward improvement. There must be agreement on the critical elements of job performance.

Factual and specific. The appraisal system must provide specific feedback to subordinates. The results of the appraisal must be communicated to subordinates clearly and completely—and sincerely, without evasion or equivocation. Raters must be alert for the introduction of bias and errors. They must describe behavior specifically and factually. They must avoid "adjectival" comments. They must tell the truth and not waffle about their evaluation.

Legal. The performance appraisal system must be job related and not a substitute for "tests." It must make use of formal evaluation criteria. It must not discriminate (negatively affect disproportionately members of protected groups). There must be a direct relationship between the performance measured by the system and success on the job in question. It must be administered under standardized conditions. Raters must have personal knowledge of and contact with the person rated. There must be a review process, including an appeals procedures, to prevent a manager from taking action alone that significantly affects an employee's career.

Meaningful and useful. The system should be meaningful and helpful to all constituencies. It should be useful in personnel planning and forecasting, in making management decisions, for training and development, as a basis for coaching, and for giving awards and recognition.

Tested before use. Finally, no performance appraisal system should be installed until it has been subjected to a full test under normal working conditions. That test should include a sample of workers at all levels destined to be rated under the system. The raters should be trained prior to the test. All instructions and forms should be used as designed. Careful analysis of results, including the reactions of raters and ratees to the system, should be made.

Factors Influencing Performance

Not all cases of deficient performance are attributable to subordinates. Many different factors influence performance: company policies, the manager, the work group, or the work itself. There are three categories of influences on the productivity of knowledge workers. (That is, people whose work is, for the most part, intellectual: planners, problem-solvers, decision makers, and managers. Typically, their effectiveness cannot be easily measured in tangible products or outputs.) See Figure 11-1.

Company policies. Substandard performance can often be traced to dissatisfaction with company policies, particularly those relating to compensation and benefits, incentives and awards, and employee relations. Discontent about limited opportunities for employee participation in policy formulation and the development of work rules is much more common today than it was only a few years ago. In any event, corporate policies, rules, and regulations can be an important source of shoddy job performance.

The work group. Performance deficiencies can also be caused by the employee's work group, including the manager or supervisor. Specific conditions that can give rise to mediocre performance include ineffective supervision, lack of recognition and acceptance, discrimination and prejudice, lack of assistance and support by either the work group or the supervisor, and interpersonal conflicts.

The work itself. People sometimes become dissatisfied with the job itself and fail to perform up to expectations. Some of the most common reasons for such discontent are that the work is too difficult or too stressful, that the job lacks challenge, that it involves hazards to health and safety, or that working conditions in general are unsatisfactory. Other reasons for substandard performance may be displeasure with geographic location or the shift worked.

Figure 11-1. Influences on knowledge worker productivity.

External	Internal	Peer Group
Government regulations	Company benefits	Recognition of technical competence by internal peers
Societal demands	Participative management	
Community needs		
Professional associations	Decision-making involvement	Recognition of technical competence by external peers
Customer requirements	Quality of work life	
Unionization	Two-way communications	Opportunity to provide assistance to group members
Economic shifts		
Competition	Clearly defined goals	
Market shifts	Mutual respect	A social environment divorced from the sociotechnical environment of the company
Educational systems	Meaningful assignments	

From Ira B. Gregerman, *Knowledge Worker Productivity* (New York: AMACOM, 1981), 15. Used by permission.

Employee shortcomings. However, most substandard performance begins with the subordinate. Motivational problems are an important source of substandard performance. They can be caused by fear of failure, harsh or extremely negative criticism, frustration, lack of appropriate rewards, work standards that are too high or too low, or lack of feedback. Sometimes the root problem lies in the employee's lack of job knowledge, inadequate reading, writing or speaking abilities, insufficient aptitude for the work (mechanical or scholastic), or limited intelligence.

Emotional problems can run the gamut from insecurity, depression and anxiety, to neurosis or psychosis. The symptoms or origin of other emotional problems may be in alcoholism or substance abuse or family difficulties and concerns. Still other sources of substandard performance include illness, whether temporary or chronic, handicapping conditions, and physical characteristics, such as disfigurement, obesity, thinness, or insufficient muscular development.

Also, family problems of one type or another can result in poor quality work performance. Among the most common are recent or pending divorce or separation, other marital problems, financial problems, illness or hospitalization of spouse or child, or death of parent, spouse, child, or close friend.

Rating Methods

There are two types of rating scales, absolute and relative. Either type may be used exclusively or they may be combined to gain the advantages of both.

Absolute

Absolute rating scales require the rater to assign an absolute value to the trait or performance being rated without any reference to any other person. In other words, the rater uses a fixed scale. There are several types of absolute scales.

Numerical Scales

The numerical scale is the simplest absolute form. Although any number of points can be used, an odd number is usually chosen so that the middle number represents the average. The number of points on the scale depends on the number of observable differentiations, the uses to which the ratings are to be put, and the ability of raters to discriminate accurately. Because few evaluators can make more than nine or ten differentiations, most numerical rating scales contain five to nine points. A five-point scale divides a group into highest, above average, average, below average, and lowest.

Descriptive Scales

Descriptive scales use adjectives or phrases to rate levels of ability, proficiency, or performance. Descriptive scales are more versatile than numerical scales because the adjectives or phrases can be varied to suit the situation. It is wise to keep in mind that for performance appraisals, descriptive phrases, rather than adjectives, are preferred. A portion of a descriptive scale used to rate the questioning technique of an instructor is shown in Figure 11-2.

Essay appraisal. This method of descriptive rating is simply an open-ended statement that describes a subordinate's performance. It can be written by the manager, the subordinate, peers, or a combination of all three. It is most effective when it is based on and cites facts about performance relating to established performance standards—on results achieved, observable behavior, or progress toward objectives. It is least effective when the statement is general and only vaguely related to performance standards. It is most helpful in rating performance of a job that involves abstract knowledge or skills, such as in HR. Ideally, it should be used in conjunction with a graphic rating scale, and in situations that provide ample opportunity for discussion by the parties involved. In the final analysis, however, the effectiveness of the essay rating depends on the rater's ability to express an appraisal in written form.

Critical incident technique. This descriptive approach is a means of refining the essay-type appraisal. The rater is asked to observe and record specific incidents of effective and ineffective performance involving each subordinate during a rating period. These observations are matched against a predetermined critical incident, often referred to as a behaviorally anchored rating scale (BARS). A numerical value can be

Figure 11-2. A portion of a descriptive scale used to rate instructors.

Instructions: Place a check mark opposite the item that best describes the instructor being rated.

1. No evidence of planning; questions unsuitable because of irrelevance, vagueness, or vocabulary level; handles responses poorly; often misunderstands trainee questions.   _____
2. Some evidence of planning; questions well formulated and understood by trainees; uses thought-provoking questions; trainee questions and responses well handled.   _____
3. Evidence of thorough planning; questions elicit interested and effective trainee responses; uses correct procedures; distributes questions and provides complete answers.   _____

derived from the scale, but that is not essential. The incidents are discussed with the employee, and are used as a basis for developing an improvement plan. Although it is time-consuming and demands a great amount of detail in record keeping, it is very useful in middle- and upper-level professional, technical, and managerial positions. An example of a critical incident log is shown in Figure 11-3.

Graphic Scales

Graphic scales combine the numerical and descriptive forms. They contain both a numerical scale and adjectives or descriptive phrases that describe theoretically equally spaced degrees of performance placed below a horizontal line (see Figure 11-4). The length of the line represents the full range of the ability, performance, or trait to be rated. The rater is usually asked to select a point on the scale that best describes each employee's performance. The rater must consider both the numerical scale and the descriptive phrases. This type of scale is one of the easiest to use. However, unless it is based on performance factors and standards, it is subject to the rating errors described later in this chapter.

Behaviorally Anchored Rating Scales

The most useful, practical, and fairest type of scale for performance appraisal is undoubtedly the behaviorally anchored rating scale (BARS).

Figure 11-3. A sample critical incident log.

Positive	Negative
06/11/87 Assumed responsibility for a subordinate's mistakes when the _____program failed.	07/10/87 Misunderstood my instructions because he did not ask for clarification of the _____assignment.
08/23/87 Exercised good judgment in establishing department priorities for development projects.	08/05/87 Showed indifference in his relationships with colleagues; preferred to work alone on the _____plan.
10/10/87 Stimulated OD personnel to meet higher performance standards through personal example and constant positive reinforcement.	10/25/87 Accepted substandard products from the clerical staff.
12/21/87 Presented a topnotch briefing to the board of directors on the _____project.	11/21/87 Failed to resolve a personal problem that prevented management from meeting an important target date for initiating the _____plan.
	12/02/87 Set inadequate performance standards for subordinate instructors.

Figure 11-4. A sample item from a graphic rating scale.

Item 9. Knowledge of subject matter

1	2	3	4	5
Fundamental knowl-edge lacking; devoid of allied information; frequent errors of fact		Knowledge limited to specific area of instructional responsibility, but clearly adequate for current duties		Demonstrates mastery of subject; genuine scholarship; rich store of knowledge of related fields

These scales focus on the *critical tasks* of a job, emphasize *observable behavior*, distinguish between *behavior* and *results,* and stress needed *improvements* in performance by providing descriptions of effective and ineffective performance.

Forced-Choice Scales

This type of appraisal resembles a test. The rater is asked to complete a form containing items assigned a meaning by someone else. Thus the rater may not know whether the rating being given is favorable or unfavorable. The method was designed to eliminate the problems inherent in the graphic scale—rater errors. This type of rating is applicable to almost any type of job at any level.

Forced-choice rating scales use two to five descriptions of behavior in each section of the scale. Both favorable and unfavorable statements are included in each section. Most forced-choice instruments contain 25 to 30 sections. Figure 11-5 shows a single section containing four descriptions, two favorable and two unfavorable. The rater is asked to select the statement that is most characteristic and the one that is least characteristic.

Checklists

A checklist is a set of descriptive statements or questions. If statements are used, the rater simply checks those items he or she believes are characteristic of the subordinate and leaves the others blank. If questions are used, the rater uses a plus or minus sign to indicate whether the performance is satisfactory or unsatisfactory. (See Figure 11-6.) In actuality, a checklist is a two-point rating scale. It is most useful when rating the performance of set procedures. Although the reliability of checklists

Figure 11-5. A single block of a forced choice rating instrument.

Description	Most characteristic	Least characteristic
1. Tells subordinates what he or she really thinks.		
2. Sets realistic, measurable, and attainable objectives.		
3. Procrastinates when faced with difficult decisions.		
4. Frequently uses criticism when providing feedback.		

is high because the range of decisions is reduced to two, only a limited amount of information can be obtained from most checklists.

The weighted checklist is a recent addition to the array of performance appraisal formats available to managers. A group of designers who are intimately familiar with the details of a particular job prepares statements describing effective and ineffective performance, arranging the statements from unsatisfactory to outstanding. Each statement is then assigned a numerical value arrived at by averaging the scores assigned to each statement by members of the design group. Appraisers use the checklist without knowing the weighted scores. The weighted scores are then assigned to the checked items and summed.

Comparative or Relative Ratings

It is sometimes either necessary or desirable to rate people in comparison with others; for example, for promotion, retention, or spe-

Figure 11-6. A portion of a checklist for evaluating a discussion leader.

Instructions: If the item is satisfactory, place a plus sign in the space provided. If the item is unsatisfactory, place a minus sign in the space.

1. Did the leader clarify and get agreement on purposes? _____
2. Did the leader get agreement on the agenda and procedures? _____
3. Did the leader set an appropriate climate for discussion? _____
4. Did the leader keep the group focused on the problem? _____
5. Did the leader help the group progress toward the goal? _____
6. Did the leader help the group balance task and member needs? _____
7. Did the leader summarize? _____

cial performance awards. Each person is rated only in comparison with others. With purely relative ratings, no attempt is made to assign meaningful values. Here are some of the more common methods.

Rank Order

The rank order method involves comparing the performance of members of a group with one another and assigning a rank to each within the group. The result is that the members of the group are arranged in order from highest to lowest or best to worst. To make rankings more objective, an average may be obtained. The group is ranked by several raters, individual ranks are summed, and the sum is divided by the number of raters.

Rank order has two advantages: (1) because someone must be at the top of the scale and someone at the bottom, the maximum spread of scores is obtained; and (2) any logical (or illogical) connection between performances is severed because the rater deals with only one behavior at a time and therefore tends to disregard ranks assigned to previous behaviors.

There are several weaknesses in rank order: (1) the rater is forced to give extreme ratings—someone must be at the bottom—and this may be interpreted to mean that the person's performance is unsatisfactory; (2) ranking does not portray the magnitude of differences in performance among the persons rated; (3) it is difficult to make meaningful differentiations among members of a large group; and (4) rankings of one group cannot be meaningfully compared with those of another group.

Equal Intervals

This is a variation of the ranking technique. It is used when many people are to be ranked. Instead of ranking all employees in order, the rater places them in groupings that seem to be equally spaced. Those who appear to be alike in behavior or performance are then placed in the same grouping.

Paired Comparisons

This method requires the rater to compare the performance of each member of a group with that of every other member, one at a time. The number of times a person is chosen (as the better of the two) is tallied at the end, which gives an index of the number of times the person is chosen compared to the number of persons being rated. The total "scores" for individuals identify reverse rank order of the group—the highest scorer is the best performer and the lowest is the poorest. (See Figure 11-7.)

Although this approach makes the method more reliable and consid-

Figure 11-7.   Matrix for rating five employees on leadership by the method of paired comparisons.

Compared with:	Employees rated				
	Allen	Betty	Carl	Donna	Frieda
Allen		+	+	+	−
Betty	−		+	+	−
Carl	−	−		+	−
Donna	−	−	−		−
Frieda	+	+	+	+	
Total	1	2	3	4	0

Donna ranks highest (rank #1) with a score of 4; Frieda ranks lowest (rank #5) with a score of 0.

erably easier to use than others, it does have two important limitations: (1) ratings tend to be influenced by the rater's overall impression of the individuals being compared; and (2) the technique is cumbersome if more than ten people are to be rated.

Forced Distribution

This is a modification of the graphic scale. To avoid rating errors, raters are instructed to force their ratings into a normal (bell-shaped) curve—excellent, 10 percent; above average, 20 percent; average, 40 percent; below average, 20 percent; and unsatisfactory, 10 percent.

Although the system may be satisfactory where comparisons of employees are necessary for such specific purposes as selection for promotion or retention, it is unsatisfactory for general appraisal purposes, such as semiannual reports of performance. It unnecessarily forces the rater to say that some subordinates are below average. If the number of employees changed, some of those formerly considered below average would become average, or vice versa.

Problems and Pitfalls in Appraisal

All too often, performance appraisal systems based on observation and evaluative instruments have failed. Mainly, these failures can be attributed to the nature of the job, inadequate planning, passive resistance, lack of objectivity, misuse of forms, and rating errors. Poor systems produce anxiety, resentment, or efforts to sabotage the program.

Contextual Factors

Often overlooked are contextual factors that inhibit or complicate performance appraisal. They include the nature of the work itself, environmental demands, and organizational characteristics. Managerial jobs, where much of the work is cerebral, abstract, and often unobservable, are more difficult to appraise than jobs that involve manual, concrete, and observable activities.

Environmental factors, such as critical tasks being performed away from the direct personal observation of the rater (for example in sales, financial or other forms of auditing, or management of a branch office), make performance appraisal more complex and challenging. In small organizations, where positions are often one of a kind and supervisors are not intimately familiar with the requirements of subordinates' jobs, managers are certain to have difficulty appraising performance.

Inadequate Planning

To be successful, performance appraisal systems must be carefully planned. That means that the details of the system must be worked out in advance: getting top-management support, making the purposes of the system clear to all parties, selecting the methods and techniques to be used, developing the instruments, describing the specific procedures to be followed, training supervisors in the use of the system, scheduling observation and reviews, trying out the system on a pilot basis, and evaluating and modifying the system.

Lack of Training

All the foregoing are critically important to the success of the performance appraisal system. But one item deserves special attention— training. All participants in the system—executives, managers, and employees—must understand the rationale and procedures of performance review, they must understand how the performance appraisal fits into the company's total process, and they must be given the skills needed to make the system work. They must be trained in how to plan, prepare, and participate in the performance review.

Forms Design Errors

Many organizations use standard forms available from commercial publishing houses and distributors. Obviously, this saves a great deal of time and effort. Yet, although many of these forms are well designed, it is wrong to assume that they are always valid and reliable and will automatically meet your needs. Remember that a rating form is reliable only when it describes and measures the traits or performance consistently; it is valid only when it describes and measures the traits, abilities, and performance it is supposed to measure and not something else. Every item on the form must be examined for how well it relates to performance of the job to be appraised. Standardized forms must be given the same detailed scrutiny as those developed in-house.

Three of the most common design errors are: (1) including too many extraneous items (such as personal traits and characteristics); (2) using items that are not job-relevant or that cannot be objectively evaluated; and (3) depending heavily on numerical or adjectival ratings and slighting descriptive items.

Passive Resistance

For one reason or another, some managers are reluctant to rate or review subordinate employees. With some, the underlying cause is fear of confrontations. Others object to being put into the role of judge and jury or playing God. Still others wish to avoid the detailed work involved in preparing for performance appraisal.

Regardless of the reason, the net result is that some managers complete the appraisal form and send it on to Personnel without discussing it with the subordinate. Other managers are vague or evasive in their comments. Others do not even complete the form or don't sign it. There are even managers who are dishonest enough to change ratings *after* discussing their original ratings with the subordinate.

Misuse or outright abuse of forms can be prevented by having the subordinate sign and retain one copy of the completed appraisal form. In addition, employees should have the right to appeal or rebut a rating in writing.

Insufficient or Improper Observation

All too often, observation of performance is a haphazard, catch-as-catch-can activity. To be valid and reliable, observation for performance appraisal must be systematic, frequent, and appropriate. The rater must have a clear understanding of the job activities that should be observed, and must get the "quality" information needed to compare present performance with past performance. Unless the manager observes the right things often enough to reach a valid judgment, the appraisal will be neither fair nor useful.

Rating Errors

There are four types of rating errors: halo, standards, central tendency, and logical. All ratees are affected when they are rated by a manager subject to errors of central tendency or standards. Error of halo affects only certain persons in the group being rated. Logical error appears only when two or more traits or behaviors of individuals are being rated. The effects of these errors can be minimized, and some can be completely eliminated, if great care is taken in designing the instruments and training the raters.

Error of central tendency. Many managers are reluctant to assign either extremely high or extremely low ratings; their ratings tend to cluster close to the middle of the scale. Even experienced raters can make this error when they rate personal qualities, abilities, or behaviors that are more or less intangible, such as leadership or instructional ability.

The tendency to give extreme ratings is the opposite of central tendency but is considered to be in the same category. Occasionally, a rater will place too many ratings at the extremes of the scale. Everyone is identified as either excellent (error of generosity) or unsatisfactory (error of parsimony).

Error of standards. Some managers tend to overrate or underrate everyone in comparison to the ratings of other qualified raters. This is because their standards are either too high or too low. Experience with a particular rating scale, and thorough training in using it usually result in similar distributions of scores by several raters, indicating that their standards are compatible.

When differences in standards are consistent and have enough stability to permit correction, the error is called *systematic*, or *constant*. Although this kind of error can be adjusted by adding or subtracting the same amount to all the scores of a given rating (of course this is applicable only to numerical ratings), a better solution is to provide further training so that the rater can correct the error.

Error of halo. Some raters are unable to prevent the general impression they have of an individual from influencing their scoring of performance. Usually the impression that clouds their judgment is the result of prior observation of the individual in critical situations. However, likes, dislikes, and prejudices may also cause errors of halo. Raters' reactions to physical features, race, or national origin can influence their general impressions. It is important to note that halo error can be either favorable or unfavorable; therefore, it can result in a higher or lower rating than the performance of the individual warrants.

It has been noted that when a person rates a close friend, the tendency is to rate the individual higher than he or she should. This is called *error of leniency*. When halo error is traced to such sources as physical features, race, or nationality, it is called error of *bias* or *stereotype*. Halo errors frequently go undetected; even when found, they are extremely difficult to correct.

Logical error. This type of error, sometimes called *error of ambiguity*, occurs when two or more traits, abilities, or behaviors are being rated. If the rater sees certain traits as related (although the relationship may be obscure or illogical to other qualified raters), similar ratings for those traits will be given. For example, some people believe that an intelligent person is invariably creative. Intelligent people may be creative, but not necessarily. Similarly, industrious people may or may not be efficient. Usually, the person who exhibits logical error is unaware of the fault.

Performance Appraisal and the Law

Some managers fail to recognize that federal[2] and state laws on civil rights, antidiscrimination, and equal pay apply to performance appraisal systems and procedures and employee development as well as to recruitment, selection, pay, and promotion. It should be obvious that performance appraisal is inevitably linked to most personnel actions. The *Uniform Guidelines* issued by the Equal Opportunity Commission, the Civil Service Commission (now the Office of Personnel Management), the Department of Labor, and the Department of Justice in 1978 not only clarified the rules for hiring, promotion, demotion, retention, training and development, and referral but also made performance appraisal a "selection procedure" for any of those personnel actions. Court rulings have repeatedly underscored the need for performance appraisal systems to meet certain criteria.

Business necessity. This criterion states that the performance appraisal system must be essential to the proper conduct of the business or enterprise, that there is a clear relationship between the rating system and the goals and objectives of the organization. It also means that the system must help managers carry out their functions and meet their responsibilities.

Objectivity. Performance appraisal systems must be based on objective and clearly defined criteria. Among other things, that means that the system must be based on job and task analysis rather than on subjective evaluation by managers, that it is rooted in important job requirements, and that job requirements and standards are stated in unambiguous terms. It also means that ratings are based on specific, observable job behaviors and not on the personal characteristics of employees.

Consistency. This criterion points to the need to ensure that performance evaluation systems are applied consistently by managers to *all* employees in the same job category. It also means that raters must be thoroughly trained and that written instructions are provided to guide

2. Equal Pay Act of 1963, Age Discrimination in Employment Act of 1967 (as amended in 1978), Civil Rights Act of 1968, and the Equal Employment Opportunity Act of 1972.

them in using evaluation forms and in conducting performance appraisals.

Validity and reliability. This means that the performance appraisal system can be proved to measure and evaluate what it was intended to measure and evaluate and that it measures those things consistently. In other words, you must be able to demonstrate that performance ratings predict or correlate significantly with important aspects of job performance, that the items rated are truly representative of important aspects of job performance, and that the system measures traits, characteristics, or behaviors that are important in successful job performance.

Nondiscrimination. You must be able to prove that the system does not discriminate against any protected group (employees aged 45 to 70, minorities, women, and the physically handicapped) and that there is no other means available to evaluate employee performance that would be less discriminatory. It also means that you must be able to prove that the rejection rates of a minority group for any favorable personnel action are comparable with those of nonminority groups.

The Appraisal Review Process

Conducting the interview is the most difficult aspect of the appraisal system. Here is where all your preparation and hard work can be destroyed in a matter of minutes. There are many things you can do to preclude disaster. (The following discussion assumes that a "collaborative" form of appraisal is being used.)

Planning

Thorough and careful planning is one of the keys to successful performance appraisal review. Prepare for the interview. Review the subordinate's job description. Focus on critical job performance activities and expected results.

Review notes made after the last review, paying particular attention to agreements reached on needed improvements in performance. Review your informal notes of observations made since the last review. Base your appraisal on facts, not on opinions or general impressions; on job performance, not on personal traits or personality; on behavior, not on gut feelings. Identify strengths and shortfalls and be ready to back up your evaluation with facts—specific illustrations of performance in the form of critical incidents. Documentation is the key.

Select a setting for the interview that is pleasant, comfortable, and private. Make sure there will be no interruptions. Choose a time that is convenient for the employee. Avoid late-afternoon sessions and Thursdays or Fridays. Allow enough time for full and free discussion. Although you may not use it all, reserve one hour for the review.

Notify the employee of the time and place in writing at least one week in advance. Remember that subordinates must also prepare for the performance review if it is to be effective. They must be ready to present their self-evaluation of performance with respect to each major function, duty, and task.

Conducting the Review

Your first task is to establish rapport with the employee. Strive for informality. Get out from behind your desk. Sit in comfortable chairs facing each other. Structure the interview. Work for an atmosphere of understanding, mutual respect, and trust. Adopt a "can do" attitude. Emphasize the need for frankness and the importance of sharing observations and points of view. Identify the purposes and objectives of the review. If this is the employee's first review, describe the process, explain the purposes of appraisal, and discuss the meaning of terms used on the appraisal form. Cooperatively review the exact job performance expected of the employee, focusing on results.

Get the employee's *oral* assessment of his or her performance of the whole job, *all* the major functions, duties, and critical tasks. Again, emphasize the need for specificity and candor. Where shortfalls are identified, ask questions to elicit the employee's thoughts about possible reasons for the deficiency and potential remedies. Listen carefully.

Give the employee your assessment of job performance. Identify specific strengths and weaknesses. Choose your words carefully. Use description rather than positive or negative evaluative comments. Be specific. Tell the truth. Don't waffle, but don't be overly critical. Don't compare the employee with others. Don't do all the talking. Consider your own role in the employee's performance. Acknowledge any deficiencies in your supervision.

Discuss the two assessments—yours and the employee's. Note areas of agreement and dispute. Avoid debate. Get agreement on how well the subordinate has met expectations. Exchange ideas. Provide information and get information. Focus on future performance. Don't lecture. Watch for nonverbal messages.

Clarify and reach agreement on what's expected. Jointly assess objectives and targets, measures and indicators, and develop plans. Make objectives for the forthcoming appraisal period specific, quantitative (if possible), observable, measurable, challenging, realistic, attainable, and targeted for a definite period of time. Put them in writing. Determine what action by either you or the employee would maintain or improve performance. Jointly identify the sequence of actions required to achieve the improvement objectives.

Get commitment to the improvement plan, and set definite times for review of progress. Encourage the subordinate to record his or her own accomplishments, in categories jointly agreed upon—such as delegating, decision making, training subordinates, planning, writing, oral communication, assertiveness, team building, and the like. (See Figure 11-8.)

Documenting Performance

Document the review by completing and signing the three-copy appraisal form. Have the subordinate sign the document and give him or her one copy. Give him or her an opportunity to add comments. Have

Figure 11-8.   Sample subordinate accomplishment record.

RECORD OF ACCOMPLISHMENTS

(Name of Employee)

Time Period: June to December 1987

General statement of what you accomplished:

I was given the task of

Description of what you did:

This information verified by: _____
                                                                  Title

---

your boss review and sign the completed form. Keep one copy and send the other one to the proper office for file.

Monitoring Progress and Accomplishment

The interview is not the end of the appraisal process; it is only the end of one phase. The manager has an obligation to help employees implement the action plan, to monitor progress and accomplishment, and to provide feedback.

The surest way to destroy the value of the performance review is to fail to follow up. Managers must be ready to provide guidance and assistance to subordinates in carrying out their improvement plan. This does not mean that the manager should be constantly looking over the subordinates' shoulders. It does mean that managers should help subordinates identify needed actions when difficulties are encountered. It also means that managers must be ready to make needed changes in the work environment, relationship with the subordinates, and the amount and kind of supervision and support given. Follow up to ensure that the action plan is implemented. Reinforce desired behavior. Make use of daily observation and coaching. Record results.

Feedback is an essential element of a performance improvement plan. Provide feedback on performance, and make it specific and job oriented. Feedback is specifically concerned with analyzing and improving the subordinate's performance of job functions and tasks. In that context, it is informal. It should be given regularly, frequently, and immediately after excellent, acceptable, *and* poor performance. It is not the same as the formal feedback of performance reviews.

Reviewing, Evaluating, and Revising the System

The significance of performance appraisal practically dictates periodic review and evaluation of the system. Even if periodic scrutiny shows the basic process is sound, the system will require revision just to accommodate changes in the composition of the work force and in the jobs being assessed. The HR manager must always be alert to indicators that point to the need for system changes. Some of these indicators are lateness of report forms, greater numbers of employee complaints and grievances, increased turnover, insufficient rating score divergence (too many "average" or "outstanding" performers), and internal inconsistencies in ratings.

The HR manager should not rely exclusively on personal observation. Enlist the assistance of all managers and supervisors in the effort. Actively solicit their judgments about the effectiveness and practicality of the system: how they use the information it provides, how it affects the motivation and job performance of their subordinates, the adequacy of the forms and procedures, their need for additional training in conducting the performance review, and other glitches and discrepancies.

Summary

Regardless of how HR managers feel about performance appraisals, they are here to stay. An objective, controlled process is far better than a subjective, uncontrolled system, which is almost guaranteed to produce both employee dissatisfaction and unwanted legal consequences.

Performance appraisal is a vital management tool. It is also a very demanding process. Essentially, it is a formal, systematic, collaborative review and analysis of the job performance of an employee, with the primary goal of improving that performance. It is important to the organization, the HR manager, and the individual employee.

Acceptable performance of the appraisal requires a thorough knowledge of job standards and requirements, ample opportunity to observe and evaluate performance, objectivity, positive attitudes toward the system and subordinates, and highly developed listening, observational, interviewing, and feedback skills.

If it is to be successful, the performance appraisal program must be fully supported by executives, managers, supervisors, the collective bargaining unit, and employees. It must be regularly scheduled, objectives and results oriented, cooperative, factual and specific, meaningful and useful, and must comply with equal employment opportunity and non-discrimination statutes.

The objectives of the system must be clear to all employees. Appraisal forms must be carefully designed and tested before use. Forms and procedures must help raters to appraise relevant and important elements of the job. Appraisal factors must be precisely defined in terms that are specific, observable, and measure behaviors and results—not personal traits. Progress and accomplishment must be tracked and documented. Finally, the system must be periodically reviewed, evaluated, and modified to accommodate changes in the organization, the composition of the workforce, and the jobs themselves.

The performance review process described here is one that has worked reasonably well in organizations of several types. It is not perfect, it is an improvement over less structured approaches. The important thing is that a structured approach will go a long way toward eliminating the negative aspects of appraisals and will have a positive impact on employee performance.

FOR FURTHER READING

Baird, Lloyd S., Richard W. Beatty, and Craig Eric Schneier. *The Performance Appraisal Sourcebook.* Amherst, Mass.: Human Resource Development Press, 1982.

Beaulieu, Rod. "An Easier Look at Performance Appraisal." *Training and Development Journal,* October 1980, p. 56.

Carroll, Stephen J., and Craig Eric Schneier. *Performance Appraisal and Review Systems.* Glenview, Ill.: Scott, Foresman, 1982.

Dailey, C., and A. Madsen. *How to Evaluate People in Business: The Track Record Method of Making Correct Judgments.* New York: McGraw-Hill, 1983.

Danzig, Selig M. "What We Need to Know About Performance Appraisals." *Management Review,* February 1980, pp. 20–24.

DeVries, David L., Ann M. Morrison, Sandra L. Shullman, and Michael L. Gerlach. *Performance Appraisal on the Line.* Greensboro, N.C.: Center for Creative Leadership, 1981.

Eichel, Evelyn, and Henry E. Bender. *Performance Appraisal: A Study of Current Techniques.* New York: AMACOM, 1984.

Frechette, Henry M., Jr., and Edward G. Wertheim. "Performance Appraisal." In *Human Resources Management and Development Handbook,* edited by William R. Tracey. New York: AMACOM, 1985.

Gregerman, Ira B. *Knowledge Worker Productivity.* New York: AMACOM, 1981.

Gubman, Edward L. "Getting the Most Out of Performance Appraisals." *Management Review,* November 1984, pp. 44–48.

Hamelink, Jack, and Jerry Hamelink. "A Numeric Plan for Performance Appraisal." *Training and Development Journal,* October 1980, p. 88.

Harper, Stephen C. "Adding Purpose to Performance Reviews." *Training and Development Journal,* September 1986, pp. 53–55.

Henderson, Richard. *Performance Appraisal: Theory to Practice.* Englewood Cliffs, N.J.: Prentice-Hall, 1980.

Holley, William H., and Hubert S. Field. "Performance Appraisal and the Law." *Labor Law Journal,* July 1975, pp. 423–430.

Kaye, Beverly, and Shelly Krantz. "Performance Appraisal: A Win/Win Approach." *Training and Development Journal,* March 1983, pp. 32–37.

Kelly, Charles M. "Reasonable Performance Appraisals." *Training and Development Journal,* January 1984, pp. 79–82.

King, Patricia. *Performance Planning and Appraisal: A How-to Book for Managers.* New York: McGraw-Hill, 1984.

————. "How to Prepare for a Performance Appraisal Interview." *Training and Development Journal,* February 1984, pp. 66–69.

Kirkpatrick, Donald L. *How to Improve Performance Through Appraisal and Coaching.* New York: AMACOM, 1982.

————. "Two Ways to Evaluate Your Performance Appraisal System." *Training and Development Journal,* August 1984, pp. 38–40.

————. "Performance Appraisal: Your Questions Answered," *Training and Development Journal,* May 1986, pp. 68–71.

Latham, Gary P., and Kenneth N. Wexley. *Increasing Productivity Through Performance Appraisal.* Reading, Mass.: Addison-Wesley Training Systems, 1981.

Malinauskas, Barbara K., and Ronald W. Clement. "Performance Appraisal Interviewing for Tangible Results." *Training and Development Journal,* February 1987, pp. 74–79.

Mayer, Richard J. "Keys to Effective Appraisal." *Management Review,* June 1980, pp. 60–62.

Meidan, Arthur. *The Appraisal of Managerial Performance.* New York: AMACOM, 1981.

Momeyer, Alan G. "Why No One Likes Your Performance Appraisal System." *Training,* October 1986, pp. 95–98.

Morrisey, George L. *Performance Appraisals in Business and Industry: Key to Effective Supervision.* Reading, Mass.: Addison-Wesley Training Systems, 1983.

————. *Performance Appraisals in the Public Sector: Key to Effective Supervision.* Reading, Mass.: Addison-Wesley Training Systems, 1983.

"No Excuses with Smart Performance Standards." *Training,* April 1986, pp. 67–68.

Parnes, S. E. *The Personnel Manager's Handbook of Performance Evaluation Programs,* rev. ed. Madison, Conn.: Business and Legal Reports, Bureau of Law and Business, 1982.

Sashkin, Marshall. *Assessing Performance Appraisal.* San Diego: University Associates, 1981.

Schneier, Craig Eric, Richard W. Beatty, and Lloyd S. Baird. "How to Construct a Successful Performance Appraisal System." *Training and Development Journal,* April 1986, pp. 38–42.

Smith, Howard P. with the assistance of Paul Brouwer. *Performance Appraisal and Human Development.* Reading, Mass.: Addison-Wesley Training Systems, 1977.

Zemke, Ron. "Is Performance Appraisal a Paper Tiger?" *Training,* December 1985, pp. 24–32.

12

COACHING
Fulfilling Performance
Expectations

Increasing effectiveness, efficiency, and productivity is one of the most challenging tasks facing today's HR manager. Managing, coaching, counseling, and training are all useful means of meeting that challenge. These are all distinctly different skills, requiring different mindsets, environments, and approaches. Yet they share several theoretical, and at the same time quite practical underpinnings: (1) people need to exercise choice and control over their work lives; (2) a sense of "owning" goals, objectives, and approaches gives employees a stake in the company and promotes responsibility, dedication, effort, and achievement; (3) the competitiveness and productivity of organizations hinges on competent and cooperative employee effort at all levels; and (4) empowering people has a positive impact on attitude, motivation, and morale. Skilled coaching can help achieve those outcomes.

Coaching is not managing. It does not mean leading, counseling, or teaching in the *formal* sense. It is an informal and continuing relationship between a manager and a subordinate. But it is much more than a senior-junior relationship. Coaching is the process of helping subordinates, one on one, to perform well—to remedy their deficiencies and improve their job performance. It is a strategy to help subordinates learn better ways of doing their jobs. It is also a means of developing the potential of people. It provides a means of developing technical, professional, or managerial skills.

Coaching involves a continuous flow of instruction, comments, and suggestions from superior to subordinate. It is day-by-day informal teaching done by the manager, involving precept, demonstration, practice, observation, correction, feedback, encouragement, praise, reward, and, above all, example. Coaching is a joint venture; it is not something done *to* somebody but a process conducted *with* somebody.

A trendy word in HR, sometimes inaccurately used as a synonym for coaching, is *mentoring,* a term drawn from Greek legend. Mentor was the counselor, adviser, and "coach" of Telemachus, the son of the warrior Odysseus (Ulysses). Mentor's influence was pervasive. He was concerned with all aspects of Telemachus's development, not just with his intellectual skills. That is why mentoring in some circles has come to mean much more than coaching.

The primary objective of coaching is to develop job-related knowledge and skills, and usually involves a superior-subordinate relationship, but a mentor can be anyone more experienced than the person "mentored," and the mentor may serve as a teacher, adviser, guide, coach, role model, developer, protector, advocate, and sponsor. In short, the mentor takes a personal interest in the junior. Modern application of the mentoring role tends to center on workplace relationships and excludes personal characteristics, values, and lifestyle.

Coaching skills are a must for today's HR manager. Young professionals want, in fact demand, individualized attention. They want access to those who direct their activities, and they demand a share in decision making. They expect to be groomed for greater responsibilities and ultimately for advancement to higher-level positions. The HR manager without coaching skills, or with substandard coaching skills, is an anachronism. More important, coaching is one of the most effective ways to improve employees' performance.

> Effective performance development through coaching forms a critical part of the performance management process. Coaching sessions make sure that performance expectations are fulfilled or that employees make desired changes in their work activities. Managers who do not engage in performance development through coaching are, in effect, betting that the performance expectations they have developed with their employees will be carried out with no problems. It's by no means a safe bet, even when expectations are clear and employees are competent.[1]

Benefits of Coaching

Coaching has many benefits for the organization, the HR manager, and the individual employees. It is centered on the real world—the employees' work activities in the job environment—and that is a benefit to the organization, the manager, and his or her staff. It is provided by the person in the best position to evaluate performance and provide focused help—the manager.

With a competent coach, the technique provides the optimum in

1. Marshall Sashkin, *A Manager's Guide to Performance Management* (New York: AMACOM, 1986), p. 38, 40.

individualized instruction. The needs of individual employees can be identified, problems and deficiencies can be diagnosed, and interventions can be tailormade to meet these unique requirements. In the coaching setting, the highest possible degree of employee participation can be achieved. Direct employee involvement in the learning, by answering and asking questions and by performing tasks under supervision, is practically guaranteed. The ability of the coach to adapt interventions to the needs of the individual employees, together with the employees' high degree of interaction and participation, make this approach extremely effective.

Coaching may be used as a strategy in all departments and at all levels of operation from technician to executive. It is also a valuable means of orienting people to their jobs. It helps subordinates understand how their superiors see organizational functions, relationships, and personalities. When analyses of specific performance are made, both manager and employee are afforded opportunities to learn why results were good or bad. In addition, specific managerial skills, such as interpersonal relations and leadership, can be evaluated, discussed, and improved.

Coaching provides HR managers with daily opportunities to get to know their subordinates—their capabilities, talents, and potential, and their values, interests, goals, and ambitions. It also provides opportunities to use those talents and abilities; to develop team workers, supervisors, and managers; to make better decisions; to get new ideas and approaches; and to improve the effectiveness and efficiency of their departments.

For subordinates, coaching provides individualized attention, a role model, and regular and frequent feedback on performance. It also provides opportunities for subordinates to articulate their points of view, express their opinions, make suggestions, display their talents, get the attention of their boss, and become achievers.

Coaching Objectives

Coaching can serve several different but complementary purposes. The manager can use coaching skills to correct deficiencies in technical, professional, and managerial knowledge and skills, and to ensure that the talents of subordinates in those areas are used to the fullest.

Technical growth. HR has its technical side. Regardless of their preparation and advanced degrees, young HR specialists, or not-so-young people new to the field, have technical deficiencies that can and should be remedied. No master's or doctoral program can possibly develop all the technical knowledge and skills needed to make maximum contributions to the organization's HR programs, activities, and services.

Consider the range of technical knowledge and skills required: strategic planning, budgeting, preparing proposals and contracts, data processing, editing, equipment maintenance, long-range forecasting, graphics production, job and task analysis, job evaluation, media production and selection, scheduling, developing statements of work, television production, test development and validation, and word processing, to identify but a few.

Professional growth. Similarly, HR junior supervisors, managers, and specialists need coaching to develop their professional knowledge and skills and to remedy shortfalls in those areas. Topics for this category of coaching objectives might well include: adult learning, needs assessment, career planning, coaching, counseling, evaluation, platform instruction, individualized instruction, instructor training, public speaking, organization development, research, team building, and training systems development and validation.

Managerial growth. To ensure a continuing supply of qualified HR managers, every organization needs to develop its own people in-house. Again, coaching provides an effective and inexpensive means of accomplishing that objective. Here are some of the areas in which coaching can make a contribution in this area: arbitration and mediation, communication, conflict resolution, cost reduction, decision making, delegation, disciplining, employee screening and selection, equal employment opportunity, ethics training, financial planning, instructional management, labor relations, leadership development, management improvement, marketing, motivating, negotiating, performance evaluation, personnel development, personnel planning, problem solving, productivity improvement, public relations, and strategic planning.

Personal growth. Personal growth and development of HR managers and specialists should never stop. Coaching opportunities abound to help subordinates develop themselves as people. Some of the most fruitful areas are assertiveness training, behavior modeling and modification training, attendance at meetings and conferences, career planning, physical and recreational activities, introspective exercises, membership in technical and professional organizations, participation in community groups, public speaking, self-evaluation, sensitivity training, small group interactions, stress management training, travel, visits to other HR organizations, and writing.

The Successful Coach

Because coaching is a personalized, individualized, one-on-one strategy, it requires some special abilities, traits, beliefs, and values. Successful coaches believe that people not only *want to* but *can* improve their performance. They also believe that improvement takes place only in a favorable climate under the guidance and assistance of an understanding manager.

Successful coaches like people and are able to empathize with them. They are unselfish. They have a deep and abiding concern for the welfare and the professional development of their subordinates. They have a sincere interest in improving job performance, preparation for the assumption of greater responsibilities, and ultimate advancement of their subordinates. They serve as role models—demonstrating the values, attitudes, and behaviors they profess. They have earned the respect of their subordinates. They are invariably patient, fair, firm, and supportive. They also have highly developed leadership abilities.

A successful coach needs at least five specific skills: observation, analysis, interviewing, intervention, and feedback. Sequentially, coaches must identify the behavior that needs to be improved. Next they must observe and record how, when, where, and how often a deficiency occurs (hourly, daily, weekly, and so on). Then they must develop and implement an intervention strategy. Finally, they must remeasure and evaluate results.

Observational skills. Effective coaching requires that managers become highly skilled in looking and listening for opportunities to help subordinates improve their job performance. They must watch how employees interact with their colleagues, respond to superiors, supervise their work teams, deal with conflict, hold up under pressure, present briefings, and write reports.

The successful coach studies all subordinates as individuals, notices the degree to which they have difficulty on the job, sizes up their alertness, interest, and motivation, and takes note of the extent to which they learn from mistakes.

Analytical skills. HR managers in the coaching role must be able to determine whether a subordinate's deficiency is caused by lack of knowledge or skills, lack of direction, obstacles in the work environment, ineptitude, inattention, lack of interest, or just plain laziness. They must be able to suspend judgment about subordinates or performance. They must be able to probe for concerns about the work and sometimes about themselves. They must be able to determine whether coaching can remedy the shortcoming. Finally, they must be able to identify the skills that require upgrading.

Interviewing skills. When the performance deficiencies have been tentatively identified, the coach must meet with the subordinate to confirm findings, determine what can be done, and place the shortfalls in order of priority for remediation. The coach must be able to ask questions and to listen objectively, empathically, and nonevaluatingly.

Both manager and subordinate need to be realistic about what can really be accomplished. Before deciding how much to attempt, they should consider each deficiency in the light of budget, work load, probability of success, and any other constraints. Then alternative methods of addressing them should be discussed.

Intervention skills. Intervention skills are the means used by the manager to change behavior and improve performance. Some of the options available are on-the-job training, cross training, formal education, training or development (in-house or outside), correspondence courses, professional and technical meetings and conferences, job or task assignments (additional duties, job rotation, job enlargement, temporary promotions, and serving on committees and task forces), professional and technical reading, visits to other departments and outside organizations, and feedback from subordinates, peers, and the manager. All these interventions require planning, and many demand some degree of skill on the part of the manager.

Feedback skills. Adequate feedback is so critical to the coaching process that it must be considered a separate and distinct skill. It is not easy to do. The manager must use description rather than evaluation; that is, make no comments that contain judgmental content, only what was *observed* about the performance. Feedback must take into account the subordinates' needs, *never* the manager's. It must show sensitivity to the differences between demands and suggestions. It must be noncritical, nonpunitive, and supportive. It must be timely and specific, and it must not ask for the unachievable.

Conditions and Requirements for Success

In addition to the skills just described, certain conditions and requirements must be met if coaching is to be successful. They include recognition and use of the principles of adult learning, ready access to the manager, self-development of the manager to permit service as a role model, the right combination of personal characteristics on the part of manager and subordinate, the subordinates' acceptance of the manager as a role model and mentor, a high level of subordinate motivation, and appropriate rewards for improved performance.

Application of Learning Principles

Essentially, a manager in the coaching role is serving as an adviser, guide, and tutor. It is critically important that the coach remember that the "learner," the subordinate, is an *adult* learner. The coach must do the coaching job in accordance with the principles of adult learning.

Learner involvement. Adult learners learn best by doing. They must be directly and completely involved in the learning process. They respond best when they help design and structure their learning activities. They must be directly involved in selecting objectives and planning. They must be provided with the opportunity to assist in diagnosing their own shortcomings and in determining their own learning needs. Otherwise they will not accept the need for behavioral change.

Adult learners must also be totally involved in planning, executing, and evaluating their own development and in assessing their own progress and accomplishment. They must be active participants in the coaching process, have a clear understanding of what they are to learn, and be given the means of tracking and measuring their own progress.

Tailored activities. Adults learn best when learning activities that are tailored to their individual needs, backgrounds, experiences, skills, abilities, knowledge, and learning styles. Coaching must be learner-centered rather than presentation-centered. Learning activities must start where the subordinates are, not where the coach thinks they *ought to be*. The coach must take advantage of the past experiences of subordinates in planning. If learning efficiency and effectiveness are to be achieved, coaching objectives and strategies must be appropriate and feasible for the individual subordinate.

Realism. Because adult learners must perceive and accept the need for behavioral change, must see an application for the learning, strategies and activities must involve real, job-related tasks, problems, and issues. The more immediate the use, the stronger will be the motivation to learn. All experiences must be directly related to the duties and tasks that the subordinates are required to perform in regular work assignments. The real occupational setting must be used at all times.

Informality. The coaching environment must be informal and humanistic. The manager must act like a helper, not a boss. He or she must be sensitive to subordinates and accord them understanding and respect. Activities must be nonthreatening, nonauthoritarian, and, where possible, nonevaluative and nonpenalizing. There must be mutual respect and confidence between manager and subordinate. The coaching environment must be pleasant, comfortable, and characterized by openness, trust, nondefensiveness, and acceptance. It must accord personal dignity and respect to the subordinate.

Structure. Learning tasks and activities for adults must be broken down into manageable units, sets, or steps. Because people learn best when they are helped to avoid errors, coaching strategies must make maximum use of guidance, assistance, hints, and suggestions. Enough flexibility must be allowed to accommodate the unique background, abilities, experiences, and learning style of the subordinate.

If they are to be retained, knowledge and skills must be related to and integrated with what subordinates already know and are able to do. Subordinates must be given immediate feedback on their performance. The total coaching experience must be successful and rewarding.

Application. The focus of coaching activities must be on direct, hands-on experiences for subordinates—*doing* rather than listening, reading, or observing. Opportunities must be provided for them to apply and practice newly acquired knowledge and skills. Again, flexibility must be allowed to accommodate the unique abilities and learning style of subordinates.

Ready Access

Subordinates must have ready access to the manager, since frequent face-to-face contacts are essential to the success of the technique. That does not mean that subordinates are encouraged to run to the manager every time difficulties are encountered. But it does mean that the manager is ready and willing to spend the time required to provide the direction and feedback needed.

Role Model

Real coaches are managers who first groom themselves, rather than their subordinates, to reflect the image of technical, professional, moral, and ethical excellence. They are real role models for proper professional behavior. They set the example. They inspire confidence because they respect their subordinates.

Personal Characteristics

Both manager and subordinate must have the right combination of personal qualities. The manager must be open and supportive, have the desire to develop subordinates, be patient and understanding, be able to delegate, and have enough self-confidence to let subordinates make mistakes.

Subordinates must have confidence in the manager, and they must be challenged by the job, interested in their own development, objective and analytical in their approach to problems, responsible, and have enough self-confidence to use the authority delegated to them.

Acceptance by the Subordinate

The success of a coach rests on subordinates' recognition and acceptance of the manager as a wise teacher and the knowledge that their relationship is based on mutual understanding, trust, and respect for each other. Real coaches do not declare themselves mentors or coaches. They recognize and respect an individual's right to choose his or her own mentor. They are mature enough to accept that not every manager is the subordinate's chosen embodiment of rationality, prudence, and wisdom. They are too busy being role models for that.

Subordinate Motivation

Subordinates must have a reasonably high level of motivation for coaching to be successful. If subordinates do not see a need for improved job performance, or if they are disgruntled, dissatisfied, frustrated, or petulant, the success of coaching is likely to be very limited—if it occurs at all. If motivation is lacking, no amount of coaching will help. Therefore, the first item on the agenda is to develop the required degree of motivation using the strategies and techniques described in Chapter 9.

Rewards for Performance

The coach must provide positive rewards for improvement—praise, credit for doing a good job, recognition, and other types of rewards—and then evaluate the results on performance. Recognition and rewards are among the most powerful motivating devices at the manager's disposal. Every adult wants to be told when a job has been done well. People tend to thrive on praise and wilt under severe criticism. Whether the rewards are monetary or as simple as a pat on the back, they are always effective in generating renewed effort to improve. It is important for the HR manager to determine what each subordinate considers to be rewards for improved performance—and then use them.

Pitfalls in Coaching

Several pitfalls await the unwary coach. Under certain conditions, coaching may be viewed as critical and destructive rather than helpful. The primary snares, though, are lack of planning, lack of subordinate involvement, lack of agreement on standards and measures of performance, subjectivity, overemphasis on deficiencies, and linking coaching to salary review.

Lack of planning and objectives. Careful and complete planning is essential to success. The manager must think through what is to be achieved in the coaching role, who will be involved, when it will be done, and how it will be accomplished. Clear objectives must be established. For each subordinate, a definitive and *written* coaching plan made after consultation and discussion with each participant, must be prepared. Without a well-conceived and detailed plan, coaching is doomed to failure.

Lack of subordinate involvement. This is the primary pitfall. If subordinates are not involved in developing and implementing the plan from its very inception, coaching efforts will amount to nothing. This pitfall has three aspects:

Identifying problems: the "Here's what's wrong" syndrome. The proper role of the manager is not to assemble information and explain what went wrong to the employee, but to work with the employee to examine the information and make sense out of it, identifying whether or not the performance is on track, nor should the manager or employee jump to conclusions about problems and solutions.

Discovering what happened: the "It's your fault" trap. The second misconception . . . is that coaching consists of fixing blame for "what went wrong" . . . While it is important to know the details of the actions that led to the problem, it's equally important to avoid evaluating the employee. The role of the manager . . . consists of giving the employee helpful feedback . . . descriptive and not evaluative, concrete and not general, and that has useful implications for further action.

Planning what to do: the "Let me tell you" pitfall. The third . . . misconception . . . is that coaching consists of telling how to do it right. . . . Rather than giving the employee a solution the two [manager and subordinate] must work together to explore solution alternatives, select a course of action, and plan to put it into practice and monitor the results.[2]

Lack of agreement on standards and measures of performance. Improvement strategies and programs must be based on standards and measures of performance that both the manager and the subordinate have agreed to. If there is confusion, misunderstanding, or disagreement about the performance criteria or differences about the yardsticks to be used to measure the performance, the improvement program will stall at that point.

Subjectivity. Objectivity on the part of manager and subordinate in describing performance and results, and accurate, unbiased, and impartial comments by the manager, are essential. If either party is subjective about the performance, there cannot be a mutual understanding and agreement, and little of value will emerge from discussions about new approaches to improvement.

Overemphasis on mistakes and deficiencies. Although it is evident that attention will tend to focus on errors and deficiencies that require correction and remediation, if those are the only aspects of the performance noted during planning meetings, interventions, and review sessions, the whole coaching process tends to take on a negative shading. Carping criticism or unrelenting disapproval will destroy the coaching relationship. It is essential that the things subordinates do well be acknowledged and recognized.

Tie-in with salary reviews. The kiss of death for the coaching process is to tie it in with salary reviews. As we saw in Chapter 11, that

2. Sashkin, *A Manager's Guide to Performance Management*, 34–36.

has long been a problem with performance appraisal. But it should not be difficult to divorce coaching from salary considerations. No discussion of salary or bonuses should enter the planning, intervention, monitoring, or review phases of coaching.

Common Performance Problems

These performance problems have been identified by Sashkin, an expert in organizational psychology:

Problems Involving the Work Context

Unclear, ambiguous, or ill-defined work roles—specifications as to what a worker is responsible for doing.

Inadequate job skills on the part of the individual worker, skills that a manager should be able to give training assistance in mastering.

Lack of experience on the part of the worker, calling for new, broader, more varied, more specialized, or more involving job assignments, such as the worker may develop through appropriate task assignments.

Inappropriate involvement in decision making, either too much involvement, involvement that is undesired and seen as a burden, or (much more common) too little, such that the worker feels little involvement in or commitment to a particular course of action.

Problems Centered on
Managerial Skills and Behaviors

Ineffective communication with workers—the manager lacks basic skills in effective listening and giving directions.

Ineffective feedback skills—the manager lacks basic skills in giving and receiving feedback such that the feedback is more likely to do harm than to help the worker improve performance.

Leadership behaviors that are not appropriate to the situation; whether one believes in one "best" leadership style or in tailoring one's style based on circumstance, there is little doubt that the specific behavior exhibited by a manager must take into account the worker and the context; research shows that inexperienced workers perceive highly directive leader behavior as helpful and considerate while experienced workers see the same behavior, quite properly, as smotheringly close supervision.

Ineffective use of rewards, such as recognition, increased job responsibilities, greater self-control and autonomy, personal praise, and any of the many other non-economic rewards readily accessible to managers who take time to seriously examine just what they have to offer.

Problems Requiring
Formal Actions by External Agents

Lack of basic job skills on the part of the employee, to the extent that additional formal job training is required.

Personal psychological problems on the part of the employee, to the extent that personal psychological counseling or career counseling is needed.[3]

Other common remediable deficiencies in some of the same categories are:

Work context

○ Writing, speaking, or listening skills: the subordinate has deficiencies in one or more of these areas sufficiently serious to interfere with job performance.

○ Numerical analysis: in recent years, a much more common deficiency; attributable to avoidance of mathematics-related courses in secondary school and college, resulting in inability to deal with numerical problems.

○ Customer relations: particularly important where contact with customers, dealers, suppliers, or the general public is a part of the job.

○ Interpersonal skills: inability of the individual to deal with others in an open, constructive way; inadequate or improper response to disagreements or conflict.

○ Social skills: deficiencies in terms of accepted norms of politeness and social manners.

○ Stress management: lack of skill in handling personal stress in difficult situations.

○ Inattention: overlooking a part of the job or task; failing to follow up; misunderstanding or misinterpreting instructions; allowing distractions to interfere with performance.

Managerial skills

○ Appraisal: failure or inability to set reasonable performance standards.

○ Motivating: inability to establish conditions that foster employee motivation.

○ Goal setting and objective setting: inability to define goals and objectives.

○ Budgeting: deficiencies in preparing and controlling budgets.

3. Sashkin, *A Manager's Guide to Performance Management*, 61–62.

- Writing, speaking, and listening: severe deficiencies in basic communication skills.
- Problem sensing and problem solving: inability to sense potential problems and inadequate skills in dealing with job-related problems.
- Decision making: lack of ability to use a systematic approach to making decisions.
- Strategic planning: inability to develop realistic strategic plans.
- Delegation: unwillingness or inability to delegate functions, duties, and tasks to subordinates.
- Coaching and team building: deficiencies in ability to perform one-on-one coaching or to develop work teams.
- Assertiveness. inability or unwillingness to assert one's self; confusing assertiveness with confrontation, dogmatism, or aggression.
- Counseling: inability to provide help to subordinates with their career, personal, or social problems.
- Stress management: inability to deal with stressful situations.
- Evaluation: deficiencies in evaluating people, materials, processes, or products.
- General management: hands-off management style, failure to follow up on the performance of delegated functions.

Steps in Coaching

Effective coaching involves a series of sequential steps, all important to the ultimate success of the technique. Certain steps of the process are redundant—and that is deliberate.

Step 1: Analyze the Task

Set the stage for coaching. Identify the major activities and results. Separate what subordinates *must* know and be able to do from what is nice to know and be able to do. Conduct a performance analysis focused on job requirements. Find out what subordinates already know and can do. If it's a complex task, break it down into its components or elements. Get agreement on exactly what the task entails. Focus on requirements, standards of performance, and measures of performance.

Step 2: Determine and Discuss Status

Observe subordinates in action. Study work products and ask questions. If there is a problem, get agreement that it exists. Ask employees what would enhance or sustain improvement. Mutually discuss improvement alternatives. Use questions that center on the what, when, where, and how. Ask questions about subordinates' experience by using probing, clarifying, and open-ended questions. Use questions to find out what they already know and don't need to relearn, to find out what they don't know and do need to learn, and to find out what they know that can be related to and integrated with the new task. Identify *specific* deficiencies or shortfalls in performance. Determine the cause. Communicate the findings to subordinates. Get agreement on them.

Step 3: Develop a Remedial Plan and Intervention Strategy

Identify the generic approach to be used—how you're going to get subordinates to improve their performance. Then identify the specific steps to be followed and the sequence in which the elements of the job or task should be relearned. Again, get subordinates' input and get agreement on the plan. Schedule follow-up meetings.

A distinction must be made here between "must" and "can" coaching actions. A "must" intervention is one where the manager believes he or she must *do* something—because of company rules, regulations, or policies, or of the seriousness of the deficiency. Subordinates are not given the option of deciding not to cooperate in the intervention. For example, the company policy states that when 10 percent of a training class fails the test, the instructor's strategy and performance must be reviewed and monitored. If more than 10 percent fail, neither the manager nor the instructor has a choice. The monitoring and review must be accomplished.

In a "can" intervention, the manager does not feel compelled to intervene, but believes the intervention will help the subordinate or the organization. For example, although a supervisor is performing adequately, the manager may conclude that performance could be improved if he or she attended a supervisory development workshop. The manager suggests that the subordinate attend the workshop, and the subordinate is free to decline.

Step 4: Implement the Strategy

Establish the conditions that will facilitate the remedy. Tell subordinates about the task and discuss the remedy. Emphasize one thing at a time. Start with the most important deficiency that can be overcome with reasonable effort. If there is any doubt about subordinates' ability to correct the deficiency, or if failure is a strong possibility, defer action on that item.

Explain the results expected. Treat subordinates as equals. Ask for their suggestions. Discuss what is to be done, why it is to be done, and how it should be done. Tell them about the importance of the task. Determine whether they know how to do it correctly. Determine whether they could do it correctly if they wanted to. Don't just give information— tell them what to do with it. Invite questions. If necessary, demonstrate proper performance of the task. Act as a model. Show, talk your way through, or get subordinates directly involved by having them talk *you* through. Have them do it. Provide tactful, noncritical feedback, and be sure to recognize progress and accomplishment.

Step 5: Monitor Performance

Observe and analyze performance. If needed, again demonstrate how the task should be performed and ask the employee for questions. Have subordinates demonstrate and give them feedback on performance. Ask for their view of progress to date. Identify areas that can be improved. Use questions rather than criticism. Review earlier plans for performance improvement and determine how they can be improved. Discuss, urge, and encourage, but use a minimum of direction. Again, provide appropriate recognition and rewards.

Step 6: Handle Mistakes

The difference between effective coaches and ineffective ones is how they handle subordinates' mistakes. When mistakes occur, as they inevitably will, the worst thing the manager can do is to criticize subordinates. The consequences are likely to be resentment, tension, denial of responsibility, buck passing, insecurity—or all those. Plus damaged communication, deception, and the need for more stringent controls.

The next worst response to error is to ignore it. It is nothing less than foolish to allow subordinates to continue making mistakes and causing damage to the department. It is unfair to them and to the organization.

It is also ineffective to take over the task, to revoke the delegation. If you do, subordinates will never learn and will become extremely reluctant to take on new responsibilities.

Still another ineffective tactic is to exercise such close monitoring that the error is called to subordinates' attention before they even recognize that a mistake has been made, or so soon after the error that they don't have time to make the correction. Again, this approach will only result in resentment.

The best way to handle mistakes is to ask subordinates how the error happened. If the explanation is weak or self-serving, they are likely to see that in describing the event. Next, ask them to tell you how the mistake can be corrected and avoided in the future, or how performance can be improved. Although you are under no obligation to accept the solution or remedy, the approach is likely to get subordinates to accept responsibility for the action and to try to prevent repeating the error.

Most mistakes are caused by lack of knowledge or skill; they can be handled with kindly suggestion and without resorting to overt and destructive criticism. Some mistakes, however, are caused by inattention or negligence. In those cases, managers have no alternative. They must let subordinates know that they are disappointed and displeased; express the criticism quietly, privately, matter-of-factly, and without emotion—and be specific about the performance deficiency.

Focus attention and commentary on the job performance rather than on the person. Avoid belaboring the point, and balance criticism by giving recognition and credit when good work is done.

Finally, support your subordinates. Help them to be winners. Encourage them to improve. Earn their trust and confidence and show that you believe in them.

Step 7: Evaluate Results

At this point in the coaching process, manager and subordinate cooperatively evaluate the effectiveness of the interventions, note performance improvements, and identify areas where additional attention is required. Evaluation should not be haphazard. It should be done regularly and in accordance with a schedule mutually agreed to.

Step 8: Modify the Improvement Plan

In this step, manager and subordinate discuss needed modifications to the improvement plan. Agreement on what needs are to be addressed and how they should be addressed is essential. At the conclusion of the meeting, a new improvement plan should be developed. A specific, positive summary statement should be prepared, and a review date should be established. Follow up with periodic, specific supportive comments in the course of normal, day-to-day operations.

Summary

Coaching is not managing. It is a totally different skill involving an informal and continuing one-on-one relationship between manager and subordinate. At all levels of organization, its purpose is to help subordinates improve their job performance, develop their technical, professional, and managerial skills, and enhance their potential.

Essentially, coaching is informal, individualized instruction. It makes use of many techniques including encouragement, observation, correction, demonstration, practice, feedback, recognition and reward, and example.

Successful coaches believe in people, in their need and capacity to improve their performance. They recognize that effective coaching takes place only in a nonthreatening environment with a fair and firm manager. They have highly developed observational, analytical, interviewing, intervention, and feedback skills, and they use them judiciously and appropriately.

In all their activities, they apply the principles of adult learning. They get the learner directly involved. They tailor learning activities to individual needs, backgrounds, skills, and learning styles. They ensure that coaching interventions involve realistic, job-related activities and problems, and that the environment is informal and characterized by mutual respect and confidence. They structure tasks and activities, relate and integrate them with what the subordinate already knows and is able to do, and focus them on direct, hands-on experiences.

Effective coaches are accessible to their subordinates, and they serve as technical, professional, moral, and ethical role models. They are unselfish, open, patient, understanding, supportive, and accepted by their subordinates. They provide positive rewards for both progress toward improvement and actual accomplishment.

Successful coaches avoid the pitfalls of inadequate planning and objective setting, lack of subordinate involvement, unclear or unaccepted standards and measures of performance, subjectivity, and overemphasis on errors and deficiencies. They do not make the mistake of relating coaching activities to salary reviews.

Effective coaches follow a definite sequence of steps in planning for and carrying out the coaching function. They analyze the job or task, determine and discuss status with the subordinate, distinguish between discretionary and mandatory interventions, develop and implement a remedial plan and intervention strategy, monitor performance, deal with mistakes, evaluate results, and modify the improvement plan.

FOR FURTHER READING

Allenbaugh, G. Eric. "Coaching . . . A Management Tool for a More Effective Work Performance." *Management Review,* May 1983, pp. 21–26.

Anderson, J. "Giving and Receiving Feedback." In *Organizational Change and Development,* edited by G. W. Dalton, P. R. Lawrence, and L. E. Greiner. Homewood, Ill.: Irwin-Dorsey, 1970.

Clawson, James G. "Is Mentoring Necessary?" *Training and Development Journal,* April 1985, pp. 36–39.

Cover, William H. "Curbstone Coaching." *Training and Development Journal,* November 1980, p. 33.

Deegan, Arthur X. *Coaching: A Management Skill for Improving Individual Performance.* Reading, Mass.: Addison-Wesley Training Systems, 1979.

Egan, G. *The Skilled Helper,* 3rd ed. Monterey, Calif.: Brooks/Cole, 1986.

"Everyone Who Makes It Has a Mentor." *Harvard Business Review,* July–August, 1978, p. 89.

Fisher, Sheldon. "The Adult Learner." In *Human Resources Management and Development Handbook,* edited by William R. Tracey. New York: AMACOM, 1985.

Fournies, F. F. *Coaching for Improved Work Performance.* New York: Van Nostrand Reinhold, 1978.

Ganz-Sarto, Keith. "The Merit of Mentors: Myth or Reality?" *Training,* April 1985, pp. 14–16.

Hill, N. C. *Counseling at the Workplace.* New York: McGraw-Hill, 1981.

Hunt, R. G. *Interpersonal Strategies for System Management: Applications of Counseling and Participative Principles.* Monterey, Calif.: Brooks/Cole, 1974.

Hurst, D. M., and C. Michael. "Mentorship: A Career Training and Development Tool." *Academy of Management Review,* July 1983, p. 8(3).

Kanter, Rosabeth Moss, and Joseph P. Zolner. "What the 'New' Coaches Can Teach Managers." *Management Review,* November 1986, pp. 10–11.

Kinlaw, D. C. *Helping Skills for Human Resources Development: A Facilitator's Package.* San Diego, Calif.: University Associates, 1981.

Knowles, Malcolm S. *The Modern Practice of Adult Education: Andragogy Versus Pedagogy.* Chicago: Follett, 1980.

Leatherman, Richard W. "One-on-One Training." In *Human Resources Management and Development Handbook,* edited by William R. Tracey. New York: AMACOM, 1985.

Luft, J. *Of Human Interaction.* Palo Alto, Calif.: National Press, 1969.

Maier, N. R. F. *The Appraisal Interview,* rev. ed. San Diego, Calif.: University Associates, 1976.

Meyer, Henry D., Bruce L. Margolis, and William F. Fifield. *The Manager's Guide to Developing Subordinate Managers.* New York: AMACOM, 1980.

Nordstrom, Rodney R., and R. Vance Hall. "The Platinum Rule." *Training and Development Journal,* September 1986, pp. 57–58.

Peters, Tom, and Nancy Austin. *A Passion for Excellence: The Leadership Difference.* New York: Random House, 1985. See especially Chapter 18.

Phillips-Jones, L. *Mentors and Proteges.* New York: Arbor House, 1982.

Roche, Gerard R. "Much Ado About Mentors." *Harvard Business Review,* January–February 1979, pp. 14–28.

Sashkin, Marshall. *A Manager's Guide to Performance Management.* New York: AMACOM, 1986.

Schneier, Craig Eric, Richard W. Beatty, and Lloyd S. Baird. "Creating a Performance Management System." *Training and Development Journal,* May 1986, pp. 74–79.

Shea, Gordon F. *Building Trust in the Workplace.* New York: AMACOM, 1984.

Stockard, James G. *Career Development and Job Training: A Manager's Handbook.* New York: AMACOM, 1977.

"The Coach's Art." *Training,* March 1986, pp. 77–80.

Tyson, Lynne A. "Coaching." In *Human Resources Management and Development Handbook,* edited by William R. Tracey. New York: AMACOM, 1985.

Zimmerman, John H. "Human Resource Management at MCI." *Management Review,* April 1986, pp. 49–51.

Zorn, Theodore E., Jr. *The Manager's Role in Developing Subordinates.* New York: AMACOM, 1983.

13

COUNSELING
Helping People
Help Themselves

Over time, the HR manager is likely (if not certain) to come in contact with the full range of human problems. Performance, career, personal, and social problems will inevitably surface among subordinates, superiors, and peers. Despondency, reclusiveness, marital difficulties, spouse abuse, alcoholism, drug abuse, divorce and separation, sexual harassment, lack of acceptance by peers, insecurity and lack of self-acceptance, neurosis, and paranoia—these problems and many more afflict employees at all levels.

Counseling by managers ("employee first aid") can help some of these employees to cope. Many managers avoid counseling employees on personal or job-related problems either because they feel incompetent to do so or because they fear the confrontation that could result. But, all managers must counsel *some* time. At those times, the proper role of the HR manager is to show sensitivity to employees, be approachable, and be willing to help on a one-to-one, face-to-face basis.

Counseling, appraising, coaching, and mentoring involve similar skills, but they are quite different in purpose, approach, and technique. All four have to do with a personal relationship between two people, one of whom is wiser and more experienced than the other. Counseling, however, is the process by which these two people come together face to face and one on one to attack a problem so that it can be more clearly defined and the one who has it can be helped to understand, clarify, and find a *self-determined* solution to it. In brief, counseling is helping people help themselves.

A comprehensive and effective counseling program is one of the keys to effective job performance, an acceptable level of job satisfaction, and high employee motivation and morale. Obviously not all the requirements of a comprehensive program can be met by HR managers; some of the needs can be met only by psychologists, psychiatrists, or other professionally trained therapists. Services of these specialists should be available (on call). However, counseling skills at the manager level are essential, and can supplement and support professional therapy. At the very least, counseling is important to HR managers because it provides them with an invaluable tool for directing and improving the perform-ance and job satisfaction of their subordinates and others in the organi-zation.

Personal problems affect job performance. An alert manager will perceive when an employee is having difficulties. No manager can avoid the counselor's role without imperiling his or her effectiveness as a manager. Managers must help subordinates maintain a reasonable emo-tional balance, control their emotions so that they can work productively and cooperatively, and receive feedback and help in improving their job performance. Counseling is an effective means of doing those things.

Steps in Counseling

Clinical counselors customarily divide the process of therapy into six interdependent and interrelated steps. Sometimes the sequence may be changed, or a step omitted, depending upon the orientation of the counselor. For example, nondirective counselors omit the diagnosis step and play down the analysis, synthesis, and prognosis steps. Here are the steps:

1. Analysis. Collecting information from all sources to gain an understanding of the counselee.
2. Synthesis. Organizing and summarizing information to identify the counselee's strengths and weaknesses.
3. Diagnosis. Drawing conclusions about the nature and origin of the problem.
4. Prognosis: Predicting the future development of the counselee's problem and the probable outcome.
5. Counseling: Taking the actions needed to bring about adjustment and a solution to the problem.
6. Follow-up. Helping the counselee with new problems or the recurrence of the old one, and determining the effectiveness of counseling.

It would be foolish to suggest that HR managers can carry out all these steps with the depth and skill of clinical psychologists, psychiatric social workers, or psychiatrists. However, all but steps 3 and 4, diagnosis and prognosis, can be performed, at least to a helpful degree, by thoughtful, alert, and caring managers.

Types of Counseling

Counseling sessions can be classified by their objectives: job performance, career planning, outplacement, and personal and social adjustment.

Job Performance Counseling

The objective of job performance counseling is simply to improve job performance. Specifically, it attempts to improve employee efficiency, effectiveness, and productivity, and in so doing achieve job adjustment, improve motivation and morale, decrease absenteeism, reduce turnover, aid acceptance of change, release emotional tension, reduce stress, and promote teamwork.

Performance counseling lets employees know where they stand, what they do well, and where they are deficient. It identifies needed improvements in job knowledge and skills and provides information and assistance in acquiring those skills and in learning more effective techniques of working cooperatively and harmoniously with other employees.

Because performance counseling is typically initiated by the manager and is usually the result of unsatisfactory or substandard performance by the employee, it is perhaps the most difficult type of counseling to conduct successfully. Remember, though, that most employees cannot correct poor performance without help, and sometimes that help must take the form of confrontation. Some managers try to avoid confrontation, hoping that performance will improve or that negative behavior will just fade away. But that just won't happen. It is almost always necessary to confront poor performance or negative attitudes. Confrontation has its positive side. Managers can use confrontation to change behavior and improve relationships and performance.

Here are some special "rules" for handling manager-initiated confrontational job performance counseling sessions:

- Engage in confrontation with an employee only when your own emotions are fully under control and you can think clearly.
- Never engage in confrontational counseling without preparation; lack of adequate preparation is certain to make the situation worse.
- Focus on the root problem and limit the time you spend talking about it.
- Use an exploratory or investigative style. "I'm concerned about . . ." or "Help me to understand . . ." or "Do I have this right?" Don't be accusatory.
- Be ready for a counterconfrontation; it's almost sure to come.
- Listen without interrupting. Take the time to calm yourself if you become upset or hurt.
- Provide feedback to the employee. Rephrase what he or she has

said. "It seems to me that you feel . . ." or "You're saying that . . . ?"

○ Always return to your original point of concern. Continue the discussion until you have resolved the problem one way or another.

○ State what has been agreed upon as needed changes and let the employee know that you are pleased that an understanding has been reached. "I'm glad that we had this conversation. I think that we understand each other."

Career Counseling

The objective of career counseling is to help employees exploit their strengths and potential and avoid mismatches between individual aspirations and capabilities and organization opportunities—and in so doing increase productivity, deepen job satisfaction, improve retention, and enhance their promotability. It helps employees know who they really are, what they really want, and what they really can do so that they can plan and operate out of a sense of confidence in their true potential.

In short, through career counseling, employees learn about their own capabilities, assets, limitations, preferences, and objectives, where they stand in the organization, what opportunities are available to them within and outside the organization, and what they need in the way of training and development to employ their talents and make the most of their opportunities.

Outplacement Counseling

The primary purpose of outplacement counseling is to help the employee identify the reasons for the termination, accept the finality of the action, identify strengths, skills, and talents that can be stressed in seeking new employment, and provide leads for the job search. Outplacement counseling is not a simple or routine task; it is an important interchange that can well serve both the employee and the organization.

Termination is always traumatic for the employee, and it is not unusual for an individual to become severely depressed. In addition to the financial aspects of termination—the real concerns about supporting one's self and family and maintaining the lifestyle one has become accustomed to—the experience is usually a severe blow to the individual's ego and self-esteem. Unquestionably, terminated employees need help in dealing with this shattering experience.

From a strictly organizational standpoint, outplacement counseling can uncover the real causes of employee failure. Of course, it is unfortunate that the cause of an employee's substandard performance was not identified and remedied before dismissal became necessary. However, there are still gains to be made in the form of key data that managers and supervisors need to decrease the potential for substandard performance among other employees.

Of course unsatisfactory performance is not the only reason for terminating employees. Mergers and reorganizations, downsizing, divestiture, restructuring, lost markets, and serious business declines also make termination of skilled and productive people necessary. From both humanistic and practical standpoints, a sound outplacement counseling program is a good corporate investment.

Personal Adjustment Counseling

The objectives of personal adjustment counseling are to help subordinates gain self-understanding, learn how to regulate their own lives, achieve insight into difficult experiences, and deal with emotional stress. Through interaction with a caring counselor, subordinates learn to use their own resources, as well as the resources of the organization and the larger community, to achieve the optimum personal adjustment they are capable of.

Personal counseling takes many forms but all have the objective of helping employees to deal with problems that affect their mental health, job performance, and personal satisfaction. Unfortunately, the "working wounded," the employees working with pain, are legion among us. They need help to rid themselves of anxiety, depression, eating or sleeping disorders, substance abuse, and a host of other personal problems.

Obviously, the HR manager cannot provide psychotherapy for subordinates. The most severely wounded require professional psychological or psychiatric care. But the HR manager can help people with less severe problems and can refer more serious cases to professionals.

Alcohol and substance abuse. One of the most serious problems facing all types of organizations today, from amateur and professional sports, through public and private organizations, to government, is alcohol and substance abuse. More and more people from all walks of life are cocaine users—they're "tooting, smoking, and croaking" or "taking a little ride."

The number of people afflicted by addiction to alcohol, cocaine,[1] marijuana, "uppers" and "downers" (amphetamines, benzodiazepines [Librium and Valium], barbiturates, opiates, and PCP), and the "serious" habits—crack, heroin, and "designer" drugs—is literally staggering. One approach to a solution involves legislation—drug testing and tougher penalties for possession and use. Another approach is education. A third

1. Also called blow, coke, fairy dust, koo koo, lines, nose candy, snow, toot, and white magic. The National Institute of Drug Abuse estimated that in 1979–1982 as many as 22 million people were cocaine users, and the Cocaine National Help Line Study conducted in 1985 found that 75 percent of cocaine users used it on the job, 69 percent regularly.

is counseling, either on an individual basis or in groups, by professionally trained counselors.

Legal. Legal problems constitute another category of personal problems, and a growing one. Litigation appears to be the way of the world. People are suing or being sued at a rate never before seen—and for anything and everything—from medical malpractice to false advertising, from trespassing to battery, from child custody to environmental hazards, from palimony to paternity. It is highly unlikely that any adult can go through life today without at some time being involved in a legal action. The complexity of the laws, including tax laws, makes it equally unlikely that people will be able to deal with the problem without trained legal assistance and counseling.

Financial. Similarly, almost no one can go through adult life without facing at least one financial crisis, a crisis that requires the assistance of a financial expert. Even such commonplace financial matters as purchasing a home, making investments, developing retirement options and plans, planning for the education of children, and drawing up wills and trusts, require the services of a financial counselor as well as a lawyer.

Marital and family. The high divorce rate is testimony to the prevalence of marital problems and the inability of people to deal with them. Divorce is often preceded by incompatibility of partners, spouse abuse, sexual dysfunction, child abuse, and a host of other problems. This is an area where professional therapists can be of great help. The difficulty is getting the people with the problems to the sources of help they need. Managerial counseling can assist in achieving that objective.

Preretirement. In the past, too many workers reached retirement without proper planning. They lacked the information they needed about health care, financial affairs, legal matters, housing and location choices, use of time, and the role of change. The result has been dissatisfaction, boredom, unhappiness, depression, and sometimes alcoholism and mental illness.

A satisfying retirement is built around various critical decisions: where to live, how to live, and what to live on. It addresses lifestyle regardless of whether an individual plans to continue working, engage in volunteer activities, travel, or play lots of golf. An effective preretirement counseling program can do much to prevent the bad consequences of inadequate or incomplete retirement planning.

Identifying Problem Employees

Changes in a subordinate's appearance, behavior, personality, or job performance are usually the first signals that something is wrong. An observant manager must be alert for the kinds of changes listed here.

Any of them may point to the need for referral to a competent and qualified therapist (psychiatric social worker, psychologist, psychiatrist, or other mental health specialist), but the items with an asterisk almost certainly do. They are symptoms of severe emotional problems.

Chronic absenteeism
Habitual tardiness
Dishonesty—theft, pilferage, lying, falsifying work records
Willful damage to company property
Significant weight loss or gain
Facial tics
Skin blemishes
Frequent hangovers
Insubordination
Temper tantrums
Frequent indecisiveness or impatience
Excessive restlessness or irritability
Inappropriate laughter or giggling
Habitual worried expression
Peculiar mannerisms
Overly talkative or uncommunicative
Exaggerated self-references
Extreme lack of self-confidence
Inability to cope with minor problems
Chronic exhaustion
Constant fighting
Compulsive gambling
Slovenly appearance
Use of abusive or threatening language
Grandiose schemes
Sexual harassment
Bizarre or outlandish clothing, hair styles, or manners
Chronic failure to meet deadlines and requirements
*Unmistakable personality changes
*Avoidance of contacts with supervisors or other employees
*Persistent apathy
*Intoxication at work
*Persistent carelessness; accident proneness
*Significant and repeated errors of judgment
*Long and deep periods of preoccupation with anxieties, fears, and guilt feelings
*Abrupt decline in intellectual efficiency; confused thinking
*Inability to concentrate; persistent daydreaming
*Difficulty in remembering or following instructions
*Ineffective or disruptive relationships with others

*Reclusiveness; friendlessness; suspiciousness
*Extreme aggressiveness
*Possession or use of narcotics
*Persistent or severe depression
*Unexplained physical ailments; hypochondria
*Unrealistic rationalization of deficiencies
*Denial of obvious problems
*Wide, frequent, and rapid mood shifts
*Strong resistance to offers of help
*Delusions or hallucinations
*Talking about suicide; suicide gestures

Some managers unconsciously use invalid or inaccurate means of gauging character, personality, or ability. Many of these "systems" are based on the assumption that personal traits and abilities are associated with certain physical attributes. Here are a few of the most common.

People with high foreheads are intellectually superior.
People with receding chins lack will power.
People with weak handshakes lack self-confidence.
People with shifty eyes or those who avoid eye contact are dishonest.
People with red hair are emotional.
People with close-set eyes are devious.
Obese people are good-natured.
Underweight people are joyless.
Short people are arrogant and pushy.

Like phrenology, graphology, palmology, numerology, and astrology (the number of their supporters notwithstanding), these indicators are illogical.

Benefits of Counseling

Regardless of the types and specific objectives of counseling, all can produce similar benefits. They revolve around the important matters of achieving self-understanding and self-acceptance, developing the ability to deal with immediate problems and problem-solving ability in general, eliminating or reducing deficiencies in personality, knowledge, or skills, and making needed changes in the environment. Although full realization of these benefits can be achieved only through professional counseling, skilled and caring managers can produce gains in these areas—at the very least they can reinforce the work of professional therapists.

Achieve self-understanding. People do not always understand themselves as well as they should or need to. They often have a distorted or inaccurate view of themselves, their needs, values, aspirations, strengths, and limitations. Effective counseling can help employees appraise themselves more objectively and achieve greater personal insights.

Gain self-acceptance. Well-adjusted employees are able to accept themselves despite the deficiencies and shortcomings that all people have in various kinds and amounts. They need to believe that they have personal value, that they have contributions to make to the organizations they serve and the people they work with, and that they are useful and important. Again, skillful counseling can achieve these important results.

Understand and deal with immediate problems. An immediate purpose served by all counseling sessions is to help people understand the problem or concern that brought them to the counselor. People with problems need to get help in solving the immediate concern.

Learn to deal with problems more effectively. Dealing with an immediate problem is one thing; learning to manage problems in general is quite another. Counseling is, or should be, concerned with both. By dealing with the problem at hand, employees should also be learning problem-solving skills that can be applied to problems in the future—and, it is hoped, on their own. Counseling should be conducted to produce changes that will not only enable people to extricate themselves from the immediate difficulty but also to make better decisions in the future.

Eliminate or reduce deficiencies. A fifth objective of counseling is to help people identify and either eliminate or reduce deficiencies in personality, knowledge, or skills. Although an adult's personality probably cannot be drastically changed without long-term psychotherapy, important behavioral changes can compensate for shortcomings that interfere with interpersonal relationships and related job performance. Certainly, concepts, facts, and principles can be transmitted from the boss to the employee through counseling sessions. Similarly, many skills, such as communication and interpersonal skills, can also be taught through the counseling medium.

Make needed environmental changes. Sometimes the solution to a problem or concern lies in changing the environment of the individual employee—a different job, a new location, a different shift, or a new team. Effective counseling can identify when such changes are needed.

Counseling Methods

There are three basic approaches to counseling: directive, nondirective (client-centered), and eclectic, a combination of both. The differences between directive and nondirective counseling lie mainly in the role of the counselor.

Directive

Directive counselors define their role as collecting, sifting, organizing, classifying, summarizing, and evaluating relevant information to arrive at a description of circumstances surrounding the problem. The counselor analyzes attitudes, motives, interests, emotional balance, and other factors that facilitate or inhibit satisfactory adjustment. However, *both* the counselee and the counselor participate in the effort to help the counselee learn about himself or herself. The counselor helps in the learning process by serving as a coach and teacher. Together the counselee and the counselor interpret the relevant facts and their implications and identify ways for the counselee to make needed adjustments.

In directive counseling, the counselor may advise, persuade, or explain. When advising, the counselor states his or her own opinion about the best choice of solution or course of action, always being sure to identify those suggestions as *opinions*.

When persuading, the counselor marshals the evidence to support a solution or course of action logically and reasonably. The objective is to persuade the employee to understand the implications of the decision or choice and encourage the counselee to follow the advice. When using the explanatory approach, the counselor explains the significance of the information uncovered, identifies the underlying cause of the problem, and provides conclusions and recommendations for action.

Directive counseling is characterized by what might be called an external frame of reference. The directive counselor thinks *about* the counselee. For example, here are the sorts of things a directive counselor might be thinking during a performance counseling session with a subordinate.

> "He seems to be very nervous. I wonder if I should help him to start talking."
>
> "Why this indecision? What could be causing it?"
>
> "What is meant by this focus on the female members of the work team?"
>
> "He's been divorced. I didn't know that."
>
> "He's a Vietnam veteran. I feel sorry for anyone who spent a year in Vietnam."

Nondirective

Nondirective (client-centered) counselors define the counselor's role as that of demonstrating warmth and acceptance and reflecting and clarifying attitudes. In their view, counselors should not interpret, advise, suggest, reason, persuade, probe, or pass judgment. They believe that the counselor must respect the individuality of the counselee and his or her capacity to solve problems.

They believe the key to success is not the counselor's diagnostic ability but rather the counselee's insight into the problem and its causes. The nondirective counselor's role is to establish and maintain the conditions necessary for the counselee to achieve insight into the problem and thereby achieve control over it. It is therefore of little or no importance for the counselor to diagnose the client's problem.

It might be said that nondirective counselors assume an internal frame of reference when dealing with a counselee. The counselor feels *with* the counselee. For example, here are the things a nondirective counselor might be thinking in the session described above.

"It's really hard for you to get started."
"Decisions are difficult for you."
"You're very upset by the actions of the work team."
"You feel rejected because of your divorce."
"To you the Vietnam experience was devastating."

Eclectic

This approach to counseling attempts to make use of the best features of both directive and nondirective methods. Some practitioners choose an approach based on the type of problem. Others use status, age, or personal characteristics or the personality of the individual to select the best method. Still others claim they decide on an approach by trial and error.

In my view, it is extremely difficult, if not impossible, for a counselor to make effective use of both methods. Their underlying rationales are far too different for one person to accept and practice them consistently and successfully.

Counseling Strategies

There is really no such thing as a "standard" counseling strategy. Strategies are specific to different problems and different people in different situations. The counselor must adapt specific approaches to the individuality and problem of the counselee. Flexibility, adaptability, and modification are called for. Every problem requires a fresh approach. Problems are never exact duplicates of one another. Here are a few of the most commonly used strategies.

Forcing compliance. This approach involves exerting pressure—job, financial, peer, or other kinds—on employees to force comformity by making it advantageous to follow a certain course of action and unwise to refuse. It is forcing compliance by threatening punishment in some form—whether it be formal sanctions or just plain disapproval. Although not uncommon, this approach has nothing to commend it.

Changing the environment. Here the strategy involves changing those aspects of the environment that cause the difficulty. Some of the options are transfer to another job, department, team, shift, or location. Others might involve removing hazards to safety and health, providing better or more effective tools and work aids, and so on.

Selecting the appropriate environment. Here the approach is to help employees choose from the environment those aspects that are most appropriate to their capabilities, interests, preferences, and the like. For example, they might be helped to select a new career goal, or choose social experiences that will facilitate development in the desired direction. In essence, this technique attempts to block out unfavorable aspects of the environment and highlight the favorable.

Learning needed skills. With this strategy employees are helped to overcome deficiencies in the knowledge and skills that caused the difficulty. It may involve coaching, training, or short- or long-term assignments to task forces and work groups. Whatever the strategy, it may have as its objective the improvement of physical, mental, or social skills.

Changing attitudes. This approach has as its objective helping employees change their attitudes to facilitate a comfortable and reasonable balance between their needs and the demands of the job environment. It does not necessarily mean that attitudes must conform to group norms. It may be simply a matter of helping employees develop compensatory or rationalizing attitudes. For example, a low-aptitude employee who aspires to become a manager may be helped to develop a more realistic achievement, one more consistent with his or her potential.

Pitfalls in Counseling

Counseling is often poorly done—or not done at all. The process is not only time-consuming and complex but also potentially damaging to both counselor and counselee. If improperly handled, counseling can destroy relationships between manager and employee, and result in degradation rather than improvement of performance. Some of the most common pitfalls follow.

Avoidance. Some HR managers avoid counseling because the process requires personal involvement. Others steer clear of counseling because it requires a great deal of time. Still others duck it because they don't want to put themselves in the position of "shrinks," or because they believe that they lack the skills to deal with the problems of others.

Lack of objectivity. Managers sometimes find it very difficult to maintain their objectivity when attempting to help employees deal with problems. They may react more emotionally than rationally. They become sympathetic toward the employee and the problem, rather than empathic.

Misconceptions. All too many HR managers view counseling as nothing more than advising, warning, ordering, forbidding, or entreating, in an effort to "reform" an employee. Others believe that counseling means simply encouraging or reassuring people that they are doing well and that "everything will work out OK." Still others believe that counseling amounts to persuading people to do better. Some HR managers try to limit their counseling to job-related problems. They overlook the fact that personal and emotional problems have an impact on job performance. Effective counseling is *not* advising, reassuring, or persuading. It must include attention to problems of personal adjustment.

Lack of skills. Perhaps the most common pitfall in counseling is lack of skills. In addition to at least a degree of personal warmth and large amounts of patience, understanding, and tact, counseling requires special skills: listening, analyzing, communicating, and providing feedback. These skills require training and practice. Ineptness in conducting counseling is certain to result in inappropriate actions, poor solutions to problems, hurt feelings, and their destructive consequences to the individual, the manager, and the organization.

Poor judgment. On occasion, managers have demonstrated overconfidence in their ability to deal with the problems of people. They have attempted to help employees solve very serious problems—problems that really require the help of professionally trained and experienced psychotherapists. The effective HR manager not only is able to identify problems that exceed his or her ability, but also knows when, where, and how to refer employees to competent professionals.

Initiation of Counseling

Self-referral. Probably the easiest situation for you as manager-counselor to handle, at least from the standpoint of rapport with the counselee, occurs when employees ask for help. Although the problem may not be an easy one to address—and in fact may require referral to a professional therapist or other helping specialist—it makes your job much more straightforward. Employees want help, and your task is to be sure that they get the best assistance available.

Third-party referral. Sometimes the need for counseling is identified by a third party—a member of the employee's work team, a staff person, or another supervisor. If the person who sees the need is able to convince the employee to seek help, the problem is simplified because it then becomes a self-referral. However, if the person with the problem sees no need to seek help, the situation becomes much more tenuous. You must either confront the employee or find some less abrupt way to get the employee to discuss the situation. In either case, the solution is not easy to find.

Manager-initiated. Perhaps the most common means of initiating counseling sessions, particularly job-performance counseling, is manager-initiated. That is because it is the manager who is responsible for ensuring optimal job performance, who has many opportunities to observe employees under a variety of conditions, has a responsibility to provide career planning guidance and assistance, and, in the case of termination, has an obligation to provide outplacement counseling.

Techniques of Counseling

There are no set formulas that will ensure success in the counseling process. Techniques that work well in one situation may be inappropriate in another. However, certain techniques are commonly used by competent counselors in preparing for and conducting counseling sessions. Those techniques overlap and do not necessarily develop in any fixed order; their relative importance varies with the counseling situation and the problem at hand.

Remember, *all* procedures are designed to get employees involved in finding the solution to the problem. The manager must give special attention to employees' feelings about the situation because feelings are usually much more important than the rational content of their statements.

Preparing

Effective counseling sessions don't just happen. There must be careful preparation so that conditions will be as favorable as possible.

Environment. A really satisfactory counseling session cannot take place where there are the distractions of noise and constant interruptions, or even the threat of interruptions. Find a place that is private, orderly, comfortable, and free from distractions. Unquestionably the most critical element is the need for privacy. Except in group counseling sessions, it is impossible to have a frank discussion if a third person is present or within hearing. People are usually reluctant to discuss even apparently simple and publicly known problems under such circumstances. Employees must feel confident that what is said cannot be overheard by anyone. The matters of comfort and absence of distractions are secondary.

Time. An effective counseling session takes time, so you must allow sufficient time for it. In any event, a sense of haste must be avoided. How much time should be allocated? There is no absolute standard, but the rule of thumb is a minimum of 30 minutes and one hour is even better. Too much time is better than not enough.

Records. Assemble and review the individual's records (personal, not official personnel records) and any other available information before a scheduled counseling session. That part of the preparation should rarely be omitted. Regardless of how pressing the problem or how short the time, an additional delay long enough to look over the records will actually save time and avoid false moves.

Establishing Rapport

The effectiveness of counseling depends in large measure on the degree of rapport established and maintained between counselor and counselee. Although there are no hard and fast rules, the following comments and suggestions may be helpful.

It is well to assume at the outset that most employees are reluctant, at least at first, to discuss their problems. For that reason, you sometimes need to begin the session with little, if any, reference to the reasons for which the counseling session was scheduled. Watch employees' comments, inflection, posture, facial expressions, and gestures to learn when they are psychologically ready to discuss the problem. Rapport must be established before the problem can be directly addressed, but once rapport has been established, the problem should be addressed without further delay. In sum, counseling sessions should begin promptly but not abruptly.

Open the conversation casually. As soon as the employee is at ease, identify the purpose of the session. Avoid embarrassing pauses, but as soon as possible guide the discussion directly to the subject at hand. Be frank and straightforward but not brusque or blunt. Keep the discussion on a professional rather than a personal level, but show interest in and concern for the individual.

The HR manager must establish and maintain a friendly, cooperative working relationship with employees. This step is particularly important in the first session. Feelings of friendliness, security, and mutual confidence are essential and must be established before the serious work of the session is begun. If rapport is lost during the session, it must be regained before any decisions are made.

Methods of establishing rapport depend on the personalities and situations involved, and stereotyped suggestions cannot be given. You must be sensitive to the subtleties of the situation and be resourceful in dealing with them. Your attitudes, posture, facial expressions, inflection, gestures, and oral expressions in large part determine the reactions of the employee. A counselor's success in helping the counselee hinges on a combination of reputation, actions, and attitude.

Reputation. The counselor must have a reputation for competence, kindness, respect for the individual, and for keeping confidences. HR managers will usually experience little difficulty in establishing rapport if they are known as consistently fair, friendly, understanding, and competent, if they are reputed to be adequately informed and intelligently concerned about employees' problems, and if they are known to respect the need for confidentiality and avoid prying into private affairs.

Actions. If you greet employees *by name* in a cordial, pleasant, and friendly way and without display of authority, put them at ease, and deal with them in a forthright and sincere manner, you should have no difficulty. A manager who listens courteously and attentively without any semblance of impatience or ill humor, speaks in terms the employee understands, avoids evidences of pressure, boredom, irritation, anxiety, and lack of compassion, and maintains an attitude of absorption in employees' welfare, should find it relatively easy to establish and maintain rapport.

Pronounced and unnecessary movements or frequent handling of papers or objects indicate uncertainty, anxiety, or lack of confidence. They also detract from the concentration and attention necessary to conduct an effective counseling session.

For best results, it is essential that the counseling session proceed with dispatch once it is started. If you waste time, you run the risk of letting the session lose direction. But don't rush. Employees need time to get accustomed to the situation, to feel at ease, and to get ready to talk. A counseling session in which employees feel the pressure of time is worse than no counseling session at all.

Attitude. Display an objective but not a cold or uninterested attitude. Convey regard for employees' ideas and feelings as important and show an interest in hearing them. You must be able to accept expressions of negative feelings and be unperturbed. Don't censure; at the same time, acceptance of employees' words and feelings should not convey acceptance of unacceptable behavior or standards.

Don't antagonize or embarrass the employee. Effective counseling cannot take place if employees are antagonized or angry. Competent counselors avoid arguing with the counselee, and they demonstrate warmth, sincerity, respect, and friendliness.

Don't try to be clever. When HR managers try to be cleverer than employees, they are likely to forget the purpose of the session and elicit attempts from employees to be equally shrewd.

Defining the Problem

During the review of the employees' characteristics, information has been collected that provides signs or symptoms of problems. For many problems, this process of identification is relatively straightforward, but it is usually incomplete. Time and lack of skill usually force the manager acting in the role of counselor to identify only major relevant characteristics. However, it is usually unnecessary to go deeper. The end result is that you make a tentative decision about the nature of the problem. The task is to get employees to identify the root of the problem for themselves.

At this point, attempt to define the problem. Encourage employees to state the problem as they see it and to relate facts, not feelings. By talking about the problem while you listen carefully and attentively, employees may be able to project the problem outside of themselves where it can be viewed more objectively. The job of the counselor-manager is simply to hear employees out completely and try to see the problem from their viewpoint.

Be on the lookout for signs of emotion: blushing, nervousness, hesitation in answering, twitching, or downcast eyes. Ask questions that require more than *yes* or *no* answers, but avoid leading questions. Don't suggest the answers to questions. Avoid sharing your own experience and giving solutions. Invite employees to talk freely, but don't trick them into revealing confidences. Don't repeat verbatim what employees say. Avoid at all costs making them feel stupid, juvenile, wrong, or silly. Don't make value judgments, and don't generalize.

Solving the Problem

When the problem has been identified and described, counselor and employee together review the factors that produced the symptoms and search for relationships. They seek to understand why the employee is in the present situation and what changes are likely to occur in the near future. By identifying symptoms, they infer the expected causes and attempt to verify or reject their diagnosis. They may arrive at a conclusion about causes by deduction, hunch, intuition, or just plain guessing, but it is always necessary to double check the conclusion by logic and the employee's reactions.

Now various solutions to the problem are proposed, considered, and discussed and ultimately a plan of action is established. Employees must be helped to come to grips with the problem, do their own thinking, and change their own feelings and perceptions. You may raise "do you think?" "could it be?" or "is it possible?" questions.

Do not make decisions for employees. Counseling involves personal problems and choices among alternatives. People should make their own decisions. Although it may seem to be easier for you to make the decision, to do so is a grave error. Decisions made by the manager cannot reflect the employees' perspective and more often than not do not solve the problem.

Restate ideas and feelings expressed by the employee. Summarize what has been said on various points, and then try to help employees mentally try out solutions and thereby anticipate the consequences of some possible decisions. Use language employees understand. Avoid technical jargon. When explaining, make certain that employees are following you. Proceed no faster than employees can follow. Don't be annoyed by pauses in the conversation. Follow leads. Don't do all the talking.

Before the end of the session, employees should have drawn up a set of objectives and some reasonable alternative action plans. Then evaluate the factors for and against each course of action. The employees' points of view, attitudes, and goals should always be the point of departure. Jointly list the factors that are favorable and unfavorable. Then sum them up and balance them, identify their implications, and encourage employees to reach a decision.

Terminating the Session

When the purpose of the counseling session has been accomplished, you should close the conversation and dismiss employees gracefully. End on a positive note. The employees should leave with a feeling that all factors in their situation have been considered and with the conviction that they have had a sympathetic hearing and a helpful experience.

Carrying Out the Decisions

The selected course of action is followed. Both you and employee take the actions decided upon at the meeting. Action by employees will vary with the nature of the problem and the objectives. Your action will be directed toward helping employees succeed in their proposed action plan. That may mean changing the environment, providing special assistance, scheduling training, referring the individual to professionals, or coordinating needed services.

Recording

It is important that at least an informal and confidential record of the counseling session be made as soon as possible, to avoid confusion during follow-up and at the next counseling session. Immediately after each counseling session, write a concise summary: facts learned, significant questions and comments, decisions reached, and follow-on actions agreed to. Don't depend on your fallible memory. Even waiting a day may cause significant gaps in the record or confusion with facts and decisions reached.

Referral

In view of the bewildering complexity of some problems, you must be fully aware of your own limitations in the role of counselor. Learn to recognize the need for professional assistance in diagnosing and treating complex problems and refer subordinates to specialized sources for information and assistance you cannot provide.

Sometimes the most appropriate action you can take is to suggest that employees see another person or agency for help. *But don't stop there.* If employees are willing, follow up by letting the person or agency to whom the referral is made know what specific assistance employees need.

Some common sources of expert assistance are:

- For financial problems: financial counselor, personnel officer, employee assistance office, public or private family assistance agencies.
- For legal problems: corporate legal counsel, public or private family assistance agencies.
- For social, personal, and emotional problems: corporate offices (employee assistance programs or employee counseling programs [EAPs or ECPs]), private or public mental health therapists (psychologists, psychiatrists, counselors), public family assistance agencies, mental health clinics, substance abuse agencies (AA, Al-Anon).
- For health problems: company physician, nurse, corporate, public, and private health providers.

Following Up

You must follow up on individual employees and evaluate results. Determine whether they have carried out the plan (or at least attempted to) and whether the desired improvement or resolution has occurred.

Summary

Counseling, or employee first aid, is a necessary and important skill for HR managers. It can help the manager improve the job performance, job satisfaction, motivation, morale, and adjustment of troubled employees. Although HR managers cannot be expected to provide the in-depth analysis, diagnosis, and treatment of professionally trained therapists, they can be of help to employees with problems.

Basically, there are four types of counseling: job performance, career, outplacement, and personal and social. The degree to which HR managers can and should become involved in counseling varies considerably with the nature of the problem and the counseling skills of the manager.

One of the fundamental obligations of HR managers is to be alert for signals that something is wrong, that employees have a problem that requires attention. Changes in appearance, behavior, personality, job performance, or relationships with co-workers are important indicators of problems.

Basically, all forms of counseling have these objectives: (1) helping employees achieve self-understanding or self-acceptance; (2) helping employees understand and deal with problems; (3) helping employees eliminate or reduce deficiencies in personality, knowledge or skills; and (4) helping employees make needed changes in their environment.

Two quite different approaches to counseling are commonly employed: directive and nondirective. Their differences lie mainly in the role and orientation of the counselor. Directive counselors define their role as collecting, sifting, organizing, classifying and evaluating relevant information to arrive at a description and diagnosis of the root problem. The directive counselor makes use of advice, persuasion, or explanation in attempting to get the counselee to follow a course of action. Nondirective counselors define their role as demonstrating acceptance and warmth and reflecting and clarifying feelings and attitudes. They eschew advice, suggestion, persuasion, and probing. They rely on the counselee's capacity to gain insight into the problem and its causes.

There are many serious pitfalls in the counseling role. Among the most common are avoidance, lack of objectivity, misconceptions of the role, lack of counseling skills, and poor judgment. Perhaps the most serious is failure of managers in the role of counselors to recognize their limitations and attempting to help employees deal with deeply rooted emotional problems—problems that demand the help of professionally trained therapists.

Although there is no magic formula, effective counseling involves the use of a number of techniques: preparing for counseling, selecting the proper environment, allocating enough time, establishing and maintaining rapport, displaying the proper attitude, defining and clarifying the problem, solving the problem, terminating the session, carrying out the action plan, making a summary record of the session, when necessary referring employees to some other person or agency for help, and following up.

In all aspects, counseling must be conducted jointly and cooperatively. One rule should never be broken: The counselee, the person who has the problem, has the ultimate responsibility for choosing the course of action to solve it. Counseling is helping people to help themselves—not doing it for them.

FOR FURTHER READING

Belkin, Gary S. *Counseling: Directions in Theory and Practice.* Dubuque, Iowa: Kendall/Hunt Publishing, 1976.

Brammer, Lawrence M., and Frank E. Humberger. *Outplacement and Implacement Counseling.* Englewood Cliffs, N.J.: Prentice-Hall, 1984.

Britsch, R. Lanier, and Terrance D. Olson, eds. *Counseling: A Guide to Helping Others.* Salt Lake City, Utah: Deseret Book Company, 1983.

———. *Counseling: A Guide to Helping Others,* vol. 2. Salt Lake City, Utah: Deseret Book Company, 1985.

DeBoard, Robert, *Counseling People at Work.* Brookfield, Vt.: Gower Publishing Company, 1983.

Dickman, J. Fred, and William S. Hutchinson, Jr., eds. *Counseling the Troubled Person in Industry: A Guide to the Organization, Implementation, and Evaluation of Employee Assistance Programs.* Springfield, Ill.: Charles C. Thomas Publishers, 1985.

Dixon, D. N., and J. A. Glover. *Counseling: A Problem Solving Approach.* New York: Macmillan, 1984.

Downing, Lester N. *Counseling Theories and Techniques: Summarized and Critiqued.* Chicago: Nelson-Hall, 1975.

Drug Abuse: The Workplace Issues. American Management Association, 1987.

Egan, G. *The Skilled Helper,* 3d ed. Monterey, Calif.: Brooks/Cole, 1986.

Feingold, S. Norman. *Counseling for Careers in the 1980s.* Garrett Park, Md.: Garrett Park Press, 1979.

Gutsch, Kenneth U. *Counselors Desk Manual.* Springfield, Ill.: Charles C. Thomas Publishers, 1985.

Hill, N. C. *Counseling at the Workplace.* New York: McGraw-Hill, 1980.

Kirn, Arthur G. "Career Planning." In *Human Resources Management and Development Handbook,* edited by William R. Tracey. New York: AMACOM, 1985.

Lewis, Judith A., and Michael D. Lewis. *Counseling Programs for Employees in the Workplace.* Monterey, Calif.: Brooks-Cole, 1985.

Lyons, Paul V. "EAPs: The Only Real Cure for Substance Abuse." *Management Review,* March 1987, pp. 38–41.

Meckel, Nelson T. "The Manager as Career Counselor." *Training and Development Journal,* July 1981, p. 64.

Pietrofesa, John, and others. *Counseling: An Introduction,* 2nd ed. Boston: Houghton-Mifflin, 1983.

Ramsey, Katherine B. "Counseling Employees." In *Human Resources*

Management and Development Handbook, edited by William R. Tracey. New York: AMACOM, 1985.

Randall, Phillip M., and Alyson Scott. "Retirement Planning." In *Human Resources Management and Development Handbook,* edited by William R. Tracey. New York: AMACOM, 1985.

Schlossberg, Nancy K. *Counseling Adults in Transition: Linking Practice with Theory.* New York: Springer Publishing, 1984.

Stanton, Erwin S. "Outplacement Services." In *Human Resources Management and Development Handbook,* edited by William R. Tracey. New York: AMACOM, 1985.

Steinmetz, Lawrence L. *Managing the Marginal and Unsatisfactory Performer,* 2nd ed. Reading, Mass.: Addison-Wesley, 1985.

Tolbert, E. L. *Counseling for Career Development.* Boston: Houghton Mifflin, 1980.

Tureen, Richard M. *Counseling Skills for Managers.* Coral Springs, Fla.: Richard M. Tureen Publishing, 1984.

Wicks, Robert, and Richard Parsons. *Counseling Strategies and Intervention Techniques,* 2nd ed. White Plains, N.Y.: Longman, 1983.

Wilson, Howard. *Counseling Employees.* Irvine, Calif.: Administrative Research Association, 1973.

Wrich, James T. *Employee Assistance Program: Update for the 1980's,* rev. ed. Center City, Minn.: Hazelden Foundation, 1980.

14

NEGOTIATING
Win-Win Bargaining

When individuals, groups, and countries are unable to resolve disagreements quickly, the disputes often grow into arguments, quarrels, and conflicts, sometimes accompanied by violence in one form or another, including open warfare. However, in our American culture, most unresolved conflicts evolve into litigation—a process in which one person invariably loses. Not only are legal battles complex, time-consuming, and expensive, they also often exacerbate the dispute and severely damage relationships.

Negotiation is an alternative to argument—not to mention fist fighting, malicious mischief, sabotage, and war. Negotiated settlements are likely to be more durable than other means of resolution. When a person or organization experiences a humiliating defeat, the natural tendency is to get back at the opponent—to retaliate in kind—or failing that, to change the settlement.

Successful organizations depend on people to reach agreements and resolve conflicts. Positive negotiations can help HR managers and their people achieve desired results. More and more HR managers find themselves negotiating for the things they need and want: the right salary and benefits package for themselves and their staffers, a decision or commitment from the boss or subordinates, a change in policy, or the price on an item of equipment or a new program or service.

HR managers must often play a negotiating role within their organizations and with outside individuals and groups. Whether they are providing training or assistance to line managers and staff personnel on how to get people to accept change, attempting to influence individual managers or employee groups directly, or trying to reach agreement with people from outside, they must have well-honed negotiating skills. The success of HR managers on a day-to-day basis hangs in the balance. Here are some common situations that require negotiations involving HR managers:

- At meetings, to get viewpoints supported or adopted.
- In planning work load and work flow, to make them efficient and equitable.
- When allocating short resources, to achieve optimum return or efficiency.
- During hiring interviews, to attract and employ the right people.
- In contract discussions with vendors, suppliers, consultants, and collective bargaining units, to consummate an agreement.
- In purchasing, leasing, or rental situations, to get the best buy at the lowest possible cost.
- During performance appraisal reviews, to get commitment to change and improved job performance.
- In interpersonal and interdepartmental conflict situations, to change opponents into cooperative colleagues.
- In salary and benefits discussions with the boss, to improve the financial position.

For example, at one time or another HR managers are certain to become involved in union negotiations, either as direct participants in discussions with the collective bargaining unit on the labor agreement or contract, or as advisers to management on negotiations. In both roles, HR managers must have special skills and knowledge if they are to represent their parties effectively or provide useful guidance.

In the negotiating role, they must come up with an agreement that is acceptable to both parties, but one that will allow the organization to remain effective, efficient, and competitive. In addition, the agreement must be administrable with a minimum of conflict, must change relationships from adversarial to collaborative, and must facilitate the management of human resources.

There are several alternatives to conflict, violence, and legal battles; four of the most common are private negotiation, mediation, arbitration, and litigation. Let's see how they differ.

Negotiation is a process for reaching agreement between or among two or more individuals or groups who have conflicting interests acting either for themselves or as representatives of organizations. It is a means of making acceptable and practical arrangements for settling disputes. It is used to decide on actual or potential disagreements between individuals and groups, such as the sale or exchange of property, budgets, rates, salaries, wages, benefits, conditions of work, and policies. Essentially, then, negotiating is conferring to reach agreement or exchanging ideas to change a relationship from adversarial to cooperative. It is communication.

Much that has been written about negotiating mistakenly stresses the skills a manager needs to get the best possible deal, to win at all costs. Words like *power, moves, traps, game plan,* and *tricks* are used to describe the negotiating process. All too infrequently do we see emphasis placed on how manager and opponent can become partners in the venture, an outcome in which both parties can be winners. The basis of negotiation is exchange—all parties to the disagreement must give and get concessions until agreement is reached.

Mediation is another form of negotiation. Although its objectives are identical to negotiating, its form is considerably different. In addition to the disputants, mediation involves a neutral third party who helps the people with the disagreement to reach a voluntary settlement. Mediators have no power to make decisions or judgments or to enforce an agreement. Rather, they serve as facilitators and expediters. They use a variety of techniques to help the people with the disagreement to focus on potential solutions, communicate openly, and arrive at fair and mutually satisfying solutions. The mediator may make suggestions, but the decision to accept or reject them remains with the disputants. Mediation does not involve rules of evidence or legal precedents; it emphasizes relationships and rules that the disputants have agreed to follow.

Arbitration is a formal process of settling disputes or resolving differences by a means short of litigation in a court of law. When the parties to the conflict agree to resolve their differences by arbitration, they agree to accept the decision of an independent arbitrator as final; in effect, they equate the arbitrator's power with that of a judge. Arbitrators do not rely on legal precedents, although they may refer to similar prior cases. Increasingly today, the arbitrator as well as the representatives of both disputants are attorneys.

Litigation is the process of settling disputes and disagreements in a court of law. In litigation, there is a large body of procedural law that specifies such things as rules of evidence, the types of questions that can be asked, the kinds of documents that must be filed, and what happens when the rules are violated. Either a judge or a jury determines the outcome, and those decisions are final unless appealed to a higher court.

Requirements for Successful Negotiations

Success in negotiating depends to a great degree on your ability to understand yourself and understand other people. You must be aware of your own emotional pattern and your prejudices and biases, particularly as they relate to your needs. In a negotiating situation you are likely to experience pressures that may provoke emotional reactions. Yet you must hold a tight rein on yourself. You must be able to identify your own needs and demonstrate a high degree of emotional control and adjustment to frustration and thwarting.

You must also understand other people, their needs and motivation.

You must be able to identify the needs that other people have and the priority they give to them. You must be able to cause people to feel new needs and then use them to advantage in negotiations.

Self-Knowledge

Effective negotiators know themselves—their strengths and weaknesses, talents and shortcomings, flairs and faults. We all have self-concepts, our own picture of ourselves; unfortunately, they are not always accurate. The problem is that each one of us has three separate and quite different selves: ego, ideal, and real.

The **ego self** is the self we *think* we are, the private self we believe no one else really knows. That self-image may be positive or negative. We may see ourselves as serious and goal-oriented although outwardly we may appear to be flippant and unconcerned about events. Or we may see ourselves as imperfect and insecure whereas others see only an assured and self-confident person.

The **ideal self** is the self we would *like* to be, the self that we want others to perceive, whether or not we truly believe that image would be consistent with reality. Most HR professionals would like others to perceive them as intelligent, articulate, creative, responsible, industrious, conscientious, and caring. It is the ideal self that primarily causes people to say what they say and do what they do. It is one of the primary determinants of behavior.

The **real self** is the most important self, whether the HR professional is acting as a manager, trainer, counselor, or negotiator. It is the self that others *do* perceive, whether at home, at work, or at play. It is the self that determines a person's satisfaction with the present and, at least in part, determines the future. For that reason, it is the real self that everyone must get to know. HR professionals must be aware of their impact on other people, and that is particularly critical in the role of negotiator.

People Knowledge

Good negotiations are built on a firm foundation of mutual respect, good will, and a belief in the dignity and worth of human beings as individual personalities. All HR managers must develop skills in relating to the situations in which they find themselves. These skills must be integral parts of their everyday behavior in dealing with others. They can be developed and improved only by understanding human behavior and its causes and its effects, and by constant practice.

What people do and why they do it are obviously quite separate things. To predict behavior, a successful negotiator needs to observe what people do, and sometimes needs to try to understand why they do it.

There is always a reason for behavior, even actions that would appear to be a suspension of the rules of rationality. A thorough understanding of human behavior—what makes people do what they do—is therefore essential to the conduct of successful negotiations.

When dealing with people in any situation, your thoughts and your ability to judge, persuade, evaluate, compromise, or whatever it is you must do are made possible by what you know (what has been communicated to you) and what you can communicate to others. Part of that knowledge is an understanding of practical psychology as it applies to your opponent, to yourself, and to your ability to communicate. Of the many facts about human nature that bear on communication in the negotiating situation, three are critically important.

People Are Egocentric

It may sound harsh, but people are self-centered—selfish, if you will. To a very considerable extent, people do what they believe is in their own best interests. That is not to say that people are never altruistic, motivated by caring. They are. But much of the time the actions people take are those that promise the most personal satisfaction, benefit, and, oftentimes, advantage. The goal of each person in most situations is to attain the greatest amount of personal satisfaction possible.

People Have Needs

All behavior is goal-oriented. In every waking moment, human beings are goal seekers. The goal is either something the individual wishes to gain—a need he or she wishes to satisfy—or something the individual wishes to avoid. To say it another way, all human actions are directed at targets, whether immediate or deferred, and those targets in some way relate to needs.

Situations—the persons, objects, and symbols that surround a person at any given moment in time—offer opportunities for people to satisfy needs; they also present challenges and threats to the individual. People bring "readiness" to situations; it consists of what they are able to do at a particular time, the responses they can make. Readiness depends upon the person's physical and mental knowledge and skills, as well as emotional maturity. Therefore, readiness actually limits what a person can do in any situation.

People are constantly analyzing the situations they face. In effect, they check them against their past experiences. They predict what will happen if they respond in different ways. Before people act in any situation, they must decide what actions are possible. Then they do what they think will lead to the greatest amount of *net* satisfaction—the greatest amount of reward and the least amount of difficulty.

Whatever happens next is seen by the individual as consequences of the chosen action. Results either confirm or contradict the person's interpretation of the situation. If confirmed, the individual achieves the goal, and in the future will tend to make similar interpretations of like situations.

If a result doesn't satisfy the needs, we say that the person thwarted. People react to thwarting differently. Some reinterpret the situation and try a new response. Some decide that the goal cannot be reached and give up. If people doubt that needs can be met, they may become emotionally upset. Some people are not mature enough to handle any kind of rebuff. They may blow up and say tactless things. Or they may mask their feelings and spend the next few hours reenacting the scene in their minds and thinking about what they *should* have said or done. In one way or another, thwarting is *always* followed by other behavior. When you thwart the other party, you do so at your own peril, and you must be ready for a reaction of some kind. When you are thwarted, you must be on guard to forestall an observable emotional response.

People Are Defensive

In an attempt to protect themselves from undesirable things, people erect barriers and defenses that they carry around with them all the time. Some take the form of offensive weapons—aggression, hostility, sharpness, imperiousness, deliberate failure to observe amenities, projection (ascribing one's motives to others), scapegoating (blaming others), repression (ignoring the unacceptable or unpleasant), or role playing (feigning charm, affability, subservience, and the like).

People tend to become rigid under conditions they perceive to be threatening. Consider this example. You go to your boss with a proposal for a completely new approach to organization development. You make your well-prepared pitch in the form of a decision briefing. Let's assume that some temporary emotional condition, perhaps an argument at home that morning, causes the boss to react unfavorably to your proposal. Instead of "That's a sound plan; let's do it," he says, "I don't want to do it" or "I don't think it will work." Possibly he feels some slight to his self-esteem, and the objection represents a tightening of his self-concept against you.

Ordinarily, when our studied proposals are not accepted and acted upon promptly, we are more than a little bit annoyed. In this case you feel that your judgment has been questioned. You are likely to say to yourself, "Doesn't he realize that OD is my area of expertise?" The fact that the boss does not accept your proposal becomes in itself a personal threat to you. This immediately makes you tighten up, so you decide, "Well, he must not have been listening." So, you try again, only this time a little louder or in a patronizing tone of voice. Of course, the normal reaction when people raise their voices, or are not as deferential as we expect them to be, is to tighten our defenses a bit more and reject the message by deliberately misunderstanding or misconstruing the message. Sometimes it is done by walking away. Either response is likely to act on you and make you more rigid—or livid. We now have a condition that might be called communication deadlock—an impasse. Solutions to communication deadlock will be addressed later.

Essential Conditions

Accurate Assumptions

The first requirement for successful negotiation is that you operate on the basis of accurate assumptions. Assumptions are the genesis of beliefs. They are not consciously learned; rather they are carryovers of information or misinformation. They are rooted in emotional contexts. There are two types: known or perceived, and hidden or unconscious. Known assumptions are relatively easy to confirm or refute; hidden assumptions are difficult to recognize, let alone test and modify or discard. People use assumptions to make sense out of what they see, hear, smell, taste, or feel.

Accurate assumptions are correct hypotheses about the attitudes, positions, and direct and indirect needs of both sides of negotiations—yourself and your opposition. Unfortunately, assumptions in negotiating are usually only guesses or gut feelings—at best, probabilities, not certainties. Nonetheless, they are essential in attempting to identify organizational and individual needs and to look beyond the words used in negotiations to discover the facts.

Effective Techniques

The negotiator must be skilled in the arts of communication, concession, compromise, and accommodation. What do successful negotiators concede or accommodate? Almost anything the opponent really needs. Less astute negotiators offer what they have the most of or are most willing to give up; the real pros concede what others *need* the most, whether or not they have it to give to begin with. Skillful negotiators develop a strategy and plan to support their bargaining position.

One of the best techniques is asking questions. Questions are powerful negotiating tools. The negotiator who knows what questions to ask, how to phrase them, and when and how to use them has a great advantage over less skillful bargainers. Here are some of the most common applications.

- ○ To get and maintain attention.
- ○ To probe for information, get the facts.

○ To get clues to the opponent's thoughts, wants, and needs.
○ To give information, make all participants familiar with available facts and assumptions.
○ To gain understanding.
○ To control the amount and kind of information given or received.
○ To control the direction or focus of the discussion.
○ To stimulate thought.
○ To prod the opposer to consider or reconsider your proposal.
○ To lead the opposition to your way of thinking or conclusions.
○ To delay or forestall decision.
○ To end discussion.
○ To get a decision.

There are several types of questions. Some are likely to result in manageable answers, responses that should cause little or no problems for the questioner. Others are almost certain to result in responses that will cause difficulty for the questioner.

• Manageable questions:

  ○ Planned: questions that are carefully thought out in advance of the negotiating session.
  ○ Open-ended: questions that cannot be answered with a simple *yes* or *no* but invite the respondent to express ideas freely.
  ○ Leading: questions that telegraph the expected reply.
  ○ Stroking: questions that compliment, praise, or flatter the opposer.
  ○ Dispassionate: questions that are calm, composed, and reflect an unemotional attitude.
  ○ Directive: questions that require a specific, clearcut, and precisely focused response.
  ○ Exploratory: questions that encourage the respondent to provide feedback or express feelings and opinions.

• Potentially troublesome questions:

  ○ Impulsive: questions that are unplanned, unprepared, and impetuous.
  ○ Blunt: questions that are curt, abrupt, or brusque.
  ○ Nondirective: questions that allow the respondent to choose the focus or direction of answers.
  ○ Loaded: questions that force the respondent to make embarrassing, discomforting, ambiguous, equivocal, or revealing responses.

- ◦ Emotive: questions that arouse strong feelings and emotional responses.
- ◦ Deceptive: questions designed to trick, snare, or trap the respondent.

Barriers to Successful Negotiations

In addition to the obvious problems of lack of negotiating skills, inadequate planning and preparation, and poor representation, there are several less obvious pitfalls.

Threats and promises. Negotiations conducted under conditions of duress or threat are doomed to failure. There can be no common ground, no meeting of the minds, no real agreements when one of the parties is placed in a totally no-win situation. Nor can negotiations be conducted when promises are made that one of the parties intends to ignore once the settlement is reached. Good faith is the only way to go.

Citing precedents. Precedents are useful guides in arbitration and in a court of law. They are not operational in negotiations. No two negotiating situations are identical, so what appears to have been workable in a past situation in all probability will not fit the current situation. Both parties giving to get something is far more likely to result in a workable agreement.

Hidden agenda. When one of the parties to a negotiating session arrives with ulterior motives or hidden agenda, any agreements that are reached during the meeting are likely to be short-lived. Negotiators must pursue agreements without dissembling. They must be completely frank and honest with themselves and their opponents about what they want to achieve.

Conducting Negotiations

Although negotiation is not a game and has few rules, there are some guidelines that will help avoid the pitfalls and obstacles and go a long way toward achieving cooperation and agreement, resolving the issue by finding ways to meet the interests and needs of both parties, and avoiding an adversarial climate.

Preparation and Planning

Thorough preparation and planning are essential. Never negotiate at the eleventh hour. Start as early as possible so that you won't be forced by the pressure of time to make concessions that you would otherwise refuse to make. Allow plenty of lead time for planning. Preparation should focus on (1) setting objectives and expectations, (2) getting to know your opponent, (3) predicting the strategy and tactics of the opposition and preparing to deal with them, and (4) identifying potential common ground or issues on which there is agreement, how to get them into the negotiation, and how to build on them.

Don't overlook such matters as assisting the opposition with travel plans and hotel accommodations, selecting an appropriate meeting place and time, choosing participants, developing an agenda, and collecting and organizing data, both specific, issue-oriented and general background data.

Setting Your Objectives and Expectations

Establish your objectives, and keep them in mind at all times. But don't set them in concrete; keep them flexible. Be honest and realistic about your needs and requirements. Don't overexaggerate them if you want to retain your credibility. But set your expectations considerably higher than you can reasonably hope to achieve.

The more you anticipate in the way of concessions, the more you are likely to receive. Always plan to ask for more concessions than you expect to get from your opponent. When you ask for five concessions, you are likely to get only two; you need the other three as bargaining chips. Don't make excessive or unreasonable demands. And don't bargain only about concessions that you truly must have. Be ready to bargain about peripheral matters as well. Get ideas and suggestions from others in your organization—executives, managers, supervisors, and your subordinates.

Gathering Your Data—Facts and Figures

Collect data to support your bargaining proposals. Be sure that you have facts and figures to support each and every one of your requirements. Of course, each negotiating situation will require different types of data.

Examples of data needed to support labor union negotiations include figures on promotions, layoffs, transfers, disciplinary actions, grievances, overtime, individual performance, and salary payments. Examples of general data to serve the same purpose include economic conditions and forecasts, cost of living trends, current and projected inflation rates, and profit outlook.

Remember that each negotiating situation is unique, that the conditions surrounding negotiations, the goals you are seeking to achieve, the strength of relative positions, and the experience and personalities of the participants differ from situation to situation. Study these variables thoroughly. Carefully review any previous agreements, and diagnose weaknesses and mistakes.

Knowing Your Opposition

Study your opposition. The more you know about the members of the opposing team and the organization they represent, the more effective you will be. Get to know the backgrounds of every member of the opposition's team: education, experience, expertise, financial status, temperament, interests, hobbies, reputation, past history of deals made, and failures and the reasons for them. Talk with people who know team members—competitors, contractors, suppliers, clients, creditors, and other contacts. Read biographical sketches in professional publications.

Find out as much as you can about the organization your opposition represents: goals, objectives, products, services, market share, profit, financial position, problems, and the like. Sources of this information include company publications and reports, press releases, media advertisements, annual and other reports, speeches and public statements, and company biographies (such as those contained in *Moody's* and *Standard & Poor's*).

Determining What You Will Compromise

Develop your bargaining position by identifying proposals in three categories: *must* have, would *like* to have but would be willing to compromise, and definitely *will not* accept or *must not* have. Anticipate the actions and reactions of the other party. Finally, prepare a written document covering all aspects of your position.

Selecting and Rehearsing Participants

The size and composition of the negotiating team are determined by the environment, conditions, issues, importance, potential difficulties, and the time available. It is important to have top management endorse the chief negotiator and sometimes the members of the team. Should you have a single negotiator or a team? Both have advantages. Having just one negotiator prevents disagreement and dissension among team members, reduces discussion and therefore saves time, fixes responsibility for progress and results, and enables on-the-spot decisions. Team negotiations provide in-depth expertise, permit pooled judgment, and enable broader representation.

For most situations involving HR negotiations, particularly over day-to-day, on-the-job disputes, one-on-one negotiations will be the rule. The HR manager will be negotiating with superiors, colleagues, subordinates, or people from outside organizations either as individuals or in small groups. However, where the HR manager is representing the organization—for example, in contract negotiations with an outside firm or agency or with an internal collective bargaining unit—there is usually a need for a team of negotiators. When that is the case, the kinds of knowledge and skills needed during the negotiations must be carefully identified. Then you must choose people with the required knowledge and skills.

Each member of the negotiating team must have definite and assigned functions, with sufficient overlap provided where necessary. In addition, each member of the team must be assigned to provide a "person-to-person" defense—the responsibility of observing carefully and listening attentively to an opposite number.

In addition to having specialized subject-matter expertise, an effective negotiator must be:

Intelligent	Inquisitive
Articulate	Knowledgeable
A good listener	Adaptable
Persistent	Systematic
Objective	Experienced
Self-controlled	Gutsy

It is important to have a preliminary meeting with all members of the negotiating team. Work out a system of signaling among team members—when to stop talking, when to change the subject, when to ask questions, when to present facts, when to caucus, and the like. It is even more important for the team to discuss roles, identify counterpart assignments, and determine how, when and what to do. And also it is critical to review the issues, bargaining positions, and the backup data to support the team's position on each issue. Practice arguments and discussion will help; so will role playing the opposition's anticipated position and arguments.

Constructing an Agenda

It will be very much to your advantage to have a prepared agenda, whether or not you can get the other party to follow it. Having an agenda will enable you to present your proposals in the best order, will help prevent your being sidetracked or blind-sided during the actual negotiations.

The agenda presented to the opposition should be general. The agenda for your own use should be specific; it should contain such items as where and how to begin the session, ground rules, assumptions and premises, a carefully sequenced list of requirements, a list of major and minor isues in the order in which you wish to have them addressed, and the questions you plan to use to defend and advance your position. Keep your agenda flexible, however.

Selecting a Meeting Site and Time

There are advantages to holding meetings on your home territory and to using the opponent's facilities. When meetings are held on your premises you can quickly get decisions from higher-level management on unexpected issues, the opposition cannot easily terminate the meeting summarily, and you have the psychological advantage of having the opposition come to you.

On the other hand, when meetings are held at the opponent's site, you can devote your attention to the session without distractions or interruptions, hold back information or delay proceedings by stating that the information is not immediately available, or appeal to the opposition's upper-level management. Also, the opposition has the time-consuming task of preparing for the sessions.

A neutral site provides the best of both worlds and probably should be selected whenever possible. It is far better to hold meetings away from the parent organizations—a hotel meeting room, for example. This gives you fewer interruptions, a different environment, and possibly more comfortable surroundings.

In any event, be sure that the room is large enough, well heated and ventilated, properly lighted, and comfortably furnished. Participants should be seated around a circular, oval, or square table. The principals of each party should be facing one another.

Arrange for suitable visual aids—flip charts or chalk boards, overhead and 35mm projectors, and, if necessary, video recorders. Also provide for telephones, refreshments, and recording the sessions, either by tape recordings or stenographic services. An adjoining room for caucusing is often useful.

Getting Underway

Although there are few hard and fast rules for negotiations, participants must be fully aware of the rituals and steps to follow, to get negotiations started and keep them moving.

Your Opening Statement

The opening is important because it sets the stage and establishes the negotiating climate. A cordial attitude and demeanor and a little humor can help relax tensions. Introduce the members of your team; keep the introductions short and simple—names, affiliations, and job titles. A part of the opening statements of both parties should establish the bargaining authority possessed by representatives on both sides.

Revealing Your Position

Start with major issues before addressing minor differences. When the opposition unreasonably insists on talking about one issue first, divert them by introducing new elements into the situation—ones that are vital to the opposite side.

Each party should present its proposals and clarify them by explaining its position and the reasons for seeking the concession. Try not to make the opening bid. After your opponents have presented their position, state your requirements and then let the opposition try to sell you their position. Never disclose the relative importance you attach to each proposal.

Sizing Up Your Opponents

Know as much as possible about the opposition's objectives, needs, and motivation. Remember that giving consideration to the needs of the other party is essential to successful negotiations. Those needs affect the opponents' feelings toward you and affect their behavior during negotiating sessions. If you ignore or block the needs of the other party, they will become frustrated. They may become sullen, uncooperative, or totally unreachable.

You should also keep in mind the dissimilarities in the competing organizations and the differences in individual philosophies, structures, goals, and objectives. Know these differences, then use them.

One of the most important things negotiators must do is to identify, implant, and use the needs of their opponents to get concessions. They must try to find out what needs are paramount to opponents and how they rate them. When negotiators know the priorities the other side assigns to its needs, they have a key to its behavior.

How do negotiators go about identifying needs? By reviewing earlier negotiations and their documented results, by identifying unfulfilled demands, and by assiduous study and observation. They take advantage of every opportunity to learn about their counterparts. They observe and listen attentively.

Sometimes opponents in a disagreement do not have the needs required to make concessions. They have not learned the "right" needs. The job of negotiators under these circumstances is to inculcate—or teach—the needs. Often this is a matter of making clear to opponents that their patterns of behavior or beliefs are inconsistent with the conditions needed to resolve the issue.

After needs have been identified or implanted, negotiators must stimulate and use those needs to induce the desired behavior or responses. The needs exploited, of course, should be those judged to be most powerful in eliciting the desired action or those most easily satisfied by current or controllable conditions. More often than not, you will have to experiment with several appeals to discover which ones work best with each person.

Win-Win Negotiating Skills

No one can give you a foolproof prescription for carrying out negotiations. Much will depend on your ability to adjust to the situation as it develops. Don't expect negotiations to proceed smoothly and according to your plan. It's usually a give and take environment, with both sides looking for an advantage.

Using Verbal and Nonverbal Tactics

Enter negotiations with the right attitude. Never threaten, confront, or demand. Keep people and issues separate. Be patient; don't try to rush things. Negotiate problems and issues, not demands or requirements. Remember that there is always more than one possible solution to a problem. Identify alternatives and then focus on consequences that will separate the development of options from any action your side may choose to take.

Never accept an opponent's first offer. Don't feel obligated to reciprocate any concessions you receive with one of your own. When your opponent sets a limit, makes a demand, asks for a commitment or a concession, you have several options. Of course you can accept, but you can also ignore it, pretend not to understand it, treat it casually, tell a joke, change the subject, or make a demand of your own. If negotiations are stalemated, look for alternatives, such as concessions that are adjuncts to the primary issue.

Some people have exaggerated notions about their powers of persuasion. They appear to believe that an argument based on logic can overcome objections or recalcitrance. They are dead wrong. Unless one of the parties to the negotiation is recognized as having a distinct edge in expertise, or except when neither party has a vested interest in the specific item under contention, reasoned argument will not prevail.

A consultant on negotiating strategies suggests the use of "exchange strategy" as an alternative to logical persuasion. Essentially, it involves knowing exactly what you want, asking for it, and being prepared to pay for it. "Using an exchange strategy requires that you state exactly what you want or need (expectation), ask about and then listen carefully to any problem your request causes for the other person (active listening), and find ways to resolve those problems or satisfy additional needs the other person may have in order to gain his or her cooperation (offering incentives)."[1]

1. David E. Berlew, "How to Increase Your Influence," *Training and Development Journal,* September 1985, pp. 60–61.

Using Questions

Questions should be used to serve all the purposes described earlier, but primarily they are used to get facts, give information, control discussion, and supplement your powers of observation for clues as to what the opposition is thinking. Have a list of functional questions ready for use during negotiations. Key them to the agenda, and be sure that they track with your strategy and tactics.

Use questions with discretion and good judgment. Always prepare the respondent for questions about sensitive areas that may elicit resentment. Tell *why* you are asking the question. If possible, avoid confrontational questions, those that may provoke anger or antagonism. Similarly, questions that may create nervousness, apprehension, or anxiety should be shunned. Avoid ambiguous questions. Be sure to make your tone of voice, word choice, and phrasing consistent with your purpose and intent. Be clear, direct, and concise; keep your questions to the point.

Don't overlook the usefulness of affirmative statements as substitutes for questions. They can help you control the discussion, communicate the information you want the opposition to have, and clear the air when an impasse is imminent.

Making Concessions

Plan to negotiate, not destroy your opponent. But don't enter negotiations with the sole intention of compromising. Don't foreclose your options. Give yourself a chance to grasp any benefit or advantage offered. Make concessions gradually. Keep them small and space them so that the other side has an opportunity to make concessions of its own. Give in on the little things. Find two or three small things to concede.

Offer enough concessions so that both you and your opposition can win. Try to create a situation where both you and your opponents can both feel satisfied, if not completely happy, with the outcome of the negotiations.

Being Assertive

Be assertive but not overly aggressive. Know when to stop pushing; that point is reached when your needs are satisfied. Don't try to demolish the opposition. You may have to live and work with them tomorrow or next week. The objective of negotiation is agreement, not total victory. Both parties to the negotiation must feel that they have gained something they want.

Keeping a Positive Attitude

Avoid the negative, including negative terminology. Keep the process of negotiating orderly, factual, and positive. Always take a win-win approach. Negotiate in good faith. Don't conclude that an opposer's behavior is irrational. It may very well be rational for him or her. You can't possibly know until you understand the postulates and premises upon which the behavior is based. Even such behavior as shouting or table-pounding may be rational because it is deliberate. When what seems to be irrational behavior occurs, pay more attention to what your opponent is doing than attempting to determine why.

Breaking an Impasse

How can you avoid communication deadlocks? Or, having gotten into one, how do you get out again? There is obviously no simple answer, but here is something that will help. Listen to the other person. In spite of what you consider to be clear evidence that he is boneheaded or obstinate, listen. Accept the fact that that's the way he sees it, although you see the situation quite differently. All you can do is say, "Tell me more." This is nonevaluative listening—listening without passing judgment, without arguing, listening fully in order to understand how the issue looks to the other person and why his resistance to your proposal makes sense to him, even if it doesn't make sense to you.

In other words, try to get insight into the quality of your opponent's experience as conditioned by his background and orientation and find out why resisting makes sense to him in the light of the kind and amount of information he possesses.

Nothing is so pleasing as being listened to. People are almost certain to relax the rigidity of their defenses. Their statements are likely to become less dogmatic, not only in tone of voice but also in actual content. Then, confronted by less rigid statements, you will begin to feel more relaxed. The change will be revealed in your facial expressions and posture as well as in your oral responses. This is picked up by your opponent, who in turn relaxes, until ultimately both of you are making sense.

The most important point is reached when, after hearing a statement you can say, "I don't agree with you but I can see why you believe as you do." This is the real turning point in the deadlock. When you can say that, you are admitting that the other person has rational processes, starting on different assumptions, and therefore coming to different conclusions, but nevertheless traceable, rational processes. Once this admission has been made, communication and compromise are again possible.

Other useful techniques for surmounting an impasse are: (1) carefully reconsider the goals and objectives your opponent is trying to achieve and try to find a common ground; (2) find a valid reason for calling for a break; (3) tell a humorous story to relieve the tension; (4) grant a small concession in another area; (5) rephrase your requirement, to give status to your opponent—without changing your position; or (6) announce that since the talks are not progressing, a break is needed—and walk out before your opposite number can reply; then be ready with a fresh idea when you return.

Answering Questions

To the greatest extent possible, negotiators must be prepared to answer (or deliberately not answer) questions posed by their opponents. Some questions can easily be predicted, and their answers, or the strategy for handling them, can be prepared in advance. Other questions, however, are totally unpredictable. The negotiator must then depend on experience and quickness of mind to deal with them.

In addition to the option of answering questions directly and fully, negotiators have several other alternatives. They can provide a partial answer, a response that is limited to aspects of the question they feel they can respond to. They can dodge the question by talking around the subject; when done successfully, this leaves the questioner with the feeling that the question has been answered. They can cause the questioner to drop the question by injecting so many conditions and variables that the question becomes basically unanswerable. Or they can respond with a question of their own, change the subject, or create a diversion. Of course, there are other less desirable options: answering inaccurately, dissembling, refusing to answer, adjourning the meeting, or walking out.

Negotiators should always remember that there are six interpretations of every question and answer, every conversation between two people:

1. What you really say.
2. What you think you say.
3. What you intended to say.
4. What he or she really heard.
5. What he or she thought he or she heard.
6. What he or she wanted to hear.

Finalizing the Results

When a decision or agreement has been reached, put everything in writing. Commit the negotiated agreement to written form and subject it to careful review by both parties. If at all possible, write it yourself or have a member of your team write it. Otherwise you may find yourself renegotiating points misunderstood or deliberately changed or omitted by your opponent.

Summary

Well-honed negotiating skills are a must for today's HR managers. Not only must they negotiate for the things they need for their subordinates and themselves, but they must also serve as negotiators for their organizations or as advisers to negotiating teams when bargaining with individuals and groups from outside.

Negotiating is a communication process used to reach agreements between two or more disputants or to change a relationship from adversarial to collaborative. In its preferred form, negotiation eschews bargaining to win at all costs, and stresses the exchange of concessions so that both parties win by having some of their needs met.

Negotiating is far preferable to mediation, arbitration, or litigation because it is less costly in time, personnel, and funds, is more likely to result in an agreement that is satisfying to both parties (and therefore longer-lasting), and avoids the inevitable win-lose outcome of most other methods.

Successful negotiating requires negotiators who know themselves, understand the motives and behavior of others, are able to make accurate assumptions, and can select and use effective negotiating strategies, tactics, and techniques. It avoids the pitfalls of using threats, promises, mind games, precedents, equivocation, misrepresentation, and fabrication. Instead, it is based on detailed preparation: establishing realistic objectives and expectations, collecting and using pertinent data, studying the opposition, identifying acceptable compromises, selecting and rehearsing participants, constructing an agenda, and selecting and preparing an appropriate meeting site and time.

During the negotiations, emphasis is placed on win-win strategies, tactics, and techniques: establishing your position, being assertive without being overly aggressive, using questions to control discussion, making and receiving concessions, maintaining a positive attitude, and avoiding communication deadlocks.

The keys to successful negotiations are positive attitudes on both sides, an understanding that at least some of the needs of both parties must be satisfied, and a willingness to exchange concessions to reach a fair and lasting agreement.

FOR FURTHER READING

Adler, Peter S. "The Balancing Act of Mediation Training." *Training and Development Journal,* July 1984, pp. 55–58.

Bazerman, Max H., and Roy J. Lewicki, eds. *Negotiating in Organizations.* Beverly Hills, Calif.: Sage Publications, 1983.

Berlew, David E. "How to Increase Your Influence." *Training and Development Journal,* September 1985, pp. 60–63.

Brooks, Earle, and George S. Odiorne. *Managing by Negotiations.* New York: Van Nostrand Reinhold, 1985.

Cohen, Herb. *You Can Negotiate Anything: How to Get What You Want.* Secaucus, N.J.: Citadel Press, 1983.

Crosby, Philip B. *The Art of Getting Your Own Sweet Way,* 2nd ed. Del Mar, Calif.: McGraw-Hill Training Systems, 1982.

Fisher, Roger, and William Ury. "Getting to Yes." *Management Review,* February 1982, pp. 16–21.

Folberg, Jay, and Alison Taylor. *Mediation: A Comprehensive Guide to Resolving Conflict Without Litigation.* San Francisco: Jossey-Bass, 1984.

Gould, Joe. *The Negotiator's Problem Solver.* New York: John S. Wiley & Sons, 1986.

Harrison, Gilbert W. "Negotiating at 30 Paces." *Management Review,* April 1980, pp. 51–54.

Hawver, Dennis A. "Plan Before Negotiating . . . and Increase Your Power of Persuasion." *Management Review,* February 1984, pp. 46–48.

Holley, William H., and Kenneth M. Jennings. *The Labor Relations Process.* New York: Dryden Press, Holt, Rinehart & Winston, 1980.

Illich, John. *Power Negotiating: Strategies for Winning in Business.* Reading, Mass.: Addison-Wesley Training Systems, 1980.

Jandt, Fred E., and Paul Gillette. *Win-Win Negotiating: Turning Conflict into Agreement.* New York: John Wiley & Sons, 1985.

Karrass, Chester L. *How to Get What You Want.* New York: Thomas Y. Crowell, 1970.

Kennedy, Gavin. *Everything Is Negotiable: How to Get a Better Deal.* Englewood Cliffs, N.J.: Prentice-Hall, 1983.

———, John Benson, and John McMillan. *Managing Negotiations.* Englewood Cliffs, N.J.: Prentice-Hall, 1982.

Levin, Edward. *Negotiating Tactics: Bargain Your Way to Winning.* New York: Fawcett Book Group, 1985.

Lewicki, Roy J., and Joseph A. Litterer. *Negotiation.* Homewood, Ill.: Richard D. Irwin, 1985.

Loughran, Charles S. *Negotiating a Labor Contract: A Management Handbook.* Washington: BNA Books, 1984.

Masterbrock, W. F. "A Model for Negotiation." *Training and Development Journal,* October 1983, pp. 76–79.

Moore, Christopher C. *Mediation Process: Practical Strategies for Resolving Conflicts.* San Francisco: Jossey-Bass, 1986.

Nierenberg, Gerard I. "Negotiating Strategies and Counterstrategies: How to Develop Win/Win Techniques." *Management Review,* February 1983, pp. 48–49.

————. *Fundamentals of Negotiating.* New York: Editorial Correspondents, 1973.

Parris, John. *Arbitration: Principles and Practices.* Dobbs Ferry, N.Y.: Sheridan House, 1985.

Schatzki, Michael, and Wayne R. Coffey. *Negotiation: The Art of Getting What You Want.* New York: New American Library, 1981.

Seltz, David D., and Alfred J. Modica. *Negotiate Your Way to Success.* New York: New American Library, 1981.

Shea, Gordon F. *Creative Negotiating: Product Tools and Techniques for Solving Problems, Resolving Conflicts, and Settling Differences.* New York: CBI/ Van Nostrand Reinhold, 1983.

Wall, James A., Jr. *Negotiation: Theory and Practice.* Glenview, Ill.: Scott, Foresman, 1984.

Wehringer, Cameron K. *Arbitration Precepts and Principles.* Dobbs Ferry, N.Y.: Oceana Publications, 1969.

15

TEAM BUILDING
Engineering Synergy

Corporate values are changing. The old ideals emphasized individualism, self-reliance, and competition; the new touchstones emphasize collaboration, cooperation, and teamwork. One of the most effective means of using the talents available in an organization and fostering collaborative effort is the use of work teams.

Workforce values are also changing. Today's employees want opportunities to participate in corporate goal setting, planning, and decision making, and they demand more meaningful relationships and interesting and challenging work. That is particularly true of knowledge workers (that is, people whose work is primarily intellectual—managers, scientists, engineers, instructors, and so on), who, because of their educational level and highly developed problem-solving and innovating skills, have a greater need for involvement and creative opportunities than workers of a different stripe or an earlier era. Membership on work teams can provide opportunities for professionals and other workers to satisfy those needs and demands.

A team is two or more persons who have a psychological relationship to each other, who are in some kind of dynamic relationship. It differs from other groups in that it is assembled specifically to perform a function. It is not a mere aggregate of individuals. It does not evolve casually through chance socializing. Given a favorable environment, competent leadership, training, satisfying experiences for members, and substantive accomplishments, it improves over time.

Work teams are composed of people who have unique abilities, aptitudes, interests, skills, and values. But teams differ from one another, just as individuals do. Every work team has its own "personality" and pattern of characteristics that distinguish it from other teams.

A work team becomes more than the sum of its individual personalities. Its distinctive structure becomes evident as members share goals and aspirations and learn to deal effectively with such nonadjustive behavior as buckpassing and scapegoating, submissiveness, lethargy, lack of acceptance of responsibility, overdependence on the leader, inhibiting expression of feelings, withdrawing, projecting, and the like.

Team building is a strategy for helping a work group improve its unity of purpose and functioning by learning to identify, analyze, and solve its own problems. Team building is the process of developing cooperative work groups so that organization goals and objectives can be achieved more effectively and with enhanced job satisfaction for the employees involved.

The underlying rationale for work-team development underscores the importance of the strategy. It is simply this: The people who are affected by any significant program, decision, or organizational change must be involved in the program or decision or participate in the change process. The ability of employees to influence planning and decision making must be integral to the processes of participation and involvement.

Teams are effective work units because their potential for productivity far outstrips the potential of any individual member. A well-coached, cohesive team can consistently outperform a group of talented individuals. Proof? Look at sports. The reason is simple. On a coordinated and cohesive team, the members work together toward common goals instead of competing with one another. They discover that they can further their own careers and achieve their own goals and objectives by helping one another perform at their top level. Team play releases synergy. But more than that, it has a positive effect on employee enthusiasm, job satisfaction, and productivity.

Purposes

The primary purpose of a work team is, of course, to perform some function related to the goals and objectives of the organization. But within that general mission, many subordinate purposes are served. Here are some of the most important.

Align personal and company goals. Membership on a work team clarifies both organization and individual goals and objectives and enables members to see the relationships among them. Employees come to realize that personal goals are best reached when they are aligned with organizational goals. Work teams can link individual and corporate goals and objectives.

Increase effectiveness. Teams multiply the effectiveness with which organizational functions are performed, problems are solved, and objectives are reached. Teams can help identify the steps needed to achieve objectives. They enable the organization to use the diverse talents of team members to increase production and improve quality. They get more accomplished by tapping available talents. Work teams can also improve the group skills of both their leaders and members. In short, work teams produce results—they get the work done.

Increase commitment and job satisfaction. Participation in a work team builds cooperation and commitment to the goals and objectives of the group and the organization. It causes members to feel positive about their work and provides satisfactions that emerge from relationships with other members of the team and the completion of assigned tasks. It improves work performance and problem solving. It enables members to improve professional and technical processes and to solve problems that negatively affect organization goals and the work to be accomplished.

Identify and build on employee strengths. Involvement in work-team activities enables the manager and team members to identify talents that might otherwise go unrecognized, and to develop those skills for the good of the individual and the organization. Most HR professionals adapt easily to work teams and function well in those settings. Their level of education, coupled with their penchant for collaboration with others to accomplish difficult tasks, makes them ideal team members.

Improve communication. The use of work teams improves communication. It promotes the exchange of information, the development of better understanding and cooperation, and the integration of diverse talents and perceptions. It provides feedback that is straightforward and tough-minded but not harsh or hurtful. It encourages employees to be more open, accepting, and inquiring. It reduces the barriers between manager and subordinates and develops closer and more collaborative relationships.

Reduce conflicts. Participation in team activities promotes conflict resolution by providing a means of sharing and integrating diverse views and experiences, searching for the root causes of problems, and identifying alternatives to conflict. It reduces dissension and negativism. It develops employees' skills in handling interpersonal conflict, and improves the general level of trust.

Improve motivation and morale. Knowledge workers typically possess high levels of self-motivation and self-esteem. Their formal and informal education and experience have usually been oriented toward identifying and solving problems in a group environment. For all workers, group settings tend to enhance motivation and provide opportunities to exercise a considerable degree of freedom in choosing the work methods and the environment in which they can function best.

When to Use Work Teams

Teams should never be used to buttress an ineffective or incompetent manager. They should be used only to supplement and complement competent managers. Teams should never be assigned tasks or functions that can be better performed by a single manager; they should be used only when they can be more effective than a single individual. In other words, the results produced by work teams must be potentially superior to those expected of individual effort in terms of time, costs, quality of decisions, fairness, or sound judgment. Essentially there are four situations that call for the use of teams:

1. When the subject, task, or action required is beyond the experience or skill of the manager, and the manager needs help from subordinates who have that experience and skill. For example, developing marketing plans for training programs and services when the HR manager lacks marketing experience.
2. When actions or decisions require broader experience and knowledge than any single manager can be expected to have; for example, when the task is to develop a completely new salary and fringe benefits package for the entire organization.
3. When the risk is too great for one manager to shoulder alone; for example, determining when and how much time, personnel, and funds to invest in a new product or service.
4. When there is risk of bias or prejudice in making a critical decision or judgment; for example, selecting personnel for promotion to key positions or for annual awards.

Barriers to Team Productivity

Several problems can arise in work-team activities that require the attention of team organizers, leaders, and members.

Team size. Can a team be too large or too small? Certainly. If a team is too large, participation will be limited and face-to-face interaction more difficult to achieve. On the other hand, if a team is too small, adequate representation of constituencies will be impossible, and the different skills and perspectives needed to carry out the functions of the team will not be available. The solution is to draw together the smallest team possible that represents at a functional level all the necessary skills, perspectives, and backgrounds. For most situations, a carefully selected team of five to nine members is best.

Participation. It is sometimes difficult to get all team members to participate fully in team activities. Failure to participate may be caused by lack of self-confidence, fear of ridicule, or just plain timidity. Such techniques as role playing, questioning, calling directly on nonparticipants, or breaking the team into subgroups are often suggested as remedies. However, those measures are more likely to inhibit the development of the team and often have undesirable effects—lack of direction, boredom, aggression, shirking, dictation, and the development of inter-group competition and hostility. The best approach is to encourage participation by showing warmth and acceptance and by positively rein-forcing even the slightest effort to contribute.

Team frustration. A common observation of those who work with teams is that they often become frustrated by the problems of function-ing. Some of these frustrations are legitimate: finding one's role and function on the team, discovering that one has inadequate skills to make the contribution expected, failure of the team to make progress, intra-team rivalries, and interpersonal conflicts. Illegitimate sources of frustra-tion include withdrawal of the team leader from required leadership activities, lack of planning, agenda, and priorities, and allowing individ-ual team members to present undue obstacles to progress and goal achievement.

Failure of members to assume leadership functions. In some in-stances, leadership functions are never shared or taken over by team members. Sometimes that is due to an authoritarian leader or to pres-sures put on the team leader by higher management. Other groups may not assume leadership functions because they find it difficult to change their concept of leadership. Such factors as the age, education, experi-ence, and status of the leader may make it difficult for the team to see its leader on an equalitarian, nonauthoritative basis.

Those problems are not insurmountable. If the limits within which the team operates are clearly defined and the team stays within those boundaries, and if the leader consistently demonstrates faith in group members and belief in their ability to assume responsibility and discharge it effectively, the problems will disappear.

Competition between groups. Work teams are formally organized to attain company goals and objectives. However, within and outside of work teams, informal groups exist. The HR manager must give attention to both formal and informal groups because they can and do interact. To ignore the informal is to court difficulty. The task is to establish the conditions between formal and informal groups that will enhance the efficiency and productivity of both. Cooperation, rather than competi-tion, must be stressed.

Differences in status. Differences in the status of team members, whether real or perceived, sometimes get in the way of efficient team functioning. Such status-determining factors as seniority, position, title, salary, educational level, or experience have an adverse effect on the behavior of the individual or on the demeanor of other team members. Sometimes the result is jealousy, envy, unfriendliness, hostility, belliger-ence, coldness, or feelings of inferiority on the part of those of lesser status, and aloofness, arrogance, or superciliousness on the part of those with the real or perceived higher status.

Interpersonal problems among members. Sometimes employees bring to team meetings grudges, ill will, or resentment for earlier offenses, either real or perceived. Occasionally there is long-term hostility centered on old rivalries, preferential treatment, or disagreements. In other cases, conflicts develop during team meetings and deliberations.

Blocked or by-passed communication channels. Sometimes teams are not given access to the information they need to deal with an issue, despite specific direction from top management that the teams are authorized to have it. The cause of the breakdown may be inadvertent—a glitch in the notification system—or it may be deliberate, caused by an employee who has something to hide.

Other times the effectiveness of teams is short-circuited by premature disclosure of the progress of team deliberations. Again that may occur either accidentally, or it may be the result of a deliberate attempt by a disgruntled employee to sabotage the team. Untimely release of information, or planned leaks, are particularly damaging when the team is dealing with sensitive problems or issues—ones that have the potential to adversely affect employee motivation and morale.

Group loyalties. Another potential barrier to effective work groups is the loyalties of members for their particular constituencies. Every organization consists of several subcultures, each with its own image and value system. The groups overlap, but they are far from identical. Each group has an important effect on work-group activities and results by influencing the views of its representatives on the work team.

Barriers arise when loyalties to the groups cause members to restrict their support of team decisions or withhold or distort information to maintain the internal strength of their group. Such actions can lead to intergroup conflict, unhealthy competition, and restriction of communications—all of which are likely to reduce the effectiveness not only of the work team but also the entire department.

Types of Work Teams

Standing work teams are groups of employees assigned to either identical or similar jobs and formed into teams based on their location, their jobs, and the structure of the organization. Work-team activity is a regular and ongoing part of getting the work of the organization done. In the HR context, supervisory development, instructional, assessment, organization development, and training system development teams are examples.

Special work teams are formed to work on specific problems or issues. They are often interdepartmental or departmental. They may be executive search teams, task forces, quality circles, employee participation groups (EPGs), or committees. They may be formed among people with diverse jobs and responsibilities or among people whose jobs are closely related. Their purposes are to engage in a cooperative effort to identify, analyze, and solve job-related problems, make recommendations, integrate organization and individual needs and goals, or improve communications and understanding.

Requirements for Successful Teamwork

The effectiveness of work teams depends largely on the spirit in which they are conducted and the methods of their operation.

Member involvement. You get a work team "up" by involving the members, by encouraging them to make contributions to the total effort. Involvement and collaboration are the keys to motivation. Participation must be real, not just simulated or peripheral. Problems and activities must be challenging.

Clear definitions. The mission and functions of the work team must be clearly defined—for the leader, team members, and other employee groups who are either interested in or affected by the team's products.

The team must also have a defined set of objectives—mid-term or short-range targets. The team will be most productive when the objectives are of immediate concern to its members. For example, an HR team will work much harder at the task of developing policies for individual employee development than at defining the relationship of the organization to the general public. Of course, the limits of authority of the team must be clearly identified to set reasonable boundaries for its activities.

Top management support. Work teams cannot flourish, or even survive, without the total commitment and support of top management. That means strong, overt, long-term, continuous, and open commitment to and support of employee participation in corporate planning, problem solving, and decision making. It also means that top managers thoroughly understand what work teams can accomplish and what effort is necessary to achieve those benefits. It means that executives must be directly involved on a personal, developmental level, must believe in the relevance of team effort and its potential, and must give work teams much more than verbal support.

Appropriateness of setting. Work teams are most productive when the surroundings are consistent with the functions and problems the team is organized to deal with and with the preferences of the individuals who serve as team members. Because most HR work teams deal largely with concepts and other intangibles, their purposes are best served by conference-style accommodations—quiet, comfortably furnished rooms, free from noise, interruptions, and distractions.

Availability of time. Clearly, collaborative approaches require more time than individual action. But the results are worth the additional investment; teams produce better results than individuals. Most important, since consensus is the aim of team action, providing adequate time to reach it is essential. Listening to arguments and taking a quick vote is not a good way to get the most out of work teams.

Informal procedures. Much promising work-team endeavor has been stifled by too much formality. Work-team meetings are best when they are unhampered by parliamentary procedures. Too much concern with status and lines of authority frequently destroys initiative and originality. Machinery for conducting work-team studies should not be elaborate.

Focus on results and action. The effective work team focuses on the end results, not on activities and processes. It is concerned with the behavior of team members, not on attitudes or personality. Team decisions should result in action of some sort. Team members must see that their deliberations and study have an effect on operations. Long-term, abstract study does not induce intense effort; deliberations must have some immediate result, such as the implementation of new or revised policies.

Noncompetitive atmosphere. Effective work teams emphasize cooperation and collaboration rather than competition, trust and confidence rather than doubt and suspicion. They employ praise and other forms of positive reinforcement, and avoid criticism. They attempt to enhance the self-esteem of group members. They emphasize the value of people and their ideas. They foster involvement and discourage contention. They encourage team members to show interest in the opinions of others and demonstrate respect for their ideas and experiences.

Cohesiveness. Without a high level of trust and loyalty—in other words, cohesiveness—teams will be unable to achieve group action. Cohesiveness is influenced by the degree to which individuals depend on the team for need satisfaction, on the size and stability of the team, on the amount of competition within (decreases cohesiveness) and outside (increases cohesiveness), progress toward goals, and participation of members in activities of the group. Cohesiveness is achieved by establishing common goals, total involvement of members, and successful completion of team projects.

Capable leadership. Basically, work-team leaders must be committed to and must fully support team building and understand and accept the limitations of the process. They must inspire team members to cooperate with one another and work as a team. They must create an environment for team development by understanding themselves, understanding and appreciating their people, communicating both verbally and nonverbally, and emphasizing the positive.

They must be able to develop an open atmosphere, promote the exchange of ideas and feelings, and build interdependence, trust, and commitment. They must get team members to develop team-building skills, adopt positive attitudes toward the organization, improve their work habits, and take pride in their work. Work teams can be productive only when there is adequate provision for the exercise of initiative and responsibility. Leaders must encourage team members to assume as much responsibility as they are capable of. That is the concept of shared leadership—the most important requirement for team success.

Able team members. Teams must have the right mix of talents, abilities, and capacities—ones that collectively can match the demands of the assignments given to it. To be effective, a team must comprise members who are good team players. Good team players like, trust, respect, support, and help others. They understand and appreciate the roles and contributions of their colleagues. They are able to communicate effectively in terms of speaking, listening, writing, questioning, and giving feedback.

They openly confront problems and know how to resolve conflict. They pay attention to group processes and monitor how the team works as a team.

Adequate support. Teams must be given the kind and amount of support they need to be productive and successful. That includes the right tools and equipment, facilities, consultative expertise, funds, and supervision and encouragement needed to do the job.

Open atmosphere. Effective teamwork occurs where a feeling of belongingness is established and maintained, where there is a sense of acceptance by members, a feeling that their contributions are important. Such barriers to communication as physical space separation and lack of face-to-face contacts are absent. The psychological climate is nonthreatening; members feel that they are not being judged or evaluated, that they are understood, and that all aspects of their personalities, both positive and negative, are accepted.

Conformity and creativity. To survive, teams must have some degree of conformity; to make progress, they need to be creative and innovative. Those characteristics are controlled to a great extent by the informal groups within the organization. Their attitudes can either support or undermine the interests and concerns of management, and strengthen or weaken team performance and productivity.

Team training. If work teams are to grow and become more productive, they must receive constant training, in addition to an initial orientation to the principles and processes of teamwork. With regular training, goal-oriented, cohesive, committed, and effective work teams will be created.

Rewards and feedback. There must be real, clear, and immediate incentives, recognition, and rewards for team progress and performance. In addition to the intrinsic rewards associated with successful resolution of problems, there must also be extrinsic rewards.

Success. Work teams have a need for constant improvement and steady performance to be truly effective. Goals that are important to the individual and the organization must be achieved. The team's success in doing what it was organized to do is a bottom-line criterion of effectiveness.

Work-Team Roles

A role is a pattern of behavior expected of people by virtue of their membership in a group. Several aspects of roles must be considered: status, formal and informal roles, role perception, and role conflict.

Status

Status is the relative rank a person possesses with respect to others in a group or work team. Status is determined by such things as titles, roles and functions, credentials (education, experience, and degrees), special abilities, and compensation. Status is often tangibly expressed in status symbols or "perks" such as size and location of office, type of furniture and furnishing, clothing, special privileges, and so on. Status is an important source of job satisfaction. If a team assignment is inconsistent with status or is perceived to be inconsistent, it is almost certain to be a source of anxiety, discontent, and frustration.

Formal Roles

Formal roles are determined by duties performed as a member of the work team—supervising and directing others, assisting others, observing group process, making decisions, or, in the case of subordinates, complying with directions, cooperating, and getting along with team members.

Team Leader

The best way for the leader to increase team productivity is not by trying to change individual team members, but by inducing the team to accept change. Knowledge-worker teams in particular tend to resist changes they consider external authoritarian pressures and accept those they perceive as resulting from their own actions.

Team leaders must have a deep personal understanding and appreciation of people, particularly of those they work with. In addition, they need to respect each person's potential for making unique contributions to the team. They must exemplify confidence, poise, kindness, and thoughtfulness.

Specifically, the team leader:

- Fully supports and is committed to team building.
- Shares leadership with team members.
- Understands and accepts time constraints and the limitations of the team-building process.
- Organizes only work teams that can perform a real service or meet a specific need.
- Defines the duties, responsibilities, and authority of work teams in writing.
- Provides a meeting place that is accessible, comfortable, and conducive to study.
- Assigns tasks that are clear cut, understandable, logical, and important enough to produce direct and purposeful work and vital enough to stimulate the interest and commitment of members.
- Makes large blocks of time available for team sessions.
- Makes use of carefully prepared agenda.
- Circulates the minutes of previous meetings before the work team convenes.
- Appoints and uses service people (recorder, process observer, and resource people) wisely.
- Helps the team organize itself and determine the rules of its own conduct.
- Helps the team define and clarify goals, objectives, functions, and limitations.
- Sets the stage for full and free discussion.
- Exemplifies ease, confidence, poise, kindness, and thoughtfulness.
- Provides a warm, accepting, and understanding emotional climate.
- Develops an atmosphere that is free and encourages all team members to contribute.
- Encourages the contributions of all team members.
- Demonstrates and encourages openness, trust, and communication.
- Draws out timid team members and keeps dominant members from monopolizing.
- Avoids the expert role and lets the team solve its own problems.
- Avoids behavioral science jargon.
- Listens carefully and conveys a sense of full attention, respect, and acceptance.
- Improves the interactions and relationships of team members.
- Uses available talents to best advantage.
- Links the contributions of team members to the central thread of thought.
- Keeps discussion to the point.

- Contributes to the work of the team in terms of his or her own talents and experience.
- Promotes the understanding of meanings and intents by restating and summarizing the contributions of team members.
- Keeps the team moving toward goals.
- Allows the team to make its own decisions.
- Furnishes expertise in the techniques of team action.
- Coordinates the efforts of the team.
- Trains team members and helps them develop power, responsibility, and leadership.
- Attempts to reach consensus on problem solutions, issue resolutions, and decisions.
- Guides the team in evaluating both team products and processes.
- Makes provisions for reporting plans, policies, and decisions to all individuals and groups concerned or affected.
- Provides for the rapid translation of accepted work-team recommendations into action.
- Provides recognition and rewards for effective work-team service.

Team Members

Individual team members must accept the responsibility for acquainting themselves with the purposes of the team session and the agenda. During the session they must concentrate on issues instead of personalities. They must discipline themselves to contribute to the activities and deliberations of the team, listen attentively and critically, ask relevant questions, make comments and suggestions, and assist the team leader to achieve progress toward purposes and objectives.

Specifically, team members:

- Accept leadership responsibilities.
- Contribute ideas and suggestions for the solution of the problem or issue.
- Are forceful and positive, but avoid equivocation.
- Listen actively and attentively to the comments and suggestions of others.
- Maintain eye contact when others are speaking.
- Provide support to team members.
- Give information and share experiences freely, but avoid evaluating; describe but not judge.
- Combine ideas and identify alternatives.
- Seek consensus; don't insist on majority rule.
- Discuss barriers and consequences, but don't look for perfection.
- Identify follow-up actions.

- Make consistent use of "we" instead of "I," and "us" instead of "you."
- Work toward common goals and objectives.
- Demonstrate trust and confidence in themselves as a team.
- Cooperate with one another and the team leader.
- Provide feedback and request clarification when needed.
- Assume the roles of recorder, process observer, or resource person as needed.

Recorder

One of the service people necessary in an action work team is the content recorder or secretary. The function of the recorder is to keep a running account of the important items discussed during the meeting and to record the solutions proposed or agreements reached. Subsequently, those minutes provide continuity from one meeting to the next, and are used to prepare decision papers for higher-level management to act on recommendations.

Specific functions of the recorder are:

- Record the main problems, issues, ideas, and decisions developed in the discussion.
- Summarize points and report to the team from time to time.
- Prepare minutes of meetings, final reports, and decision papers.

Process Observer

One of the most important services that can be provided for a work team is assistance in improving itself. Process observers look at team processes, record what they observe, and report findings to the team. They observe and record not the content of team thinking but the procedures the team uses. They use the record to develop hunches as to why the team behaved as it did and to make suggestions for improving team procedures. The process observer observes and reports on the following:

- The effectiveness of the leader.
- Clarity of goals and objectives.
- The degree and kind of participation and interaction.
- Use of resources.
- Actions taken by team members that enhance or reduce the self-esteem and satisfaction of other members.
- The extent to which members show appreciation for the ideas of others.
- The extent to which the team focuses on behavior and performance rather than on personalities.

○ The degree to which members try to inform or persuade, convince or control.
○ Progress toward goals.
○ The degree to which members demonstrate responsiveness to others—use open-ended questions, direct questions, or active listening.

Resource Person

Although resource people or "experts" are not always necessary, there are times in work-team deliberations when they are really needed. The function of the resource person is to supply information on request when it seems pertinent to discussion. Before a resource person is invited to a team session, the group should determine whether its own members can provide the information. If the resource person is essential, the team should decide the areas in which the person is needed, the type of person to be invited, and the way the person is to be used.

The resource person should:

○ Become acquainted with the functions of the team, the nature of the group, the purposes of the meeting, and the way the team wants him or her to function.
○ Prepare contributions in light of the preliminary work.
○ Deliver remarks succinctly and within the time allocated.
○ Sustain participation of team members through adroit questioning and substantive answers to questions.

Informal Roles

In addition to their formal roles, team members often assume informal roles: analyzer, summarizer, devil's advocate, compromiser, team comedian, team complainer, bleeding heart, union leader, and so on. Pecking order determines the relative status of these players within the group.

Role Perceptions

The roles of team members are affected by their role perceptions. That is, roles are determined in part by how the individual perceives he or she is expected to perform. Obviously, the perceptions of the leader and group members are not always congruent—and that usually results in discontent and discord.

Role Conflict

Managers and team leaders expect to carry out company policies and procedures and are typically more concerned about company goals and objectives than team members. Team members, for their part, expect their leaders to protect them, support them, be loyal to them, and look after their interests. That produces conflict for both leaders and members.

Strategies and Techniques

Although the organization, functioning, and processes of work teams are largely matters for individual decision with regard to the special problems and needs of the organization concerned, there are several points which apply to most situations. Successful teams are built through an active process. That process involves preparation and planning; clarification of purposes, objectives, roles, procedures, and relationships; participation of members in finding solutions; and evaluation and follow-up.

Pre-session activities. In a memorandum to members of the work team, the HR manager or team leader should describe the purposes of the team, the time and place of the first meeting, and the agenda. Stress the importance of attendance. Arrange for a quiet and suitable meeting room, preferably away from the workplace, and furnished with a table or tables arranged so that team members can communicate face-to-face, comfortable chairs, facilities for visual aids, and flip charts or chalkboards.

Getting started. The initial meeting of a work team is probably the most critical of all; this is where any reservations about the process should be laid to rest, expectations made realistic, and the stage set for productive meetings in the future.

Keep introductions brief and simple. Have participants introduce themselves by giving only their names and affiliations. At this point, no one should be permitted to discuss his or her background, experience, motivations, or biases.

Establish how the work team will function—the ground rules. Discuss such mundane items as coffee and lunch breaks, smoking, and so on. Then move on to more substantive matters: the roles of participants, the agenda, how decisions or recommendations will be reached, and how the results of team deliberations will reach top management. Underscore the importance of cooperation, collaboration, and teamwork.

Emphasize that all team efforts should be directed toward attaining commitment and achieving results. Some of the results include improved control over group processes, procedures, and practices, development of a sense of "ownership," generation of new ideas, objective evaluation of proposals, and development of solutions. Members should be encouraged to deal with issues, not personalities, to openly confront conflicts and problems, to eschew finger-pointing, scapegoating, nitpicking, putdowns, pussyfooting, and mind games. They should be helped to avoid embarrassing anyone, to accept responsibility, and to listen attentively and actively.

Get each team member to reveal his or her mindset: What's on your mind about this meeting? What do you expect to happen? What reservations do you have about the session? What are realistic and reasonable expectations for the team? What can make the session worthwhile? What barriers could interfere with progress?

Areas of concern. The work team should develop a list of major concerns shared by all. Some examples of common areas of concern to HR professionals are: long- and short-range planning, allocation and distribution of resources, communication with line managers, participation in corporate goal setting and budget preparation, decision making, and management practices, identification of barriers to intergroup cooperation, training and developing subordinates, productivity improvement, cost reduction, and generation of new ideas.

Purpose and objectives. Unless the team was organized to work on a specific problem, it should itself select one area of concern for attack. The best way to do that is to rank the items in priority order for attack. The objective should be set forth in terms of the results desired. For example, "To increase the participation of the HR department in developing and controlling the training and development budget." Record the objectives on a flip chart. Then the team should determine the who, what, why, when, and where of the assignment, identify the tasks that need to be completed, the problems and issues that need to be solved or resolved, and the strategies to be applied to achieve the objectives. Again, these items should be placed on a flip chart.

Task assignments and data gathering. The team allocates the work to be done by members. The team members should develop a schedule for using the information available and pushing toward the results they want to achieve.

The team then identifies current conditions, practices, or events that characterize and clarify the area of concern. Both "good" and "bad" conditions should be identified. Brainstorming can be used to advantage in developing the data. For example, "The budget is currently developed from the top down. Funds are allocated by quarter. The HR department must submit all purchase requests to the controller for approval. Monthly reports of expenditures are furnished by the controller." Those items should be recorded on flip charts.

Barriers and problems. Here the task is to identify blocks to resolution or solution. Are departmental goals and objectives clear? Are they in conflict with individual goals and aspirations? Is the route to the attainment of the goals and objectives clear? What needs to be done to make departmental and individual goals compatible?

Conflict. Work teams must identify and show understanding of differences in members' experiences, expectations, wants, needs, and ideas. They must look for points of agreement and disagreement and also for the feelings team members have about them and why. The leader must make sure that dissenting members have a chance to voice their objections. Team members must try to determine the reason the dissenting member views the issue differently and try to arrive at a mutual understanding of opportunities, problems, and challenges. It is important to get differences out into the open and to search for alternatives that take everyone's views into account.

The leader should attempt to get members to support an agreed-upon solution or alternative and to exchange, share, and adapt points of view. Members should listen, and when they disagree, do so without putting other members down.

Problems and solutions. At this point the team reviews each current condition, identifies all conditions that could result in improvement, and discusses the relative importance of each condition in achieving the improvement. The team then brainstorms possible solutions to the issue or problem. The solutions are placed on flip charts, no matter how far-out they may appear at first glance. Solutions are not evaluated until all possible ideas have been recorded. Then, and then only, each solution is reviewed and discussed from the standpoints of appropriateness, effectiveness, costs, including potential hidden costs, and probability of acceptance and success in solving the problem.

Action plans, reports, and briefings. Here a detailed plan of action to solve the problem or remedy the deficiency is developed. The action plan must include specifically what is to be done, why it must be done, who is to do it, when and where it is to be done, and in broad terms, how it is to be done.

A written report of the work team's findings, conclusions, and recommendations should be prepared by the recorder. The report should be succinct, but it should include a statement of the problem or issue, the factual findings, analysis of the facts, alternative solutions or remedies considered by the team, conclusions, recommendations, and the action plan.

The team should also select someone to present a decision briefing to higher-level management on the team's findings, conclusions, recommendations, and the action plan.

Evaluation. Members evaluate all the team's decisions and the processes used. The team leader evaluates and summarizes key information about the decision-making process and results. Observers give feedback to the team. Evaluation and feedback sessions address such matters as clarity of objectives, effectiveness in roles, commitment of members, extensiveness, quality, and frequency of participation, quality of team leadership, acceptance of leadership roles by members, interaction of members, group cohesiveness, and quality of solutions and decisions.

Summary

The complex problems involved in the operation of the modern organization demand the full use of the talents and special abilities of all employees. Applying the energies and skills of personnel of all levels depends substantially on their understanding of and contact with substantive issues and problems. The enthusiastic support of employees for the organization's programs, plans, and policies is contingent upon the extent to which these programs, plans, and policies are their creation.

Good morale is enhanced when staff members have opportunities to participate in solving problems of common concern. In this way, a feeling of belonging, of security, of adequacy, and of worth is developed, and it manifests itself in sound morale throughout the organization. Furthermore, well-organized and well-operated work teams inevitably obliterate rivalries, misunderstandings, and jealousies.

Team building requires an understanding of the team as a psychological and social entity, a knowledge of the factors that influence the relationships and behaviors of individuals on the team, and skill in applying those understandings to the development of productive work teams.

Sometimes internal factors work to make teams unstable. However, teams have the capacity to adjust to those disruptive forces and achieve a high degree of productivity, if problems are dealt with properly.

Several conditions are basic to the release of team potential for productive effort. The most important is shared leadership—where leadership becomes a function of the entire team and not a trait that resides in any one individual. Other factors are opportunities for members to use initiative and responsibility; and a proper emotional climate, the essence of which is a feeling of belongingness, security, acceptance, and success.

Several service roles are important: the content recorder, the process observer, and the resource person.

Among the more important problems that impede the progress of work teams are proper group size, obtaining participation, avoiding group frustration, and overcoming the failure of team members to assume leadership functions. Those obstacles are not insurmountable.

The process of teamwork involves the following strategies and techniques: (1) pre-session activities; (2) making introductions and discussing ground rules, mindset, and expectations; (3) identifying areas of concern; (4) identifying purpose and objectives; (5) making task assignments and gathering data; (6) identifying barriers and problems; (7) resolving conflict; (8) reviewing and discussing problems and solutions; (9) developing action plans, reports, and briefings; and (10) evaluating process and results.

FOR FURTHER READING

Adair, John. *Effective Teambuilding.* Brookfield, Vt.: Gower Publishing Company, 1986.

"Anatomy of a Team Player." *Training,* October 1986, pp. 14–15.

Baker, H. Kent. "The Hows and Whys of Team Building." *Personnel Journal,* June 1979, pp. 367–370.

Barone, Frank J. "Can Conflicting Values on the Change Team Work?" *Training and Development Journal,* August 1986, pp. 50–52

Beardsley, Jefferson F. "Quality Circles." In *Human Resources Management and Development Handbook,* edited by William R. Tracey. New York: AMACOM, 1985.

Blake, Robert R., Jane Srygley Mouton, and Robert L. Allen. *Spectacular Teamwork: How to Develop the Leadership Skills for Team Success.* New York: John Wiley & Sons, 1987.

Carew, Donald K., Eunice Parisi-Carew, and Kenneth H. Blanchard. "Group Development and Situational Leadership: A Model for Managing Groups." *Training and Development Journal,* June 1986, pp. 46–50.

Cooper, Colleen R., and Mary L. Ploor. "The Challenges That Make or Break a Group." *Training and Development Journal,* April 1986, pp. 31–33.

Dyer, William G. *Team Building: Issues and Alternatives.* Reading, Mass.: Addison-Wesley Training Systems, 1977.

Galagan, Patricia. "Work Teams That Work." *Training and Development Journal,* November 1986, pp. 33–35.

Gerber, Beverly. "Quality Circles: The Second Generation." *Training,* December 1986, pp. 54–61.

Harris, Philip R. "Building a High Performance Team." *Training and Development Journal,* April 1986, pp. 28–29.

Hines, William Watson III. "Increasing Team Effectiveness." *Training and Development Journal,* February 1980, pp. 78–82.

Johnson, Cynthia Reedy. "An Outline for Team Building." *Training,* January 1986, pp. 48–52.

Kanter, Rosabeth Moss, and Joseph P. Zolner. "What the 'New' Coaches Can Teach Managers." *Management Review,* November 1986, pp. 10–11.

Littlejohn, Robert F. "Team Management: A How-to Approach to Improved Productivity, Higher Morale, and Lasting Job Satisfaction." *Management Review,* January 1982, pp. 23–28.

Marguiles, Newton, and Anthony P. Raia. "People in Organizations: A Case for Team Training." *Training and Development Journal,* June 1981, pp. 58–69.

Merry, Uri, and Melvin E. Allerhand. *Developing Teams and Organizations.* Reading, Mass.: Addison-Wesley, 1977.

Miller, Barry W., and Ronald C. Phillips. "Team Building on a Deadline." *Training and Development Journal*, March 1986, pp. 54–56.

Miskin, Val D., and Warren H. Gmelch. "Quality Leadership for Quality Teams." *Training and Development Journal*, May 1985, pp. 122-129.

Oberhammer, Maureen. "Training the Team." *Training and Development Journal*, August 1986, pp. 70–72.

Ouchi, William. *Theory Z: How American Business Can Meet the Challenge.* Reading, Mass.: Addison-Wesley, 1981.

Palleschi, Patricia, and Patricia Heim. "The Hidden Barriers to Team Building." *Training and Development Journal*, July 1980, pp. 14–18.

Patten, Thomas H., Jr. *Organization Development Through Teambuilding.* New York: Wiley-Interscience, 1981.

Reitz, H. Joseph. *Behavior in Organizations*, rev. ed. Homewood, Ill.: Richard D. Irwin, 1981.

Rubin, I. M., and others. *Task-Oriented Team Development.* Del Mar, Calif.: McGraw-Hill Training Systems, 1978.

Schermerhorn, John R., Jr. "Team Development for High Performance Management." *Training and Development Journal*, November 1986, pp. 38–41.

Shaw, Malcolm E. "Work Team Development Training." In *Human Resources Management and Development Handbook*, edited by William R. Tracey. New York: AMACOM, 1985.

Shea, Gordon F. *Company Loyalty: Earning It, Keeping It.* New York: AMACOM, 1987.

Strong, Graham. "Taking the Helm of Leadership." *Training and Development Journal*, June 1986, pp. 43–45.

Szilagyi, Andrew D., Jr., and Marc J. Wallace, Jr. *Organizational Behavior and Performance*, 2nd ed. Santa Monica, Calif.: Goodyear Publishing Company, 1980. See especially Chapter 7.

Watkins, Karen. "When Co-workers Clash." *Training and Development Journal*, April 1986, pp. 26–27.

Woodcock, Mike. *Team Development Manual.* New York: John Wiley, 1979.

Index

action plans
  characteristics of, 136–137
  development of, 161, 342
  implementation of, 161–162
adult learning, principles of, 267–271
advertisement, employment, 169, 172–173
AIDS (acquired immune deficiency syndrome), screening for, 179
alcohol abuse, counseling for, 287–288
analysis paralysis, effect of, 146
applicant specifications
  elements of,
  format for, 70–71
  writing guidelines for, 66–68
arbitration, characteristics of, 307, 313
ARC (AIDS-related complex), screening for, 179
artificial intelligence (AI), characteristics of, 126–127
assessment centers, function of, 190
assumptions, types of, 311
authority
  delegation of, 151–152, 223, 227–233
  sources of, 152–153
  types of, 153–154

behaviorally anchored rating scale (BARS), characteristics of, 247, 248–249
behaviors, psychological determinants of human, 308–311
biographical inventories, use of, 179
body language, uses of, 13–17, 28
brainstorming

purpose of, 124–125
rules for, 125, 134
briefings
  formats for, 39
  purpose of, 100, 135–136
  types of, 4–5, 38–39, 98, 342

career counseling, objective of, 286
checklists, as appraisal technique, 249–250
Civil Rights Act of 1964, employee selection regulations of, 168
Clinard, Helen, on listening, 1
coaching, 264–282
  benefits of, 265–266
  characteristics of, 5, 264–265, 273
  need for, 265
  objectives of, 265, 266–267
  pitfalls in, 272–274
  requirements for successful, 267–272
  steps in, 276–279
  types of, 268–269
compromise, guidelines for, 315, 318–319, 320
conferences, see meetings and conferences
conflict resolution, see problem solving
controls, importance and categories of, 76–77
counseling
  avoidance of, 294–295
  benefits of, 283–284, 290–291
  definition of, 283
  identifying problem employees for, 288–290
  initiation of, 295–296

counseling (*continued*)
  listening effectively during, 5, 12–13
  methods of, 292–293
  misconceptions about, 295
  necessity of, 283
  ojectives of, 285–288, 293–294
  pitfalls in, 294–295
  referrals for, 295–296, 301
  skills required for, 295
  steps in, 284
  subjectivity in, 295
  time requirements for, 297
  types of, 285–288
  see also counseling process, techniques of
counseling process, techniques of:
  documentation, 300–301
  follow up, 301
  implementation of decisions, 300
  planning and preparation, 296–297
  problem identification, 299
  problem solving, 299–300
  rapport, 297–298
  referrals, 301
  termination of session, 300
  see also counseling
creativity
  applications of, 120–121, 124–126, 334
  definition of, 125
critical incident appraisal tecnnique, characteristics of, 247–248
critiques, guidelines for, 55
crunch factor, search for, 157–158

data analysis, methods of, 113–114
data collection, *see* information gathering, methods and sources of
deBono, Edward, on lateral thinking, 125
deception, forms of, 14–17
decision(s), types of, 145–150
  crucial, 150
  group, 149
  individual, 148–149
  intuitive, 145–146

logical/analytical, 146–148
  mathematical and scientific, 147–148
  nondecisions, 145
  nonmathematical, 146–147
  routine, 150
decision briefing, function and format for, 39, 125–126
decision making, 141–165
  barriers to, 143–145
  bases of, 145–147
  errors in, 154–155, 162
  importance of, 141, 142–143, 150
  kinds of, 141–142, 151–152
  listening and, 4–5
  see also decision making, steps in; problem solving
decision making, steps in, 155–162
  assess tentative decision, 159–160
  determine purposes and objectives, 155–156
  develop action plan, 161
  evaluate alternatives, 157–159
  follow up and evaluate, 162
  identify alternatives, 157
  implement decision, 161–162
  make final decision, 160–161
  make tentative decision, 159
  prioritize objectives, 156
  see also decision making
decision papers, function and format for, 55, 58–59, 135
delegatee, duties and skills of, 228
delegation, 220–237
  accountability for, 221, 227–228
  barriers to, 222–224
  benefits of, 221–222
  conditions for effective, 230–231
  definition of, 220
  elements of, 220–221
  extremes in, 229–230
  failure of, 224–225
  levels of, 153–154, 228–230
  methods of, 225–226
  as motivator, 211, 215
  need for, 230
  for policies and rules, 227
  principles of, 226–228

scope of, 231–232
steps in, 230–235
see also delegation, types of
delegation, types of:
autonomous, 230
counterfeit, 225
functional, 226, 228
incremental, 226
sequential, 226
tight, 229
delegator, authority and responsibilities of, 227–234
discrimination, avoidance of, 168, 169, 257
discussion groups, functions of, 106–107
documentation, functions of, 98–102, 300–301

Ellis, Albert, on motivation, 198
employment interview(s)
characteristics of, 6, 12, 180–182
documentation of, 170
types of, 181–182
see also employment interview(s), elements of
employment interview(s), elements of:
closing, 188
detection of deception, 187
information sharing, 185
interpretation of responses, 185
preparation, 182
questioning, 183–185
rapport, 183
reference checks, 189
see also employment interview(s)
equal intervals appraisal technique, characteristics of, 251
essay appraisal technique, characteristics of, 247
Eureka factor, in decision making, 146
evaluation reports, guidelines for, 55
exchange strategy, purpose of, 319

feedback
barriers to, 8, 9
uses of, 11, 205, 211, 260, 269, 278, 334

feedback theory, decision making and, 148
financial problems, employee counseling for, 288
forced-choice appraisal technique, characteristics of, 249, 250
forced-distribution appraisal technique, characteristics of, 252
forecasts, problem sensing and, 84–85

game theory, decision making and, 148
gestures, interpretation of, 16–17
goal(s)
as motivators, 201, 208–209, 213
need for, 309–310
setting of, 214
grapevine, function of, 82
group discussions, function of, 86

halo, error of, 255
handicapped persons, interviewing of, 187–188
Herzberg, Frederick, motivation-hygiene theory of, 201
hidden agenda, impact of, 313
hiring process, 166–195
characteristics of, 6, 167–168
cost of, 166
importance of, 166–167
legal aspects of, 168–170
misconceptions about, 167
see also employment interview(s); hiring process, elements of
hiring process, elements of, 168, 169–181
decision to hire, 191
documentation, 170, 191–192
follow up, 192
interviewing, 180–189
recruitment, 169, 170–173
screening and selection, 169, 173–180, 189–190
testing, 169
see also hiring process

incentives
function of, 202–203
types of, 205–207

individual differences
   forms of, 199–200
   importance of recognizing, 210–211
information
   analysis and interpretation of, 113–114
   categories of, 96–97
   nature of, 94–95
   uses of, 94–95
information briefing, purpose and format for, 38–39, 98–100
information flow, barriers to, 8, 9
Information gathering, methods and sources of, 97–113
   document review, 98, 99–102
   inspections and reinspections, 107–109
   interviewing, 103–105
   meetings and conferences, 105–107
   observation, 102–103
   questionnaires, 109–110
   self-audits, 110–112
   snowflakes, 110, 111–112
   staff briefings, 98, 100, 102
   surveys, 109–110
   taskers, 110, 111–112
in-house proposal writing, guidelines for, 57, 59, 61
inquiring skills, applications of, 95–96, 128, 314–315
   see also information gathering, methods and sources of
inspections, purpose and procedures for, 85–86, 107–108
interventions, functions of, 269, 277
interview(s)
   drawbacks to, 104
   formats for, 104, 179–180
   functions of, 86, 103–105
   procedures for, 104–105, 186–187
   see also interview(s), types of
interview(s), types of:
   coaching, 268–269
   exit, 6
   group, 103–104, 182
   individual, 103–104, 182
   nonstandardized or nondirective, 181–182

schedule versus nonschedule, 104
   standardized or directive, 104, 181
   stress, 182
   television, 37–38
   see also employment interview(s)
interviewer, traits of skillful, 183

job application forms, characteristics of, 175
job descriptions
   characteristics of, 173–174, 213
   format for, 68
   writing guidelines for, 66–68
job interview, see employment interview(s)
job performance counseling, objectives of, 285–286
job satisfaction, as motivator, 203, 207–208

knowledge workers, productivity of, 244–246

language problems
   solutions to, 7
   types of, 9–10, 11
legal problems, counseling for, 288
letters, writing guidelines for, 51–53
Likert, Rensis, on participative management, 123
linear programming, decision making and, 148
listening
   barriers to, 3, 7–10
   characteristics of, 2–4
   hearing rate for, 10
   importance of, 1–2
   improving of, 17–18
   management uses of, 4–6, 82
   see also listening techniques, elements of effective
listening techniques, elements of effective:
   active listening, 10–11
   context clues, 7
   detection of propaganda and deception, 14–17
   evaluative listening, 12

listening for meaning, 11–12
listening with your eyes, 13–14
nonevaluative listening, 12–13
litigation, characteristics of, 307

marginal analysis, function of, 147–148
marital problems, employee counseling for, 288
Maslow, A. H., needs hierarchy of, 200–201
Mayer, Norman, on group problem solving, 123–124
MBO (management by objectives), characteristics of, 214
mediation, characteristics of, 307
medical examinations, preemployment, 178–179
meetings and conferences
    functions of, 5, 83–84, 86–87, 123–124
    procedures for, 105–106
memo(s), characteristics of, 54
mentoring, definition of, 265
    see also coaching
messages, guidelines for, 54
minutes, guidelines for, 55
moderator, responsibilities of, 34–35
motivation, 196–219
    definition and characteristics of, 197–199
    determinants of, 207–209
    effective systems of, 209–210
    importance of, 196–197
    individual differences and, 199–200, 207–208
    professional values and goals and, 208–209
    skills for, 199, 272
    steps in, 215–216
    strategies for, 209–215
    theories on, 200–202
    see also motivation, forms of; motivation strategies, elements of
motivation, forms of:
    external, 203–204
    extrinsic, 202–203
    feedback, 205

incentives, 202–203, 205–207
    intangible, 204–205
    internal, 203
    intrinsic, 203
    rewards, 203
    tangible, 204
    see also motivation; motivation strategies, elements of
motivation strategies, elements of:
    delegation, 211, 215
    feedback, 211
    goal and objectives setting, 213–214
    job enrichment or enlargement, 215
    leadership of managers, 212–213
    MBO programs, 214
    organizational environment, 210–212
    participative decision making, 211, 215
    rewards and recognition, 212
    stress reduction, 213–214
    triggering action, 214
    see also motivation; motivation, forms of
multiple management strategy, uses of, 149

needs hierarchy, of Maslow, 201
negotiating team, selection of, 315–316
negotiation
    arbitration versus, 307
    barriers to, 313
    characteristics of, 6, 306–307
    litigation versus, 307
    mediation versus, 307
    situations requiring, 305–306
    see also negotiation, conditions for; negotiation strategies, elements in
negotiation, conditions for, 307–313
    accurate assumptions, 311
    effective techniques, 311–313
    people knowledge, 308–311
    self-knowledge of negotiator, 308
    see also negotiation, negotiation strategies, elements in
negotiation strategies, elements in, 313–322

negotiation strategies (*continued*)
agenda, 316
compromising, 315
data collection, 314–315
knowledge of opposition, 315
objectives setting, 314
opening statement, 317
participant selection, 315–316
preparation and planning, 313–317
response to needs of opposition, 318–319
revealing your position, 318
site selection, 317
time selection, 317
win-win skills, 319–322
written agreement, 322
see also negotiation; negotiation, conditions for
negotiator, qualities of effective, 316
Nickerson, Raymond S., on thinking process, 125
nonverbal behaviors, characteristics and importance of, 13–14, 16–17

observation
characteristics of, 103
purpose of, 102–103
steps in, 103
types of, 102–103, 120
uses of, 82, 85, 190, 254, 268, 338–339
one-on-one dialogues, characteristics of, 33–34
see also interview(s)
operations research (OR), decision-making application of, 148
oral presentations
critique of, 30
parts of, 24–25
to transcultural audience, 30–31
see also public speaking
Osborn, Alex, on brainstorming, 125
outplacement counseling, purpose of, 286–287

paired comparisons appraisal technique, characteristics of, 251–252
panels and symposiums, roles and responsibilities in, 34–36

paragraphing, criteria for, 47
parsimony, error of, 255
participative management
characteristics of, 149, 211, 215
rationale for, 123
perfectionism, dangers of, 120–121, 144
performance
factors influencing, 244–246
sources of substandard, 244–246
see also performance problems
performance appraisal, 238–263
benefits of, 240–241
characteristics of, 242–244, 256–257
criteria for, 243–244, 256–257
definition of, 238–239
legal requirements of, 244, 256–257
need for, 256
problems in, 8, 253–256
purpose of, 239–240
skills for, 5–6, 242–244
types of, 241–242
see also performance appraisal, methods of; performance appraisal process, elements in
performance appraisal, methods of:
absolute, 246–250
behaviorally anchored, 247, 248–249
checklists, 249–250
comparative or relative, 250–252
critical incident, 247–248
descriptive, 247–248
equal interval, 251
essay appraisal, 247
forced choice, 249, 250
forced distribution, 252
graphic, 248, 249
numerical, 246
paired comparisons, 251–252
rank order, 251
see also performance appraisal; performance appraisal process, elements in
performance appraisal process, elements in, 257–261
assessments, employee and employer, 258

documentation review, 257–258
document performance, 259–260
goals and objectives setting, 258–259
monitoring of progress, 260
planning, 257–258
rapport, 258
system review and evaluation, 260–261
see also performance appraisal; performance appraisal, methods of
performance problems
  handling of, 278–279
  sources of, 274–276
  see also performance
perquisites (perks), as motivators, 206–207
personal adjustment counseling, objectives of, 287–288
planning, importance of, 76
policy(ies)
  definition of, 59
  types of, 62
policy statements, format and guidelines for, 59, 63
preemployment inquiries, *see* screening and selection procedures
preretirement planning, counseling for, 288
press releases, guidelines for, 68–69
press room, guidelines for, 38
probability theory, decision making and, 148
problem(s)
  cause of, 77–80, 133–134
  characteristics of, 118–119
  definition of, 118
  identification and statement of real, 129–131
  types of, 121–122
problem analysis, steps in, 132–134
Problem Analysis (Specification) Worksheet, function of, 129, 130
problem identification
  steps in, 128–130
  uses of, 273, 299
problem sensing, 74–93
  characteristics of, 128

definition of, 74, 118
in HR function and management, 77–79
obstacles to, 75–76
procedures for, 89–91
see also problem-sensing strategies, casual; problem-sensing strategies, planned
problem-sensing strategies, casual:
  grapevine, 82
  incidental observation, 82
  listening, 82
  meetings and conferences, 83–84
  questioning, 80–81
  records, 83
  reports, 83
  suggestion systems, 83
  tests and surveys, 83
  see also problem sensing; problem-sensing strategies, planned
problem-sensing strategies, planned:
  books and journals, 89
  catalogs and brochures, 89
  consultants, 87
  forecasts, 84–85
  group discussion, 86
  inspections, 85–86
  interviews, 86
  meetings and exhibits, 87–88
  observation, 85
  spot reports, 87, 88
  staff meetings, 86–87
  surveys, 87
  see also problem sensing; problem-sensing strategies, casual
problem solving
  barriers to, 120–121
  characteristics of, 118–119
  definition of, 119
  need for, 117–118
  options in, 143
  skills for, 96, 118, 119–120
  steps in, 138
  uses of, 299–300, 342
  see also problem solving, approaches to; problem-solving strategies, elements in

problem solving, approaches to:
artificial intelligence, 126–127
creative, 125–126
group, 123–125
individual, 122–123
see also problem solving; problem-solving strategies, elements in
problem-solving strategies, elements in, 127–138
action plans, 136–137
alternatives, 134, 139
analysis of problem, 132–134
approval, 135–136
criteria, 131–132
follow-up, 137
planning, 127–128
problem identification, 128–130
report on results, 137–138
solution selection, 134–135
statement of real problem, 130–131
see also problem solving; problem solving, approaches to
procedure manuals, writing guidelines for, 62–66
process observer, responsibilities of, 338–339
propaganda, forms of, 14–17
proposal summary, function of, 136
proposal writing, guidelines for, 57, 60–61
public speaking, barriers to, 8–11, 14–17, 211
public speaking, preparations for:
analyze audience, 23–24
check setting, 26
control stage fright, 23
dress properly, 25–26
rehearse, 24, 25
set objectives, 23
write out talk, 24–25
see also public speaking, presentation elements of
public speaking, presentation elements of:
body language, 28
control of resistant audience, 29–30
eye contact, 27
handling questions, 29

humor, 24, 28–29
introductions, 27
language, 25, 27, 30–31
style, 27–28
visual aids, 26, 31–32
voice and speech, 27
see also public speaking, preparations for; speaking skills, uses of

question(s)
handling of, 29, 322
in negotiations, 320
techniques for asking, 80–81, 183, 311–313
types of, 183, 312–313
questionnaires, characteristics and procedures for, 109–110
queueing, decision making and, 148

rank order appraisal technique, characteristics of, 251
rapport, rules for establishing, 297–298
rap session, characteristics of, 106–107
rating scales, types of, 178
reasoning, types of:
inductive versus deductive, 119–120
specious, 15
vertical versus lateral, 125
reference checks, function and methods of, 189
reports
guidelines for writing, 54–55
problem sensing and, 83
types of, 55
requests for proposals (RFPs)
format for, 50–51
guidelines for, 57
types of, 57, 59
résumés, as screening device, 175
rewards, functions of, 202, 212, 272, 334
rigidity, effects of, 120
role, definition of, 335
Rowan, Roy, on decision process, 146

screening and selection procedures
documentation of, 170

legal aspects of, 169
see also screening and selection procedures, forms of
screening and selection procedures,
forms of, 173–180
applicant specifications, 174
application forms, 174–175
assessment centers, 190
interviewer evaluation forms, 179–
180
job descriptions, 173–174
medical examinations, 178–179
observations, 190
rating scales, 178
résumés, 175
self-reports, 179
tests, 175–178
see also screening and selection procedures
self-concept, types of, 308
self-reports, uses of, 110–112, 179
servo theory, decision making and,
148
snowflakes, format and function of,
110–112
speaking skills, uses of:
briefings, 38–40
one-on-one dialog, 32–34
oral presentations, 23–32
panels and symposiums, 34–36
television appearances, 36–38
see also public speaking
spot reports, function of, 87, 88
staff studies, characteristics of, 55,
58–59, 135
status, characteristics of, 152–153, 335
stock option plans, description of, 206
stress, reduction of, 213–214
substance abuse, counseling for, 287–
288
suggestion system, function of, 83
summaries, guidelines for, 55, 113,
136
surveys, characteristics and procedures for, 87, 109–110
symposiums, *see* panels and symposiums, roles and responsibilities in

tabulation, steps in, 113
taskers, function and format of, 110–
112
teambuilding, *see* work teams
team problem solving, characteristics
of, 123–125
see also participative management;
work teams
television appearances, guidelines for,
36–38
termination of employment, counseling for, 286–287
tests, preemployment
documentation of, 170
legal aspects of, 169–170, 177
standards for, 176
validity and interpretation of, 177–
178
thwarting, nature of, 310
training course descriptions, writing
procedures for, 66
triggering action, characteristics of,
214
trip reports, guidelines for, 55, 56

*Uniform Guidelines on Employee Selection
Procedures* (1978), employee selection regulations of, 168

value, characteristics of, 200, 208–209
video recordings, guidelines for, 38
visual aids, use of, 31–32
vocabulary, choice of, 47–48
vocabulary problems, solutions to, 7

waiting-line theory, decision making
and, 148
win-win negotiation skills, elements
of, 319–322
work teams, 326–345
barriers to, 339–341
characteristics of, 326–327, 329,
335, 342
concerns of, 341
criteria for, 332–335
functions of, 339–342
productivity of, 329–331
purpose and objectives of, 327–328,
341

work teams (*continued*)
  rationale for, 327
  roles in, 335–339
  strategies and techniques of, 340–342
  types of, 331–332
  uses of, 328–329
worst-case planning, technique of, 158
writing style, definition and selection of, 46
written communications, 43–73
  cost of, 43
  importance of, 43–44
  improvement strategies for, 49–51
  limitations of, 44–45
  see also written communications, elements of; written communications, types of
written communications, elements of:
  appearance, 49
  clarity, 48–49, 50
  conciseness, 48–49, 50
  form, 45, 50
  format, 49, 50
  grammar, 48, 51
  graphics, 49
  layout, 49
  organization, 46–47, 50, 51
  paragraphing, 47
  punctuation, 48, 51
  sentence structure, 47
  spelling, 48, 51
  style, 46
  tone, 45–46
  vocabulary, 47–48
  see also written communications; written communications, types of
written communications, types of:
  applicant specifications, 67–68, 70–71
  course descriptions, 66
  critiques, 55
  decision papers, 55, 58–59
  job descriptions, 67, 68
  letters, 51–53
  memos, 53–54
  messages, 54
  minutes, 55
  performance appraisals, 55
  policy statements, 59, 61–62, 63
  press releases, 68–69
  procedures manuals, 62–66
  proposals, 57, 60–61
  reports, 54–55
  staff studies, 55, 58–59
  summaries, 55
  trip reports, 55, 56